Table of Contents

3

Tags: businessperson, undergrad founder, hiring

Foreword

Background

The idea for this book started out as something completely different. My dad said I should write about my experience of starting a company and selling it after I went through Y Combinator while I was an undergraduate. I pocketed that idea and thought, "Maybe some day I will." In my spare time, I jotted things down that I would have told my younger self with the intent of some day putting it on a blog.

Finding good cofounders, for example, is something that really interests me because it's such a difficult problem that so many people face. I built Hacker News Directory (http://www.hndir.com) over a weekend so that I could find other students at UIUC who were reading Hacker News, maybe I could hang out with them and see what kind of projects they were working on. That web site is now open for all schools and has close to 1,000 hackers from schools like Stanford, MIT, Cornell, Harvard, and others—so if you're a student you might find someone from your school that has similar interests on there.

Finding cofounders is still a difficult problem—even after I've interviewed all of these founders, I'm still not completely sure what I'd recommend. I was kind of surprised to see that many founders were approaching the topic casually: they weren't out hunting for cofounders necessarily; they let serendipity happen. Granted, several founders like Josh Greenberg from Grooveshark and Ryan Junee from Omnisio had very high expectations and wouldn't just start a company with anyone, but that's not to say that luck and chance didn't have its role to play in everything.

Whenever I would start writing about a topic like "How to find good cofounders", I found myself wanting to ask other founders what they did in their situation. I realized that I could only offer anecdotal advice, and while this was good, it might have helped to get more anecdotal advice to try and find some patterns. This cascaded into the rest of my other topics that were relevant to people who wanted to start a startup or even to those already involved with one. I had lots of questions that I would have wanted answered as a high school or college student. I reached out to my immediate network and started talking to founders, and then I got introductions to other founders and it took off from there.

Audience
While this book is a great read for anyone interested in startups, I think people who benefit the most are high school and college students. Business students might stand to learn the most from this book: the tech startup world is not an easy place for business students, yet founders like Evan Reas from LikeALittle have shown how even non-technical students can surround themselves with very smart engineers and build a successful company. You also will notice a very clear pattern from today's startup founders: there are no business plans or financial projections; there's only room for execution.

If you liked *Founders at Work*, you'll probably enjoy this. While the two books aren't associated with each other, part of the motivation for writing this was driven by a desire for another *Founders at Work*. I use the same Q&A I'm talking to aren't quite at that celebrity status yet, but some of them seem to be headed in that direction. I think we'll be able to look back at these stories and get an accurate snapshot of where they were back when they were still a small startup.

My motivation for this book
I wanted to know *how these startup founders got to where they are today*. Did they start at a young age? Was everything intentional and planned out or was the success of founders driven by serendipity, as Paul Buchheit poses? Some startups such as Grooveshark are the product of meticulous searching for cofounders and personality matches while other startups such as Octopart and Gobble are more coincidental.

How difficult was it? My interview with Dennis Crowley of Foursquare—now one of the media's most sought after speakers—will reveal how the media is very good at making startups look easier than they really are. How were all the difficult decisions made? This is the core focus of this book: trying to understand how founders got started with entrepreneurship; how they found their cofounders; how they got the idea for their company; how they raised money; how they grew their product;

how they resolved problems in challenging times; how they started generating revenue; how they allocated their time and what kind of hacks they used. Some founders offer conflicting advice, so I leave it to the reader to draw conclusions on some of these more difficult topics.

Be inspired into action
The book doesn't just serve a utilitarian purpose of educating and informing. I hope it inspires people into action and reminds them that the "trough of sorrow" is something that happens for lots of founders; don't get discouraged and think you're the only person failing or not doing something right. The world of startups is messy and chaotic as T.J. Rodgers would tell you, but it's also extremely efficient.

One of my favorite memories of Y Combinator was the weekly dinners. Each night, a guest speaker would come and share their experience—how they started their company and how they solved their hardest problems. These talks were special because they were off-the-record, so the speakers would typically share more than they usually would. But the anecdotes turned out to be incredibly valuable. They made me realize that the stress and difficulty in a startup weren't unique to just our group. It was an experience shared by most other startups, and that was encouraging to us. When I spoke to Ricky from Crowdbooster, I was reminded of the early days of GraffitiGeo—along with other companies in our batch, we found it difficult to define ourselves at times. We iterated through three distinct products during our three months at Y Combinator, and that's okay. When we met other founders who had similar problems—that actually motivated us.

I think the single most reassuring thing about doing a startup is knowing in advance how difficult it is going to be. From one of Y Combinator's very first meetups, Paul Graham told the group something to the effect of, "There will be times when it gets really difficult; you think you're going to fail and you're going to call your parents and tell them you're quitting. But just remember the trough of sorrow is something that happens to almost everyone, and you just have to keep going. Remember when I told you that it was going to be difficult and just keep moving forward despite that." Those words have stuck with me ever since, and I think hearing stories from other entrepreneurs in similar situations will help you keep going even when times are at their worst.

I've noticed the conversation lately on Hacker News has been somewhat critical of founders spending their time on doing things other than hacking, but I think reading is underrated. You should be reading blogs and stories of founders to get inspired and encouraged. Startups are a lot of work, and it's going to get lonely and depressing sometimes. There's a reason YC wants everyone together in the same room each week—it's easy to think that you'll spend 100% of your time heads down just programming or doing deals or pushing pixels, but the reality is that sometimes you need to recharge and put your keyboard down. I hope this book delivers on that value. Don't get me wrong—you should be working your tail off while you're doing a startup, but take time to look around. Read stories about other founders if you can't get stuff done; figure out what's going on. And then get back to work.

Terminology

For those who are unfamiliar, I want to try and explain some of the phrases used throughout the book and often abbreviated during the interviews. You can probably just skip to the interviews if you're already familiar with everything here.

"YC" stands for Y Combinator and is referenced a lot because most of my personal network consists of founders of YC funded companies. A majority of the founders interviewed in this book have gone through Y Combinator, and many of them were in my batch (Summer 2009). YC is an accelerator lead by Paul Graham ("PG"), Jessica Livingston, Trevor Blackwell, and Robert Morris. The "trough of sorrow" is a period that nearly every startup is expected to go through after they launch and their traffic tapers off and many founders refer to that since it's one of the most difficult times a startup will face. To provide additional context, there's a whiteboard on the wall when you walk into the Y Combinator office; in permanent marker is written "The Process": TechCrunch of Initiation, Wearing Off of Novelty, Trough of Sorrow, Releases of Improvement, Crash of Ineptitude, Wiggles of False Hope, Spike of Misconfigured Mixpanel Code, Acquisition of Liquidity, and Upside of Buyer.

Yuri Milner is mentioned and some people may not be familiar with the terms he recently offered Y Combinator founders as of January 2011. Yuri Milner is an investor offering $150,000 to every team accepted to Y Combinator in the form of a convertible note with no cap and no discount (these are considered to be very favorable terms for the founders). As part of my questions I ask founders whether they think the offer is a good or bad idea.

There are several "tags" I use to describe each founder and their company. When I sent the manuscript to people and was receiving feedback, they wanted a quick way to understand who a person was, or what a company was about—a reason why they should read every single interview in this book. There are lots of interviews here, and it's a long read, so I'll try my best to briefly describe each founder and their company with a set of tags. Maybe you'll read something and then forget what the exact context was, but you'll remember that they had dropped out. So you can scan through the book for founders that had the "dropout" tag. I'll describe these here, in no particular order.

Acquired – the founder either had a previous company that was acquired, or the company being interviewed was acquired.

Y Combinator – the founder or the company was part of a Y Combinator batch

Anti-school – founder had mentioned that they didn't attend classes often, or made a habit of skipping classes. This isn't meant to discount the value of education—in fact, Amit Sudharshan is one of the smartest engineers I've ever known and he only showed up to class to take the exams. It might just go to show that the material was too easy for him. This tag is mostly to show that a founder may have had different priorities in school, such as their projects.

School worker – founder mentioned paying for their own tuition in school or working jobs as a student; some advice may be particularly relevant for other students in similar positions.

Programmer, Designer, or Businessperson – founder played a key role as someone who was programming and writing code, designing interfaces or creating a strong user experience, or handling the business operations and negotiating deals. It's interesting to see founders carrying only the businessperson tag, or only the designer tag—this might challenge the notion that you must be a programmer in order to start a technical startup, or that the role of design isn't important in a startup.

Undergrad founder – founder started their startup as a project during their undergraduate years in school

Ramen profitable – founder either mentioned—or in a few cases I might assume based on their profitability they described—that the founders are making enough money to pay their own personal living expenses. "Ramen profitable" is a concept that Paul Graham created as the goal for your startup to have: to not be in a position of neediness where you need investors and are required to raise money.

Profitable – a level above "Ramen profitable"; founder either mentioned—or in a few cases I might assume—that the founders are generating enough profit to cover personal living expenses in addition to hiring expenses (salaries, benefits, etc) and business expenses.

Hiring – company is actively hiring. You should definitely go apply to the startup if you see this tag, and pay attention to what the founders say about 'standing out as an applicant.' If you're just sending a resume, that's probably a dead end unless your resume is actually really impressive. I know many of these founders personally and I'd have no hesitation about joining their companies to do an internship if I were brand new to Silicon Valley.

Side project – the founder worked on their current startup on the side or part-time while working at another company or startup full-time. These are always interesting because they challenge the conventional wisdom that you have to commit fully to doing a startup in order for it to be successful; really good example would be GitHub. If you're an employee at a larger company, I would recommend paying attention to these stories.

Self-funded – founder has not raised outside money whether it was from angel investors or venture capitalists; the startup is 'bootstrapped.'

Funded – startup is funded by angel investors or family/friends, not necessarily by VC investors

VC funded – company has raised—in most cases—a large sum of money and has experience with that process. If you're currently raising money, you might want to pay attention to how the founders describe their fundraising process.

Cofounder search – founder had mentioned looking for cofounders and might have looked for personality matches, for example. If you're currently out looking for cofounders, these will probably be good stories to read, although most founders I spoke with don't carry this label.

Dropout – founder dropped out of school to do their startup. I don't think any of them have any regrets; so if you're considering dropping out for a startup, these stories will most likely encourage you to dropout, rather than discourage you to dropout.

Iterate quickly vs. Iterate slowly – if the founder mentioned iterating through several products in rapid succession, or pivoting a lot, I would assign this tag to them. If they spent more time on product-market fit, I'd tag them as "iterate slowly." Sam Odio is a great example here as someone who would iterate slowly while he did Divvyshot. If you're uncertain whether you should change your idea, you might want to watch for this tag.

Design-focused – founder or startup made an effort to focus on UI and user experience. Disclaimer: this is more subjective in nature, so I try to use my best judgment and think back as far as I can to the earliest memory of the startup's website or application. I think every startup needs to pay attention to these stories; design has become increasingly important whether it's making your product easy to use or building trust and sending the right impression.

Ivy League – founder attended an Ivy League school. I talk to lots of founders from "public ivies" but don't tag founders from schools like Stanford as "Ivy League", despite many schools having top engineering, business, or design schools. Notice that several founders aren't from schools that are prestigious or entrepreneurial; challenges the conventional wisdom that you need to go to a really nice school to make something happen.

Major league player – startup is considered to have significant users, traffic, growth, revenue, or influence. Mostly this is looking at Alexa.com traffic—you can assume that the numbers are U.S. only; worldwide numbers are stated explicitly.

Coincidental – founder mentioned they weren't intending to do startups or I thought they didn't seem likely to do a startup coming out of school; seemed accidental.

<u>Solo founder</u> – founder is working alone without other cofounders. I think solo founders will in general be discounted because people will wonder why they don't have cofounders—is it because they're not friendly or fun or smart to be around? Nobody knows, but you also have more work to carry on your own, so you might be at a disadvantage. These are great reads for other solo founders and it challenges the conventional wisdom that you *have* to have a cofounder to be successful.

<u>Laid off</u> – founder was laid off in their job, which may have led to them doing their current startup. If you're laid off, read some of these stories and realize there may be something positive that comes out of that situation.

In general, the tags are mostly to guide you to specific interviews if a certain topic interests you. If any of them are inaccurate—I didn't explicitly ask founders to tag themselves, I did this based on reading and re-reading all of interviews—then I will make corrections on the blog and in book updates.

You should intern or join these startups
Most of the companies interviewed in this book are hiring. Some of these companies have put considerable time and effort into their recruiting and retention efforts, just look at Wufoo (now part of SurveyMonkey). As many founders have said, joining a startup as your first step might be your best way into the startup world; it definitely was for me. When you intern at a startup you'll learn a lot, you'll get strong connections, you may get equity early on, and you'll get the chance to work in an environment where bureaucracy simply doesn't exist. If I were a freshman in college, my summer would be spent interning at one of these startups rather than the typical office cubicle jobs. One summer at a startup could possibly teach you more than your entire undergraduate education could.

Special thanks
The book is the result of many people's contributions. First and foremost, the founders who took time to do these interviews: thank you for sharing your knowledge and experience with the rest of us. Startup founders are "the men in the arena" as Theodore Roosevelt said. These are the people moving the world forward and impacting the way we use technology.

I owe a lot of thanks to Y Combinator, a great group of people who are out there doing what they love. The partners at YC genuinely want to learn and understand this entire process as best as they can. Every dinner they are there to help founders diligently fix whatever problems they're having. They go above and beyond. Paul's essays have been some of my favorite reading material throughout the years, starting from when I had moved high schools and discovered *Why Nerds are Unpopular*. I didn't know anyone when I went to California in the summer of 2009 but I've become good friends with many of the people from my YC batch and to this day I still go to them for advice and help.

I also want to thank my parents, family and friends for being supportive. My dad encouraged me to write what would eventually become this book and I probably wouldn't have done it otherwise.

Need help?
As long as I have the time, I'm always happy to help people out whether it's reviewing their applications, making introductions, suggesting internships, or anything else I can do to enable entrepreneurs to achieve their goals.

You can reach me at jmtame@gmail.com. I'll try to respond as quickly as I can. Also, let me know what you think about this book. I'll read every single e-mail I get.

You can also follow any new interviews and updates on the site at http://www.startupsopensourced.com.

Josh Greenberg, Grooveshark

Tags: programmer, cofounder search, undergrad founder, hiring, VC funded, school worker, undergrad dropout, design-focused, major league player (Top 50 ranked site, Alexa top 1,000)

Overview: Grooveshark started in 2006 with the goal of competing with piracy and becoming the #1 destination for listening to music online. Having raised less than $1 million, Grooveshark consumes more bandwidth than most Internet Service Providers with over 27 million active users streaming music. Time Magazine has rated them as one of the 50 best web sites of 2010.

Can you tell me about how all of this got started for you? What was your earliest experience being an entrepreneur?

I don't know if there is one, specific answer to that question, but at the same time, I'm constantly in search of it. It has puzzled me for quite a while: what makes someone an entrepreneur and how do you really define that characteristic? The reason I find it so fascinating is because you can see it in someone.

When you meet someone you can tell in five seconds whether or not they have it, and yet at the same time, you still can't put it into words. It's somewhat coupled with things like dedication, perseverance, or passion for a cause, but at the same time it is none of those things. There's no unique combination, there's no magical formula for entrepreneurship. I am just as lost when trying to look inward and do self-analysis, and I really don't have any idea what makes me an entrepreneur. At the same time, I know that it goes as far back as I can remember; even when I was a little kid I was doing things that were somewhat entrepreneurial.

The first thing I ever did was in the second grade. I had collected shells on the beach and I was back at my house, coloring on them for some reason. Later, I tagged along with my mom when she went out to do errands and, for whatever reason, I asked the gas station attendant if he would buy one of the shells; he did, for a nickel. He took it out of the free change jar. I think that set off a little spark and I realized, "wow, I can do something to make money." At the time I had no sense of the value of money. I didn't really understand what it was, but the overall concept intrigued me. I colored more shells and started going to more places and selling them, and before I knew it I had a little jug full of change.

Fast forward a few years, I'm at my dad's electronics repair store—where I used to go with him every Saturday—he had this grapefruit tree out back, behind the store that had begun to grow in such a way that it was a little obtrusive. Just so I had something to do, he asked me to go out and pick the grapefruit. Again, I can't really tell you why, but for some reason once I had picked all of these grapefruits, I decided it would be a good idea to sit out front, with my dad's colleague's son, and sell them for a quarter each.

We made $50, went next door, and bought a bunch of video games at Blockbuster. So it's little things like that. I really don't know what motivated me to do them. It wasn't financial; it wasn't that I had some lifelong hunger for money. I suppose I just enjoyed the process of creating value.

My first, real entrepreneurial endeavor was in high school. I was 17 at the time and, by that point, I had already begun to build websites for people. It wasn't really substantial income, I made maybe $100 here and there but, in high school, that was a lot of money.

Eventually I got a day job working at a medical management institute and my boss' husband came in every now and then. He was a very experienced lifetime entrepreneur, and he and I would chat. I told him about my aspirations to start a company, do more web development and really get paid for it; he said, "Well, there's nothing holding you back so let's start one." He said "let's" because I wasn't 18, so I couldn't legally be on my own board of directors; he helped me get the paperwork signed. I think I actually ended up having my grandpa serve as chairman.

That at least got a company name behind me so instead of saying, "I'm Josh Greenberg" I could say, "I'm with DevelopedWeb, Incorporated." I got $20 worth of business cards printed at Office Depot and that was what started everything, back then. So, I guess I took myself a little bit more seriously and that helped me to be taken a little bit more seriously, which is a requirement if you're 17 and trying to solicit money from people.

That first endeavor got me through high school and gave me a true taste of dealing with clients and managing expectations. I was building lots of websites, here and there, maybe 50 or so over the course of high school.

Later, I went to the University of Florida for college, and I was always interested in technology but figured it would be easier to learn everything technical on the side; I wanted to learn about business from people who've been there before. Shortly after freshman year began, I started a project with a few other guys: an online community for sharing class notes. We wanted to make it easier for people to collaborate. By freshman year standards, it blew up. We made the local paper a few times, had 75 signups in one day, and were ecstatic. We thought it was gigantic. That gave me a taste of community building, which carried over to Grooveshark.

That experience was more of an advanced web project, and unlike my work in high school, we weren't making a website for a chiropractor or a funeral home, we did it for ourselves, for fun, to define our value and then create it, as opposed to seeking out bits of value other people defined and seeing how we could help.

I went on to found my second company, a little later in my freshman year. We were still doing web development but we were reaching further. Instead of going after lots of little mom-and-pop websites, we tried to do a few big sites, and we were successful in landing a few. I spent most of my freshman year developing a few web applications for some local companies and entrepreneurs. All of that ended up leading to the start of Grooveshark.

I was involved with an entrepreneurship club at UF and I was looking for someone who had the next good idea, so I could help them on the technical side. I heard a lot of ideas, most of which were not too inspiring—kids wanting to start a website to sell Gator merchandise and things like that. It was sort of what you'd expect, but nothing groundbreaking.

Then I met Sam, my cofounder and partner at Grooveshark, and he pitched me this idea on revolutionizing the music business and competing with piracy by offering a better product. I found it fascinating and he and I hit it off from day one. We were both kind of interviewing each other at the same time without calling it an interview. I could tell—not only that he had his stuff together—that he was very passionate about his idea, he truly believed in it, and I knew from the moment I met him that he was going to make this happen one way or another.

At first, the way that we approached each other was that I would be building Grooveshark and selling it to him, and I'm glad I didn't; that would have been a terrible mistake. After getting to know each other a little better, we decided to partner and we realized there was definite synergy between us.

Were you taking a heavy course load that freshman year?

I was taking a pretty average course load. I went into college with just enough AP credits. I ended up figuring out that taking a very steady course load of around 13 credits per semester would allow me to graduate on time, which is what I was looking to do.

I didn't want to get out early. I was enjoying the college experience, because at the same time I was also making connections and I knew I was going to be working a hell of a lot through the whole process. I didn't need to cram four years' worth of college into two, and then not be able to really get any work done.

The entrepreneurship class I took was definitely my favorite one, taught by Professor Rossi. He had a very realistic mindset about entrepreneurship. It's not like I came out with a bunch of notes along the lines of, "here are the nine items I need to do to become an entrepreneur." He just gave good overall insight about what it takes, that there is a certain risk vs. reward balance—that you've got to be a little crazy to be an entrepreneur, but that's what it's all about. He bridged the gap between the traditional business classes I was taking, where we would learn about business management and marketing and all those other things that are taught as how to make a company, with the entrepreneurial mindset: *throw all the rules out the door and just get it done.* He served as a real point of inspiration for Grooveshark, and both Sam and I have kept in touch with him.

Did you know anyone going into UF? Did you do anything else outside of class?

I came up to UF with a lot of close friends. Many of the people I graduated high school with, came up here. I had a nice social circle going into school, but I didn't have any business connections. I was doing the whole Ramen noodles for dinner thing, for quite a while.

The entrepreneurship club was the only organization at UF that I was ever affiliated with, and I'm very glad I picked that one. If I hadn't joined the entrepreneurship club, Grooveshark wouldn't exist because I wouldn't have met my cofounders, and I think of that organization, in particular, as the thing that really got everything started.

How did you pay your way through school? Did you work while you were there?

I worked on the side, building websites, but I didn't have a day job up here. I also had some financial aid when I started at UF, but aside from that, from the time I got up to Gainesville until now, I've just been self-sustaining by building websites for companies, and now from Grooveshark.

Did you take time to relax or was it mostly academic?

I definitely made time to keep my social life going. My freshman year was when I was really trying to get everything off the ground at once. I had this project I mentioned before, where students could share course notes online. I had my second company up here for doing larger web development projects where we would actually be bringing in tens of thousands of dollars at a time, and then I also started Grooveshark.

So, during most of my freshman year, I don't know how, but I was balancing all that. I had a girlfriend *and* I had a social life. When my sophomore year started, Grooveshark went from a cool idea and fun brainstorming to, *we have an office and we need to start hiring people*; as soon as that happened, things really started to change.

I went from working 10 hours a day, to 16. A few months into my sophomore year, Grooveshark was my life. I would do Grooveshark and sleep, and that was about it. On weekends I'd still go out and have fun, but Monday through Friday, if I was awake, I was doing Grooveshark. Obviously, school was missing from that equation.

Sophomore year I almost exclusively took online classes or classes where, at the very least, I wouldn't get penalized for not showing up. I was passing them all, but after passing by like that for two semesters, I realized my heart was no longer in it and, more importantly, there was nothing I was really chasing after. I didn't feel like I would get anything out of a degree that I had earned without paying any attention to the underlying material.

I used to pride myself on how I did in school, at least to some extent. I suppose I felt that if I did want to earn a diploma, I wanted to do it right. So I took an "indefinite leave of absence" after the second semester of my sophomore year. I still say that, eventually, I'd like to go back for fun, take classes in psychology or statistics, something like that.

Did things take off your sophomore year then?

Yeah. That was when things started taking off. But that was still a very, very slow ramp up, overall. In our first meetings, we'd sit around our whiteboard; we were projecting that by the end of

2006 we would have our product out the door. Then, by the first month of 2007, we were going to have VC funding and then, I don't know, we were going to be millionaires a few months after that. But, things did not go as planned. I had to learn that *projections are usually complete bullshit*, especially in an entrepreneurial environment; we had to temper all that with reality.

We founded Grooveshark on paper in March 2006; it wasn't until March 2007 that we got our first product out the door. But it was in a very limited, test environment. That was our alpha, and it was garbage. It was terrible, but it was a proof of concept. It showed us that, at the very least, we could come together as a team and implement something. So, we scrapped it entirely and then from March until September, we were developing our beta, which we pushed out the door in early September.

Compared to the alpha it was much improved, but it was still terrible. It was basically lipstick on a pig. It looked a lot better, but the underlying functionality was not where it needed to be. By that point, we had thought about all the different components of an ideal, music service. We listed all of them and tried out every, single one. We were thinking about comments, reviews, tags, rating, playback, syncing, social, all different stuff. But we lost sight of the *less is more* mentality, which I think is really critical to software development. It was a tough pill to swallow but, by early 2008, we realized that the beta was not getting the type of adoption that we needed.

We went back to the drawing board and thought about what people would *really want*. What's the *one thing* they would want out of a music service? Then we looked back at our core value, the whole reason we started Grooveshark, the elevator pitch that Sam gave me that we, in turn, passed on to every employee we hired after that: that we wanted to *compete with piracy by creating a better product*.

Our first attempt had been to compete with piracy by having an ecosystem where, in essence, you get paid back to download, but it was too complicated. So we thought, "okay, let's approach this on a broader level. What if we make downloads obsolete? What if we make it so that you don't *have* to download?" And that really got the juices flowing. We looked at sites like YouTube and got a lot of inspiration from that. We thought of the main silos of content on the Internet: if you want photos you go to Flickr or Google Images; if you want videos or shows you go to YouTube or Hulu; *but if you think music, there is no place to go to.*

There are lots of smaller sites. There is Internet radio on Pandora, there's a social experience on Last.fm, there are artist biographies on Wikipedia, etc. But there's no single, cohesive destination and, most importantly, there's no destination where you just listen and eclipse the value proposition of what people get from piracy by providing a faster experience, therein, legitimately competing with and creating a business model around what pirate sites have been effective at doing. So we took that really basic concept of *on-demand streaming* and built up from there.

We made a visualized funnel of how people come in to Grooveshark, and how many of them get down to the actionable steps we're looking for. We realized that for every, let's say, thousand people who visit Grooveshark.com, a certain number of them would understand the marketing message that we had posted and would keep going; a certain percentage of those would decide they want to request an account; and a certain percentage of those would come back after they got approved; and it keeps going down, down, down and we isolated each one of these drop-off points, and removed most of them. We made it so *you don't have to sign up, you don't have to download a helper application, you basically don't have to do anything.* You just go to the site, enter a query, and you're playing a song in two seconds.

When we launched that version of the service on April 15th, 2008, Grooveshark went viral. Ever since, we've been growing steadily and our graphs all look like hockey sticks.

Just to backtrack a little, how did you come up with the idea for Grooveshark?

The credit definitely goes to Sam. Sam's vision was to compete with piracy. He drove by a buy-sell-trade CD store and the first thing that popped in his head was, "I wonder if we could do that, but online." We obviously had to deviate a bit from that initial concept since the economics of the physical world and the digital world are worlds apart. We thought about how there is zero marginal cost online, and how that affects things.

By the time we met he had already broadened the concept from solely "buy-sell-trade, but online" to "let's compete with piracy"—this can't be impossible. That's when I started adding a lot of the technology aspect, thinking about the way that different services like iTunes and Rhapsody work, the way all the legal sites work; identifying what each of them really do well and what they don't do well. We realized it's not impossible to compete with free. It sounds impossible, so much so that the vast majority of our competitors completely ignored piracy—attempted to turn a blind eye to it, and only competed with each other.

We were entering into a space that was unbelievably fragmented, but that's not a bad thing. That's the way that search was, before Google entered. We saw all of these different companies that were competing for a tiny slice of a gigantic pie and we realized the money isn't in creating a better iTunes or a better Rhapsody, it's in taking 1% or 2% of the pirate market away; then we'll be bigger than iTunes plus Rhapsody plus all the other legal services combined. So the idea definitely had to evolve quite a bit from its early days.

We went through a lot of different iterations but we kept a laser focus on competing with piracy and, over time, we kept having all these different epiphanies that continued to assure us that, it was indeed possible. One was when we came up with a great analogy that we used to use in our early pitches. Often, when we'd go pitch a potential investor, they'd offer us a bottle of water or something, and we'd always accept the water and then use it as a prop because when we'd say "yeah, we want to compete with piracy" we would always get laughed at and told "okay, well it's impossible to compete with piracy, everybody has tried this, you can't compete with free." That comment always opened the door for us, we'd say, "Well, what about this bottle of water right here, did you pay for it? Why did you pay for it? You can turn on a tap and get it free", and I really love that example, because value is a funny thing.

Value is really in the eyes of the beholder, *it comes down to whether or not someone is willing to pay*. There are a lot of reasons why someone would be willing to pay. In the case of water, it's not because they can't get it for free, it's because there's the convenience, there's the packaging, there's the perceived quality, and any of those 'reasons' could be applied to traditional music. So, even if CD sales are tanking—and now downloads are hitting a plateau—that doesn't mean that there isn't money in music. When I think of all of the friends I have who haven't bought a DVD in years and they pirate their movies all the time, those same people are the ones that, every single Friday night, will spend *$10 or more on a movie ticket to see it once but they won't spend $5 to own a copy forever.*

The Internet has definitely turned traditional economics on its ass, and the way that every single monetization issue should be approached, is from a starting point—from zero, because the way things used to work just does not apply anymore. All of that said, the position that we're in right now, as a global community, is that more people are listening to more music than ever before, and there is money in that somewhere. So, we've been in an endless pursuit to make sure that we are on top of finding it and providing that value to users and artists and labels.

How do you guys get growth? It's certainly impressive that in a couple of years you're now one of the top-ranked web sites. Do you spend money on advertising?

We have never spent a dollar on advertising. As far as we're aware, at least for much of the past few years, we've been the fastest growing music service on the planet—not counting piracy, because those numbers are really hard to get a handle on.

I think the real reason is because *we created something that people want* and in early Grooveshark, back when we had the alpha and then when we had the beta, we had a marketing team; we weren't doing advertising but we would send a guy dressed up as a shark onto the UF campus. We would see little spikes every now and then, we would get a blog to talk about us and would see traffic go up, but then it starts to go back down. And we thought that what we were doing wrong was poor marketing. But at the end of the day, marketing includes product. It's the core of all marketing, and because it's the core, it's also the starting point. *You can't market something that people don't want.* That's not sustainable; it only works in the short term.

What we really had to do was to make something that people wanted and once we did that, we've relied on word of mouth. We certainly could have grown faster, especially back in the day, if we had done a lot of advertising and really pushed it harder, but, we were a startup, so operating on low amounts of capital made us less inclined to make that decision in the first place. Beyond that, I really do like the fact that the vast majority of people that hear about Grooveshark, hear about it from a friend. You don't hear about Grooveshark because you've seen an ad on TV or because we're constantly talking to the New York Times. No, you hear about Grooveshark because your friend opens it up at a party, or says to you, "you haven't heard about Grooveshark yet? Check it out", and that is the best marketing we could ever ask for.

Tell me about the fundraising process. I'm sure a lot of VCs have been skeptical especially considering you're in the dreaded music industry; you might sound like just another Napster to them. Was fundraising a positive or negative experience for you guys?

It was negative in the short term, positive in the long term. It's never good when you're first getting started, you've never pitched a VC before, you're a little bit intimidated, you don't know what to expect and you go in and they say "no." It's especially negative because, usually, they don't even say no, *they imply no but they want to keep the door open in case something changes.*

It was a new experience and we were getting a bit disheartened at times, seeing that people weren't interested in investing. But we did end up finding investment, so it was by no means the end of the world and, more importantly, it gave us a lot of perspective. We didn't come out of most of those meetings thinking, "god this sucks, maybe Grooveshark isn't right, maybe I should have stayed in school." We came out of those meetings thinking, *we need to do a better job at pitching, we're not explaining this well*. We've had the utmost confidence since day one that there is a problem that we see and there's a solution that we have in mind.

There were a few instances where we just had serendipitous moments of self-assurance, which came out of nowhere. During one pitch that we were giving, a VC told us, "You will never see DRM drop in your lifetime, I guarantee it", and he was referring to DRM on downloads because, at the time, every single major service had it. A week later, one of the four major labels, EMI, announced they were dropping DRM, and we thought, "okay, so maybe we are onto something—these guys do have millions of dollars and they have experience investing in companies but our gut seems to be right. Things are really moving in the direction of what we are talking about."

It was a challenging process finding the right fit on the investment front, but the same thing goes for hiring. At the end of the day, the type of investors that we're looking for are investing in people; not in our idea, not in our product, not in our potential to earn the money, at least not just in that. Not every investor fits that bill. There are a lot of investors out there who do invest for other reasons but, in my opinion, *the really good investors are the ones who invest in teams*.

How do you explain how all of this is legal to a user or investor? I still don't think a lot of people understand it.

First off, I'm not a lawyer, but I'll do my best to speak on this subject. Essentially the main governing law is the Digital Millennium Copyright Act (DMCA), which is very long and very complicated. But there are a few parts of DMCA that, in particular, govern over services like Grooveshark, Myspace, Google, YouTube, eBay, Craigslist, Facebook—any place where users are posting content or sharing information in certain ways. Prior to this law going into effect, there was a paralyzing amount of ambiguity regarding the rights and responsibilities of consumers, service providers, and content owners. There were no defined parameters for services to operate under.

The way that the DMCA arbitrates everything is basically by saying that *content owners have a right to their content at the end of the day*. So, if a content owner points to a specific piece of content on a service and contacts the service provider using specific parameters, then the service provider has to take that content down.

There's also a lot more to it, including obligation for service providers to notify infringing users and to ban repeat infringers. I think what everything boils down to, is that the law recognizes that in a community of millions and millions of users, some will end up breaking the rules, but at the same time, content owners always have a right to point to their content to have it quickly removed; service providers have protection from what their users are doing as long as they comply with certain responsibilities toward content providers; and users have an obligation not to pirate or upload infringing content.

So do you guys make that explicit? Do you say, "don't upload to the site"? What happens there if a user uploads and they're not supposed to, can they get into trouble?

Yes, we do make our policies explicit. Our terms of service tell users what they can and can't do with Grooveshark but, naturally, there are a lot of people who don't read them, or just decide to ignore them. So, if we ever do get a take down notice for content someone uploaded, we notify them immediately, we do follow the take-down procedures, we follow the repeated infringer procedures. A lot of times, the process can be scary to users, but it's still our obligation to carry it out.

How do you guys get your money? Is it advertising?

We make money through advertising and through subscriptions.

Was there a point where revenue just started to take off?

I think, to some extent, we need to hit a critical mass on the monetization front for it to be really effective. If you're a small service, you don't really have enough ad impressions coming in, and there aren't many advertisers who want to give you the time of day. Once you get to be big enough, you attract more of them. Then, you can start setting price floors and having different advertisers bid against each other, which really drives up overall revenue. So, the scale of Grooveshark really helps. As we've grown, we've been able to monetize much more easily.

There was also a learning process. Early on, we didn't really know how to balance our remnant versus premium, or how to handle ad operations for when we're implementing a campaign, and making sure it doesn't fall apart midway through. It was basically trial by fire.

Were there any points in Grooveshark's history where you thought, for whatever reason, either Grooveshark is going to fail or stress levels were really high?

To the former, no, to the latter, yes. At no point in Grooveshark's history did I ever believe Grooveshark was going to fail. The same goes for Sam. Grooveshark is more than our product and Grooveshark is more than our ideas. Grooveshark is the group of people that we have in the company. If tomorrow, every record label and every large technology company all partnered up and launched a service that they've secretly been developing for ten years, that is Grooveshark but a thousand times better, and for whatever reason we couldn't compete with it, we would turn on a dime.

We'd have a meeting tomorrow and we would both come in together and we'd say, "okay, the bad news is this business model isn't sustainable. The good news is we're all still here, so what are we doing now?" and that would really be it. I'm a very big fan of Jim Collins and I loved his philosophy on business, about how everything comes down to the team. Over time our team has only gotten better, the people that we've had since the beginning have only gotten sharper, smarter, and more honed in on their abilities; we've obviously also expanded and added a lot of people.

In terms of whether or not there have been any stress points in Grooveshark, hell yes, all the time! But at the same time—and, maybe it's just because I'm a little bit crazy, I kind of thrive off of that—I like a fast-paced environment, I like having to make a lot of quick decisions, I like being able to deal with it. I've been a natural procrastinator since I was a kid; I'd always do my homework the class before it was due and that kind of instilled in me a mindset in which I actually perform better when there's a little stress involved, than when there isn't any.

What is Grooveshark's biggest challenge today?

Grooveshark's biggest challenge right now, is scaling. We're morphing from just being a small little enterprise—we could all yell across the room and see each other at the same time—to having offices in multiple cities and trying to plan for growing into hundreds of employees. It's definitely challenging to think about, because the most important thing to me, is maintaining the culture that we have, and as we grow further and further there's a lot more room for that to go wrong, if we don't think about it beforehand.

How many users do you have now, on the topic of scale?

We have about 27 million people using Grooveshark, per month, right now. By traffic, we're one of the top 500 or so websites on the Internet. Apparently, we consume more bandwidth than most Internet service providers. Because of that amount of usage, we have had to scale that operation significantly. We have two different data centers right now, and we're thinking about opening a third one. It has been a challenge, but it's a challenge like any other.

It's come to us one step at a time, so it's not like overnight we thought, "shit, we've got to get three data centers up." We started off with a single server in our closet, and then that server didn't work so we get a second one, and then pretty soon we rented a little space in the local colo facility. Pretty soon, we used up all of the bandwidth that Gainesville had to offer. We moved to Jacksonville; we used up all the bandwidth Jacksonville had to offer, then we expanded to a Denver facility, and we've continued to scale since.

Has anyone at Grooveshark or have you ever had any productivity brick walls or motivational problems?

We work with each person individually. A lot of times, there's a temptation to throw blanket solutions on problems. Even widespread issues are not necessarily symptomatic of single problems, which imply single solutions. Often, it can be a single problem that requires multiple solutions. It could be multiple problems that require multiple solutions. I think it's always best to deal with each person, individually. Whenever there's any kind of a crisis in productivity or motivation, what it comes down to, is, *there is a conversation that needs to be had that someone isn't having*.

There's someone who feels as though what they're working on is not what they should be working on. There's someone who feels that somebody else in the company isn't doing the right thing. It all comes down to communication and really, just having little, isolated instances of disagreement and discontent and taking care of them one at a time, has a huge bubble-up effect.

The opposite is also true; trying to deal with some collection of individual issues with an impersonalized touch could be very detrimental. It could leave everybody actually feeling worse off than they were before.

You've hired quickly, the product scales well and it's a great product—do you have any tips for hiring?

Absolutely. It all comes down to the people. You're not looking for a tool. You're not looking for a set of experiences. *You're looking for a human being, and the most important thing is personality.* I've turned down numerous people with PhD's in computer science, who have written code for years and years. I've accepted many people who have never written a line of code in their life—it sounds crazy, but *everything comes down to personality*. When we're interviewing someone, we're essentially thinking, "is this someone that we want to be a part of our family? Do we want to adopt them? Do we see us hanging out with this person and going out with them at night?"

By day we all work together, by night, my roommate is a Groovesharker, the two guys next door are Groovesharkers, and there are probably 15 other people in the same complex. We hang out at night and we go out drinking together on weekends. That's really what it comes down to. It sounds like it's ridiculously oversimplified, but it's not. It's not as though experience isn't good and technical skills aren't good, it's just that *the starting point is personality. The personality has to be perfect* and if that's not, the person is not the right fit.

What advice would you give to an undergraduate who wants to do a startup?

Just do it. Once again, it sounds stupidly oversimplified, but I think that's the advice that everyone who has ever done anything entrepreneurial understands, and everyone who hasn't, doesn't understand. There is no magic to it, it's just a self-realization that there's no one holding you back, and there are no invisible brick walls in front of you if you have an idea. Granted, if your idea is, "I want to build a better space shuttle", you're probably going to need some funding for that, so there is some variance in terms of how much time is required before your idea reaches its fullest potential. But one way or another, if you want to create something and form a startup, there is always a first step: go ahead and take it.

Alexis Ohanian, reddit

Tags: designer, businessperson, acquired (Conde Nast), Y Combinator, undergrad founder, profitable, funded, iterate quickly, major league player (Alexa top 150 worldwide), coincidental

Overview: reddit launched in 2005 as a customizable social news web site where the community votes on stories and comments. reddit went through Y Combinator in 2005, raised $100k and was acquired in 2006 by Conde Nast. reddit is now ranked as one of the top 50 web sites in the US and one of the top 150 web sites in the world by traffic according to Alexa.com.

How did you get the idea to start reddit?

The really long version of the story is that when Steve Huffman and I applied to Y Combinator, we had a totally different idea. Keep in mind this was in 2005. We wanted a way to order food from your phone to avoid waiting in line. We thought you should be able to place your order when you are a few blocks away, so you can just walk into the Starbucks and pick up your latte; just say your name and go. The idea is that you don't have to wait in line; all the payments are handled; you don't even need to take out your wallet. So this was quick and convenient. We applied to Y Combinator; they said they thought it was a cool idea. Paul seemed to like it the first time we pitched him on it. But when we actually went to Y Combinator and interviewed, they were less pleased and they ended up actually rejecting us. That night, we got drunk and the next morning we were hung over, on a very long train back to Virginia where we were going to school. Both of us were hunched over our laptops working on our senior theses.

It was a really depressing train ride and then Paul called me when we were somewhere in Connecticut and said, "Listen, we liked you guys; we didn't like the idea. Come back and you can do Y Combinator." This was the first class of YC, so no one knew anything about it. "But if you want to be in it," he said, "come on back and come up with a new idea"; so we jumped at that chance. We had been working on this idea for almost a year, just thinking about it. I'd been doing research and talking to restaurants around Charlottesville. I had taken it very seriously—even incorporating an LLC—with the expectation of diving in with Steve after graduation. But as soon as Paul said "drop the idea, come up with something new", we both jumped at the chance.

We got off that train and took the first one back to Boston—I'm still proud of the fact that I talked the Amtrak agent into not charging us for the new tickets back, just minutes after asking Paul to buy us plane tickets back to Charlottesville for that night. We met with Paul, chatted with him for about an hour, and what came out of that conversation was essentially what would become reddit. Somewhere in the midst of that brainstorming session, Paul decided he really liked this train of thought we had gotten on, and said, "Yes, that's it. You should try to create a front page of the web", and those words really stuck in my head.

For a long time we used that as a description for what we were trying to build, and it's nice that it has actually come to fruition. Now, with over a billion page views a month, reddit really has become a place for so many people to go and get informed about what all the rest of their friends will be talking about, a day later.

How did entrepreneurship get started for you?

I don't know if it counts but when I was in high school I started and very actively managed a number of Quake 2 and Half Life clans. It started, actually, as a way for me to practice web design, because every clan needed a website. I guess there was also a bit of startup-style management because when it comes to organizing things like practices. I know this sounds absurd, but if you've been in a clan, you know how serious it can be—a well-organized clan makes a difference.

What started with wanting to make a cool Quake 2 website on Geocities later spawned a little not-for-profit—never actually registered it, just did it—that I ran during my senior year of high school. I would just go on message boards, random-ass forums of non-profits, and offer my services to make free websites for them. Just making websites for clients, I thought, would be a fun way to practice my skills. It certainly wouldn't hurt my resume or college applications; it was just a fun way to practice and create stuff with a good purpose.

So I did a few of those, started to really enjoy more of the design process than the programming side of it, and I had taken enough community college classes and done really well in my high school Pascal class to think, "I could totally be a programmer." Then I got to college and I met Steve and realized I was not a CS student; Steve is a CS student. So I continued to focus on the design side of things and after a semester abroad in London I started and moderated a small PHPBB forum.

I came back from that trip rather politicized—the United States had also invaded Iraq during that period—and inspired by Speaker's Corner. The Internet seemed like such an obvious—and much larger—platform to do what folks did on Sundays at this corner of Hyde Park, only all the time and with a global audience. So I started a forum with this in mind. It would later get me vetted by the US Government as "approved with concerns," I would later learn.

It was just a place for people to come and have discussions about world news, politics, and philosophy—a really fun exercise in community management. I managed it until the end of college, at which point it had maybe 500 active users, so we are not really talking about a significant user base at all, but it was a great experience for me.

There was always this part of me that really enjoyed doing these kinds of projects, whether it was my first Quake 2 clan website, or running and maintaining this community and forum. Ultimately, they all appealed to me because I could do them in my underwear, from anywhere I had an Internet connection. Combine that with the fact that—as juniors in college—my buddy Jack and I looked at each other about thirty minutes into an LSAT Prep class and walked out of it, to go to a Waffle House, because it was too depressing to be there on a Saturday morning.

That's where I had this epiphany—I think all epiphanies should happen in Waffle Houses—that I *didn't really want to be a lawyer* and that if I were going to invest three years and a lot of money and hard work into becoming a lawyer, I really ought to, at least, *really want* to be a lawyer.

So, that's when I stopped being *Alexis, the aspiring immigration lawyer,* and started being *Alexis, the aspiring entrepreneur,* which really just meant not having to get a real job, at least one where I had to be accountable to anyone other than myself and my cofounder.

Well, it just so happened that I was a good friend with Steve and he had tons of ideas for ways that technology could improve his life—and presumably other people's lives—so my insidious business mind was thinking of all the ways that we could make them popular and make a living from it all.

I'm absurdly optimistic, so I was pretty convinced, *especially* after he lent me a copy of Masters of Doom. This book absolutely inspired me to become a startup founder and I'm pretty sure Steve would say the same. The book is about the founding of ID Software that went on to create some of the most impressive computer games of our time: Wolfenstein, Doom, Quake. ID Software defined the first person shooter genre. And it all seemed so damn fun. I saw Carmack and Romero as this fantastic duo and I thought, "Uh huh, this could be like Steve and me, except I won't be the asshole crazy guy."

Unfortunately, unlike Carmack, Romero isn't much of a role model, but so it goes. It just seemed like a lot of fun and of course every gamer's dream is to design video games, but we figured, "Well that's going to take a little more work than two guys in an apartment, let's just try this mobile phone ordering thing and see what we can do."

We went from there. Steve already had a really comfortable job offer from a small company in Virginia that he'd been working on for years. Basically, as long as Steve passed college, they were going to hire him, and Steve is the kind of guy that always gets stuff done at the last minute and still does great on it; he was certainly not obsessing over his GPA and pulling long hours in the library like I was. But eventually, I somehow convinced him that it would be a good idea to live a near poverty, college-style existence for some indefinite period of time, with the hope that one day we could have a successful exit or at least a successful company.

How did you meet Steve?

I met Steve my freshman year of college on move-in day. He lived across the hall from me. Think stereotypical dorm hallway setup, and I was really excited when I met him because he was playing video games and I was so convinced I was not going to find anyone like me there. I didn't have any siblings; I didn't have any older friends who could tell me what it was going to be like. The perception I had of college was pretty much based on movies. I really expected it to be all about popped collars and beer pong, which is actually true at UVA, but I genuinely didn't think anyone played video games.

I was so heartened to see on my first day that Steve was playing Gran Turismo—even though it's not a great game, but nobody's perfect. We shared plenty in common in terms of gaming, and I thought, "This is wonderful." He however, was much less excited to see me because he thought—based on my name, which was on the door—that he was living in a co-ed hall and there was going to be a girl living across the hall from him. But he got over it.

There was a little disappointment, maybe?

Definitely.

I remember being the Webmaster for a clan called When Darkness Falls for Natural Selection. I also started the largest game hacking site for another game Westwood Studios released, called the Nox Hack Archive. Much of my childhood was ruined by gaming.

That's hilarious. So our clan was called Clan Nocturnal. God, we are so unoriginal with our names. You know what I miss? Let me really go off. What I really miss is how modding communities used to be such a big deal, like Planet Quake, Planet Half Life, I would go there to check up on these fantastic mod projects and that culture, I mean it's dead, right? As far as I know—and my God, so much fantastic stuff, fucking Team Fortress, if you want to go back to Quake.

The great stuff for me was even before Counterstrike. I adored Q2RocketArena, Q2CTF, and Action Quake. I can still hear the echoes of the hand cannon.

Anyway, in high school and even in college, we would bring our CRTs and our desktops over to each other's houses and the seven of us would have these fantastic LAN parties. We did this a couple of times at college where they would drive down to UVA— my friends all pretty much stayed in Maryland, so they'd come down to Virginia—and we had these LAN parties where we just wouldn't shower for four days. It was spectacular.

Oh those cathode ray tubes, those were the days.

Kids these days don't fucking appreciate what we went through.

They don't, not one bit.

Just even setting up the goddamn network was a pain in the ass sometimes.

What kind of classes did you take at UVA?

Well, when I was in school I was still taking a couple of community college classes over the summers. I think freshman and sophomore year it was, Java—oh God, I remember Steve teasing me about that one—just to keep up with programming stuff, but while I was at school at UVA, I was taking history classes. I declared a history major after my first semester and I did an honors program for history; absolutely loved it. I also majored in business, partially because I was really intrigued by the people who do it. I had seen lots of them around campus and, at that time, everyone was talking about their futures and finance—poor guys, it was such an alien thing for me to be a part of that. I just had to do it, and it was a lot of fun. I can't say I made a lot of lifelong friends in the business classes I had, though, but did have a handful of great professors who tolerated my green hair—among other eccentricities—and understood that I was just trying to hack the business world.

Pretty much all of my friends from college are either engineers or humanities majors. But all my best friends were engineers, so I was the weirdo who would bring excellent stories from business classes. If you ever want to see a bunch of engineers look appalled, tell them that the average finance professor tells his students how smart and exceptional they are.

Did you take any East Asian history classes?

I studied modern China. Well, I took a class in modern China and Japan.

Do you remember Yukichi Fukuzawa?

That's Japanese, Fukuzawa. What did he do?

He immigrated to the United States and he did some entrepreneurial things. He started one of the leading schools. He is known as one of the founders of modern Japan.

I totally forgot; I'm reading Wikipedia now. Thank you.

I loved reading his autobiography. I took a history class and that was my favorite historical character.

Son-of-a-bitch, my professor didn't do him justice. Granted, there's quite a lot of Japanese history to cover in one semester, but still... Well, we never stop learning, right?

When you were in college, were you thinking you wanted to do a startup?

No, I was going to be an immigration lawyer. I was 100% sure of that. I was doing history because I liked it and then I figured, "Well, that's a good degree," It's not like it's an awful degree to prepare for an LSAT with, because of the reading, critical thinking, and writing skills, etc. I was just planning on going to law school and doing immigration law primarily to help immigrants get citizenship.

How did you pay your way through school?

I actually was really lucky. I was an only child so there was only one kid for my parents to pay for, and they actually were able to afford the out-of-state UVA tuition, thanks to my great aunt who had put together—I guess that makes me kind of a trust fund kid— she put together a trust fund for me to use for school. She had no children of her own and so that fund paid for me to go to UVA.

I've been pretty active in giving back to UVA as a result. She's since died, so I figured I would pay it forward with the scholarships at the university. I wanted to make it right.

Did you party and relax and do stuff outside of class, or was it mostly academic?

No, I spent all of my time in the library. My senior year I think I had 24 credits. I had to get a dean to sign off on it because it wasn't supposed to be allowed. My advisor, Professor Midelfort, also ran the distinguished majors program and informed me on graduation that he'd never actually seen anyone do both a distinguished major and a degree in the business school. Coincidentally, both departments had their graduations at the same time, even though I was only getting one piece of paper— and it had to be the B.S. in Business for a bunch of bizarre reasons—I obviously chose to attend the History Department graduation.

I suppose it's unorthodox because most business school students aren't terribly interested in much else. But I figured I was going to squeeze every possible bit of knowledge out of those four years—I also minored in German, too. Naturally, all of these things help me every single day. (Laughter)

What were you thinking about doing, right as you graduated?

After I decided I wasn't going to go to law school I just figured I really had to convince Steve or someone to build a company with me. It was going to be a software company, and whether it's web or we make the next Quake, Steve or someone like Steve was going to absolutely have to be there, because I was not going to build it alone. I just started talking to him and trying to talk him out of that job he was going to take and once he agreed to it, I used most of my spare time during senior year to think about this company, incorporating the LLC, and doing all the non-technical, cofounder mandatory bullshit that just has to get done to start a company.

I have always been fairly optimistic, so I was never terribly concerned. I just figured I had so little to lose because, as Bob Dylan wisely pointed out, we really have nothing—not that I had nothing, but I didn't have a family, I didn't have expectations; and I was living on a fairly reasonable, typical student budget. I figured, "As long as we can do some consulting work on the side"—and this was before Y Combinator was announced—we can pay the bills and then focus the rest of our time on building the startup and hopefully it will be profitable pretty quickly and I'll keep going. I also had two extremely supportive parents who never really questioned or wondered about what kind of life choices I was making. So, I really was not ever too worried; let's hear it for naïve optimism and ignorance!

When you were in college was there anyone in particular that inspired you?

I had professors. That was actually the best thing that I got out of business school. I really don't feel like I learned a lot from a lot of the finance classes, for example; I didn't learn anything terribly useful from them. But there were individual professors that were great. Professor White, actually, was the first one I ever pitched on Steve's remote food ordering app idea and we were in Singapore. I guess that was quite a pivotal moment, actually. I'd gotten accepted for a summer internship at Ogilvy in New York and I was thrilled because I was going to be able to live in New York the city of my birth and home to the best falafel in the US.

Ogilvy is a pretty big deal advertising agency and at the time I was like, "Oh this should be great. I can learn the ins and outs and then apply this towards the startup we'll be doing" and Professor White, at the time, was like, "Hey, I've got to bring this group of UVA students to Singapore for a technopreneurship forum. It's going to be a competition where schools from all over the world are going to compete. Oh, and by the way, UVA is going to pay for it so it's like a week and a half free in Singapore with travel stipend." And I was like, "Dude! Fuck Ogilvy, I am going to do it."

I love traveling. It was a paid trip to Singapore and so I jumped on that and the first night we were there I was out with him and his wife and I pitched him on the idea and he said, "You know what Alexis? I get pitched all the time but this actually could work", and he gave me some great feedback. I have this awful email; I can't believe I published it. I sent an email to Steve the next day or a couple of days later in the middle of this "technoprenuership forum"—I love Singapore for having "technopreneurship forums"—so enthusiastic about what we were doing together and how I absolutely needed him and we could take over the world, and so on.

This was the food ordering idea?

Yeah, this was food ordering. This is the summer between junior and senior year.

Is this when you applied to Y Combinator?

We saw Paul give his talk and then start Y Combinator during our spring break, senior year because, what else would we do on our senior year spring break? We went out to Boston, heard his talk, met with him, and he agreed to come out with us for drinks, after. He signed Steve's Lisp book and I followed, saying we had come all the way from Virginia, and that it would be totally worth the cost of buying him a drink to get his opinion on our startup and he said, "Sure." So we met with him, which was thrilling. He loved the idea and he said, "You have a pretty good chance of making something happen." A few weeks later he announced Y Combinator. I persuaded Steve to email him and Paul got back really quickly.

He was like, "Hey, you know what? You've got a pretty good shot, you should apply", and it went from there. So, after almost a year, at least six months of thinking about this other idea really seriously, we got up to Y Combinator sometime in April and once we heard Paul's offer, we immediately dropped that idea and started actually working on reddit up at Boston, in June.

Did you guys end up raising more money after that? Was it positive or negative?

Positive, we got money. We only took one angel round of $70,000. So, in total we raised $82,000.

Did you split the work? Did one person fundraise while the other worked on the product?

Unfortunately, that did not work as planned.

I was dealing with some personal stuff; my girlfriend was in hospital and so I was actually in Germany for a lot of that communicating via email and occasional phone calls. So, Steve had taken that mantle. We weren't actively looking but folks started approaching us and we raised without too much trouble.

Our would-be angel Paul Graham was like, "You know what? I like what you guys are working on. I know you are going through a lot of stuff right now, here is enough money, here is 70 grand that will give you guys another year to live and keep working, will you take it?" And I remember having this email conversation with Steve I think, from some hospital in Freiburg, and we were just like, "This is one thing to not have to think about anymore. Paul is a valuable advisor to have, so why not?"

So, on the whole it was solid and what we needed. In hindsight, in a perfect world, we probably could have been more strategic about it, but there were so many other things outside of our control. I have no regrets.

However, a year later, when we sold reddit, I was actively running that entire process. Anything that's not programming-related for someone like Steve really just is a waste of his time.

Did you have any advisors?

We didn't. I've actually spent a lot of time looking for advisors. There are people I found in my life who I go to for certain things. Throughout reddit, Steve and I really were just kind of bullshitting our way through stuff. I would try the thing that seemed like the best idea at the time and if it worked out well then I'd make a note that this thing seems to work out well in certain situations, and we really made it up as we went along; now seeing it with Hipmunk, we have this fabulous advisor pool and we have people who can actually use their experience to say, "In this situation, consider doing X, Y and Z", and that is very helpful. And of course we ourselves are far more experienced, so I'm seeing the benefits every day because I'm not doing *nearly* as much stupid stuff. But I know I'll be saying the same thing in five years about my present self, though.

I'm sure reddit would have benefited from something like advisors. But of course we were also working on something that was fairly new, and I think people hadn't even talked about social media at that point; most of us who were building stuff in this 'social media world' were just faking our way through it. See what works, see what doesn't, iterate, and always stick to the vision.

How long did it take to get the beta version of reddit built?

I think we launched in June, a little less than a month after we got started. It was a really rough version of the site and it was basically a version that we just finally got online because it was tough. It's not like there were a lot of people clamoring to see what we were about to do. We were just two random kids out of UVA. There were people who were curious to see what Y Combinator was going to produce, and it helped being the first YC company to launch.

To get that initial traction we benefited from those Paul Graham fans that were just curious about what Paul was doing, what YC was doing, and Paul made sure to mention us whenever he was talking about Y Combinator. A couple of his early essays helped out because he would link to us and, certainly, having Paul Graham readers as your first users on a social news website is a great asset, because the links that they are going to submit are generally high quality and pretty thoughtful and so it sets the tone very nicely.

As for growing it outside of that, I begged a lot of my friends and I definitely emailed that old list of folks from that PHPBB forum, announcing it. But the rest of it was just a lot of grunt work. Every time someone wrote a blog entry about reddit— and this is, of course, pre-Twitter—good or bad, I was going to leave a comment there and engage them, talk to them, make a note of them. I just worked my way up the food chain, so to speak. The funny thing is, nowadays, TechCrunch is considered the place to launch your site. reddit never got a single mention on TechCrunch until the day we got acquired.

I always stress to startups that they shouldn't be building and working for TechCrunch appearances because those don't really mean anything in the end. You can still have a successful startup without ever having a write-up on TechCrunch, for instance.

Did you build fake accounts to get user growth early on?

Yes, I've said this publicly, usually to some laughter. It certainly helped. This was also one of those things that fell within the purview of the non-technical founder. Steve made this nifty little way—a form field—for us to just type in a random username that came to mind, along with the URL, and the title, and that's who it would be submitted by. That definitely helped, but it really only mattered for the first three weeks, and then there was some point when Steve and I didn't actually have to do anything, and we were so thrilled.

We didn't have to submit or vote; there was no commenting back then. The site just worked, and the trick with a social site, especially one like reddit, is: if people come to it and it's empty, the incentive for them to want to contribute to it is really, really low, especially when it's a totally new thing. Even now, when new reddits are created all the time, it's really tough to feel interested in submitting to a lonely, empty new reddit, but once there is a little bit of momentum, once there's a few new users, there is some social proof and this is now what, six years later?

Back then you show someone an empty reddit and they just see a blank website and they can't even comprehend what or why they should ever consider participating in this, so I really have no qualms about having done that, in the beginning. It would have been a different story if we had commenting and I was writing comments like, "What a brilliant comment, Alexis, your genius is unmatched!" That would have been crossing the line. And obviously fake.

Did you ever think reddit was going to fail?

Oh yeah, every day. Yeah, it's extremely bipolar. There were mornings when I woke up thinking, "Oh fuck, we're fucked", and other mornings when I was like, "Oh, this is going to be awesome. We're kicking ass and taking names."

Server failures? Bad PR?

You should talk to Steve about all the nights he had to spend sitting with his laptop because the site was written in LISP back then. He actually had to leave a friend of ours' birthday party, because the site went down. He ran into, I think it was an Apple store, because he knew he could get online there easily and reset it.

Was there a point where you guys noticed revenue picking up?

No.

I'm half joking. We didn't have ads on the site for a while and that was part of the appeal; that it was a very user-focused, content-first site, and at some point, Federated Media said, "We'll run some ads for you guys, we'll sell. You guys just put up the ad space", and I was like, "Alright, this could be kind of cool", and I negotiated a good deal with them and we just had ads running on our comments pages. That was an interesting little start because it was surprise checks every month, and that seemed fun.

I'll tell you what really got interesting was when we started getting into the white label game and that was because Condé Nast reached out to me because of a mutual friend I had with their head of M&A. He dropped me a note and said, "Hey, I am from Condé Nast"—which I had never heard of at the time—"We publish Wired and the New Yorker", and I was like, "Okay, cool. I know who these guys are" and he said, "Let's do a deal together and basically create a pink version of reddit for celebrity gossip." So we worked up the terms for this licensing deal and then we started; between the setup fee and the recurring monthly we were like, "Wow, we can live for a while on this", and I'm sure we would have experimented more with licensing had we not gotten acquired, but that licensing business model was sort of just the early flirtations, the testing of the water by Condé Nast, to see if they could work with us.

I wanted to actually ask you about that because I know when we got acquired by Loopt it wasn't one of those sudden emails where they say, "Hey, we want to acquire your company." What was the process like for you guys?

The first email was just that. It was, "Hey, we've got a mutual friend in common. I'm from Condé Nast, give me a call, and let's talk." I was definitely trying to walk that fine line because I think, like all founders, you are intrigued by this idea, but you are also really just trying to focus on your product because you spend one day thinking about acquisition and before you know it you are spending three months thinking about it and you haven't been thinking about what actually matters, which is your product. So trying to balance that was tricky.

Eventually, I remember my one day of vacation—a buddy of mine had rented a place for a bunch of us from college in the Outer Banks—and I got an email from Kourosh that said, "Hey, why don't you come out to San Francisco, we're having the RAVE

Awards, and then we can go get breakfast in the morning" and when the M&A guy from Condé Nast says that, you don't say "no."

So I was like, "Sure, I need a ticket from Norfolk", which was the closest airport. Fortunately, my dad is a travel agent, so he found the closest airport with a flight to San Francisco—which is still a fucking four-hour drive from the Outer Banks. So I had one night of vacation; the next morning I'm in the car driving to the airport to fly to San Francisco to spend the night, to wake up, have breakfast, talk with Kourosh, during which I finally approached this acquisition subject, and then fly back home; so it goes. Totally worth it, but these things just kind of happen sometimes and the first conversation is never, "Hey, we want to buy you."

How long did it take from start to finish?

About six months.

How did you split the work early on?

When it was just the two of us in the apartment the work flow was pretty much, "Let's talk about the stuff we want to do", and then a little dry erase action, and then I'll basically shit out a bunch of different ideas, all with Paint Shop Pro 5.0 ugly-ass mock-ups, because I'm not a good designer; I'm like, a good *enough* designer.

With logos: between reddit, Breadpig and Hipmunk, it's clear that I cannot be associated with anything that doesn't have some kind of cute logo that I designed. But I'm talking about UI kind of stuff, like you give me 24 hours and maybe I can come up with a cute logo, but really good design is something that I'm just not capable of. I'm good enough. It was a miracle that we finally got rid of Verdana on Hipmunk, and I was overjoyed. Steve still defends that font; it's unconscionable. It's jut not right.

Anyway, I'd shit out all these ideas and Steve would be like, "Well, that's not feasible, that's not going to happen. I can't do that, but this could work." At the end of the day, when it's only two people in an apartment, you have to draw a line somewhere. So when it was a technical decision, I deferred to Steve, and when it was a non-technical decision, Steve would defer to me; whether that was ordering Chinese food or pizza, or moving forward with some kind of non-technical thing when it came to the more touchy-feely aspects of the product, and the community aspect of reddit.

As the site grew, and as we took more people on, even after we got acquired that pretty much stayed. Like any smart tech company, though, we hired far more programmers than we hired non-technical people and all those people just kind of started working under Steve.

Was the schedule chaotic? Did it change over time?

I was going through a bunch of other stuff during most of reddit, and so work for me was extremely therapeutic. I found myself diving back into it at any opportunity. If I was awake I was probably thinking about reddit and I was probably working on reddit. It helps when you're handling all things non-technical. Basically, in my Gmail I can find an excuse to be doing work at any given time, and if it's in some way helping reddit advance towards some end of getting larger and really becoming a front page of the web, it's worth it. It felt really, really good to invest all that time in something that I enjoyed doing.

Any time something went wrong, it was great to know that I was responsible for it because that also meant that anytime something went right, I would also be responsible for it. Working *with people* and not *for someone* made such a difference. Knowing what I was doing there in Boston, working on a startup, as opposed to being at home with family, I wanted to know that I was putting that time in for a good reason and not squandering it. It was pretty much all the time. I do prefer to work at night though, and I do keep a pretty awkward sleep schedule. I love sleeping in during the day; I don't give a fuck. It's just really frustrating running your startup when you have to go to the bank too, and apparently they are not on our schedule.

I've read some of the stories. You wonder if it would have made the situation worse for some people, but for you, you basically worked more or you stayed involved even through it. So that's really impressive.

I had a lot of very supportive people in my family so I never felt guilty taking out my laptop in the hospital. In a lot of ways I really see it as an advantage that I had because no matter how much press competitors were getting, no matter what we were going through, no matter what, I still felt like I could outwork everyone we were going up against. It didn't matter; I didn't care. There was no way that we were going to be beat, and there was no way that reddit was going to be thwarted. Let's hear it for *that* startup delusion.

You guys continue to grow enormously. Everyone is on reddit. Did you do anything to promote it?

I'm finally writing this blog entry and it will be up tomorrow because everybody has asked me that, especially now that reddit has gotten so big. Keep in mind: reddit really grew more in the last year than ever before. So, as soon as Steve and I left, that's when reddit really took off; whether that's correlation or causation, I leave up to your readers. It was a technology that gave power to the users—though I know it sounds so trite. If you look at where reddit started and where it is now, we have done nothing but give more and more authority to our users. We've let them create their own communities. They have moderator controls over those communities. We even open-sourced the site.

They are actually creating content on the site now, I think a third of the links submitted to reddit are actually just self-posts on reddit. They are discussions, like, "I'm a nuclear engineer, ask me anything." It's fabulous content that the rest of the Internet talks about a day later. I'm really proud of the fact that everything about the technology—everything about the product—actually marched toward that ideal that everyone was spouting about a democratic front page. The product walked that talk. On the community side we really gave a damn. Everyone we hired was from the reddit community. They were all redditors and there were lots of reasons why I think that was a good idea.

Every person who joined reddit got onto the program and they understood that what we were trying to do was create a fabulous community, where people really believed in this site so much that, not only would they spend their time submitting links—voting on them, and commenting—they could even go a step further and take ownership within the site; actually create communities of their own and start coming up with projects of their own. At first this was tough, that I had to kind of nurture, whether it was various, end-of-the-year fundraisers we'd do with our buddies XKCD, where we'd let redditors vote on which charity we donate the funds to.

But a few years later, we started acting on reddit comments. One of the first, one that I think sort of sets stuff in motion, was about the guy who spotted Gordon Freeman at CERN (it wasn't really Gordon Freeman but it sure as hell looked like him). And the comments on reddit to that post where they found the photograph, said, "We should send him a crowbar", and it didn't do even that well. I think it was a pretty high-scoring post, but it got me thinking, "That's a great idea." So I went on HomeDepot.com and I ordered a crowbar, bought red and silver spray paint, painted it, and got in touch with the redditor who worked at CERN who could deliver it. I think we got a head crab hat as well, and the dudes at FARK also sent a Half Life strategy guide so Gordon would know what to do, and we mailed it to him.

We actually sent it and sure enough, a month later—and we kept the community abreast on the blog with photos, and Chris Slowe dressed up as a Head Crab Zombie and we actually got a fantastic photo shoot back from this random-ass Italian Physicist who had never even heard of Gordon Freeman, and he's like, "Oh yeah, Gordon Freeman! Cool, I'll put on a lab coat and act this out for you." So he's running around CERN, bashing scientists over the head with a crowbar for the pleasure of the Internet. That was one post where, once we finally came around full story and said, "Look what happened", I think a lot of people on reddit thought, "Holy shit, this actually worked", and it wasn't long after that, I think, that they realized we were just something that got in their way and they didn't need to wait for a moderator to get in the way. They could just do this.

I think back to the very first fundraiser we did for the EFF and we raised a modest sum of money but it was all very orchestrated, and redditors contributed a little bit when they voted on the non-profit, but my god, they raised almost a million dollars last year between DonorsChoose.org and Haiti's Direct Relief, and admittedly the Haiti Direct Relief one was another one where the community was interested in this and did a little bit of coordinating on the back end, because it was easier for me to get in touch with a couple of the important people at Direct Relief.

Jump ahead five months later and all of a sudden reddit is entirely, entirely, running this massive DonorChoose.org fundraiser that gets the attention of Stephen Colbert. It wasn't long until they realized that this was possible, and now it's like a daily occurrence on reddit that there is some crowd-sourced awesomeness going on, and it's just fabulous.

I used to be a Digg user—

Ohhh, Jared. Well, nobody's perfect.

Well, back before reddit existed I think Digg was around for a while, but I didn't feel that strong community effect there; I feel it at reddit.

It's the same, and some of that is definitely a culture we instilled where, yeah, I really was obsessive over every comment, everything. Everyone who worked at reddit needed to be in a conversation at some point, and we'd go out of our way to send each other messages, so if some random user was complaining, we would make sure the admin saw it so that he could chime in and be like, "How can I help you?" Just to let people know that we cared. Not enough startups really give a damn.

It's like throwing a party and trying to be an attentive host, but you take that kind of dogged determination to make sure that everyone was having a good time (and downvote assholes), to sort of show the rules for this community, and to be the change you want to see in other people; to be the redditors that you wanted to see in other redditors, combined with the fact that we had a system Steve invented where good conversations actually float up to the top, and so when you're having a really thoughtful pun thread, a lot of people see it and thus it gets reinforced that this is an appropriate way to behave in a comment thread.

We definitely started with a really good sample of users with Paul Graham's following that came to the site. We were fortunate with the users that we got to start with, and as much as I love shamelessly praising redditors for their intelligence, cleverness, and overall awesomeness, the fact of the matter is: we've got software that really does a good job of separating the wheat from the chaff; that's just going to happen and then it's going to discourage the trolls unlike on YouTube, for instance, or pretty much any other site with comments, and I wish more people would steal our goddamn commenting system.

The commenting and ranking system is genius.

Well, that was all Huffman. Although I will say there was a debate for a little while about whether or not we should even have comments, because the thinking was that links were a little too ephemeral, anyway, and that good conversations couldn't happen. But I was really, really hell bent on it, and once we finally had it at the top of the to-do list, Steve was like, "I've got an idea" and then he just disappeared for a week and when he came back and I saw it, I was like, "Oh, my god, this is game over right here."

What advice do you offer to non-technical people interested in doing tech startups?

Here's the thing. I don't think Steve would have ever started a company with me if I needed him to show me how to set up my FTP client. If you are at least technically competent, let's say you got A's in your high school Pascal class for instance—or whatever it is they are teaching now—and let's say, you've taken a few classes and you have an interest In programming, I think there is a test. Jeff Atwood wrote about this fantastic test like, "Are you a sheep?" It's a really basic programming question. If you're a sheep you're technically competent, if you're a goat, you're fucked, you don't understand anything about programming.

Let's say you've never programmed in Python or Ruby or any of those suitable languages. But I at least know what programming is and have some experience doing it—granted, just Pascal, Java, and Visual Basic. I think it's totally, totally worth getting some background especially with shit like Heroku and I'm sure there's some Python equivalent now. For 99% of web-based startups, you're going to need a technical lead on the founding team and that's the requirement, so if you are a non-technical founder and you have some programming aptitude, it's totally worth picking up some chops in the way of programming.

45

If Steve did not respect me, he would not have been my cofounder. It is a really tough world right now for non-technical cofounders, and it's a bit frustrating for me, especially in New York—I hear plenty of them who come to me and ask me the same thing and unfortunately, I'm bummed out because I can't give them a good solution. It's either, become technically competent yourself, or re-do the last couple of years you spent in college and become friends with engineers.

Can you talk about the time you most successfully hacked a non-computer system to your advantage?

I think one of my skills is in social hacking. I know that can have kind of nefarious tones. I'm not talking about calling the credit card agency and somehow getting them to divulge all kinds of important information. More like, I think the fact that I was able to get in that first round of Y Combinator probably demonstrates some level of social hacking, because I was the only non-technical founder and I know deep down Paul probably was skeptical of me for some time just because I was a new breed. I was *friends* with a technical founder but not technical myself. Fortunately it worked out OK. Getting into Y Combinator was definitely one of my best hacks.

Tom Preston-Werner, GitHub

Tags: programmer, designer, profitable, laid off, grad school dropout, side project, self-funded, hiring, design-focused, major league player (Alexa top 1,000), coincidental

Overview: GitHub launched in 2008 to make it easy for many programmers to work on the same project, or as they call it, "social coding." It's like Wikipedia meets Google Documents meets Facebook for programmers: it uses the collaborative editing features of Wikipedia, everyone works on the same document—or program—with Facebook-like social features so that developers see what other developers—their friends—are working on. As of 2010, GitHub hosts over 1 million projects and has operated profitably since its launch. Founder Tom Preston-Werner turned down $300,000, in addition to a retention bonus and a base salary from Microsoft to start GitHub.

Can you recall your earliest experience doing something entrepreneurial? I'm curious where this all started for you.

When I was a little kid, maybe 6 or 7 years old, I made little booklets and tried to sell them to my parents. They just had drawings on them, but I pretended that they were legitimate publications, and then I tried to get my folks to buy them from me so I could have a little more allowance money.

I never really did lemonade stands or anything. As a kid I wasn't like a lot of people who are entrepreneurs now, who were selling stuff and doing legitimate businesses when they were really young. I didn't really ever do that as a kid.

The first real business I started was called Cube6 Media. I had been working at a web consulting and design firm that also did some PR, with two other people. We perpetually disagreed with the decisions being made at the company, but couldn't do anything about them, and we were constantly talking about starting something ourselves as a way to explore the things we were interested in without having to answer to a corporate boss.

We actually all three ended up getting laid off, and once that happened we decided to start Cube6 Media. So we did that and did a few things with it, here and there, but we didn't know many people, so it was hard to drum up business. Eventually the other two quit and went to do full-time jobs elsewhere, because business was not great and it was difficult, scary, and we didn't know what the hell we were doing, but I carried on for three years.

It was a really good experience. I learned a lot about how difficult business can be and how you have to deal with finding your own clients, and doing your own taxes and accounting, and all that stuff that you don't think about when you are working for someone else. It was a kind of trial-by-fire for me. I bought a bunch of books and just jumped in and tried to do it; I screwed a lot of stuff up and I'm sure I paid way too much in taxes, but it was a great experience to just get into it and see what it was all about.

While you were in school, did you do anything outside of your class work?

I was really into physics. I wasn't really entrepreneurial and I wasn't much of a programmer at the time. I was mostly interested in theoretical particle physics. I read a lot about quantum physics and tried to understand it as much as I could without having the math background you really need, to understand it. That took me all the way through to college, so high school and college for me were mostly about trying to learn as much as I could. I had also been programming since high school, on the side, which I always enjoyed.

What were you favorite and least favorite classes?

I actually enjoyed the computer science classes more than the physics classes once I got to college, because college-level physics is just about math, and I was never that great of a mathematician; I could never do proofs very well. Some people were really good at them and I just wasn't, so really hardcore math while I could do it, I never really enjoyed it. But the computer science and Java we learned were awesome because you could write stuff and then stuff would show on the screen and you could really affect things in the real world immediately.

Physics was about this endless struggle to find some new piece of evidence to describe the physical world, whereas programming yielded an immediate result from a very small amount of effort—it was so much more to my liking that I could get something done right away than physics was. So I loved the CS classes; humanities classes were probably my least favorite—that was just what you had to do, those core classes.

Were you consciously thinking about doing startups or looking for cofounders in college?

No, I never really thought about starting a business in high school or college. That was never really something I wanted. At that time, I just wanted to be a researcher doing physics stuff because I didn't really know what that meant, but I knew that I thought physics was awesome. Business stuff was not on my radar at all until I started working for a startup out of college.

I went to Harvey Mudd College in Southern California for 2 years. The first year I majored in physics, the second year I switched to CS and then after that, 2 graduating seniors were going to do a startup and were looking for programmers. A couple of my buddies and I knew them so we started working for their startup, which was called Infostry at the time, and that eventually became Mindcruiser.

This was in 1999, towards the tail end of the dotcom bubble. They were like, "We are going to make a *bazillion dollars,*" so I worked for them that summer. At the end of the summer things were looking pretty good, we had some investment, and they told me I was welcome to keep working there if I wanted to drop out of school. So I was faced with the decision of continuing on with the startup, or going back to Harvey Mudd to finish up my CS degree. The discussion I had with myself was really, "Does it make sense to go back to school for 2 years so that when I get out I can basically be doing the exact same thing I am doing right now?" It didn't make sense to me, so I dropped out after my second year, kept working for that startup, and learned a lot. I learned more practical information than I think I would have, by staying in school.

Did you ever go back and graduate?

No. I never went back.

Did you take time off to relax from the classes while you were in college?

In all the books about colleges that you have and pore through, when you are in high school, Harvey Mudd was always identified as *the college in the United States with the highest average number of hours of homework per night.*

So, I studied a lot, but I think Harvey Mudd was study hard, play hard. So while we studied a ridiculous amount and did a ton of homework, we also had some pretty great dorm parties for which we were actually able to buy alcohol through money given to us by the college itself. I don't know how this happened, but you could basically raise money for your dorm and then apply it to buying booze for parties, and that was the way we did it. So we had the most ridiculously amazing parties; we had bars and the students would bartend, and Harvey Mudd is part of the 5 Claremont colleges, so people would come from all of the colleges to any of the parties that were around.

The school was giving you money to party. This sounds like a hack that somebody figured out.

I think it might have been. It lasted until about 2000, after I had already left, when someone at MIT drank himself to death. On campus during one of the parties, he died from alcohol poisoning and that is when they cracked down at Harvey Mudd. They stopped doing it; you had to have external bartenders, check IDs, have a beer garden, and all this stuff. So after that tragedy they really locked things down. But before that, when I was there, it was crazy; the parties were crazy.

I had a car that had died and we decided that a good use for this car would be to push it into the quad. Because the battery was dead, we hooked the headlights up to a socket with just a DC converter on it, and powered the headlights off of that. So the headlights were on and the car was sitting in the middle of this party where all of the people were; people were dancing on it and it got completely destroyed.

I use GitHub for many projects and I think it's great. How did you come up with the idea?

The idea for GitHub came from attending the Ruby meetups here in San Francisco. We have several different kinds of Ruby meetups; one, we had created because the existing one was attended by a lot of VCs and it sort of became a meeting for VC pitches, where they were looking for people to invest in, which is okay if you are looking for that kind of thing, but that is not what it was supposed to be about.

So we created our own which was called *I Can Has Ruby* about three years ago. You had to know someone in the group in order to be invited. We tried to keep it open enough so that a lot of people could come in, so it wasn't super elitist it was just intended to keep VCs and other business people out. We wanted to really have the talks focus on technology and what people were doing with Ruby.

We had a really good group of people and we'd meet up at some office around town every two weeks, and a couple of people would give presentations about what they were doing and what they were interested in; during these meetings, my co-worker—

Dave Fayram at PowerSet, where I was working at the time—had started using Git on his own and had introduced me to it. He thought it was amazing and I didn't really know what it was about because we were using Subversion. So it was pretty unfamiliar, but he insisted it was the best thing ever and so I kept trying to use it and eventually got to figure out how the branching worked—this is three years or so ago, when Git was not even as usable as it is now.

It was kind of complicated and there weren't a lot of resources to learn it. So I struggled through and kept using it and at the meetups, we would spread this around and say, "Hey, check out this new system Git, it's distributed, you don't have to have a centralized thing, branching and merging is way simpler than Subversion," and I think people started to realize that it was really powerful. Git could do a lot of things that Subversion couldn't and it was technically superior in a lot of ways, but you did have to struggle through it to figure it out because there was no GitHub at the time; there weren't a lot of learning resources or videos or books. We would always talk about how great it was, except there wasn't really a good way to work on it on a single-code base with other people, which is ironic, because that is what Git is supposed to be good at: projects with other people.

Yet, if you wanted to share a repository with someone, the only way to do it was to setup a Linux server somewhere, give people user accounts, and have them log in and use that for coordination. It was always a huge pain in the ass. We would throw around ideas during this group and talk about how we could make this system better and the kinds of things that Git could do, being distributed, and I would try to come up with ideas that would make it easy to use. They all tended to be complicated, though.

I don't remember exactly when it was or how it occurred, but I thought that really all you needed was the ability to upload a repository to a server, and a lot of people joke about this, that GitHub is centralized—using Git in a centralized way even though it is distributed. But that is really what Git needed in order to be successful, a common place that key people could agree on to put their code to share, because in a completely distributed world where nobody knows where anything else is, you can't get anything done; you have to have some agreed-upon collaboration point. So the idea, at first, was "Let's just create a good place that is very simple, where you can upload your repository, view it online, and be able to share it with other people." That was the crystallization. That was the initial concept.

I always tell people: these language meetups are a great place to find cofounders for companies because they are going to be like you. They are interested in the same things you are and it's really easy, when you are interacting in person, to know if they have a personality that is going to mesh with yours, if they have a good sense of humor, if they know different things—it's a perfect place to find a cofounder. That's how I ran into Chris Wanstrath, who I originally started it with, and then P.J Hyett, who worked with Chris on some stuff, previously, came on shortly thereafter as a cofounder. We were all part of the same Ruby group, we would hang out together.

Did you guys ever raise money?

No. GitHub, to this day, has never raised any external funding at all.

Did you ever have any advisors?

Not really. We've done pretty much everything without a lot of external guidance. I think that is just the way we are, though. We are very independent; we don't trust what other people say, even if they are supposedly experts on things; we like to think about things from first principles and say what makes sense to us, even though we may be inexperienced. We want to use logic to go through different things and decide which one is the best.

How long did that first beta take you to build for GitHub? How did you spread the word?

We started working on it in October of 2007. That was the first commit to Grit, the underlying Ruby library that GitHub is built on top of. I had actually started working on that library on October 10th, 2007 with the idea of, "Let's build a website, I'm a web programmer, I know Ruby, I can write this library to let me interact with Git repositories through Ruby. So let me see if that is possible and then with that I will build the rest of the site."

I think October 16th was the next Ruby meetup, which I attended. Afterwards, we went to a bar called Zeeks in San Francisco and I was separated from the group, getting another beer or something. I had my computer with me and was just sitting down for a second, and Chris Wanstrath walked in; he hadn't been at the meetup but came in for the drinking part. We always loved the drinking part afterwards, it was my favorite part because that is where you really got to socialize with people and talk about ideas; during the meetups it was mostly presentations.

So these drinking sessions afterwards were where the real action happened. So, I had been working on this for a week or so and I had gotten it working in a basic fashion, interacting with Git repositories and programming some stuff from Ruby, and he walked in and I didn't really want to do Rails anymore to do front-end stuff, I wanted to do the library back-end stuff, and I did a lot of graphic design for Cube6 Media so I was pretty good at doing front-end design work, HTML, CSS, JavaScript kind of stuff.

I thought it would be great to start it with someone else who was really good at the Rails stuff. Chris and I had been working on some projects together using Git so we both understood the problems inherent in using Git and Chris had some ideas of his own as far as making sharing of Git repositories easier, but they were a little more limited in scope. So when he walked in, I thought, "Chris would be perfect to partner with on this project."

He came over, said hi, and I said, "Dude, check this out." I pulled out my laptop, showed him this library that I was writing, and said, "I want to make a very simple website for sharing Git repositories, called GitHub. I have registered the domain already and I need someone to do Rails." He looked at it and said almost immediately, "I'm in, let's do it" because he knew. He knew Git was going to became popular, it was just a matter of time, and what it really needed was an easy way for people to share the code, that's all it needed, just that one little thing that nobody was doing.

I had a feeling it would eventually be very popular but I thought it would take a long time because, at the time, it was so much different than it is now; nobody was using Git, there were a few projects, the Linux kernel and a few other little esoteric projects, that was it. Nobody was using it.

So it took 6 days to build a prototype?

All I had at the time, all I showed Chris, was a few commands that I ran in my terminal—in my shell—saying, I can pull information from a Git repository into a Ruby object and query it that way. That's all I had, I had no interface; I had nothing. Maybe I had a Photoshop mock-up of what it might look like or something, but that was it.

When you showed him the prototype, were you able to get some kind of repository somewhere else onto your computer?

It wasn't even that, it was simpler than that. Really, it was: I have a repository on my computer already, a Git repository that I have created and with Ruby I can read commits out of it and say, "Show me the list of commits and their command messages." It was just to retrieve the information from an existing repository on disk into data structures that you could then deal with, programmatically.

Over the next couple of months we only worked nights and weekends because I was working full time on PowerSet and he had quit Seanet, where he and P.J. had been working together before, and started doing their own stuff. So while they were doing that to pay the bills and I was working full time at PowerSet, we would just work and get together, nights and weekends; I would make mock-ups in Photoshop and then do HTML for them and send them over to Chris, who would put the logic behind them and interface with the Ruby Git bindings that I was writing on the back end to create the full system.

It was a lot of back and forth, there was no structure. It was just the two of us, initially, and then P.J. came on, but that was really what it was—a hobby project, a fun side project that we thought would be cool.

Was the approach of working on it just nights and weekends good, or should you have committed full time?

I think it was great the way it was, because Git wasn't very popular and nobody else was doing anything with it. There was enough time and it wasn't this big rush to get it done; at the same time, we would have had to take some kind of investment because I didn't have any money in my bank account. I needed my full-time job to support me when I was doing this, to pay off my credit card debts that I had racked up when I was doing Cube6 Media, because that was not very lucrative. So I had to work, I had to get money from somewhere and I don't think anyone would have invested in us anyway. They would have looked at us, like, "*You are all insane, what are you doing?*"

When did you take the leap to doing this full time?

I think it was about six or seven months in. We had gone through the private beta, launched the public; started charging. So we were already making money from it and I was still working full time at PowerSet. For me, it was when PowerSet got acquired by Microsoft and it had come down to having to either choose to become a Microsoft employee now or go and do whatever the hell I wanted. For me that was the decision point and it was an easy decision point because it had arisen naturally and it happened to coincide with a good time for GitHub, since Github was already making money, though not enough money to pay my salary the way I was used to.

But it was a hard decision, and I have a blog post about this. Microsoft was offering me $300,000 over the course of three years, as a retention bonus, to stay there in addition to a pretty decent salary.

So the question was: do I go and take a bunch of Microsoft stock and a bunch of money over the next three years and a good salary to work at Microsoft doing stuff that I don't really care about that much, or do I quit and take the big risk to do GitHub which is making *some* money? So it's not that huge of a risk and it looks like it's going to keep making money but it certainly wasn't making anywhere near the kind of money it needed to in order to pay the three of us, full salaries.

So why turn down 300K from Microsoft?

Well, the decision came down to *what do I want to do with my life and what is most valuable?* Is it more valuable to be comfortable and make some really good money, pretty much guaranteed, but do something that is not so thrilling, or go out on a limb and build something for myself on my own terms that is reliant just on myself and the other people I started it with? *And that, to me, is an adventure. That's where life becomes interesting.*

How long did it take to get something online to where you could point someone to GitHub.com?

It took about three months to go from the initial idea and the first commits on that Ruby Git library to a private beta that we started inviting our friends to.

We spread the word through the Ruby community and the meetups we went to. We were working on this and showing people at the meetup, what we were up to, and they would be looking over our shoulders while we hacked on it during these meetings and they would say, "What's this?" And we would explain, "This is a way to share Git repositories with friends." And they would say, "That sounds awesome; let me know when I can use it." So that was may be 30 or 40 people right there that we could sign up immediately, once we went into private beta, some of which were pretty prominent in the Ruby world. This is San Francisco, and a lot of very talented, prominent, open source developers in the Ruby community live here and go to these meetups. So we had some really nice connections just from these meetups.

It sounds like you have two problems at this point: GitHub.com is a new site, so you have to convince people that GitHub.com is a good idea. Second, Subversion is popular so you have to convince people to use Git instead of Subversion. How did you address that problem?

Yeah, that has always been a problem. At that time it was even more of a problem because nobody had even heard of Git, but a few prominent projects started moving over to it. So Merb, which is a Ruby web framework, was one of the very first projects to move onto GitHub; we knew the primary author, Yehuda Katz, through the Ruby meetups and he thought it was awesome and wanted to get on board. So we signed him up and he was the first user on GitHub that was not one of the founders; he moved the Merb project over to that very early, during the private beta.

Also another project called Rubinius, which is a VM for Ruby, had been using Git for a little while as well but they had it just on their own server; they were using it in the primitive way. But that was helpful because they came over pretty early on as well, also during the private beta.

I think the main thing was just being in San Francisco and knowing a really good group of Ruby people that could then come on board and say, "Hey, this really is worthwhile," and now any of the contributors to those projects or people who were following those projects saw that happening and asked, "What is this GitHub thing? Let me go check it out," and they could then immediately see the value as well.

We would show you the branches, the network graph, all these things that you could then use to visualize what Git was doing, whereas before, you never had any of that stuff; you had some pretty crappy clients like Git K that were not very good. All these tools were not very pretty; they did not work the way that a lot of us expected them to. So we tried to really expose the powerful pieces of Git in a simple way, via the web UI that people were used to seeing.

Did you guys ever have any big pivots?

Not really. A couple of decisions have been critical to our success. I think one of them is that we namespaced things on a site by user instead of by project. So, on GitHub you go to GitHub.com/mojombo/grit. Mojombo is my username and Grit is the Ruby Git binding that I wrote, and that means that you don't have to have permission to put stuff up in your name space, there's no naming conflicts on projects. So, if two projects on the site want to be called anything, then two different people can have the same repository name, the same thing—you couldn't do that anywhere else. Sourceforge, Google Code, none of these places let you do that. Those are all namespaced by project, so any time you put code up on one of those sites, you had to think to yourself, "Is this name that I am about to take in this project that I am putting up, worthy of consuming a top-level name space?"

And that is a pretty big overhead for someone to throw some code online; having that responsibility of knowing you are about to consume this name forever and always. So that was a big decision, just reducing the mental overhead for people to put stuff up on the site. So any code that you have, just throw it up there, why not? Because it's namespaced to you, it doesn't matter, it's under your account, no big deal; just put it up there, now you have a backup, now you could share all this good stuff with people.

Another key decision was to really bake in some social features. The idea is that you can follow other developers and then get notified when they put new code up, come into your project, create a new Wiki, or any of these kinds of things. Knowing what your friends are up to and adding that to GitHub, that was important because it was a pretty rare feature on other sites.

Did you ever think GitHub would fail? Did you ever have really stressful moments?

It has actually been a pretty easy ride for us. We haven't gone through the ups and downs that a lot of people do and I think a big reason for that is that we never took investment. When you take investment, you are essentially setting yourself up to have those kinds of roller coaster moments, because you are relying on this big chunk of money in the bank; you are burning through it, your investors want you to hire people so that you can get product out and use up the money so they can invest more money in you and take more of your company.

That whole world is designed to have you burn through money, whereas you've probably taken an investment because you don't make money in other ways. We always made money, we've been profitable every single month that we have charged since we launched publicly, except for one and that month is when we hired two people; that was in the old days. So hiring two people was a big thing for us back then, but when you do that, when you are profitable every month and you use a subscription model and people are just giving you more money every month regularly and you have a very predictable income, then you don't have to have these crisis points where you only have two months of runway left. We are never faced with that, we have infinite runway.

Do you think it's bad to take investment? Did you intentionally avoid it?

An investment is not an evil thing; it's just something that you have to understand. For us, it didn't make sense because we bootstrapped; we did it as a side project and started making money, but a lot of what we make is enough for us to grow the way that we want to and there is no real need to take outside investment. We have the money that we need. If you are someone like Twitter or Facebook, taking investment for those companies is critical because they can't exist the way that they did and grow like they did by charging people money or having a bunch of crappy ads on the site.

So, for those kinds of companies that need a critical mass in order to be successful—people that are trying to make new communication mediums or that kind of thing—you have to take investment, and that's okay, you just have to understand that there's a lot of risk that comes with that and you just have to know what it is. You have to understand what the VCs want, and as long as you understand what they want—which is to make a profit at the end of the day—then you can be okay working with them but it does mean that you are giving up control, it does mean that you can't necessarily do everything the way that you want to, and it especially means that if you start out doing not so well, you will probably be kicked out of the company as a founder. So it puts founders at risk.

What does your revenue growth look like?

We've never experienced any kind of hockey stick growth, so far, it has been relatively linear; very slightly exponential but not anything that is crazy, it's really kind of shockingly predictable.

How did you guys split up the work in the early days? Has that changed?

At first, I worked on the front-end and back-end and Chris did the Rails stuff. I would make UI mock-ups and either do them in HTML or just hand them to him and he would do the HTML and then I made whatever needed to happen on the back end and storing Git repositories and accessing them. So it was a really great feedback loop and then we were both trying to create stuff that the other person then had to implement. That just went back and forth, and it was a challenge to outdo the other person and say, "Hey, I made this up thing, now you have to catch up by implementing it," or vice versa, and that is how we split up work initially. It was pretty natural.

P.J. initially did the billing code and then he started just doing Rails stuff as well and I kept doing front end because the back end had gotten to a place where mostly we just needed interface stuff so that's how it started, work on whatever is necessary, and that is how it has remained through today. We now have 22 people and we still work that same way.

Did you make UI a priority from the beginning with GitHub?

I come from a background of doing graphic design and usability for websites. I did that when I was working at Cube6 Media; that was all self-taught. It was something I was interested in doing and I learned how to do it, and that was the big focus I had.

I think that's essential and anyone starting an Internet company needs to have someone who is a designer. That is why a lot of these websites are terrible, because they have a couple of programmers and none of them have ever done any graphic design or usability or UX in their lives and they are not familiar with those concepts or are not thinking about them when they are developing these interfaces. They are basically developing the interfaces after they develop the code and you can't do that; you have to develop your interfaces first, the interface needs to drive the way the code works, not the other way around.

For programmers, do you think they should learn UI and UX? Is it easy to pick up?

I think that if you are intelligent, you can pick it up without too much trouble. Mainly, it's just about staying away from the code until you know what the interface is going to look like. Draw it on a napkin, draw it on a piece of paper, get some Photoshop mock-ups, and don't ever touch any code until you've done that, as far as the middleware stuff.

Now if you're designing access layers for other external things, they need to be libraries, fine, that can be all code-centric, fine, but when you are designing what people are going to see—if you are writing Rails, for instance—don't write a single line of Rails code until you know exactly what every single page is going to look like, or at least the pages you are about to start implementing.

It needs to dictate how your database is laid out, what things need to be accessed quickly as opposed to other things that could be accessed slowly if they appear on the same page or if you need to join a certain way, *all that stuff is dictated by what the views are going to look like.* So you have to know what that stuff is first, and I think you need to have someone on the team that has that capability. Whether you go and learn it or you hire someone to do it for you, it's probably a mistake to outsource that stuff; someone on the team should be doing that stuff.

What was the schedule like when you started GitHub? Was it day and night?

We worked a lot. My wife was doing her fieldwork in Costa Rica at the time. So she was gone for almost a year and I was looking for stuff to do and I had recently sold Gravatar, which is another one of my projects, to Automattic, and that was my side project for a long time. Once I sold that, I was looking for something else to do. GitHub became that thing, so after work everyday I went home, opened my computer, and programmed from probably 7 o'clock until midnight, almost everyday.

I spent a lot of time on nights and weekends doing it, because I didn't have a ton of friends back then since I didn't know that many people when I first moved to San Francisco.

Did you work on GitHub remotely or out of the same apartment?

Some of both. Chris would often come over to my apartment and we would sit around on a Saturday and program for a few hours; then we would go our separate ways. During the week, we would mostly work separately. We always used IRC to communicate back then and we switched to Campfire after about six months, because you could paste images in and that was the main thing—you gotta' have images. Campfire, which is the chat client from 37 Signals, really defines how we work to this day. So that decision has made a big impact for the company because when you are working remotely and you don't have an office—we didn't have an office for two years—you need to have communication and you need to always have very easy access to other people. So, to this day, Campfire is our true office and the physical office is just a place that people can go when they want to hang out and talk in person.

So being remote, you had no productivity issues?

Yeah. I have always had that ability to work on my own. I worked for three years out of my house when I was doing Cube6 Media and never had a problem getting stuff done because I liked to program, I like to write stuff; I liked to make things a reality.

It's a matter of motivation, of finding people that are motivated in that way, which is another reason why the meet-ups are so great, because those are the exact same people who care enough about programming to do it on their own time. They are self-motivated; they are not doing it because it's a job, they are doing it because they love it.

Did you guys do anything to promote growth?

The primary marketing that we do is going to conferences, speaking at conferences and doing what we call 'drinkups'; a drinkup is like the part of the Ruby meetups that we used to have when you really wanted to just talk to the people who were there instead of watching a presentation about something that really wasn't that relevant. So, we said, "Let's do our own kind of meetup except let's just make it the drinking part, the social part of it." We started doing that, probably a year and a half ago, under the GitHub banner and calling it 'GitHub drinkups.'

So, the best way to get to know somebody is to go drink with them?

That is absolutely the best way to really get to know a person and what they really like and are interested in because if they are interested in technology, then they will have no problem geeking out with you about Ruby or Node or something for three hours, over drinks; that's when you know that you found someone that could be a really successful cofounder.

I think there really is something to doing business in bars. In the early days when there were four of us—we had hired Scott Chacon—we would go to this bar called O'Reilly's, up in North beach. We went there almost every week and that's where we would talk about what we had done. This is after we had started full time and it was where all the decisions were made. A couple of drinks in, you start to just say what you mean instead of thinking so much about whose feelings you are going to hurt or whatever, you say things very bluntly, like, "I think we should do this, and I think you are wrong for saying we should do it a different way," and now you can have an honest argument about what needs to get done and what the concerns are about the company or how it's structured or how the stock is going to be split. All this stuff will come up over drinks and as long as you are not *too drunk*, it can be helpful.

What is your biggest challenge today with GitHub?

I think the biggest challenge is going to be maintaining the culture and working style that we have enjoyed so far, while we are hiring more people. We've hired eight people so far this year.

The culture is pretty unique in that it's almost entirely flat, there's really no org chart, no departments; the only obligation is what you think needs to be done. So, we have a couple of support people and they mainly stay in support but they also do some development. We have an Ops team and they do mostly sys admin stuff but they also do some development and they can do other things if they want. For instance, I do all kinds of stuff: I run the merchandising part of the company, we sell mugs and T-shirts, and we actually make pretty good money off of that.

I do business development, conference talks, a lot of stuff; a lot of people in the company do a lot of stuff. It's whatever people are interested in. So, some people will do front-end development, JavaScript, HTML, CSS, Rails, and then they will go back and work on the deep back-end libraries, infrastructure, profiling and performance, or they will go and design a T-shirt for the store. I mean anyone in the company can really work on whatever they want that they think they can contribute to.

Do you guys have an open or closed floor plan?

Right now the office is about 2500 square feet and it's basically a giant rectangle with no walls. There is one small, enclosed room in the back that has a couple of chairs in it used for phone conversations or Skype or something like that. Otherwise, we have two big tables and a desk along one of the walls that has a bunch of Mac monitors on it, so everyone in the company gets whatever computer they want, usually it's a Mac, a MacBook Pro or a MacBook Air, and they come into the office or work at home or from whatever country they happen to live in. We have people in Australia, Greece, Croatia, around the world—you just work from wherever you are comfortable, and in the office it's the same way.

I usually sit down at one of the big tables because I like using my laptop monitor instead of a big monitor, I'm fine working in that way. Other people like the big monitors so they'll go and claim one of the desk monitors, but there's not assigned places. There are certainly no cubicles and no doors. So it is open and I think that's important for disseminating knowledge and having good ideas spoken about things that aren't necessarily what you are working on, right then. That is how good ideas come about organically; by being in close proximity with other people who are having those ideas.

Is there a risk that productivity might drop because people might talk, more than work, with an open floor plan?

It can be distracting. If you don't want to be distracted you put on your headphones and nobody bothers you. They'll talk to you through Campfire. So even in the office, often the office will be silent or, we'll have something on the big speaker system that we have, and no physical talking will happen, but the discussions in the Campfire room will be endless. We are those people who will have conversations on Campfire while sitting in the same room.

Do you do any unit testing at GitHub, when you push code?

Yeah, we have a lot of unit tests; we have continuous integration servers that run for all of the branches that we push up, that are tested anytime you push a branch to GitHub. That allows us a lot of flexibility to deploy. So, it's not uncommon for us to deploy to the site a dozen times in one day and every day. People are constantly deploying stuff, little fixes, experimental branches that are enabled only for staff, etc. We have a fair amount of stuff on the site that normal users can't see and that we can still play around with because it's not enabled for the general public; that allows us to test the usability, start using it early so we can get good feedback, make sure there are no bottlenecks that we were not thinking about, that kind of stuff.

What's the work schedule like?

There is no set work schedule. You work whenever you feel comfortable working and we don't keep track of hours. We make sure that we hire the kind of people that are doing what they are doing because they like doing it, not because they have to do it, and as long as we maintain that, I think we're fine. We have this culture of shipping code and doing great work and when you do that, you get accolades—then people really want to do it. If you are not doing that, then you feel bad and if you are really not doing that for long enough then you get fired.

Do you ever have any motivational problems or productivity brick walls?

Not generally. I think working with really smart, motivated people who are passionate about what they are doing is a great way of not getting burnt out especially since we don't have departments and you can switch around what you are working on from day-to-day or week-to-week. That eliminates a lot of those motivational blockades because if you are not being productive at something, then you go work on something that you will be productive at.

Do you have any hiring tips? Is there anything that makes you say "This person is good" or "This person is bad"?

So far we've mostly hired people that we already know, or who have written code that we are already using on the site. Most of the people that we've hired are people whose code is a known quality, and I think that is where most people have a hard time hiring for technical jobs—it's so hard to interview someone and really understand what their code is going to be like.

If they have a bunch of open source code already, and I am guessing it's on GitHub, then it's a lot easier to know whether that person is technically competent or not. And once you have answered the question of competence, you don't have to waste a bunch of time in an interview asking them stupid riddles about programming crap, right? That is useless. You are not going to get anything worthwhile out of that. So the way we do it is we find people who are already technically competent because we are using code that they've written already, or they've written stuff that we know about and that other people say is really good and we can look at their code and know whether it's good or not.

So reputation of code is really important and once we know that, then we will ask them to come drinking with us. That is the second part of the interview, which is, are you going to be a good cultural fit? Are you the kind of person that I would go and have a beer with or sit down and talk about stuff with casually, the kind of person that can communicate in that way and is passionate about what they are doing and knows their stuff? So those are the 2 things. We don't generally ask technical questions during our interview process.

Let's say a student is looking for a cofounder, do you have

any advice for them? Should non-technical people learn how to program?

I would say it is extremely useful for a businessperson to have an understanding of what programming is like. So go learn some Ruby; go learn some Python; go learn some PHP. Make a little website or something. Understand what it means to be a programmer and the same thing for technical people that might want a business cofounder. Go and take a business class or two, go get some books about business so that you have some understanding of the complexities of those things. I think the big problems arise when those two very different kinds of people don't appreciate how difficult it is to do what the other is doing.

That is the biggest reason that a lot of these things fall apart and why a lot of business people try to hire tech people for pennies or for free or for stock trade or whatever and really are just treating them as people, implementing their ideas, as opposed to true cofounders, because they don't understand what it's like to program. They think programming is easy, the same way technical people often think that business stuff is just pushing a bunch of paper around, but it's not. I mean, there's a lot of creativity as to how things go and a lot of knowledge that you have to know and build up just like you do in programming.

That, to me, is the biggest thing. I think you should have some understanding of every component of what your company is going to be doing; understand and have done some of what every person that you are going to hire is doing, whatever that means. I have done business stuff, I have done UI stuff, I have done back-end stuff, I have done merchandising stuff, I have stuffed boxes and sent them out to customers, I have done sys admin stuff, I have done accounting, I have done almost everything that is done as part of the company and I think that that is really valuable—to have an understanding of those things allows you to hire better and to appreciate those people properly.

Can you talk about the time you most successfully hacked some non-computer system to your advantage?

I would say the biggest hack in the real world is going out and meeting people. Drinking is absolutely a hack. I think another hack is agreeing to do things before you've really thought them through, and by that I mean, agree to go and give conference talks even if you've never done it before or even if you haven't written the presentation yet or you don't know what the hell you are going to talk about, just agree to do it because that is a great motivational hack.

Is GitHub hiring? Why would someone want to work with GitHub?

We are hiring. The reason you want to work at GitHub is because we work how people work, naturally, that are passionate about what they are doing, meaning we don't put a lot of blockades in the way, it's not all on process; there are no meetings, no deadlines, no set vacation days, you work when you want, you go and have time off when you want, I mean it's about treating people as adults and really giving our employees autonomy to work how they think is best on what they think is best. As long as we are having good communication about it, that is the main thing. You can work on stuff that you think is important but you'd better be able to convince other people that that's true.

The company is organized, and we function in a culture, such that it's a company I always wanted to work for; I think it's silly for companies to evolve to the point where the founder would no longer want to work there as an employee. Why would you want to create a company like that? So that is really important to us, keeping the company such that, we ourselves, would like to be hired to work here if we weren't already founders.

We are also working on stuff that affects the future of development on this planet. It's really important getting people working better together, especially now that systems are becoming more and more complex, and to do something unique, you do almost have to work with other people because all of the easy stuff is already done. Now it's the hard stuff that's left and hard stuff requires multiple people and really good collaboration.

Don't just send in your resume, that's useless. A couple of times we have put out requisitions for jobs; the people that are most impressive to me, that I don't know, are the people that have web blogs and write. That, to me, is extremely important. I need to know how a person thinks and I need to know that they can write well because that is indicative of having good communication skills and having thoughts they think are important enough to share with other people. Really put forth the effort; craft your response to the individual company, don't just blast a bunch of resumes out to a bunch of places, that's useless.

If you want to work at GitHub, make a website with some awesome JavaScript on it that is designed specifically to get our attention and calls us out specifically by name. Do the research necessary to display that you know what we do and talk about what you would improve, what you would add to the team, what kind of side projects you have worked on that are awesome, just ideas that you have. Put some time into it. That approach is so much more valuable and more effective than just sending a resume. If all you send me is a resume I am probably just going to delete it.

Dennis Crowley, Foursquare

Tags: businessperson, hiring, VC funded, side project, major league player (Alexa top 1,000), acquired (previous company acquired by Google)

Overview: Foursquare launched in March 2009 at South by Southwest as a fun way to explore your neighborhood. Foursquare was novel when it launched because it introduced the idea of badges, points, and mayorships for checking in at your favorite venues. In its 2 years, it has grown to 8 million users with 2.5 million checkins per day and over 250,000 businesses using the Merchant Platform. Foursquare has raised $21 million since their start in 2009.

Can you talk about the earliest entrepreneurial experience you can remember?

Well, my dad had his own electrical contracting business. I knew he was the boss and that there were people who worked for him. I grew up understanding that, and in elementary school I was fascinated with publishing, so during that time I did a little school newspaper and handed it out. I used to create "fanzines" in high school, and I would sell those. I really started wanting to do magazines and wanting to create newspapers, and I got sucked into the Internet when I went to college because it was a means of publishing and distributing stories—that led into the Foursquare stuff.

With Foursquare, I think it's just a matter knowing and building the stuff that we wanted to use and there not being companies that—there weren't companies to work for that were doing the thing that we wanted to do.

Did you work on anything in high school or college?

Well I had a blog since 1994 that has everything I've ever done in my life. I could easily backtrack what we're doing now into that. I can easily track who the people were that I would hang out with on a given weekend and I would chart it in Excel and be like,

"These are the people that I hang out with now," and "These are the people I used to hang out with." I was really fascinated by the stats behind a lot of that stuff.

Why media in college, why not engineering?

I'm just not good at math. I wasn't able to take computer science courses in college because I'm so bad at math. I wasn't interested in programming per se because it was much harder to program back then: you would sit down and program in C++ or something, and I didn't want to do that.

Do you think school was helpful? Did it help you to do your startups?

I don't know. I didn't take any classes on entrepreneurship or any classes in business. But I think school is valuable. I went to communications school at Syracuse—arguably one of the best programs around—and I've learned about newspaper and TV and PR and magazine. I came out with a major in advertising because I wanted to be a copywriter since I really like the creative side of things. I definitely can see it helping out now because I understand how it all works. New York is a big media town.

How did you meet Alex Rainert back at your last startup Dodgeball, which was acquired by Google?

We had similar stories. We graduated at the same time in college and moved to the city the same time. We worked in the startup so I kind of had a little past in the way we both got laid off and we both went back to grad school and we met the first week of grad school, and Alex was one of the reasons I stayed in ITP [NYU's Tisch School of the Arts]. ITP was a little bit too arty for me at first, and I was concerned that it wasn't the right place, but then once Alex and I met and started working together, we just clicked very well.

What about Naveen, your cofounder at Foursquare?

After I left Google, Naveen and I shared an office where I worked at another startup that my buddy used to run. He worked at a startup that some friends of mine were running, two different companies sharing office space, and he was the one guy that knew how to program iPhone stuff. I was itching for another project, and he was experimenting with city guide stuff, and so we just started working together.

After you left Google, you joined Area/Code. What did you do over there?

Area/Code was making big games that touch the real world, and so it was very location-based. It was starting to do a lot of stuff with social, so it was really interesting, and so I was there. I left Google on Friday and started Area/Code on a Monday, and I was at Area/Code for about 9 months—just looking for projects and helping them out, and they were doing some really interesting work. That's where the game dynamic bug bit me.

Did anybody influence or inspire you in particular in college?

Yeah. I had this professor—Professor Steven Moziclof—and he taught the first design course I ever took. I was in college in '96 and he was one of the guys that really got the Internet. He was a big inspiration for a lot of the stuff that we're doing—the stuff is important, interesting, and we can push it in any direction that we want to.

How long did it take to build the Foursquare beta for South by Southwest?

3 months. We were dicking around with it for about 6 months, but it wasn't until January 2009 when Google announced that they were going to turn off Dodgeball. And at that moment Naveen and I were like, "We've got to stop screwing around. Let's just build this thing." And then from that point it was bang. It took us three months to put the thing together.

One of the coolest things about Foursquare—you guys pretty much came up with the idea of badges and check-ins. How did you come up with the idea of badges for example? Were there games that you played that inspired that?

I was at Area/Code and we designed a game called SharkRunners and we designed an achievement system and they weren't badges, they were called achievements and you got them for doing random things within this game. The game was about being a marine biologist studying sharks, and I got hooked on a game that we created and the same way that I got hooked on Legend of Zelda as a kid and I was like, "Wow, this is really, really powerful." I was itching to do more real world stuff and thought that we could add game dynamics to a thing like Dodgeball, and we get something that's really, really sticky.

How about the check-in concept?

I got laid off from my job in 2001. Actually all of our friends were getting laid off in 2001 and these were the only—the only friends I had were the ones that I worked with at my job. And so when we didn't go to work anymore, I didn't see my friends anymore. So I built the tool where if you're at Central Park, and if you're watching the Yankees game in the afternoon or if you're going to go to the museum, you just check in, and we know where to find you, and then we would just all show up at the park. "Oh Lucas was at the park?" Five of us would show up. "Oh someone is here drinking in the afternoon; they're watching Yankees game. Yeah, I'll go there and chill." We had nothing to do with no jobs.

There were just no jobs in the city. It was right before September 11th, and so we built things for ourselves that were going to make our lives better for 10 friends.

You were scratching your own itch right?

Yeah. I don't know how people do it the other way: I can't imagine sitting in a room and coming up with 15 ideas of what could be a profitable business. That's not the way that we think about it. We approach it more as, "let's build stuff that we love here, and when we're done building that stuff, let's look at the merchant across the street and ask, 'What do you want? We go to your bar five times a week: how can we help you bring in more people in here?'" And that's how we approached things: solving problems that real people have.

One of the most impressive things about Foursquare is definitely the growth. You're 2 years old—you're a mobile application so the barrier to join might be higher than a standard web application where you just fill out a form or click the "Facebook Connect" button—you have *8 million users*; many of them are very engaged. What did you guys do to grow so quickly?

We didn't do anything. We didn't have a marketing plan when we launched. I think—people ask this question all the time and I don't know what the answer is—it has something to do with that we're just genuinely interested in solving these problems. We're trying to build things that our friends want to use and that real people use, and I think people can just latch on to that idea. I think that there's—and this sounds kind of corny—something bigger behind the stuff that we're building. Just the idea that we're trying to build the things that will change the way people experience the world; the end goal is not to have this crazy exit, but the goal is to build these things that we're really excited about using to make people think about the role of software in their lives differently and to push the limits of what is possible with mobile phones. I think we're pretty genuine about it, and people have latched onto that idea.

But you have to wonder, why is Foursquare doing so well? Why not some of the other companies? Is there something you're doing that they're not?

I think we're being original and inventing this stuff. A lot of other things are derivative of the product—for example I think Dodgeball was one of the first things that was out there, and Loopt came after, and then Brightkite came after that, and one of the reasons that we started Foursquare was because I just couldn't use Loopt. It just didn't do what I wanted it to do, and I couldn't get behind Brightkite for the same reason. I was like, "I think we can make stuff that's different than these things, alright." And so even the stuff that came up after us, like Gowalla launched around the same time—it was a different product and they pivoted it to become a little bit more like Foursquare. Scavenger is also similar. You can see them being slightly derivative of or inspired by some of the stuff that we're doing.

Our biggest challenge is just keeping the company focused and we try not to look left to right. I'm not watching what Facebook is doing and copying them; I'm not watching what Google is doing and copying them. We have an idea of what the world is supposed to look like six months from now, and we're just chasing after that instead of chasing everyone else.

You mentioned other companies pivoting. Did you guys ever have that point where you guys took a big change in direction?

We've never done it defensively. For example, we're about to launch a whole bunch of stuff with South by Southwest which I think is going to change the way that people think about the company, but that's been on the roadmap from the beginning. There's never been a point where it's been, "Oh god, this person is doing this, now we have to do that." Again it's like, we set these goals for things that we want to do. We just chase after them.

What is Foursquare's biggest challenge today?

It's hiring good engineers; hiring a team. It's just getting the people in here, and then once the people get in here it's finding a way for everyone to work together. Scaling a company from 5 to 50 employees is a lot harder than I thought it was going to be, and the company breaks every time we add 5 people to it. You add 5 more engineers and the team just breaks because you need to restructure it. And the same thing happens with product. The whole company is like that: you have to babysit it a lot.

Why do a startup on the East Coast?

It was where we live: my parents and I lived in New York for years, my family is in Boston, and Naveen's family is from Connecticut. It didn't even cross our minds that we have to pack up and move out west. We were like, "No, we live in New York, we'll start a company here."

Was there a point where revenue took off? Did something happen to cause that?

We're generating revenue right now, but we're doing it through brands and media partnerships, which was a complete surprise. We didn't think that was going to be the case. We didn't even see that as a revenue stream. We've always thought, "we'll build tools for local merchants, all the coffee shops and all the cafes and the parks and museums and whatnot." And so I think that's going to be a big revenue stream for us eventually. We're not monetizing that yet because the tools aren't ready, but it has been a surprise that we've been able to generate some revenue with some of the things that we offer already.

What was the schedule like in the earliest days of starting Foursquare? Has that changed?

In the early days before South by Southwest, it was Naveen and I at my kitchen table 14 hours a day. It was awful, and it's better now, but we're still working a lot. We're gearing up for South by Southwest now, and people are here until two in the morning and we're just—it's tough. This is a weird time because we're launching a whole bunch of stuff. It's near Austin where everyone is working together, which is great. But I think the early work ethic from the company has transferred over. It's been nice to see.

I definitely worked at places where you're there all night and you're like, "I don't want to be here," but I feel like a lot of the folks here get it. They're on board and they realize what we're doing is interesting and important.

And when you're not preparing for South by Southwest?

It's still the same. This is our most ambitious launch. I think we have a whole bunch of stuff that we're launching as opposed to just one thing. But when we launched photos and comments in December it was just as crazy. When we were launching a bunch of stuff in September it was just as crazy. The environment is pretty intense, but at the same time it's—I think we have a really incredible group of people here, and again I'm sure everyone says that, but we did really, really well in hiring. It's very rare that you get to 50 people and you don't have any bad apples and it's been—we've gotten really lucky.

What was fundraising like? Was that positive or negative?

It depends. The Series A took a long time but we got it done and we raised the first million dollars that took us to build the company. That was positive: the Series B, we were very hot and we dragged it out and we got distracted by acquisition rumors and we weren't very focused and it took a long time. And that was slightly more negative. It depends on what you make out of it: we're in a unique position where since we took money in the beginning, we've been relatively hot so it's been easier for us than it is for most. But getting that first million from Union Square and O'Reilly, it took us six months of fundraising, six months of knocking on doors and saying, "Hey, this is what we're doing, are you interested?" And there were a lot of "no's," so that's really tough.

I think the media makes startups look a lot easier than they actually are. Have you guys had any points where you got really stressed out or you thought Foursquare is going to fail or anything like that?

Yeah. It's definitely under-reported. Everyday is like that. You can see in my face: my girlfriend was telling me I'm breaking out in little hives under my eyes since I always have my hands on my face because I'm so stressed. Everyone is saying, "you guys are so successful" *but we're not successful yet*. We're hustling and we're doing good things, but we're not where we need to be, and we're not sitting around just soaking it all in. We're hustling. We see a big opportunity and we're trying to reach it. I saw that quote—they make their way around on Tumblr and Twitter—and one of them was like, "the media will glamorize the successful startups and make it look easier than it is." It's tough—it would be fun to go to Austin and have everyone using Foursquare and be like "Okay, this is cool, like we get it, we're into it." But it's a lot of work.

How would you describe Foursquare's culture?

It's a lot of fun. The product is fun and playful and I think the culture of the company is the same way. But it's intense: everyone here is very smart, and everyone here is working a lot. You go to lunch and people are talking work, you go to drinks and people are talking work, people are here on the weekends, but the idea is that you build this stuff all week long and then when you leave the office regardless what time it is, it's what you use when you're out on the streets. And I think that's rewarding to people. It's awesome to build something that you use everyday and you come to work to make it better and when you leave work it is better.

Do you have any advice for students?

I think if you can get an internship at a startup just to see what it's like or to see how it works, that helps. I think when startup culture glamorizes it, people are just like, "Oh yeah, I'll just do a startup," and they don't realize what's involved in it. And people think it's the 90210 version of startups where it's, "Oh, we sit around, we play pool, we get drinks, we do stuff." No, we're hustling all the time here and I think that gets off in the translation. I think seeing it from the inside—like I can tell, I can see it already, there are 50 people here and there's eight guys at Foursquare who will leave and do their own startups eventually and I know they'll be successful. One of the reasons they'll be successful is because they'll try to make whatever company that they do work the same way this company does. And they're learning some of the lessons: they understand about the hours and the commitment and everything that goes into it.

I think the other thing is there definitely is not a culture of "I have done this before, I'm smarter than you," and I've fallen into that trap too. I've had a lot of people tell me they don't like the stuff that we were thinking about, that we have stupid ideas and no one is going to do that, or phones will never do that. And I think at some point you just have to—you've got to build the things that you think are interesting and you have to prove to yourself that they're not going to work. If you can convince yourself that things are a bad idea, then you move on. But don't let other people convince you of that.

Do you guys have any advice for hiring? Is there any way that you could say, this person is definitely good or this person is definitely not good?

Good people will bring in good people, and so if people want to work here I think it's because of the product and the culture and because we have a really good group of people here. And there are a lot of ex-Google people at Foursquare. When people found out that, "oh, four of my friends from Google are doing a startup," they want to go join those guys, and now it's like, "Hey, 20 of my friends from Google are at Foursquare, we should just go there." Because we have a lot of ex-Google people here, there's a little bit of Google in the culture. When people come in they go through six different interviews; they're coding on whiteboards. We're using a lot of the Google practices for hiring and evaluating candidates, and I think that's allowed us to keep the quality of the people that we bring in really high.

Was there anything that Google could have done better when they got Dodgeball? Was there anything they could have done differently?

Well, Google was in weird spot. They were just after their IPO, we were just two kids in New York and there weren't a lot of product development or product resources out in New York and it was a tough spot for us and it was a tough spot for them. There are things that could have been done better but you realize those things in hindsight. I don't know what we could have done differently while we were there and it's hard to know. I chalked it up as a failure or a write-off but doing those, going through Google has definitely helped structure the way that we do things here. And it's providing us with some clarity and some drive to do the things that we're doing now.

Foursquare is hiring right now—why would someone want to work with you guys?

I honestly believe that we're doing some of the most innovative stuff in mobile and social. Those are the three things I'm most excited about. Those are the things I'm trying to focus my whole career around. We run the shop that's doing the most interesting stuff in mobile and social, and I think it's what a lot of the folks that we've hired have had: they have side projects and the side projects are, "Hey I made a restaurant mashup with Google Maps," or "I allowed people to bookmark places" and those are the people that are very successful here. They have these outside interests about making cities easier to use, and they come here and they put all that work and drive and passion to use.

Brian Chesky, Airbnb

Tags: designer, Y Combinator, coincidental, school worker, VC funded, profitable, hiring, design-focused, major league player (Alexa top 2,000)

Overview: Airbnb is a new type of marketplace that allows people to list and book unique spaces with real people online. You can easily book anything from a private apartment to a private island, and "book" means an online transaction with a trusted community. Airbnb supports over 10,000 cities and is used in over 175 countries. I first met Brian Chesky at a YC dinner and he was one of the most passionate speakers I heard of next to Guy Kawasaki. Brian was part of the 2008 Y Combinator class. Airbnb has since raised over $7 million and as of 2011, their users have booked over 1 million nights.

Take me back as far as you can and tell me how all of this got started for you.

Growing up, I was very interested in the act of creation. I was an artist and artists are, I think, very much entrepreneurs at heart because they're creators; they're creating their own work. I started in high school as an artist and illustrator. When I got into the Rhode Island School of Design (RISD), it was an entrepreneurial-minded school. They used to give us projects where we would essentially have to come up with creative solutions to *seemingly impossible* problems. Through my education at RISD and the activities I was involved in on campus, I started going down this entrepreneurial path.

The way the story starts is that I was running probably the largest student organization on campus. It was a club hockey team; RISD didn't have intramural sports. My cofounder, Joe, ran the club basketball team which, I believe, was the second largest organization on campus. For us, sporting events were huge because there was nothing else to do on campus; they brought the whole school together. We had a budget; we thought about how to market the games to get fans; the entire thing was a little enterprise we had to run to and that was a pretty amazing education. I ran it for five years. There wasn't that much capital involved but a lot of people were involved, so it was a great lesson in really inspiring people. We worked on a lot of different projects together as well.

Additionally, I spent a semester at MIT's Sloan School of Business, where I did product design and development studio. Through that, I got quite a bit of training.

Why did you choose art? What was it about art that you enjoyed? You could have studied engineering or business, for example.

It's something I just discovered at a very young age. It was kind of how I thought. People think in different ways. Some people think through sounds or dance; I thought through drawing and through art—it was a great way for me to express my ideas and myself because I didn't know how to communicate in other ways. In many ways, it was an escape to a world of my own creation. Maybe that's another way of saying I have no idea. I just loved it and as I was growing up, it's just something I always did. The thing to do when I was growing up was to play sports. I participated in those as well but art was more uniquely my interest. I realized early on that I was pretty good at it; it was something I was interested in and I got the results I looked for.

You mentioned that RISD gave you very difficult problems to solve. Can you give examples of problems they would ask you to solve and how would you come up with the solutions?

I remember one of the first days of class we got a project, one of the projects RISD is most famous for. First, they give you an assignment to do a self-portrait. You can draw yourself using any medium you want and you have a week to do it. On the first day of class, everyone wants to impress everyone else, so they're going to do really over the top drawings, put in a lot of work and a lot of time. When we came to class the next week we presented what we had done during a *crit*, short for critique—every week you have a crit, freshman year.

So the teacher critiqued everything and then gave us the next week's assignment. If he had asked for another self portrait we would have spent another 10 hours doing another self portrait and he knew that, so, what he said instead was, "what I want you to do for next week is *200 self portraits*"; that kind of teaches you to develop a new process. In other words, it's a seemingly impossible assignment. It's not *actually possible* to do 200 self-portraits under normal means in a week. It could take a year, so you have to come up with a new process to get to 200. It's an entire sketchpad.

I think the lesson was that things that seem impossible aren't impossible; there's always a creative solution to them.

I've taken design studio classes and have drawn portraits—those are some of the most time-consuming assignments you can get in school. Were you taking a lot of classes at RISD? What were you favorite and least favorite?

I think my favorite classes were the drawing classes or the sponsor studios—studios where you basically got a problem and had to solve it. I actually enjoyed one of my three-dimensional design classes. We had a few different assignments. One of them was to construct a five-foot bridge out of only cardboard—and I think we weren't even allowed to use tape or glue—to see whose cardboard bridge would hold the most bricks. Another famous assignment I didn't have but which was very cool, was to create a violin out of cardboard: it was a single piece without any glue, can you imagine that? There are a lot of interesting challenges you have to solve and I really liked the collaborative problem solving.

Did you go into RISD knowing a lot of people?

I didn't know anybody going into RISD.

Were you thinking you should find cofounders or do a startup in school?

Absolutely not. Even after I graduated RISD it wasn't going through my head. I did not ever aspire to have a web or Internet startup, at all.

Besides the hockey group, were you doing anything else outside of class?

I was also very involved in developing a school fitness program. When I got there, there was no gym on campus and you had to go to Brown University to exercise; it was silly. I worked with the school to build a new fitness facility. We basically just got a budget, thought through how we want to spend the money and what we wanted out of the facility and equipment, and built a program to have people monitor the space. There were various personnel challenges and operational challenges we had to deal with.

When I spent a semester at MIT, I was in the industrial design program. I worked with a team of engineers and MBA candidates to rethink, redesign, and remarket a common household item. The common item was a sugar canister that you actually would see at diners. We had to rethink the product and basically improve upon it.

We went through this entire process exploration of the benefits and, most notably, the disadvantages of the existing product and realized that it's imprecise: you try to pour out a little sugar but a ton comes out; it's messy; you have to keep refilling it; it's slow; condensation builds up; it doesn't look clean. These were the issues that we identified. Then, we had to think through what the product could be, that could solve a lot of problems and we decided to really focus on coffee shops. In diners, these sugar canisters work but in coffee shops, canisters are *terrible* because there are hundreds or people coming through every hour, maybe more, and this sugar canister is getting sprayed everywhere. They were made for diners, not Starbucks, which was a new phenomenon then.

We designed a sugar dispenser, which eventually dispensed a teaspoon of sugar. We came up with—what I would argue was—an aesthetically pleasing glass canister that was mounted to the wall. It was pretty cool looking and when you tapped down on it, it would give you *exactly* a packet of sugar. If you wanted two packets of sugar you just tapped on it twice. It was really a pretty cool product so we made a prototype.

We basically got a budget of $1,000 to make a prototype and we had to create a business plan around it—what that business would look like, how we'd sell it, who we'd sell it to, etc. After the class, I entered the MIT $50K entrepreneurship competition with the product; it was another great lesson. I think it was second in my education, to funding the hockey team, which has to be the greatest lesson I ever had. It was such a great experience.

How did you pay your way through school?

I worked at the fitness center. I basically helped develop the fitness center and then I built it.

Did you take time away from classes to party and relax?

Unfortunately, RISD doesn't have any fraternities, but we certainly had our fun. Most activities I did were through the hockey team. The team would actually throw huge parties. Beyond that there wasn't really much. RISD is a school for people who already know exactly what they want out of their lives, so it wasn't as much an *exploration* of what you wanted to do, like other college experiences.

RISD was definitely more of a focused environment. We already knew what we wanted to do and—people who are obsessed with art would rather do that than party. It was the thing that preoccupied all our time and energy. We definitely did a decent amount of fun things but it wasn't too crazy.

When you were graduating, what was going through your mind? Did you know what you wanted to do? Were you thinking, "I want to do a startup at this point"?

I knew that I wanted to be an entrepreneur when I graduated. I definitely knew that, I just didn't know *what* I wanted to do. In other words, did I want to start a company making sugar canisters? I wasn't sure, but I didn't think that was the thing I would end up doing with my life.

I wasn't really exposed to the startup world. In contrast to other founders at Y Combinator, I wasn't really familiar with Hacker News or Paul Graham or YC before we applied. I came from a completely different world and I was kind of thrust into this world or, perhaps, got myself into this world when we came up with the concept for Airbnb, which was originally called Air Bed & Breakfast. But before that I was living essentially in the product design and industrial design world. I was making physical, tangible things.

When you graduated then, did you go work somewhere?

Joe and I were both very well known on campus and I actually gave the commencement address at my university. It wasn't because I was valedictorian; at RISD they don't really measure you in that way. They determine the commencement speaker through a competition to decide who has the best address, and I didn't have too much competition. I had a fun message I wanted delivered to the students, parents, and alumni. The reason I bring that up is because I think there were various things along the way at RISD that prepared me for the kind of life I live now; one of them was we got the opportunity to do lots of public speaking and presentations, and that was an example. Another, was we got the opportunity to constantly refine our skills, to use creative solutions to solve problems—as cliché as it sounds—to think outside the box. Really, what they mean is that the first solution you come up with is the obvious solution and typically not the best. You have to keep digging to get to the more complex solution, which means peeling back layers and that's really what AirBNB was about. It was about taking a process that was very, very complex, the process of being able to stay with another person on a short-term basis, and just removing all the complexities.

What was the message of the graduation speech?

It was primarily humorous, speaking on behalf of the students to all the parents and professors in the audience. Before I gave the address, I attended a few local university commencement ceremonies. Actually, one of my friends had just graduated so I got the opportunity to see another address and there was something the student did that I didn't really agree with. He used the opportunity—you see this a lot with students—to almost give lessons to the other students, you know what I mean? Probably what happens is they listen to other graduation speeches by notable people and they try to do speeches like them. But if you're graduating, the last thing your peers want to hear is a life lesson from you.

But they often do that; think about how frequently people try to offer lessons. That's not what people want to hear. In fact, they don't want to hear anything other than a humorous retelling of what they have experienced over the last four years. The people that really needed insight were the parents and so I basically went through the entire RISD experience and told them, I think, in a humorous way, the absurdity of what we had all been through.

I had this funny prank where I told the sound guy to play Michael Jackson's Billy Jean when they called my name. They called my name, but I didn't get up right away. Everyone in the audience was kind of confused like "what's going on?" So I eventually walked up on stage in front of 5,000 people, and I rip off my gown, and below it I have my tuxedo and my pants are hemmed too short with white socks underneath and I do the moonwalk. It was kind of an inside joke because everyone thought I was going to do something crazy, but I basically was aiming to shock the parents. Essentially, I created this whole production to confuse the entire commencement, but I did it in a way that added to the event. I don't think it made anyone uncomfortable. I had everything setup for it.

When you graduated, is that when you moved to Silicon Valley?

When I graduated, I realized I wanted to work for an industrial design firm. I liked the idea of working for a consultancy for a couple of years, to be able to touch a lot of different industries, so I moved to Santa Monica, California to do that.

I think the reason I ended up in Southern California, is I had a friend who was also interested in going out there. We were looking at both cities and we both talked about how it would be fun to go to Southern California. It just seemed like a fun change of pace from RISD because that was very much a professional, creative, work-centric environment. I would say San Francisco is much the same way, or it feels that way relative to Los Angeles.

It was a pretty grueling and rigorous five years at RISD and so I think that going to Santa Monica and the warm weather was a nice break from that. The industrial design firm I worked in was a 10-person camp, but there were only two or three designers. When I got there, one of the other designers had just quit and so for a very short period of time I think I was the *only designer,* which was interesting, but then it was me and one other person.

There are different ways of learning; one way is to work with really experienced people—I wouldn't say I completely got that. The other way is just to be given all these projects and challenges and be thrust into a huge opportunity. That's exactly what happened with me. There were all these projects that came in from this consultancy and, as a junior, unseasoned designer, I had to take on a lot of different projects. They varied from stuff for the military to the medical industry. I did a toy line for ESPN; a line of dog toys for a Swiss company; I even designed a guitar for rock stars. That was a really cool project. I did women's handbags and one of those teeth-whitening lamps.

I was a designer on a reality TV show on ABC that Simon Cowell produced called American Inventor. Basically there were contestants—I wasn't a contestant—and they had these inventions. Over the course of the show they turned their inventions or their prototypes into much more functional prototypes that resembled a real product, to eventually get manufactured. We had to essentially design the final prototype before it got manufactured. The whole process was really funny; we all went to a hotel room and I think they rented out 20 different rooms in a hotel. So 20 designers bid on the work and each design company got a hotel room as their presentation room, like musical chairs. The contestant would go from room to room presenting what they had in a few minutes and then we would show them our portfolio and they selected which firm they liked the most.

Each inventor would come in and basically just present what they were working on. We bid and they bid, and eventually I got matched with a guy—funny enough there always seem to be people with toilet inventions—who had this invention for a new toilet seat for people with suppressed immune systems, primarily in hospitals or adult homes. It was a funny project but I actually was pretty proud of the result that we came up with.

So essentially the job was: people would come into the office with either ideas—whether they were established corporations or aspiring entrepreneurs with just a little bit of capital—and they'd want to turn their visions into functioning products and prototypes. We would have to think through their vision, what kind of problem they were trying to solve, what markets they could go after, and develop a strategy for a product and bring it to market. After having practiced at that for a couple of years, I was sort of thinking to myself, *what is really stopping me from releasing a product of my own?* And the only difference between them, and me, was that they had done it and I hadn't. It was literally *just a decision*. They decided to do it and I had not decided to. I hadn't taken that leap yet and that was really *the only difference*.

So you decided *you* wanted to build something at that point?

Yes. I decided I want to build something, and I started to. I began building furniture; I actually built this crazy lounge chair, out of foam. It was going to be a mold and I was going to create a fiberglass lounge chair that I never ended up creating, but I almost finished it. I had this whole line of furniture and tableware. Now the reason I was taking this approach was because you as an entrepreneur essentially can't start your own hardware company, right? There are too many complexities. You *cannot* start a mobile device company the way you can start a site like Airbnb. You can't just create a minimum viable product; you have to invest heavily in manufacturing. That's probably why you don't see a bunch of young hardware startups, a bunch of young Apple companies. It's so much more capital intensive and, more importantly, it's operationally intensive, so I knew I couldn't do that. I knew if I made something it had to be something I could make myself. The only thing I could make myself was something low tech, that didn't involve a huge team and that's the problem with startups, typically they involve hardware. A lot of things I had worked on involved huge teams and also required many types of engineers with the expertise to be able to solve that problem.

Why didn't you pursue your furniture idea?

The only reason I didn't continue to pursue it was because one day, Joe called me up—Joe had been calling me up for two years by now. He was trying to convince me to move out to San Francisco; he had been telling me how much better San Francisco was and how it was just like RISD and I was like, "sure Joe, I have a whole life here", and as far as I was concerned, I did have a whole life in Los Angeles but, sure enough, when I did go to San Francisco, I realized he was exactly right. At the time I was not exposed at all to the Internet, although I do remember sitting in front of my computer in a cubicle—we had these unfortunate cubicles in the design firm that I worked at which was not a startup environment—and, I remember I was fascinated by what people then called "Web 2.0."

I was getting more and more fascinated by all these new websites being created. I was one of the early users of YouTube, when few people knew what it was. I can't remember how I stumbled upon it. I loved the product. I just thought it was amazing, as a democratic product. For the first time, you had access to all this content you didn't have access to before and I was like, "wow, this is absolutely going to change everything." I remember contrasting this tiny, almost worthless website which, in a year a half was a worldwide phenomenon, valued at $1.5 billion, with the various products I was working on for entrepreneurs who I knew would take many more years and would never make the kind of impact that YouTube had made. That was my first taste of the Internet world; it resonated with me just how powerful this world is.

It's easier to take for granted but let's say you want to start a t-shirt company. Let's say you want to start a fill-in-the-blank household item company—you want to manufacture your own garbage can; that could take years to develop. It could take many, many years or even decades to reach scale, and for you, scale is never the kind of success you would achieve through a company like YouTube or Facebook. With scale, you'd be lucky to ever get to Airbnb size today. That's assuming you get every target because how do you get distribution to millions of people? That's a major accomplishment; it's so much more complex. So it's really interesting to look at the hardware world, which I think is so much harder.

So, eventually, Joe convinced you to move to San Francisco?

Yeah and with no plan at all. I didn't know exactly what I was going to do so Joe had started this other website called Ecollect.net that was a sustainable materials library. The most notable part was that it was a website. It never really occurred to me before that that this was a viable path, because I was an industrial designer. I saw what he was doing and thought it was really cool. Separately, he convinced me one day to move to San Francisco, and the way he convinced me was: he had to renew his lease and he said if I didn't move up to San Francisco he was going to get rid of his apartment which is the apartment we're in now.

So this apartment I'm in now—which is the reason we started Airbnb—he was going to get rid of if he couldn't find a roommate. He wasn't having luck finding a roommate he thought maybe it would be easier to get a studio, but he said, "here's a chance, it's now or never. If you want, I know we've been talking about starting a company together." The reason we are friends was we did a lot of projects together at RISD in the industrial design department and we did internships together after graduation. So we knew we worked really well together—it was really inspiring working with him—so I thought it would be amazing to work with him on a company or a project. I wasn't sure what we were going to do but he convinced me to move up to San Francisco and I committed to it. I quit my job, packed all of my things in the back seat of a Honda Civic, and drove up to San Francisco in the middle of the night.

The funny thing is, I didn't realize until I got to San Francisco how expensive it is. My rent was $1,150 and I had $1,000 in the bank account. You have to remember RISD and the self-portrait challenge, right? So it's not *impossible*, it just *seems impossible*. In other words, it's seemingly impossible to do 200 self portraits and often times even today at Airbnb we propose things that *seem impossible* and we need to teach people to *think like designers* which is to think that *there's always a solution*. If you can imagine it you can create it. You just have to come up with a different solution, so for us it was just a creative challenge. It turned out—and this was *completely coincidental*—that there was an international design conference coming to San Francisco that weekend. *All the hotels were sold out on the conference website.*

So if you go to the conference website—just like any conference website, there was a hotel/housing section tab, but you clicked on the hotels tab and all the hotels they had listed said they were sold out. So, there were designers leaving comments on the page like, "We need a place to stay." We noticed there were people that needed places to stay and we loved the idea of making a splash at our local conference when we had just moved up. We wanted to do something that would get everyone's attention and come up with a very novel creative solution to a challenge that also happened to allow us to pay rent. So we decided that we were going to create a bed and breakfast for the conference, we thought it would be a really funny idea. We were like, "well, we can house them" and it wasn't going to be a hotel, it would be a bed and breakfast.

Joe was walking past my bedroom one day before I moved up there and he realized it was an empty room and since I didn't have furniture he told me that he had a bunch of air mattresses in his closet. So we blew up the beds and we called it the Airbed and Breakfast. That's where we got the name from, originally. This, essentially, leads into the story of Airbnb.

This international design conference came to San Francisco in October 2007. We created this website in two days or 24 hours, maybe even less. It wasn't a full website, it was just a very low-tech website. Neither Joe nor I are coders by training. Joe can implement some front end, he knows basic HTML but we are both designers by trade. So we weren't going to create a complex platform and that was not what we really needed. We created a fun little website with a fun story and I think the story was key to the product. We put the product out and design blogs picked it up. They thought it was just incredibly funny and quirky and they loved the creative solution that we had come up with.

So we built the site and to our surprise there was an overwhelming response to our place. Because we had told the conference about it and the conference put a link on their website, a bunch of people wanted to stay at our place. So we decided to pick the people that were really passionate and wanted to stay with us. The three people we picked were: a 35 year-old woman from Boston; a 45 year-old father of five, from Utah; and a third guy from India. So we had a pretty wide demographic of people to stay with us and honestly they came and they said they just had an unbelievable experience with us; I think they said it was like they were staying with friends. We took them all over the city. We basically became their gateway to an inside view of living as a local in San Francisco. We gave them an insider's guide to the city. They came with us to parties, we hung out together and we provided them breakfast, it was like the ultimate local experience.

Eventually you applied to Y Combinator—how does that fit into all of this? How did you hear about them?

There was quite a bit of time that had lapsed between that point and Y Combinator, like 15 months. So we had created this website for this conference. Three or four months passed and we went home for Christmas and, you know as an entrepreneur, people ask, "well, what are you working on?" That's the first question they ask you if you say you're an entrepreneur. We were in the early stage where Joe and I each had a bunch of things we were doing. So I was thinking about other ideas.

I had ideas for iPhone apps before iPhone apps were available but I thought if Apple creates a platform for applications, I had this idea for a health application that would customize fitness programs for you. There are various things like what you see today but I had a very specific vision of what I wanted to accomplish and I had a couple of other ideas that were more product-centric. But I told people the various ideas and most of them didn't seem super interested, but *everyone loved the idea of Airbnb* and I realized that maybe there was greater demand here and people continued asking for it.

There was a lot of momentum. We always liked the concept. We just were somewhat insecure about how many other people were like us, that would want to do this, and it turned out there were a lot of people that thought it was really cool and were really interested in it. We kind of unknowingly tapped into something greater than ourselves by creating Airbnb. We decided in the beginning of 2008 to build a platform or a real website and I asked Joe, "Who's the best engineer you know?" Well, it turned out that the bedroom I was living in belonged to a roommate before me, named Nate, who's now our third cofounder. I had not met Nate but Joe was friends with him. Nate, Joe, and I came together and started AirBNB. We launched our first version in March 2008 for South by Southwest. It was this tiny little website: "airbeds for conferences all over the United States."

I take it the South by Southwest launch went pretty well?

Actually not really, not many people noticed. No, I think we only had two people book rooms and I was one of the two people. So it was cool but we realized that we had a lot of work to do. We had not nailed the product yet; this wasn't something that was just going to take off. We regrouped and thought about the vision, then we started using the product and through using the product we realized that the vision we had come up with was too narrow. There were a few observations I made. So I used the product and I stayed with a guy who was a PhD candidate at the University of Texas at Austin. We hadn't built payments yet, so we still had to transact through cash just like Craigslist.

So I showed up at this guy's house; I had a great experience. His girlfriend prepared a Vietnamese dinner for me, the whole thing was really funny and kind of cool and so I had a great time with him. I think later at night before we went to bed he asked me where his money was. It was kind of a cold exchange, only because, here it was, it felt very personal, suddenly it immediately felt very financial and I also think I didn't even have the money at the time! I had forgotten to go to the ATM and I just remember the experience feeling not very streamlined and not very great overall. You have to exchange the cash, then you've got to get change, and there was no real transactional record of what was happening.

The whole thing just felt very illegitimate and under the table and so we realized that we had to build payments and we thought building payments would be the thing that really created our business and so *that was the first thing*. The second thing we realized was *airbeds for conferences was insanely limiting*. People immediately said, "do I just have to rent an airbed? Can't I just rent out a bedroom or a real bed?" and we were like, "oh, that would be kind of cool" and then someone said, "Does it have to be for a conference?" Originally we wanted it to be for a conference because we didn't think people would feel comfortable booking with complete strangers. It turned out there were plenty of people that were comfortable and so we removed the idea of conferences. We still use them as promotional or public relations opportunities, press opportunities. But we don't exclusively limit the housing to events.

Pretty soon, we changed the concept from a listing service renting out airbeds for conferences, to a site where you could easily book a bedroom anywhere around the world the way you book a hotel room. This is a pretty revolutionary product; at the time, we thought, it was a two-sided marketplace. We built this platform in the summer of 2008, basically the early version of the website you see today, we launched for the Denver Connecticut International Convention in Denver. We got a bunch of bookings for the conference or the convention but then after the convention we were back to zero traction.

We were at that *trough of sorrow* that Paul Graham talks about, it was the Fall of 2008 and we didn't know what we were going to do. We had been friends with the guys from Justin.TV through a roommate of mine who worked with them. He introduced us to the guys at Justin.TV who would become unofficial advisors or mentors over the summer, and they recommended we do Y Combinator. We ended up doing YC, and Paul Graham told us to not focus on events but on cities. We started focusing on New York City and that was the city that potentially proved this model. We started it as a website to—well, really rent out our airbed. We started as "airbeds for conferences", then to "renting out a bedroom around the world", to today, its any type of space *and that was very gradual*. Essentially what would happen is every time we created a platform, people would want to list things outside of the parameters and every time that would happen we got kind of excited. Instead of saying, "that's not really our vision" we'd say, "oh cool, we never thought of that, let's create a category for that and that's how it happened."

For me, this is where Airbnb's story gets exciting because I see New York as your major turning point. This is the tipping point where Airbnb made it out of the trough of sorrow and exploded into the successful model that we hear about in the news today. When Paul Graham told you to focus on cities instead of events, you went to New York. Can you talk about how you started Airbnb in New York?

We literally would fly to New York every Thursday or Friday during Y Combinator. We did this every week and we would be there throughout the weekend. There were a myriad of tactics we used—we went as far as knocking on people's doors. We did everything we could think of. We would stay until Monday and fly back Tuesday. Sometimes we'd be going straight to Y Combinator with our luggage.

How did you find those first few people to get started using Airbnb?

Because of the Democratic National Conventions, some people were using the site in New York and listing places. What we would do is reach out to the very few people we had and basically talk to them, get to know them, figure out what products they needed and what we could offer them. We tried to build loyalty knowing that if we did that, they would tell their friends. We'd host parties and meetups and all sorts of different things. We'd just visit all of our users, we'd go to their homes and talk to them and do interviews. Through that process, they'd get very excited and tell their friends about Airbnb. It was mostly about generating as much buzz and excitement to get them to tell their friends about us.

Did you guys ever dress up in gorilla suits or pass out fliers on the streets?

We never dressed up in gorilla suits but we passed out fliers in coffee shops, train stations—we did all sorts of things. I don't know what tactics worked more than others, but I think press was always the number one tactic for us. The press would spark another group of users, then we'd go visit those people and talk to them and get them excited. It was a pattern that repeated itself.

Did you ever hire a PR agency? Did anything ever cause revenue to spike?

We briefly hired a PR firm but 99% of the press we generated was generated on our own. We primarily focused on building a world-class product, focused on getting people to use it, and getting the press to periodically talk about it. There were numerous press cycles where we'd reach out, we had enough people to create a story, and then it grew organically from there.

What is Airbnb's biggest challenge today?

I think scaling the organization.

You're not talking about technology—you're talking about how to add a person to the team and keep the company from breaking?

Yes—even how to add the people to the team in the first place.

How many people are at Airbnb today?

We have about 35 full-time people, and we will soon have 20-30 customer support people working remotely.

You and Foursquare seem to be on the same level of scale. Dennis Crowley mentioned that was a big challenge: adding people to the organization without things breaking. Can you elaborate there? Is it a matter of cultural fit; are there potential problems from hiring a certain type of individual?

There are a number of things, and these are all going through my head right now. The first thing is finding the talent. When you start to build an organization, you need to have seen your talent. It's not as hard to *find* the talent, it's knowing: when you see someone really good, how do you *know* they're good? How do you know when you meet a director of marketing that they're actually a *good* director of marketing? How do you know when you meet a communications person that they're the best communications person in the world or that they're merely average? How would you know? How do you know if they're the right stage person for the stage your company is at?

I could go down a list—like staff accountant. Clearly, it's one thing if you're an engineer or a designer. You've done the job and you feel like you can evaluate people, but what if you've never done the job yourself? What if nobody in the company has done the job and you don't even know what you need? There's a certain leap of faith even being able to evaluate who the people are that you need. Then you have to ask yourself, "do I now need young generalists or do I need specialists? Do I need senior people? How senior should they be?" These are all interesting questions we wrestle with very frequently.

And then there's integrating them, whether they're junior or senior. Keeping the culture—if you're growing quickly, there's going to be a point where a majority of the people in the room are not going to know much about your company; they're not going to know much about the history. Some people will not have been there from the start. If you're doubling in size every quarter like what we're doing, what that means is 3 months from now, if the people in that room haven't been fully assimilated and trained, half the room isn't fully on board culturally. When the organization changes that quickly, it has a profound impact on people's positions, responsibilities, who everyone works with, and so on. You have to manage all the things that happen with those changes, whether they're good or bad.

Can you talk about culture a little bit? What's it like working or being at Airbnb? Are there lots of meetings, for example? Is the floor plan open?

We have an open floor plan. We have a weekly product meeting and a weekly engineering meeting. There may be daily meetings, but those are impromptu for a few minutes where you just huddle together over a computer and call that a product meeting. We really believe in sharing ideas—a meeting can mean a lot of things, it could be a very formal accountability meeting where things don't get done, or it could be a few people having a conversation about a challenge. Depending on your definition, I'd say we only have formal meetings a few times a week. The collaborative meetings happen very frequently and they're usually not scheduled. This probably has to do with our open floor plan. We're moving into a new office and that new office also has an open plan, so there are no private offices. People could work from the kitchen if they wanted.

We don't typically have set hours. Most people get here by 9 AM and leave at 6 or 7 PM. It varies though. Some people are here during weekends, but it's very flexible. People's schedules are dictated by the projects they're working on and the deadlines they have.

Are there any cultural values you're afraid of losing in all of the hiring you're doing?

Yeah, I worry about losing values. I think there are a couple of things: it's important for us to hire people who are passionate about Airbnb and the community and our mission. When you're growing fast and becoming a hot company, there are numerous things that can attract a person to a company. When you're really small and not successful, you can argue that the only thing that attracts people to you is you can pay them and they need a job—that's also not a good motivation. To an extent it's easy to be passionate about Airbnb: people in Silicon Valley are very ambitious and they want to be successful. They see this could be a vehicle to them having a lot of responsibility and becoming very successful.

You want to hire the right people who are very ambitious. Would they truly want to work here over any other hot company if they had the exact same offer? That's something we ask ourselves a lot.

We have a lot of core values that we measure people on that affect hiring, but one thing that's hard to understand is: how do you know you're hiring the right person given the stage you're in? For instance, if we need a finance person, should we hire the CFO of Google? Would that make sense at this stage of the company? There are a lot of questions to ask from there. There's a risk of hiring people who are too senior to "roll up their sleeves and get their hands dirty" as some people might say.

The other risk is hiring people into positions with lots of responsibility if the individual isn't as experienced—they can get overwhelmed too quickly. That's the challenge: keeping a balance somewhere in the middle.

I think it's hard to stand by your values *and* have the same level of standards when you need to hire quickly. What if you *really need* someone for a position, you have 3 candidates, and none of them are perfect, what do you do? Do you say "no" to all 3 and then wait? What if saying "no" to all 3 means waiting months? What if waiting months could cost you millions of dollars in opportunity costs? This is what's going through my head when I'm interviewing people.

To jump to a different topic and go back a little bit, you decided to sell cereal to try and make some money. Why did you decide on *cereal* when Airbnb was still struggling to take off? Why not books, consulting, or design?

We originally were thinking of making the cereal and sending it to our hosts for the Democratic Republican National Conventions. We were already considering this, but then we thought it'd a really interesting welcome kit where the host could give to the guest. We thought about how to design the entire experience, including the breakfast.

We had what we thought was a funny concept. We had a marketplace and not a lot of traction, so your mind can wander in that situation so that's the idea we came up with. We did think it was something that was still related to the brand because at the time we were called "Air Bed And Breakfast" and it might not seem obvious today, but back then a lot of people provided breakfast. It was in our name and in the description of the listings: what kind of breakfast did you provide? So breakfast wasn't an afterthought, it was core to the experience and now that's changed—today it's just an amenity.

Around the time when investors wouldn't give us money, we thought we could make a lot of money doing this fun thing selling cereal. So we ended up making a decent amount of money from it—it was low hanging fruit, it was a lot of fun, it was tangentially related to what we were doing, and we put the logos on the boxes.

Why did investors turn you guys down? What was the objection?

Airbnb seems like a crazy idea when you first hear about it. If you were to tell people today about Airbnb, some people are surprised people do this, let alone millions of people could be using our site this year. But when nobody has done this before and it is just a concept, then it does seem especially crazy. It's one thing to say "oh it's crazy I'm surprised people are doing this today" but it's another thing to say, "it's crazy, nobody is *ever* going to do this." At the time it seemed crazy and the product had not progressed to where it is today. It seemed even crazier back then and it wasn't clear that we would get any traction. I think everyone believed if we got traction there would be a huge business model, but the whole concern was the total addressable market. There was no evidence that a lot of people would be doing this. The most we could point to were people doing couch surfing on Craigslist, but nobody saw this becoming even a $100 million business, let alone a $1 million business.

Joe and I were primarily the ones pitching investors and we had never—Joe had done a web startup before, but Joe and I are both first-time founders. Both of us were trying to do something very ambitious and we both have unorthodox backgrounds—we come from design—so I'm not sure in the early days that our backgrounds were viewed as strengths. I think today maybe they are. People might look our site and say "*oh,* that's why the site is great, it's well-designed" and things like that. But in the early days, I think people were concerned that we didn't have the technical background. I remember some investors saying "you have a lack of a technical team" and of course we had Nate, but they were used to seeing *multiple technical founders*. I think investors were not seeing the whole picture: first, they were undervaluing design by saying that, but also they were not recognizing that when you build a marketplace, all the *nontechnical* challenges exist to build it. It's one thing to technically build our web site—that's the easy part. Get the marketplace going, get traction, and build a community—that's the hard part.

Do you have any advice for an undergrad student interested in a startup? Let's say they were in your position and came from a design background.

That's a good question. I don't have any regrets for my path, clearly it has worked out well for me. I think that if I could have done it over again, maybe Joe and I would have started a company even sooner. I certainly wouldn't tell this student to work for another company, although I don't think it'd be bad to work for a startup for a year. I think what I'd recommend is just doing a startup as soon as you have a cofounder. If you don't, I'd go work for a company that has lots of really smart and ambitious people. You'll learn what it's like to build a startup and you'd grow faster because you'll know what it's like to be in a startup. You'd also potentially meet your next cofounder doing this.

If someone from RISD were in this position, I'd say, "Develop your UI skills and to look for a technical founder." If someone doesn't have the skills to contribute to the product, I'd have them think through what they can actually add and build as many skills as possible. The last thing I'd ever want to tell a designer is to learn how to code. It's kind of like telling an engineer to learn how to design. I think the two should learn about the other, but to say a designer should learn how to code—great engineers have been doing engineering for over a decade and many of them grew up with this. Same thing applies for a designer. I started drawing when I was 5 years old. I'm only 29, but for 25 years I've practically spent every moment thinking about design. For the design undergrad: find a technical cofounder as passionate about engineering as you are about design.

If you got an offer from Google or any major tech company tomorrow to get acquired would you accept it?

No.

Even if it was ridiculously good?

Even if it was ridiculously good, I'd say "no." I think we can build a company like Google. When I said "like Google" I mean I think we can build a company that—success for us is people forgetting what the world was like before Airbnb. I don't think it would exist as a business unit inside a large conglomerate or as a subsidiary. I think for us to truly accomplish what we want—which is to connect millions of people and give them access to all these experiences and spaces around the world—I think we need to remain an independent company. I'm pretty forthcoming and open with people about how big I think we can become. I think we can become at least as big as eBay, and maybe even bigger. What I like to say is "if eBay can become a billion dollar company by monetizing *stuff in their house*, how big could a company be if the monetize *the house*?" We're in a multi-billion dollar market. How big could a company be if they became a marketplace for unique experiences and spaces? With our growth trajectory, I couldn't imagine a reason to sell. We didn't start Airbnb to make money; we started it to do something significant for the world. I think all of us on the board and the team feel that way.

Mike Lamond, Husky Starcraft

Tags: antischool, school worker, undergrad founder, profitable, side project, self-funded, dropout, major league player (YouTube #1 Most Subscribed Reporter [All Time], 100 million+ upload views)

Overview: Husky Starcraft is an Internet sensation. With nearly 500,000 subscribers and close to 200,000,000 views, almost everyone who plays computer games knows who Husky Starcraft is. In college, all my friends in CS would talk about is which Husky cast they liked the best. As e-sports pick up momentum in the United States, companies like Justin.TV are getting involved in live streaming of e-sports. Husky Starcraft has created video broadcasts ("casts") of the most elite and competitive players in the world for the past 2 years.

Can you describe what you do as an "e-sports broadcaster"?

Starcraft 2 for those who don't know is a computer game—the first version has been out for about 13 years, and the newest version has been out for about a year. Essentially what I do is spectate games; it's called an e-sport game because it has the same elements of the regular sports you hear of, such as tennis.

How did you come up with the name Husky Starcraft?

I've had the Internet since I was 10 years old and I've had that name as far back as I can remember. I decided when I was starting out on YouTube making videos to keep it because there's so much confusion with the name Husky alone, so it ended up being Husky Starcraft. I like two-syllable names, it's easy to make a logo for, and I had not seen any pro gamers that used the Husky name anywhere. Mostly, I just decided as a kid to go with that and I've had it ever since.

When did you start playing Starcraft and when did you move into doing casting?

I bought Starcraft about 6 months after it came out and I was playing Warcraft 2 around that time. My friends bought Starcraft, so I didn't want to get left in the dust. I had an NES and an Atari when I as a kid, so I was playing those consistently. I played Starcraft a few times a month from 13 years ago through today. I never really followed the competitive scene for Starcraft—it was huge from day one in Korea. The reason for that is because at the time America had AOL which was fantastic (sarcasm) but Korea already had broadband Internet for their entire country, so they're like "what do we do with this crazy fast Internet? Well, let's make a sport out of it." So I've played it since I was a kid, then I got into the competitive scene around 3 years ago when I was still in college. I was watching the GSL, which is hosted by a commentator called "Tasteless" and I loved watching that so much that I wanted to watch more. The only way I could watch more was to commentate on my own, so I found replays and then showed them to my roommates and friends. I had a lot of fun doing that, so I kept doing it and here we are 2 years later and I haven't slowed down at all.

What was your college experience like?

I was following the competitive scene my third or fourth year in community college—yes that's only supposed to take 2 years, but I had no idea what I wanted to do—and I was switching majors pretty heavily. At one point I was going to be a nurse, then a veterinarian, and then I switched to computer science. I was all over the place with my school studies; towards the end I just wanted to do something computer-related because I never get tired of that. I eventually went to University of Oregon for 2 terms and that was for computer science, but then I realized I had to take 9 math classes and 2 programming classes, which are both things I did not want to do for a living.

When I was at the university, that's when I started doing the commentaries. It was more fun, it felt like I was making something, and it was kind of a good excuse not to go to class—not that I recommend that, but it was an outlet for me and a hobby.

I spent a total of 5 years in college, and I never found something I really liked because I'm not a fan of someone telling me "you have to write a paper of the history of this clay pot." I was really bored by that. I wanted to make video games work for me, so I stuck with it.

Did you take time away from casting to party, or was this 24/7 for you?

I don't even drink alcohol and my friends are total nerds, so this is more of a 24/7 thing for me. The only parties I would have would be LAN parties, so that's where I socialized. All my roommates and friends would play games all day and eventually I was spending 8 hours per day making videos. In college, I was making 100 videos per month, which is a lot of casting to save my voice and sanity, but I still do it full time. It takes longer to cast now because the video resolutions have increased; it takes longer to make and upload the views. I also had a job in college, so I didn't get much sleep or go to most of my classes. I've been casting at least 40 hours per week for over 2 years now. I'm going on 2 hours of sleep for the past 48 hours because I was working with my good friend Kurt—he has twice as many subscribers on YouTube and he's one of the most talented people I have ever met. We're working on two upcoming songs for a project called Nerd Alert.

How much of your time is spent playing Starcraft 2 vs. casting?

Playing consists of about 5% of my overall time, which is unfortunate. I love playing the game—I'm a huge Blizzard fan and I've played them all, including the ones made for the consoles and most people don't remember those. I played World of Warcraft for 4 years, Warcraft 3 for 2 years, Diablo 1 and 2—basically every game they've released, I've played into the ground.

I spend at least 80 hours per week related to gaming or casting, and a majority is related to casting.

What was the very first thought that came to mind when you decided you wanted to start casting?

I remember there were other YouTube commentators before me who were doing it for about a year or longer. On YouTube, if you jump into something a year later it might not be as interesting. If someone started the channel "Epic Meal Time" (a popular channel today) a year ago, how interesting would that be today to watch? When I started out, it was just literally to show my roommates what I was doing because we had always played against each other. I wasn't really stressing about it; I was thinking, "I'm going to have a ton of subscribers and that will be awesome." I saw that Tasteless was doing it and there were other casters, so I decided to choose YouTube as my main focus where I could upload videos and make it public. YouTube makes it very easy to do this kind of stuff, and there's no strings attached.

I enjoy learning how to use the editing programs and learning how stuff works. After the first day I never stopped.

It sounds like this was something you started as a fun side project, but eventually you decided to commit fulltime?

I've always thought that whatever you want to do, you can make it work, even back in high school. Within the first couple of weeks, I wasn't thinking "I'll be making money doing this" but I definitely knew I'd be doing it for a long time. There's not a lot of money in it, so for a year I was working a part-time job just to pay for food. Over time, it grew bigger and I never looked too far into the future, I just stuck with it because I'm passionate about it.

I didn't like the current college system, personally. I can make something that I enjoy doing work, and I don't need someone to tell me how to go about it. I know nothing about business, so I might be the worst entrepreneur ever. As far as money goes, money is just a number and I've always been good at saving money so I could live off that. Luckily, my parents were very supportive when I dropped out of college.

Did you know anyone else when you started out casting?

I teamed up with another channel called HD Starcraft starting out. The reason that fit really well is because we both were getting started at the same time. Our channels started within the same day of each other, which is a funny coincidence because the game was still 9 or 10 years old.

Over time, I worked with other channels such as Ahnaris Starcraft who is a real life friend of mine. Collaborating is a lot more difficult than people realized because in Starcraft 2, replays cannot be watched together, which means they can get out of synch. What that means is: if there are 2 or 3 commentators with a football game, you'll be watching different points of the game—so one person sees a touchdown 20 seconds before another person. It makes for an awkward casting experience.

I enjoy traveling around and doing live events such as MLG's events (Major League Gaming) as well as TSL. I have a tournament coming up with Day9, another popular commentator.

There's no beef with other casters? It gets voted up a lot in the comments, for example people think there's a rivalry with you and HD.

I think a lot of people out there like drama and relationships, as I'm starting to learn. I think a lot of magazines like TMZ get started for this reason, because people love the drama. There's no beef really between any of the casters that I know. The casters completely support each other; we get what everyone in the scene has to go through. It's a lot of work, dedication, and commitment, and we all get that. Behind the scenes, I talk to a lot of the casters and pro gramers quite frequently. HD and I definitely don't have any beef, but our schedules just don't match up and it has happened in the past with no hard feelings, but sometimes it gets hectic and the schedules don't always work out. I'm not sure if we'll cast much together in the future, but I'm sure people will always post about drama since they have been doing that for the past year now.

Hopefully that helps clear the air though.

How did you get the word out at first? How did you get your first 100 subscribers? Then how did you get your first 1,000 subscribers?

That was a long time ago. Basically I told my roommates and I made all of my real life friends subscribe. I can be very convincing—not in an intimidating way, but I have the best puppy eyes ever. I was able to get 30 of my real life friends subscribed; it felt more like a Facebook at that point rather than having fans.

I wondered how I could get other people interested, so I had a friend at the very beginning who convinced Team Liquid to mention me in one of their news articles. For those unfamiliar, Team Liquid is one of the biggest competitive gaming sites for Starcraft. I got featured in an article—it wasn't a huge deal, but for someone starting out, I was very thankful. Getting featured in that article got me my first 100 subscribers and it actually caught the attention of someone who was running a semi-exclusive tournament and they had no caster lined up for it. It was called the Valor Tournament, this was back in Starcraft 1. It was backed by my favorite caster, Tasteless, and so I got involved with that. I stayed involved and casted in any tournament that would accept me or that I was interested in, and I stayed consistent there.

On YouTube, the number increases over time as you gain more subscribers. It's just important that you stay consistent. You very rarely lose subscribers vs. gaining subscribers.

If you go on YouTube, each caster has a different personality.
You're very energetic; someone like HD is more analytical. Was that intentional, or was that just part of your personality?

I think my casting reflects my personality in real life—the only thing really different is that I yell a lot more when I cast than in person. Overall, I'm an excitable person and the smallest things give me nerd chills. I wasn't faking any of my excitement; just watching Starcraft is fun for me, so I'm genuine in my reactions.

I never preview games before I cast them. Whatever comes out from casting is not planned, I just talk about what I know in the game. I've been pretty lucky with my fan base, I really enjoy interacting with them and they seem to enjoy the casting style so hopefully that doesn't change. It's a nerd loving a video game way too much and talking about it all day, that's what it comes down to.

You originally started out casting Starcraft 1. Why decide to focus on Starcraft 2 exclusively? Have you expanded into other games?

I realized Blizzard essentially makes the best games out there. They don't make a lot of games, and they spent 10 years building Starcraft 2. Whenever they release a new one, I get really excited. I'm always in line at the midnight releases, so when Starcraft 2 came out, I had played Starcraft 1 for 12 years and I was so excited about the sequel that I got a beta key the first day and played nonstop. It's not something I planned, but once that game came out, it was love at first sight and I started uploading videos for it. Luckily I was able to upload videos right from the beginning and people were anxious to see what the game was like. Overall, Starcraft 2 was the most entertaining so I stuck with that.

Do you have plans to expand into other games in the future?
In my opinion, Starcraft 2 is the most exciting e-sport to watch—which is kind of like saying "what's the most interesting sport to watch" and nobody will agree—so I cast that one 99% of the time. If I cast other games, it's usually with friends and its done more casually. It might be a single player game or an online deathmatch game such as Team Fortress 2 for fun. But I'm a gamer at heart, so I enjoy checking them all out. I have a second channel at YouTube.com/Husky, and that's the channel where I upload casual games such as Mario. It's not competitive like, "oh no! He's going for the mushroom! He's going to be twice the size!"

I support all games, though. I think for nerds to be mainstream if they aren't already—everyone has their own game that they like, and I like to try them all out and see what's up.

A lot of startup founders I've spoken to have had stressful moments where they almost failed. Has that ever happened to you? Have you ever thought "this isn't picking up enough subscribers fast enough" or "I can't pay next month's rent" or something along those lines?
I'm not a business-minded person. I always thought I can be a hard-worker, so worst case scenario I get a job at a fast food place again and I can live off of that. There's no doubt in my mind that whatever happens, I can always go back to something like that and I'll be fine. I don't need a lot of money, so I could always move back to Oregon where rent is cheap and I'm happy with that. As far as money goes, anything I can get doing something I love is purely icing on the cake. It's never my goal—it's just coincidental to what I'm doing.

As far as getting stressed out, I would never start making gaming videos saying "Ok, in one year I'll be making $1,000 per month." There's no overhead for what I do, it's just time commitment and having fun, so even if I was working fast food 40 hours per week, I'd have all my spare time for gaming and I've love that. I'm blessed to be working with The Game Station so I can do this full-time.

My car the other day got broken into and they busted out my back window, and my friends were freaking out and saying "oh my god! Are you freaking out? This is horrible, you're going to have to pay so much money to fix it! You're car is ruined." But what's getting stressed about it going to do? I think I tend to be *too calm* and collected in a lot of situations, but overall I'm just a relaxed nerd playing video games. I tried changing it with this whole college thing, but it didn't work out.

I don't really get stressed—I think that's a bad business trait, but I think that's just how I am.

Is this the Lamborghini that got broken into from the Banelings video?

Unfortunately, I don't own the car from that video. Maybe some day I can afford a ridiculously priced sports car that I would be so terrified to take out into the streets and it would just stay covered in my garage all day. The car we got was through a business contact; Justin.TV helped facilitate getting that Lamborghini. I don't know much about business stuff, but I love working with other companies who enjoy giving something without expecting anything in return. Justin.TV said "hey, here's a Lamborghini—we're huge fans, have fun with it!" So they hooked that up and since then I've been working with them doing show matches, and so that's how I "do business": I meet with them in person, if I vibe with them and they seem like cool nerds just trying to make a living, then I really enjoy working with them. There have been a lot of major companies wanting to sponsor me or do a big event, but to be honest a lot of their motives are not very good and so I've rejected a lot of those things. I'm not here to make a lot of money, I'm just here to have fun and spread around e-sports to as many people as possible.

I don't feel like I've "worked" given I spend about 80 hours a week on it, but doing what you love is amazing. Whether you enjoy bicycling, skydiving, or playing video games like me, you can turn it into a fulltime job and you can interview me again in 60 years and see if it worked out.

What's the biggest challenge for you today?

To make a 20 minute video takes 4 hours to get uploaded from start to end. A lot of people say "well, you say you work 80 hours a week on this, but you only upload 2 or 3 videos a day" but there are so many restrictions in terms of rendering and uploading videos. Each file is 1 or 2 gigabytes, so that can take up a lot of time.

A lot of it is finding good games to cast, *which is difficult for me because I don't preview the games.* One thing that happens a lot is I'll cast a game, it'll be 40 minutes, and I'll be like, "wow that was the most boring thing I've ever seen—absolutely no one is going to watch this." A lot of times I'll scrap games like that because I don't want to waste people's times. I don't want to say that every single game on my channel is super exciting, but they have to at least be interesting.

Overall, the challenging aspects are finding good games, rendering and uploading every day, and working on music videos. It's also a lot of time management for traveling around for live events too. Another commentator—his name is DJ Wheat—holds a fulltime job, travels around the country, and has a family, and I have no idea how he does it. I'm not sure I could manage my time that well.

I know you're not intentional about growth, but do you find that there's anything you do that really bumps up your subscriber count? Did you notice Nerd Alert cause any spikes in growth?

As far as why people are subscribing, I think they like my personality. The thought process I had behind Nerd Alert was: I was that kid in middle school and high school on the bus playing Pokemon, I was dressing horrendously, and everyone was making fun of me so I totally get the whole nerd thing. Some kids get made fun of, and so Nerd Alert was a good way to—Kurt actually contacted me—legitimize being a nerd, be proud to be a nerd. I'm the type of person who thinks being a nerd is the coolest thing ever, so if anyone ever makes fun of you, just point to NASA and tell them "they're all nerds and they're making crazy amounts of money and inventing things like Ziploc bags, so you need to back off." So I think Nerd Alert legitimizes nerds, maybe it does set us apart a little because nobody else is doing that.

Do you ever have any motivational problems where you wake up one day and think, "I just don't want to do any casting."

If you asked me 2 years ago if I'd be tired of doing this 2 years in, I might have told you "yeah, probably." But honestly, ever since I started, I don't think there's ever been a time where I haven't uploaded a video in more than 4 days.

It has always been in the back of my mind. If I'm gone from the house for 2 days, I'm like "oh god, I can't wait to get home and make a video." When I'm going home at 4 in the morning, I can't wait to wake up and make a video. I would have thought that at some point I'd be telling myself "it's time to take a break, go on a vacation" or something, but I've never lost that motivation. It took my first year to gain 10,000 subscribers, and now it's my second year it has grown much faster than that, but I actually didn't know where to find my subscriber count for much of that first year. I was just making videos because every day feels like a vacation for me.

The only time I take breaks is when I've been yelling for 8 hours and I literally cannot talk anymore. One time when that happened, I actually made a cast that was using the Microsoft Sam voice and people did not get the joke. That was me trying to make videos when I physically was not able to. I highly recommend it to anyone thinking about jumping in.

Justin.TV once said "e-sports is going to be bigger than golfing"—are we going to see Starcraft 2 in those big screen TVs in bars instead of football and golf? Where do you see e-sports in 5 to 10 years?

In America, gaming on TV does not do the best. There's G4 TV, but how much of that these days is gaming? It's like MTV, how much of that is actually music?

As far as that being on TV, it would be amazing—if G4 one day called me up and said "Husky, we're going to cast this tournament, it's on at 4 AM so nobody is going to watch it, will you do it?" I'd say, "absolutely, yes, let's get it on TV!"

The thing with e-sports is that it's global. It's not centralized in one country or anything, so to have it on TV you're not even hitting most of the demographic. With American football, how many people outside the U.S. watch it? That's why you'll see a lot of success on web sites like Justin.TV with the livestreams. The most recent tournament I cast on TSL, when me and the other caster were casting, there were 50,000-60,000 people watching at once, and that doesn't include people trickling in and out, so overall it's around 100,000 people in one session. That's pretty cool for a couple of nerds talking about a video game. It'd be awesome to see on TV, but I think the main focus should be "how popular is it online?" because there are millions of views on Starcraft-related content every day. Whether you sit and watch with your grandparents on your TV or not—to me, that's an older-school model and it should be focused on the live events and online streaming if you're going to try and directly compare it to the popularity of current sports.

I'm sure that you get more viewership than many TV stations—you're consistently in the top 10 or 20 most viewed videos on YouTube.

It's not even specifically me, but if you look every day at the top 100 most viewed videos on YouTube, I'd say at least a third if not half of them are gaming. So that includes Starcraft, Minecraft, or any sports game, it's really freaking popular. It's definitely becoming mainstream. My generation—I'm currently 24 years old—I'd say anyone around my age spends more time on the computer than on the TV. I'm not hitting that 65 year-old female demographic, but as far as the male demographic goes, I'd say gaming has gone mainstream.

When I was first started to realize that is when I first visited one of my friends in college who had lived in a dorm. I walked down the hallways, and *everyone* was playing either their XBOX or Playstation, and even a couple of years ago that wasn't the cool thing to do, but now it is.

On the topic of predictions—Starcraft 3? What would you give it? Another 10 years?

I'm hoping 10 years! I feel that with Starcraft, it's such an awesome sport that there's no reason to change it very often. If you look at popular sports like American football or soccer, they don't change that much. The important thing is to keep an even playing field, that's what Starcraft has been known for in the past. As long as it's balanced, that's when the interesting stuff happens.

Think about any sport, like Rugby. It's the same rules, same setup every time and you'd think it would get boring but it doesn't because anything can happen during those games which is the same thing that happens in Starcraft. They're going to release two Starcraft expansions eventually, so people getting bored have something to look forward to.

Do you still stick with playing as Protoss?

I'm sticking with the Protoss because that's the race I've played as a kid, and that's what I understand best. I'm not saying I'm a good player, but I'm not going to play gross bugs or boring humans.

How does someone beat Spanishiwa (a popular player with a unique play style who Husky covers)?

Either play Zerg, since he has admitted that he's very bad at Zerg—and he has talked to me about some of the strategies he loses against, but I'm sworn to secrecy and I don't want to tell everyone how to beat him.

For those who don't know who Spanishiwa is, he's a very popular player right now because he's really good and he has a unique style of play so he's very entertaining to watch. As far as beating him, I think on someone's channel, they uploaded a best-of-three series where he ended up losing that, so if you're looking to dethrone him so you can check that out.

A lot of younger people listening to this, and many of them might not want a job right out of college. Any advice to someone who wants to start putting videos on YouTube?

Well I don't know anything about business, so I've been able to do my own thing. I've mostly stayed consistent and I've been lucky to have my parents' support, so there was a bit of a safety net there. I was 5 years in college and still living with my parents, but if they're supportive that's the best thing ever. If you think you can make something work and have a passion—even not related to your major—hell, give it a shot and go with it, have some fun. It's like the saying we've all heard "you only live once" and I sure don't want to spend my life in a cubicle doing nothing, but if you need to do that for a while to save up, do that and find a way to launch your own company. Everything in your room was made by some company all started by individuals who wanted to do that.

You'll be surprised how much money you can save not living in a major city and not having a high cost of living with expensive hobbies. I've always believed that gaming is a ridiculously cheap hobby compared to riding dirtbikes or painting. If you're a nerd, buy a fancy computer and come up with ideas, it's about being consistent, having fun, and being genuine. If you're not genuine and you don't love it, I think that's going to be of huge detriment to what you're going to do.

Maybe we're creating some casters here, but let's say somebody's more introverted, should they go with that instead of trying to be extroverted on their casting style?

That's an *insanely good* question because I'm a huge introvert, and a lot of people don't realize that about me. That's why I spend so much time on the computer. You asked me earlier, "oh did you party in college?" and I thought, "nope, I don't think I've ever been to a single party in high school or college" because I personally don't get energized by going to parties like extroverts tend to. I spent a lot of time in my room on my computer, and it's amazing what you can do. People may tell you "oh, that's antisocial" but I just feel better after using a computer. If you're an introvert, I think computers are your best friend; I'm not saying you shouldn't go out and meet people, but I'm a huge introvert with a few extrovert qualities because I love meeting my fans at Blizzcon. I'm excited beyond words when it comes to that stuff. Being an introvert—there's nothing wrong with that and I'm 99% introvert.

Even then, a lot of introverts might get demotivated because they're forced to go to a job or interact with people who drive them crazy. My thing is: I *hate* being told what to do, so my manager would say "no, you're doing these fries wrong" and I would think, "oh my god, I don't care, I just want to go home and play video games." So if you're an introvert, this is a surprisingly good job.

As far as public speaking goes, I'm actually not a good public speaker but I'll be the most confident speaker. I'll probably ramble and have no idea what I'm talking about, but making these videos makes me so much more confident in social situations.

I remember in high school or middle school, they said "you talked very clear, you were on topic, but you talked *way too fast*" and so now I'm kind of getting the last laugh. I found something— even the negative side of my personality—that worked out for me.

David Rusenko, Weebly

Tags: Y Combinator, VC funded, programmer, profitable, hiring, design-focused, major league player (Alexa top 500 worldwide), iterate slowly, undergrad founder

Overview: Weebly allows anyone to easily create own web site whether it's a personal blog or online store for a business. Weebly started in 2007 and has raised over $600K. Weebly was ranked as one of Time Magazine's Top 50 Websites. With over 6 million web sites launched from Weebly.com, the sites collectively receive over 40 million unique visitors per month. In other words, about 5% of the U.S. visits a Weebly website every month.

Take me back as far as you can remember—how did you get into entrepreneurship?

I have two cofounders, Dan Veltri and Christopher Fanini. We all met at Penn State as undergrads; all three of us had previously toyed around with entrepreneurship and tried to start companies. In high school I started a hosted-security email provider. I grew up in Morocco and, at that time, the state of technology and development was really different than it is today. Gmail wasn't out; the other hosted offerings weren't operating over HTTPS or anything like that, and I kind of realized that no one was filling this widespread need to get communications from Morocco to the U.S. securely. Eventually, the landscape changed and doing TLS and secure IMAP, SMTP and HTTPS on web mail became a de-facto standard. So nothing ended up working out for me personally, but it was definitely a great experience.

My cofounder, Chris, had started a regional ISP in the Philadelphia suburbs in high school, and our third cofounder, Dan, early in college, had started a travel social network. Each of us had a little bit of experience with entrepreneurship in high school or early in college so when we all met, that collective experience helped us eventually start Weebly.

Once you got to college, what was your experience like?

I was studying for two majors: IST, which is Information Science Technology—a degree combining technology and business that's specific to Penn State, and MIS, which is Management Information Systems, primarily a business degree. As for my cofounders, Dan was a finance major and Chris was an IST major.

I didn't know anybody going in to Penn State since I moved from Morocco to Pennsylvania to go to college; I didn't know a single person when I started. But I did meet a lot of absolutely amazing people there, including Dan, who I met my freshman year, and Chris, who I met my junior year. Dan and I lived in the same dorm and hung out with the same group of people, so that's how we met. During our freshman year there were a bunch of really great guys in our hall and we all formed a pretty tight-knit group. Chris had gone to high school and was friends with several of the guys in our hall so we met through them. I met plenty of people through my classes too, but one of the most valuable things to me about Penn State was the environment really encouraged and facilitated social interactions. It was a lot more than learning from textbooks, it was about engaging in 'social intelligence.'

I didn't start working on Weebly until the spring semester of my junior year; initially, it was part of a class project. During my freshman and sophomore year, I spent a lot of time working on the company that I started in high school; I also spent a lot of time just socializing. I actually deejayed throughout college which, in addition to being a great way to meet people, was a pretty fun job. That's how I paid the bills. I took loans to pay for the basic stuff, obviously, like tuition, books, supplies, and part of rent, but I was able to get by comfortably, by deejaying, and just living inexpensively.

Once we got accepted into Y Combinator we moved out to California in the last semester of our senior year. We each had just a few classes left but luckily, at least in my case, the professors were really accommodating and let me take the classes from out here. This doesn't always happen, but I think most professors try to be accommodating in these kinds of situations; I just went to them and explained the situation: that this was a major opportunity and that I was willing to do whatever it took on my end to be able to make it work and still graduate if they could just help me a bit on their end. They did and I ended up ditching my extra major so I only had two classes to finish out here. Dan had a few classes left and finished some from out here that semester and the rest, the following summer. Chris still has one or two classes left; we're still trying to get him to graduate!

Can you offer any advice to students looking for cofounders?

I would absolutely say that your best bet in general is just to get out and meet as many people as possible. You tend to meet a lot of people in classes and a lot of people through more social interactions as well. So, not spending too much time in any one arena is probably key. Other than that it's pretty hit or miss. That said, Penn State didn't necessarily have the strongest technical curriculum or reputation in terms of computer science programs, so I would imagine the academic and social environments are different at schools like MIT or UIUC.

In general I think it's always going to be kind of hit or miss but just by trying to meet as many people as possible, hopefully, you end up finding someone that's a potential cofounder.

So, what was your work-life balance like in college?

I would say it was a good mix, but I did spend a whole lot of time partying. Personally, I think that's one of the most important things you can do in college, just because you always learn new social skills through different interactions, like meeting people socially, partying, and such. Obviously it's a lot of fun but it really does give you some truly fundamental social skills that I think are really important to learn.

Realistically, I'm just not sure there are many other points in life when it's socially acceptable to spend that much of your time having fun, without a whole lot of responsibility. I think it's definitely something to take advantage of. In terms of classes and then trying to balance the startup life with classes—and this is just my perspective—you don't actually need to spend that much time in your classes actually doing the work. You obviously want to try to master material that you think is going to be important to you, but in most classes you just need to get by, and there are a lot of different ways to do that. I mean, aim for, let's say, a 3.75 instead of a 4.0 GPA and you save a whole lot of time. That was my strategy. I graduated with a 3.76 and didn't actually have to spend that much time doing class work or attending classes, but I still managed to master the material that I knew would be most helpful to me outside of school.

My least favorite classes were the ones with mandatory attendance policies or pop quizzes because, and I'm generalizing here, I found those to be more foundational classes where the majority of the material wasn't super advanced so I didn't take much out of them.

I had a business law class that I really liked a lot; the professor was awesome and she got me really engaged in the class. At first I went to every single class but she was pregnant and when she had her kid she went on maternity leave. The substitute professor was absolutely horrible and after one class with him I knew I was not going to want to go anymore. I literally did not go to another class for the rest of the semester; I figured I would just show up for the session right before the midterm to get the study guide, but when I walked in I found out they had moved the test up by a week! So I walked into the midterm without having been to any lectures and still managed, somehow, to squeeze out seventy five percent on that exam. So, that was pretty lucky but for the majority of the classes I took—especially the ones that were more basic or were topics I didn't feel were going to be that useful to me—I would say I probably only attended a third, or maybe half of them.

Can you describe your experience raising money?

We got accepted into YC and moved out here that January. We raised our angel round right after demo day, at the beginning of April 2007, that actually lasted until we became profitable.

I think it's situational; there's not really a one-size-fits-all model for funding startups. I definitely don't think that everyone would or should do it like us, but I do think our experience shows you can do a lot with a pretty small amount of cash.

But, even just to raise that amount, we were fundraising all the time. In our class, we were the fastest to close a round. We got a term sheet within five days of meeting the very first investor; from start to finish we closed in 30 days. I know that it's been a lot faster since then especially with convertible notes. The whole experience was incredibly distracting because when you're fundraising you have to think about possibilities and when you're programming you have to think about constraints and they're two completely different mindsets to be in.

When you're *programming* you think about all the problems with your system, how to solve them, and then how to build the solutions. When you're *fundraising* you can't think about the problems—how would you feel if you met someone and all they were talking about was the problems with their startup? So it's really hard to get work done when you're struggling to balance that sort of business versus programming mindset. That constant struggle and the fact that it takes up so much of your time is why so many people just try to start and close; get it done as quickly as possible.

How long did it you take you guys to build your first beta and how did you spread the word?

When we applied to YC we had already built an alpha version. At that time I think we were one of the more advanced companies applying, unlike now, when it's fairly common for people to have completely finished or even launched products before YC.

We have always been extremely product-focused, though. We spend a lot of time on product improvement; really it's just a lot of time thinking about UI and usability and keeping the product simple. We are always thinking about how to add features and still keep the simplicity of the whole process, which we definitely see as one of our major strengths.

Press, early on, also helped us. One thing about our business is that it spreads by word-of-mouth so it's almost viral, except the word-of-mouth feedback is usually a lot longer than the viral couple-of-day feedback loop. But press definitely helped get the word out; from there, it was all about generating awareness; people told other people and that's where our growth started.

I think there is a different user-growth story for every start up, which is super frustrating because it's maybe the number two or three problem for any startup. Our user growth has been slow and meticulous, and I wrote a blog post about this that basically said, "Even if you have a great product, it can take a lot of time to get the word out."

You see too many people that spend three or four months working on a product, launch it, and shut it down a month later, when the problem is just that it hasn't had enough time to reach people; to get that awareness out. So that's definitely something to think about. There are those rare success stories, where user growth is just exponential from day one, but I think for the vast majority of companies that's not the case and it's something that you just have to work incredibly hard at.

Generally speaking, hiring a PR firm or a publicist is really not going to work for startups. It depends on the situation. For example, a lot of the initial growth for Dropbox came about because of that video they made that became this kind of viral hit within the tech community. Once you plant that seed and have established some growth I think PR can be helpful in accelerating that growth, but I don't really see the value in PR from day one; you can get a lot of the same benefits by doing it yourself.

It's also really expensive for a small startup. You are talking on the order of $10,000-$20,000 dollars a month and that's supposed to be a fixed retainer even though some months they don't do any work for you. Really, you're only doing a couple of major stories per year and, like I said, there is a lot you can do.

Even just being in the Valley helps, getting into the tech events, and coming at it honestly rather than hitting people with some huge marketing campaign. Just email people with a summary and highlights, maybe a couple of screenshots or a video attached. It basically tells them you respect their time but it also gives them something they can use really quickly to explain why it's cool if they decide to write about it. I think journalists really appreciate the fact that it's you interacting with them; that the founders are writing to them directly, just being open and interacting normally goes pretty far.

Did you ever think, "This isn't working, we've got to do something different"?

No. We are still working on the same concept that we've been working on since day one. The idea has definitely evolved but it's still that same idea from day one. That said, pivoting can be a really, really important part of the startup process. I guess we got lucky that what we were working on initially turned out to be what is successful for us. But again, I think that's probably not the case for the majority of startups.

Were there any really stressful situations or fears that Weebly might fail?

Oh yeah. There were tons of moments like that. One thing that really helped us was that we appreciated modest growth in the early days. We were driven by this sort of naïve excitement about getting 200 new users a day. It was awesome for us and it was one of those things that you can't un-see; you can't go back to the norm once you get to that level. That makes it really tough because you never want to discount any growth but once you get to the levels we're at today—I mean, one hundred seems like a joke. But, at the time, 200 new users a day was absolutely amazing.

Having said that, there were a ton of 'oh shit' moments. Before we raised our angel round at the end of April 2007, I think we had about $45 in our bank account and couldn't make the next month's rent, which was coming up in a couple of weeks.

Or in December 2008—we were close to being profitable but knew at the rate we were going we'd be pretty far from making next month's payroll. We just had to keep looking at our expenses and trying to figure out where we could play with them to make it work. It was a really tight month where we basically squeezed by and then things really started picking up so it wasn't a problem after that. But there definitely have been some pretty scary moments along the way.

Fortunately, we didn't have to deal with any founder conflicts. We've always been really good friends—I would imagine it would be a lot tougher if you were just business partners and not friends. I think at least for us it has worked out very, very well because we were friends for a few years first and then began working on a startup together. That way, throughout the whole thing, if there's ever any tension you just go out and grab a few beers and it kind of rolls off your back. We never had any major conflicts and there was sort of this assumption that you're sticking it out together and no one is going to bail.

When did you notice revenue taking off? What happened?

There was a point when revenue started to take off. That's when we actually started charging money for things and revenue growth has been absolutely phenomenal ever since we launched paid features in mid-2008. We are very profitable at this point and there's no one specific moment that I can say we did this one thing. It's just a lot of incremental work and incremental improvements; just a lot of individual things that have collectively built massive revenue.

How is your time allocated at Weebly?

Fifty percent of my time is still programming. So, I still build out new features. I built our entire billing system. This is the third billing system I've built in my life and I hope never to have to do that ever again. What else? I just did some major infrastructure overhauls; rewrote our database abstraction layer a few weeks ago. So I still spend a lot of time coding but more of my time is spent dealing with things at the higher levels.

The work schedule is fairly relaxed for most of the people in the company now. We've been going at this for a little over four years. I would say somewhere around the year to year and a half mark—maybe even sooner—you have to take a little bit of a step back and adopt a more sustainable schedule.

From day one it was always really important to us to take at least one day off a week. So even throughout Y Combinator we always took Saturday nights off. We'd stop working about 9:00 or 10:00PM on Friday night and go out. Saturday was just a lazy day; you got to bask in the glory of doing absolutely nothing: sitting on the couch and watching stupid TV or whatever you wanted to do. We'd go out Saturday nights, sleep in a little on Sundays and start working again after lunch or in the early evening and then work pretty hard all week. So that's the formula that worked for us.

Nowadays, as a company, we're really focused on productivity while in the office. In my mind, you have to spend as much time as possible in the early days. But once you are able to settle down a little bit, the focus on productivity is much more important. Some people work 40 or 50 hours a week. It's not a lot of hours for most of the people in the company. I really enjoy what I do; I really enjoy working. I probably work about 12 or 13 hours a day, but then I take the weekends off. So that's what my schedule looks like now.

What's Weebly's biggest challenge?

There is no one 'biggest challenge,' a lot of things are challenging. Growing the company is challenging; recruiting is incredibly challenging, especially these days. Scaling is an adventure. There are a lot of challenges but I don't think I can single one out; they're all surmountable.

How would you describe your culture to someone unfamiliar with the company?

I think the number one thing about the culture is that we're very results driven, so the goal is just to have a bunch of people in the room that are being super productive. And then the second part of that is that as long as you're being super productive we don't really care about much else. There are obviously a ton of perks: everyone has their ideal machine setup, sits on comfortable Aeron chairs, has Bose headphones to block out the noise of an open plan. Everyone has a company credit card, there are plenty of snacks in the office—it's always stocked, all the meals in the office are paid for, so lunch, dinner if you are in the office, gym membership, really awesome health care plan, the usual stuff.

We have no vacation policy, and that's something we were doing before anyone really started talking about it. You take whatever amount of vacation is reasonable, and everyone understands what level that is. There is no approval process, you just let us know a few days ahead of time that you want to take some vacation and, assuming there are no fires to put out, you take it.

All these things really boil down to the fact that we start with the assumption that all of our employees are responsible adults. It's interesting, I was talking to someone about our credit card policy for example, and he was talking about what an awesome way that would be to learn if someone was untrustworthy, by catching them abusing the credit card privileges. That would be one of the cheapest ways that companies could learn that an employee is not trustworthy.

To elaborate on that, everyone uses the company credit card as they see fit for business expenses, keeping it reasonable. A perfect example is: lunch in the office is paid for. We are not big enough to have our own chef, so a lot of times we'll order lunch into the office. If you want to go get something on your own, you walk down the street, go wherever you want, and put it on the company credit card. If you're doing something for the company and you need a cab or whatever, as long as it's reasonable, everyone has a credit card so no one ever has company-related expenses coming out of their own pocket.

What do you look for when you hire people?

We look for people who can make magic happen. So far, we mostly hire front-end guys because the back-end stuff is not a lot of work and most of it is pretty easy. So we hire a lot of front-end guys and we are also really looking for productive people. People who can just get an abnormal amount of things done in a week and not everyone is like that. But I think a lot of people, put in the right environment without distractions—without any meetings or anything like that—can focus and crank out new features, new code.

Does the open floor plan detract from productivity?

With the open floor plan obviously there are challenges but I think there are really significant benefits for office culture and even for productivity. You definitely get a certain buzz just by walking in the office. You get that with an open floor plan, you don't get that with more of a private office approach and, to tell you the truth, I think each type of layout has its own challenges.

With open offices, obviously the challenge is distractions, which I think can be mitigated to some extent. But I think the private office—even in my time working in a private office before I started Weebly—challenges productivity in its own way. So I think both can be challenging, but an open plan has definitely worked out for us so far.

Since you've reached an interesting level of scale, I'm curious what kind of development stack is Weebly using?

We are all based off LAMP (Linux, Apache, MySQL, PHP). It has scaled beautifully for us so far. We've written most of the glue in PHP ourselves. So basically we've written up a mini framework that works really, really well for us. PHP actually gets a pretty bad rap but especially since 5.3, it's really moving very quickly toward becoming a much more pleasant language. Most of the bad rap it gets is really based on its history as a simple wrapper over C. That's why a lot of naming is off; that's why a lot of various conventions are sort of weird. But I think PHP does a lot of stuff right, which makes it really easy to quickly crank out features, get stuff done, and be productive.

What advice do you have for college students interested in startups with no specific direction? Maybe they're just vaguely interested, what's that next step?

You need to be working on something. So if you don't have a specific idea, the easiest thing to remember is that all you're trying to do is make something that used to be hard, easy. That's the core of the majority of business. You're basically taking frustration away for the large majority of businesses.

With that in mind, if you don't have an idea, what you need to do is get into this mindset where every single moment of every single day, you notice every single frustration you have. The funny thing about frustrations is that a lot of time you actually don't notice them because who tries to pay attention to their frustrations? A perfect example is: Dell has finally come up with the ultimate rails for racking servers.

They're amazing and now, all these things I didn't realize were a problem that I was doing before, just using this new Rails I was like, "Holy shit, this is awesome." There are certain pains I didn't even realize just because I never took the time to notice that I was spending time doing that. So I think just getting into a mindset where you're noticing what is taking time in your life and what's frustrating and just making mental notes, writing it down and starting to come up with ideas on how to make those things better, is a great first step towards finding an idea.

Once you have an idea—*and this is I think the most important piece of advice—nothing matters except for making progress on the product.* In the early days, absolutely nothing else matters. I spent a lot of time in college, especially with the first business, constantly thinking about why you need to incorporate, how you're going to raise money, where you're going to find lawyers, and so on.

The fact is that the only challenge you have is *successfully solving a problem for a lot of people.* That's the *only* challenge you have; that's already an incredibly difficult thing to do and if you can do that, then everything else is easy. I mean, there are lots of companies that know how to make money from a potential idea, but their potential idea just isn't a problem that a lot of people have, so they don't meet that challenge.

On the whole, if you actually solve a problem that a lot of people have, you're going to figure out a way to make money from it.

I saw on your blog a popular post about hacking an electronic entry system. How did you discover that?

We had a lot of fun when we moved out to San Francisco. So during our last semester of college, we lived in the Y Scraper. Some other YC startup was helping our building manager program the Semtex locks and so she basically taught him how to program them and then the word spread that you could get into the secret menu by typing star, star, star, and six zeros. I think its ninety-nine pound and then star to get away from it.

Little did we know that pretty much every other Semtex that we tried to use throughout the whole city all had zero, zero, zero, zero, zero, zero as the default password. So if you knew this code, then you could type in almost anything and get into almost any building or do much more than that, like search or reset the address in the system. This still works today.

Can you talk about the time you most successfully hacked some non-computer system to your advantage?

I remember Chris' answer. Chris, my cofounder, set us up because he was doing a lot with Voice Over IP. He was a small-to-medium-sized ISP in the area and he had these connections straight into the phone network that aren't terribly difficult to get and he built this app where you could spoof your caller ID.

So you would put in the caller ID number that you wanted it to look like it was calling from, and then you put the person that you want to call, and then it would call your phone, you would answer and then it would call the other person's phone. This actually still works, so it's really fun to play pranks on people where basically you can have it look like—and this is 100% indistinguishable from what it normally looks like—it's calling from any number. You can make it look like someone's girlfriend is calling when it's totally not. So that was pretty sweet.

I'll have to keep the website secret, but it's out there and a lot of fun.

Weebly is hiring right now—why would someone want to join Weebly today?

The reason you would want to work for Weebly is basically twofold. First of all, it's a really awesome place to work. We spend a lot of time trying to make it that way. We went over the perks earlier but what I didn't mention is we have exactly one meeting per week. And that meeting is just a prioritization meeting.

You set your own schedule; no one is going to be timing you, like you have to get this done by next week. You set your own schedule. Everyone tries to make it a little bit aggressive and then tries to get everything done that they set out to. And there's a lot of freedom to be productive and do what you really love, which is to build things. It's a really small team, so you'll be able to make an impact.

We pay very well and it's a huge opportunity for anybody just in terms of where the company is at now and how small we are. Your goal ideally is to get as much equity as you can on as large of an expected outcome as possible, and I think from that perspective there is probably no better company than Weebly right now in all of Y Combinator. I think it's a great opportunity to get in while the team is still small in a company that, even right now, revenue-wise, is starting to be fairly massive.

It's my personal goal to see everyone in the company be as successful as I possibly can make them and, to that extent, if you're thinking about starting a company but you are not sure about the idea or about the timing or about your cofounder or anything like that or even about how to do it, or you don't really think you necessarily have the experience do it, a great option is to go and work at a startup for a few years and just get out to the Bay Area. We love moving people out to the Bay Area from other parts of the U.S. and we help to make that process really easy. Just get out here, get acclimated, get to know people, start building your own personal network—we can definitely help with that—and then when the time is right, jump in and do your own thing.

Dan Gross, Greplin

Tags: Y Combinator, programmer, hiring, VC funded, cofounder search, dropout, iterate quickly

Overview: Greplin is a search engine for all of your data in the cloud: Gmail, Facebook, Dropbox, Evernote, BaseCamp, Salesforce, Google Apps, and many others. Greplin was created as a last-minute iteration a mere 30 hours before YC's Demo Day in 2010—the earliest investors interested in the idea tried sending e-mails, but the DNS was so fresh that those e-mails bounced. At 19 years old, Dan Gross is one of the youngest founders to go through Y Combinator and has raised over $4 million from Sequoia and other angels including Bret Taylor, Facebook's CTO.

You're still very young, so this might be an easy question: how did you get started with entrepreneurship?

I guess my parents were entrepreneurs; they moved from the United States to Israel because they believed in the cause. But I wasn't really thinking about that when I wrote the YC application. I was getting ready to draft to the Israeli army; I was in this army prep program at the time, which gets you mentally and physically in shape for service. I'd seen this thing on the Web called Y Combinator and I was kind of curious about it. It seemed like people were having a lot fun doing it and, I'll be honest with you, I was most excited about the fact that, even if you don't get in you get a paid weekend in San Francisco, just by impressing a few people over email.

I thought it would be awesome. So—and this seems like it happens often—I filled out the application not thinking I would get in, and they sent me an email and said they'd like to talk to me. I grabbed my buddy and we hopped on a plane to San Francisco, obviously not thinking we would ever pass the interview, same story. We did the interview; I vividly remember sucking at the interview. The product we came in with was a piece of crap.

What was the product?

Another e-commerce, social shopping thing. PG was like, "Okay, I'm not getting it," and I remember feeling kind of flustered and trying to invent new product ideas and implement them within that 15 minutes of the interview. I was like, "Oh, you want that? Sure!" So I'd open up Firebug and say, "Sure, that works now."

That didn't really work well and I think the interview was kind of bad. They asked us to step out and we were sort of bummed. We were about to leave and then PG turns around and says, "Hey, can you come back in for five minutes?" I went back in—actually, it was kind of awkward because I stumbled and I fell on my head on the floor, which is kind of weird—and then sat back in the chair. PG looked at me with this weird face and said, "Look, we kind of like you. What you are working on sucks. Here is an interesting idea for you to do." I thought about it for a second and part of me, initially, was like, "That's a bummer, I kind of liked what I was working on" and the other half of me was like, "Holy shit, this is Y Combinator, what the fuck am I thinking?" And I said, "Sure!" Honestly, he could have finished the sentence by saying, "And we want you to mop the floor for the next two months," and I would have done it.

So I agreed, went back to Israel, packed up my things, hopped on a plane, and that's the beginning of the YC story. Previously, in Israel, I had worked at two different startups; that was my only other experience. The one small advantage I had was, in Israel in 12th grade, you spend a lot of time on finals. English finals are the most important piece of your 12th grade exams. Since I was American, the exams were a joke. So I had a lot of time to hack. So I worked for one startup, leading up to that year, and the next summer, I worked for another startup— incidentally, that one went public.

Which startups did you work at back in Israel?

One was called Vringo; they are actually a public company now. I think they are still building video ringtones. So when someone calls you, you don't hear Kesha, you see Kesha, which is so much more interesting.

Did you do anything that might be considered entrepreneurial when you were younger?

I sold candy on the bus. It's interesting because I grew up in Israel, a culture where you are constantly bargaining; you are constantly checking and asking yourself, "Is someone ripping me off? Am I ripping someone else off?" I guess that was a cultural norm.

I have been hacking since I was about 10 years old. I think all technical founders have similar stories; I went through all the iterations, going from GeoCities to Bravenet to Angelfire, doing my own hosting, getting a server in my house, figuring out how to mess with the ports, then it gets broken into; IRC networks, Trillian, starting my own IRC network, and so on.

Throughout high school, there was this highly technical Israeli army intelligence unit that I really wanted to join.

How does the army draft work?

So the way it goes in Israel is, when you are 16, you go to this army base and they give you an IQ test and a physical and make some determinations about your skills. If you are physically able, they prefer to send you to do something physically challenging, like flying a plane or driving a tank or running in the battlefield. Then, there are a few units in the Israeli Army that are considered to be so awesome, that they are willing to take someone who's very healthy and completely physically able, and put him at a desk job, hacking, because he is so awesome at what he does. So the bar was set really high.

This actually helped out at Greplin, incidentally, because that was my real first experience doing serious computer science work, and it happened in 9th grade. This was more about circumventing firewalls or writing C code, than just putting up sites on Angelfire. I spent a year interviewing for this unit and I got in, but once I got accepted to YC, I decided to do that instead.

How did you hear about YC?

I didn't know about Paul Graham or Hacker News prior to sitting at the airport on my way to SF. I read about them in the Wall Street Journal. But I have always been around startups. Israel is number two in the world for startups, per capita.

I would say the mentality in Israel is very favorable for startups, not only tech ones, but just starting your own business, doing your own thing, in general. Maybe it's a Middle Eastern thing—it seems that people are less afraid of risks there, or more willing to take them.

Did you take CS courses in high school?

I basically maxed out the CS they would give me. I doubled up on any computer science exams we could take and that gave me a pretty strong understanding of, at least, the basics. They put me through the same drills people seem to experience during their first few months in college; not incredibly exciting, but important programming drills, like, how to think about recursion, functional programming, and so on. I had that and what I learned at home from my dad.

Were you breaking any rules to go to the United States?

The back-story here is that service in the Israeli Army is mandatory, for the most part. The basis, on which I'm here, currently, is that I'm both an American and Israeli citizen.

If I had flown out here without American citizenship, it would have been difficult because they try to bring you back home to do your duty. The way I see it is, with Greplin's success—if I'm able to cultivate a position of power in the Valley—I think I will be much more valuable to Israel and the Israeli Army than if I am just another random 18-year old kid, of which they have many. That is my long-term goal as well, to help Israel do something, in exchange for all of this.

Did you know anyone, coming to the United States?

My parents moved from New York to Israel but the extended family didn't move. So most of my cousins, aunts, and uncles live in New York, as does my sister, who moved back about four years ago. But when I came out to California and to Mountain View, specifically, I did not know a single living person, I have zero family out here.

Did you find cofounders here?

I came out here with a buddy of mine. We collaborated on two different things and then he returned to Israel. Unlike me, he wasn't American-born. I think the cultural and language barriers frustrated him. So I was pretty much stuck here alone. I was forced to actively meet people and the Valley seems to dictate this reality where you need a cofounder. For the most part I was able to avoid it. I think Greplin raised half a million dollars without a cofounder.

It's a very big risk, and it seems like the more established the person that I was talking to was, the more he had to lose. So if you are at Google right now, you are making $120K; if you even talk about leaving, they assume you are going to Facebook and they will offer you a retention bonus, and that's a lot to leave on the table.

So I found that to be one problem. The other problem I had with finding a good cofounder is, unlike someone you hire, you end up spending about 22 hours out of the day with him or her so you need someone who is very technical but that you can also mesh with. It's almost like dating in that sense.

It's really hard to figure someone out within five minutes of meeting them. So, you have to go through this process, and that was particularly long and annoying. At some point I was like, "Screw it, I'm not doing this; I'm just going to do it on my own. I raised enough money for it not to matter." Ironically, the day I said that, someone introduced me and Robby, and that sort of set things off in the right direction.

Did you meet most of the people you know through YC?

You meet anyone important that you'll have to meet, through Y Combinator. It's funny, whenever I trace the way I met people, it always traces back to Y Combinator, or YC alumni. Even the way we met; we met through Blippy. Blippy came through Ariel Poler, for me; he came through Y Combinator's Angel Day.

I know Blippy because of Bill Clerico at WePay, from my YC class.

The other really interesting thing is, everyone is in the exact same position you are. Most people who come out here don't know anyone and are forced to network. So it creates this really odd social effect.

When you were in Y Combinator you pivoted a lot.

I came in pretty much with eBay, but social. The one time I ever bought something on eBay it became very emotional for me because this dick from Arkansas was outbidding me every minute and I was like, "Okay, I don't even care about these shoes that I'm buying now, *I just want to beat this guy*." I thought, "Wouldn't it be neat if we created a site where this was actually public information?" Then you can just laugh at someone, like, "Hey, you got a really bad deal on this." So we essentially built that. It was like Shoppify, in a sense, where you can start your own store if you like.

I worked on that during the summer and then applied to YC that winter. Once I got it in, we beefed it up a little and actually made it feel presentable. I showed it to PG and I remember his first reaction was like, "*Open a store? Who'd want to open a store? Are you kidding me?*" I said, "That's weird considering you made all your money from people opening stores on the Internet." Then Robert Morris (RTM) came in and said, "You are building a better eBay? eBay is really simple to use, I use it all day." I remember telling him, "Hey, RTM, you wrote the *first computer worm*; you're not an average user."

So that was my experience with the majority of the interviews. I think that is what they actually liked about me, that I was able to hold my ground even though they said ridiculous things to me.

Do you think they just said them to test you on whether you really liked the idea or not? Or were they like genuinely saying, "Who would open a store?"

I think both. I think it's something they believe in. I think the reason that they say it is, for the most part, they don't accept

123

people based on their products; they accept founders. PG told me, post mortem, that one of the things they got excited about with me was my reaction when they offered me this golden opportunity to work on something else, right after they had just told me they didn't like what I brought to them. I guess that happens with a number of startups, and they tell me that conversation could have gone one of two ways.

There is the guy who says, "Yes" to the new project very quickly, and PG will say, "Alright, why are you agreeing to do this so quickly? Don't you care about what you are doing now?" The other end of the spectrum is the stubborn guy who says, "No, this social networking website is awesome; I'm going to build it no matter what." I took the middle ground.

After I did that, PG suggested a few more product ideas for us to build. Did that. One interesting thing is that Paul has a fantastic reality-distortion field (RDF), and when you are in his 'office hours' you are like, "Okay, I'll take the check now," because you are public tomorrow.

Yeah, PG definitely has the RDF.

For that matter, by the way, Sam Altman has another really good reality-distortion field.

Yeah, Sam has it too.

You are just *convinced* that something is happening and if you don't move quickly you'll miss it. Another person who has it is Mike Arrington, and Mike's is actually pretty interesting because he can do it over text, which is kind of rare.

I've only talked to Arrington on the phone once; I didn't really feel like he had it.

The more I speak to him, the more I realize he is actually quite good at selling.

Another thing Paul pitched us on was his request for startups (RFS) for product space—let folks curate catalogs online. It's similar to Viaweb in the sense that you build stores, except instead of selling the actual product you sell a link to the product. So, I can build this virtual store for wines instead of selling the actual wine, I'll sell affiliate links to the wines. It's a really easy way to sort of curate the products you are interested in, online.

That didn't take off and we got sidetracked. At this point, my cofounder was also about to leave. I had this neat idea. I'd spent the bulk of the time building our product; it was unfortunately, not technical, but it was getting affiliate accounts to thousands of sites, which is hard to do. It's easy to do initially, like Amazon and Zappos are really easy to do, but if you want to get an affiliate account at some mom-and-pop wine shop, turns out there's a significant amount of work involved in convincing them to let you in.

So I thought, "What can I do that involves that type of technology?" So I built Browsarity fairly quickly. I can't say it's that impressive; it's an extension on Chrome or Firefox. You install it, pick a charity you want to donate to, and then every single time you buy something online money gets passively donated to that charity. What it does behind the scenes is convert every link you visit into an affiliate link.

I got a nice amount of initial traction, but didn't work out because it became illegal! Interestingly enough, a few hours after launch, Amazon changed their terms of service to add one line that basically says, "You cannot donate affiliate proceeds to charity" at which point you're fucked.

Amazon pretty much brought the axe down on you.

Yeah. I don't think it was like, "Oh, *that kid!* Fuck him." I think it was just bad timing. The real bummer was, now my cofounder had gone home and demo day was like, *48 hours away.* So I went over to PG's house and we did the walkabout.

The walkabout is fun, I remember doing that.

I had this stack of ideas I was pitching off this Google Doc that I made. Oddly enough, some of them were in the next batch. At some point, he said something quite genuine: "Out of all these things, what do you want right now?" I pitched Greplin at that point and he thought about it and said, "Alright, would you use it?" and I said yes. He said, "Do you know anyone else who would use it?" and I said yes. He was like, "Okay, do it. Build it."

So I biked back home, took the 23 down El Camino because I was too lazy to bike, and I built out a really basic prototype in the remaining few hours. That night I went over to YC and realized I hadn't bought a domain name yet because this thing had no name. So I was hanging out with PG, Steve Huffman and Adam Goldstein (Hipmunk cofounders) and a projector, and we thought, "What names can we give what we're working on?" I don't know if you've had the PGinstantdomainsearch dot com moments, but those are pretty key. So this is a relatively new thing that he does a lot. He tries to name your site, based on available domain names.

I did the domain searches when we were both hanging out at Blippy—we would have these long analytical conversations about the perfect domain name. After 3 hours of the right combination of syllables, letters and abstractness, and finally coming up with it, Ashvin from Blippy would register the domain. He'd be eavesdropping in the corner, and as a prank,

he'd register it as soon as I landed on the perfect name. He later transferred them over, but when I tried to finally register it I think he got a laugh from watching me attempt to register my own domain that I just discovered.

It's a funny process. Most of the names that Paul comes up with carry some significant academic value, like a certain word's Latin translation. I think it was actually Adam that said, "What about Greplin?" PG got really excited about Greplin. We bought the domain; I got up on stage and demo'ed this really basic demo. In all honesty, I had five searches prepared. Who knows what would have happened if I had tried the sixth search. And, funny enough, some investors emailed me right after my pitch on demo day and the DNS was so fresh that it bounced their e-mails back! So I actually missed the earliest e-mails.

Anyway, after demo day we got some positive response and now came the more curious phase of actually building something that would work. So I spent, I don't know what it was, three months building product out at night and fundraising during the day for what would become the 'legacy version of Greplin,' as I like to call it, also known as the 'scrappy version that didn't really work for more than 20 people,' mostly because it was written in a platform that didn't do anything asynchronously, nor could it thread. So it would fork every time, for every user, which would kill the machine. So you have one to twenty users; okay, now we've got to purchase new machines. At that point, it's probably worth shipping every user a MacBook.

So I hacked around; we jammed a little bit; I jammed it with a few other guys. It was at the point where nothing was perfect for anyone; I don't think there was a mutual, perfect click. There were people who were the opposite, really great hackers but kind of awkward people, personality-wise. Harj from Y Combinator said, "Hey, you should meet Robby, from Zenter. He's a genius." I go to meet Robby at the coffee shop and he gets super excited. Long story short, Robby joins.

We launched the site on a Tuesday on TechCrunch. It crashed about a week in; too many people. We rewrote everything from scratch and brought on two more people: Kevin Clark was at Powerset before it sold to Bing for $100 million; fantastic engineer. And Shaneal joined us. We put out this programming challenge. Shaneal's answers were just way over the top, like, ridiculously way over the top. So we spoke to him and got him to join.

Was the fundraising a positive or negative experience?

It was fun because you get free food, that's a win. Regardless of whether or not the guy invests, you get free lunch or breakfast or dinner.

I've heard other founders say the same thing.

When I told this to PG he shouted at me for like 20 minutes. He said I was wasting my time.

On a more serious note, I had no real product to show and no users, no team, or anything else for that matter. But what I managed to hopefully impress people with was fast turnaround. I would say that the most impressive thing I was able to get from people was the delta between things because I think in their minds they thought, "Okay, he did this in 24 hours. What does he do in a year?"

That was probably the most important lesson I learned. Other than that it was fun, I have to say. A lot of people find this very frustrating and it's hard because you get rejected and some people who reject you are real douche bags; they make a big deal out of it, whereas they shouldn't. For me, I felt like I absolutely had nothing to lose, and I still don't. It's like, as you gain more friends and people think more of you, you have more to lose as a result.

Did fundraising take a lot of time away from coding?

Yeah. Unfortunately, it took most of the day. Basically, coding was 7:00PM until whenever.

The $4 million was recently announced, did that take a long time too? Did you have a similarly positive experience? Did you get more free food?

Got more free food actually! The $4 million happened, if you factor in dollars per minute, exponentially faster. Basically, we were happy with the $750K that we raised and then Sequoia was interested and we very quickly managed to create a competitive environment. I think it all happened in a three-week period.

I think honestly, all of these people are animals and they respond like animals, to other animals. So, Sequoia responds really well to competitor interest because I think it validates their interest, more than anything else.

Is the $150K from Yuri Milner a good or bad thing?

I've thought about that a lot. I think, actually, Yuri Milner did to fundraising what YC encourages founders to do to products.

Do something really unexpected and bold; just break stuff and see what happens. That's effectively what he has done. I think he personally invested, not DST. For him it doesn't seem to be a big expense, but the way he thinks about it is like, "Okay, this is a really interesting idea. I don't know if I'll make money or not, but I think I'll definitely get a lot of information out of it."

Do I think it's a good idea or not? It definitely breaks the model for bad investors because they can't con entrepreneurs as easily because, as a founder, you now have more time to gain information and wisdom as to what should happen in the Valley. I think what a lot of people don't understand is that this wasn't YC's doing. It's a perfectly open marketplace; Yuri Milner could have made this offer whether PG gave his blessing or not.

My only fear is that being scrappy does lead to great things. I worry about this today. Obviously, things are slightly more secure now and we're not going to die tomorrow. But I always try to worry, "Does that make me decide slowly or does that make me make the wrong decision?" Because, it seems that the attitude of sleeping on a futon that you bought for $40 on Craigslist in some bullshit apartment you found in Mountain View, and hacking in a coffee shop because you don't have an office, encourages great things to happen. I worry that as you get more comfortable, it gets more difficult to recreate that environment.

Did you have any advisors?

Besides PG, Sam Altman was pretty clutch. There were a few times where I'd basically text or call Sam from a bathroom stall in some coffee shop and say, "Okay, the guy is asking for X, *what the fuck does X mean, man*?" Sam has this really good sense for those kinds of things. He will tell you, "Hey, all you have to do is just—repeat after me—just tell the guy *'the chicken is on fire.'*" So you walk back over to the guy and you tell him, "*The chicken is on fire.*" And he says, "Alright, here's the term sheet."

In all seriousness, Sam understands people's motivations very quickly. Having him on board was insanely key.

How long did that first Greplin beta take to build, when Adam Goldstein told you to get the Greplin.com domain?

Probably 30 hours or something like that.

How did you get people to use it?

No one else could use it because it had my Gmail password hard-coded into it. That edition of Greplin was mainly for demo day and existed for a week. So, if anyone came up after demo day and said, "Hey, can I sign up?" I would say, "Sure. Why don't you put an email in a field somewhere and I'll record that and email you when I'm ready." That was basically what I could offer.

Did you ever have any major points of stress?

Today we constantly worry about whether or not the product is good enough—how we can make it better. I think the thing that worries me most is the idea of getting stuck in one way of thinking about something, because that seems to be where companies fail. When that happens, you sort of get arrogant and invest in product decisions, and you don't understand why you're arrogant about it, you just are. So the important thing we try to ask ourselves every day, is, "If we were building this from scratch, would we still be doing it the exact same way?" It's hard because it requires you to not hold a bias to yourself.

Another hopeful thing, which seems to be happening slowly but with growing force, is that we sort of get what Google got back in its day, where the techie people will tell the non-techie people and almost feel proud of having this insider information, "Hey, you should use this. I know you've been having this problem." I feel like a lot of people talk about how, back in the day, everyone would tell everyone else to check out Google. If you were the techie guy looking over the shoulder of someone else, and he went to Altavista.com, you'd be like, "Hey, no. Check out Google; it's where the techie guys go." And then you would go to Google.

Same thing with Internet Explorer. You would say, "Oh, you're not using Firefox? You're not using Chrome? Alright, let me install that for you." So that seems to be happening and there's a lot of ways we can make Greplin at least interesting, if you invite friends, if not actually a viral product.

Our biggest challenge is more deeply rooted in psychology. Our biggest challenge, I think—and I might be wrong—is that even for someone who signed up, linked up all of his accounts, and the search responds in 20 millisecond speed, we have this interesting challenge of, "How do we enter your mind when you want to find something?" because, unlike Google, we're redefining the idea that you can search through all of your information. So next time you're looking for directions to somewhere, our challenge is identifying, "How do we break that old habit of looking through all the different pieces and running bullshit iPhone searches that don't work?"

There's a few neat ways to do it. On the iPhone this will be easier to break because there's an app that sits on your home screen; hopefully it will catch your eye more, and on the Web there's interesting things you can do, like, if we build a Chrome extension so that any time you type into the search box you're already searching Greplin so you don't have to go to our site separately. Or what if, for the Mac, we build something where you could just hit Command G and that opens a Greplin box and you can quickly jump to whatever you need.

Does Greplin have its own culture? How would you describe it?

Yeah, it's very nerdy I think, but we've made an effort to try to set a culture early on because it seems like every company has. If you look at Amazon's culture, the signature there is very, very scrappy and money-conscious; no one splurges. If you look at

Facebook's culture it's "Break, move very quickly, don't optimize things for too long." Google's culture seems to be more academic. I hope that ours melds those but also throws in "Work hard at what you do and make something that people like using and feel gratified because you worked hard building that."

Have you ever struggled with productivity or motivation? How do you get around it?

Some of the code base is really painful, and some of it is a lot of fun to write. So, when you have the right code that deals with Salesforce's API it's inherently going to be painful to do. Everything is obviously going to be more sluggish for you, because you're not having fun. We try to mix it up as much as we can, and I hope we reach a point where we can—at least some of the time—give our guys, including me, a chance to work on something they're excited about that's related to Greplin; not what has to get done.

Another thing is, just in general; I think it's important that everyone appreciates everyone else's work. Not like, "Oh, you did the bullshit CSS, fuck you." We value that as well. We almost try to set that up in our team meetings—I don't know how YC does this, but they have the perfect version of it. Like, for Tuesday, you feel pressure on Monday because you're like, "Tuesday is coming, what are we going to show? What did I build?"

We hacked up this script we call the 'commit machine.' When no one has committed code for a while, it gets increasingly desperate and says, "Hello? *Hello!?*"

Can you talk about the time you most successfully hacked a non-computer system to your advantage?

I have more of these now. I don't know what I said in the application. The hack I'm most excited about is getting angels to invest. That was a personality hack. As I said before, I realized that angels cared about me moving quickly. So I said, "Okay, I'm going to iterate quickly now, goodbye world."

I had one that was computer-based. I lived in the Crystal Towers for three months and they have this really annoying Semtex system. You have to have a keycard. It's really annoying. We had our office there originally and every day I'd have to let Robby in and Kevin in and be like, "Okay, this isn't working. How do I let you guys in automatically?"

You used to be able to hack the Semtex, but they installed a new one. We couldn't hack the new one. The hack Robby came up with was: we realized the Semtex system can call this number and if you press the right combinations of digits it lets someone in because you authorize them. So, we set up a Twilio account. So you dial this number, and Twilio responds, which lets you in. The only bummer is it now costs 1 penny every time you do it. It's good if your time walking down and opening the door is worth a penny.

Greplin is hiring right now—why would someone want to work for Greplin?

I think the product is really interesting. We're trying to build a new, different way of thinking about search. It's not a new Google or a new search engine. It's an area that no one has really ever thought to think about, as one collective group. So, ranking those search results proves really hard, and it's also a technology no one has ever really built. That would be my main reason for an engineer or a designer, is that's a really hard problem and if you think you can solve it, try it. It's not easy.

The second reason is: I think we're in this really interesting sweet spot as far as the company goes. We're pretty well funded, so we won't be dying tomorrow. But we're also a fairly small team so we can be much more generous in equity than, say, Facebook or Google. So, if you're looking for something that's stable but also encompasses the aura of a startup, I think we're a pretty good choice, if not the best.

Noah Kagan, AppSumo

Tags: businessperson, undergrad founder, profitable, hiring, funded, solo founder

Overview: AppSumo started in 2010 to help distribute great software and web apps to customers. Before starting AppSumo, Noah Kagan was one of the early employees at Facebook and worked as a Product Manager, and he later was the Director of Marketing for Mint.com. Since launching, AppSumo has acquired over 100,000 customers and has hundreds of bundled software deals on their website.

What you guys do has a Groupon feel to it all—you bundle software together at a discount price?

Yeah. It's interesting because a lot of our competitors use words like "discount" and "cheap". I really never use those words because they're Walmart words; I use Target words.

We're not *cheap*. We're bringing *good* software to *good* customers. It's not necessarily *bundled*, it's more like, how do we help startups succeed and how do we connect great shit that people build with great people who will pay for it?

Can you talk about your earliest experiences in entrepreneurship?

I hate generic, cheesy stories, but I'll say it's because I'm a Jew. I remember when I was a little kid my dad sold copiers and he'd put me in the van and I would just wait outside while he went into these random places. When he came back to the van I'd say, "dad, it has been two hours and I'm hungry" and he'd say, "let's go get burritos!" So we'd go get tacos and burritos. So I always rode around with him and he'd bring me inside for the sales.

When I was in elementary school I started selling pencils and school supplies and candy because I would go to Costco, do the margins, and I knew I could double the price of this candy and sell it. That was the first thing I did.

Elementary schools was pencils and junior high I was more involved in school. In high school I gained interest in tech. My stepfather is a computer programmer so I came up with business plans and started an entrepreneurship club. I was an Eagle Scout and there are a lot of successful people who are Eagle Scouts. I guess I'm just intrigued with that—I'm from Silicon Valley so it's kind of all around me. It's just a way of life. I grew up a block from Apple's campus so I guess I assumed I'd be involved in startups and technology.

My first entrepreneurial stuff, I guess, was more in college. In elementary school I was the top magazine sales guy. They made the kids go door-to-door selling magazines and they gave you candy for doing it. I won the limousine ride, right?

While you were in college, what kinds of classes were you taking?

I went to Berkeley and double majored in business and economics. My favorite class was a South Park class; that was pretty fun. Most business classes I took were pretty useless. It was all this generic shit that wasn't real.

I took a few different classes. One of them was the history of economics in the U.S. and it was interesting because I actually had to work. I thought, "I'm an A minus kind of guy." Everybody else wants A's; A minus, to me, is the ultimate grade because you got the good grade but you did just enough work. A 96 and a 93 are both A's, but a 91 means you didn't work too hard but you still got a good grade. I was always really excited about that.

With this class I thought I would just do the minimum amount of work for my A minus and I got a C on the first test. I've never gotten a C and it taught me that you have to actually do work.

I'll go back in time a bit, my favorite teacher of all time—this is probably my most interesting story—Mr. Bataglia, in high school, wore the tightest jeans. He coached college football for fun on weekends. He was kind of a stickler and I remember one time, my sophomore or junior year, I had an 89.3 in his class and I went to Mr. Batolli and said, "hey 89.3? Come on dog, where's my A minus?" And he told me: "Life is not fair." I've remembered that ever since.

Was that a moment in your life where your work ethic changed?

I was just like, "wow, life *really* isn't fair." So it's not going to be fair for everyone—it was more of a selfish realization, but I think that was a really good experience to have.

Did you work on any projects in college outside of class?

I did stuff that I always wanted. So I knew that I wanted a group for people that were like, "I like tech but I also like business." So Sarthak and I started the Computer Science and Business Association. I guess we could have had a better name.

We started that group and built a textbook exchange, which is like what the guys at Chegg were doing. I knew them when they were nothing. We created a discount card called a ninja card. We had a consulting business where we went to Dell and local businesses and said, "Hey, we'll help you market to college students." I tried to do a college site called Collegeup, which was a Craigslist for college kids. That totally failed. I might have built one or two other things, I got a lot of random shit and nothing really worked and then I graduated college.

Did you know people going into college at Berkeley?

No. I didn't really think I would get in. I didn't think I was smart enough. I had that philosophy of doing the least amount of work for a grade, so I thought I would get into Davis, but then they let me into Berkeley. I was like, "fuck it, I'll take it."

Were you looking for cofounders at Berkeley?

No, I never really looked for a cofounder. It's interesting, I don't know what it is but I always manage to just meet people. I don't know how it happens. I really don't, but I always do. I'm just kind of chill and I meet people. It's funny how that works out.

Is that a better approach than intentionally going out to find cofounders?

Absolutely. I think the best thing college kids have is they have their innocence. They can approach big-wigs and get access to companies who wouldn't give it to older people as they likely have ulterior motives, and they always do!

But the thing is they're not innocent, because they might want to get stoned and have sex instead, which is also a good idea. But it's funny because more and more now, I feel like younger people are doing startups. I'm seeing a lot of, "yeah we formed a company at 14." My kids are screwed.

How did you pay your way through school?

It's not too bad. I lived in-state so we got it cheaper and I was an RA in the dorms so I got free room and board, and then I got some scholarships. I would say the best thing for young kids is apply to a lot of scholarships. Ask yourself if you even need college, I think that's a bigger question now. No one cares about college when you get older. I think it's mostly from a social and maturity aspect, and then take advantage of your youth. Go out and talk to as many people as you can. Even now, most people approach me and say, "can you review my marketing plan?" I'm like, "fuck no", but then I hang out with some college kids who are like, "hey man, I really loved your blog post about X and I'm kind of thinking about this" and I'm like, "he's in college, of course I'll help him!" I think more people in college should try to take advantage of that. You can talk to anyone, even famous people, and they'll respond to you

Take advantage of the free time you have and the access to do almost anything at that time.

Did you party in school or take time to relax?

I definitely enjoyed my school experience. I think you learn a lot about yourself and how you want to live your life. Do you want to be organized? Do you want to be sloppy? Do you want to be responsible for things? If I had to do it again, I think I would probably go study stuff that I was really excited about. I thought econ and business were the most prestigious and might be useful, but if I could go back I'd probably do industrial engineering or psychology; stuff that is probably softer at that time but I think it would be more useful now.

I'm reading all these books on copywriting now and I wish I had become a better writer. So, focus on learning more fundamental stuff that you can use in any profession. It's all about what you enjoy doing. Even now, I work a lot but it's not work. I'll play disk golf for two hours tomorrow and then maybe I drink or maybe I don't. I'm not a material person, which is kind of the weird thing. People like money whereas I just like the process of making it, but spending it isn't very interesting to me. The jacket I'm wearing now is from junior high or high school but I'm almost 29. So I think eventually my girlfriend will help me throw out my clothes.

Right as you graduated, what were you thinking about doing? What did you want to do?

Make money. My ultimate goal was to start my own business. My dream in life was to start a company that I can run from the beaches in Thailand. I wanted to have a startup where I'm on my laptop drinking a Mai Tai or a piña colada on a beach, working with friends.

The best job I could get out of graduation was Intel. I appreciate them hiring me and they paid and believed in me, but I knew it was a means to an end. Even walking around I was like, "I have a lot of free time to work on my ideas because I'll get all my work done in an hour." I lived at home so I didn't have that many expenses. The nice thing about working for someone else is, at five you stop thinking about it. Yesterday I was drinking with a buddy of mine and I'm like, "oh fuck, I have to get this thing ready for tomorrow and guess what, if I don't do it it's not going to happen." So that's a whole different thing about what I'm trying to do. Now in the business, I'm trying to get the business to run itself but until that happens, it doesn't stop at five, for me.

You also worked at Facebook, Mint, and other startups. How did that happen?

Back to how it happened was just pure luck at Facebook. I just browsed the job page and they had an opening for a product manager. Never heard of that role before but it seemed like what I was already doing with building my websites for college students.

Mint was a bit more interesting where Dave McClure originally brought me in to just check out the product. I fell in love but Aaron Patzer did not want to hire me. I persisted and annoyed him because I really wanted it, and eventually got the job. I spent 1 week, unpaid writing their marketing plan and presented it to him. Then I said pay me for 3 months and if you like me, I stay, if not you got some marketing out of me and it didn't cost you a lot.

If I were in college today, I would try to build my own stuff every year so hopefully, by the time I graduated, I would have some of my stuff to go on or do internships. The problem with most people is they're like, "I love doing internships" but then they say they can't get one; they'll half-ass try and maybe 1% will actually be hard core enough to get it. I even know a lot of people who are like, "hey man I heard your stories and it sounds like you're a hustler", in a good sense hustler, "you make things happen and have had lots of success" and people are like "man, I'd love to be a part of it." The key is just hard work and then everyone pussies out. That really is it.

Why do you think that happens? Is it the media's fault? Do they glamorize the startup world and then people are shocked when they realize how difficult it really is?

I was actually telling my buddy that yesterday. I don't know if it's the media's fault but it's like this nerd lifestyle of the rich and famous, like, "Oh man, you build a startup and it's a worth a lot; you get funding!" Sometimes, at Facebook I used to look at myself as a rock star. I was like a startup rock star—I'm partying, I'm making money and I'm working on awesome stuff. But what you come to realize is that 95% of it is just work, either bitch work or thinking or work, and only 5% is blog posts. 95% is just bitch work. Coming back to the college students, it's, "Find the stuff that you're interested in learning and really explore that." That's the best thing to do at that time. So go intern, start your own thing and then, after college the biggest challenge is not getting sucked into a job consulting or accounting. We have this pressure from our peers to have a job. When you're saying, "I'm going go work at a dot com," it might be kind of cool, but it's still a weird thing for the majority of society.

I consider you to be one of the best people at marketing and promoting companies. Did you get really good at marketing by brute force or was there something strategic there?

Facebook is the first place I ever learned that there are a number of really, really smart people out there. It was like, "Wow, these guys are smarter than I am." I felt really bad, but I learned a lot from them. I guess I'm less interested, lately, in what made me good; it's not necessarily tactics but the *strategy and the reason behind things*. So trying to understand stuff like that, helped me think about not just doing the marketing but "What are the most effective ways to do what I'm trying to accomplish?" Then I just surround myself with good people and listen to what they say. Generally, my best ideas just come from listening to others, doing it, and then taking the credit for it. I do it and people say, "Noah, you're such a genius!" And to them I'm like, "Yes!" Then I say, "Thank *you*, Jared!"

Were there any particular things that worked really well at Facebook or Mint? At Mint, you had really gamed Digg. Did any strategies in particular work really well for you?

I did all the marketing at Mint, and at Facebook, I was like this bitch product manager. I think it's less about what worked best and more about who the audience is and what's their big problem? So, I read all these things from Gary Halbert and he wrote that, "It's less about the product and more about a hot market for the product."

Mint just came out and blew up and Mint, fundamentally, was a great product, so marketing that was a very easy thing to do; it was understanding *who is the ideal audience and where are they*? Those are the only two elements.

We found that personal finance readers and geeks, 22 to 35 with high disposable income that trust giving their info to places like Facebook, don't know really what to do with their money. So we figured out the best approach is to build trust and get those audiences to come check out Mint. So, sponsoring blogs, going to the sites that they're on and figuring out how to write creative content to get featured there. Guest posts are still the most underutilized PR tactic in the world. Every site wants more great content and if you can just bring them stuff, they'll let you write about it.

I would rather be on Lifehacker than Hacker News; as great as it is, it's a very fickle audience of moochers—they're more like jealous people, I would say. It's like, "Oh look, this startup is successful." There's a small pocket of them that are supportive, like Patrick McKenzie—amazingly nice. Hacker News has a great thing and a bad thing, but it's more about *where* the right audience is. So Digg, Reddit, personal finance sites, and really targeting, "How do we get our word out effectively through those channels?"

The problem with Hacker News, for me, is it is a decent channel but I'll spend two to five hours on an article, which I swear to god is very fucking useful. Anybody who reads it will walk away saying, "Alright, here are things that I can think about and do," versus an article I saw on Hacker News about how to go viral. The article was about how this guy put a like button on his page. I was just like, "Why do I bother making good content that's supposed to help my site and help other people?" I think that's one of the things where in marketing you need to have *predictability* versus hope.

You said at some point Digg was entirely gamed?

I think this was Mint. That was after I left; I'm not a big infographics marketer. It's just not my thing. Haven't gotten into them, I haven't ordered one. I just think they're kind of cheesy marketing tricks. It works. I think that's been a lot of Mint's success and I don't think they're horribly evil but it seems like such a cheap way of getting traffic. People will disagree with me and that's okay, I just think there's other ways of getting traffic.

Is every news site gameable?

Yeah. You know when I first realized that? There was a great article about Dan Greenburg on TechCrunch and how he gamed YouTube. It was the first time I realized that for every system, there's a way to go viral through it, or there's a way to engineer or setup the framework of taking advantage of systems. So it's not being unethical or doing anything shady. It's more about understanding how you set up a process for success. So, viral has always been around, just unscientifically. Five-year guys like Andrew Chang put it out there, "Hey, here's how you mathematically make viral work." So, you can engineer viral; it's not just an accident. I think that's the bigger thing with marketing and infographics work; "How do you engineer things so that you know what's going to happen?"

I look at, "How do I guarantee that it will work?" Even with Digg, I want to know that I can keep doing it, versus one-offs. I also don't want to have to buy or do anything that I would feel weird if people knew about.

We had talked before about productivity hacks—what kind of productivity hacks do you use?

Everyone should focus, number one thing, on how to be more efficient with their time and so I'm not going to cover the fluffy shit. How to use your keyboard effectively, what's your word-per-minute typing speed? That's one of the first tests I give people now.

Here are a few easy ones. One, speed up your mouse, so go to system properties and make your mouse faster. Get your typing speed up to like 80 WPM. If you're lower than that, learning anything else, like how to do marketing, is good but little stuff like this adds up. If you just save five minutes a day, that compounds to years of your life. Know basic shortcuts like Control L to jump to your URL bar or launcher app. If I don't have to use my mouse and I can just hit two buttons and get Gmail open, that's good.

I think another thing is being reactive on emails. I found myself running my day on e-mail. I spend a lot of my time responding to emails versus getting anything done that I want to do. So I force myself to only check email twice a day. Basically, it's just thinking about how you're spending your time and whether or not there are ways to make that faster, and then specific hacks on marketing. But I think everyone should, first, figure out how to get the most use of their computer. If you can spend $500 getting a faster computer, if that boots faster and loads things faster, think about how that will compound things. This is the number one biggest problem.

In marketing it's less about efficiency and more about effectiveness. So I like to do about 10 different marketing things and then see which one is the most effective and run with that. So it's like, "Alright, what's my objective? Where can I get this objective? Let me prioritize and try them all and then choose the ones that accelerate and grow my objective the most." That's where I think people are missing out. They're doing random shit hoping it works. With AppSumo I can either do X or Y. I can either buy ads or do affiliates and then seeing which ones are more effective I can say, "Alright, right now it's affiliates, so let me focus everything on doing more affiliates than trying to write blog posts." Instead of writing blog posts for Hacker News, right now I'm writing posts for other blogs where I know they have readership and I'll get page views. I know I might get on Hacker News but, regardless, I know it's going to get me something. So I think people need to *guarantee* themselves success.

You cofounded a company called Gambit, a payments solution for social networks. This was a top five app on Facebook with 7 million users and was generating

presumably millions of dollars of revenue each month. Did you have any takeaways from that experience?

I think you need to have a purpose for what you're doing. It's okay if you need to make money, but then you don't have a purpose; your purpose is to make money. In anything you do you should be really excited to be doing it.

With AppSumo it's to help startups succeed and it's rewarding. I help people get tools, I help companies sell their tools; it's a really fulfilling opportunity. With Kickflip/Gambit I was like, "Cool, this is a money-making experience." And I think when times get tough it's hard to stay with it and have a vision about where that goes because your vision is always just to make money. So you do short-term things to make money. With AppSumo I try to do everything in a five-year decision framework; I'd rather sacrifice short-term revenue for long-term profit. So that was a big takeaway.

Other takeaways are just being a lot more thoughtful about who you work with and how equity works out. You need to work with people you really enjoying working with. With AppSumo I've let go of people who are very good but just didn't fit our company values. Our company value is not greed; it's about growth and people liking us.

Do you think it's best that you have an even equity split?

It depends with the skill set. I always think young founders don't have enough confidence in themselves, which they should, and then I think you want to make sure that there are very clear expectations, because in a lot of startups, the business guy just doesn't have as much to do, depending on what the startup does. AppSumo is more of a marketing sales company than a technical company. Google and Facebook are technical companies. Our company relies on sales to survive. So, as much as I'd love for us to be a full technical company, we're more of a marketing company and in that case, a business guy, sales guy, or a marketing guy, is just as valuable as a tech person.

I think 50-50 is fine if you're both bringing equal value. I think there's always resentment from the engineer side where they're like, "Fuck, I built all this," and then if it's a sales guy, he's like, "Well, I fucking made all this money, your tech is a commodity I could have gotten any programmer or monkey." So each person sees the other as a monkey, but what I've seen in terms of successful 50-50 companies is, they spend three to five months just testing each other out, working together, and then they finally commit to starting a real business, incorporating and doing 50-50 splits.

Should non-technical people learn how to program if the idea is technical? Should someone spend all their time looking for technical founders?

Dustin Moskovitz was an economics major. Some of the best programmers I know are econ majors. The best people are the most resourceful people. All business people should have some fundamentals of programming.

I think people use cofounders as an excuse for not starting. They are very helpful and critical at most times but I'd prefer to start and recruit one while I have something shiny to show them. It's much easier on the biz side to get technical people vs saying "I have a great idea and you should do all the work to build it for me."

Zuckerberg was psychology.

Yeah, but he had been a developer for a long time. Dustin had no developing skills. Dustin was not a developer whatsoever, but Dustin said, "I want to be a part of Facebook enough that I'm going to learn how to code." I think he took two weeks to learn how to code and ended up being the CTO of Facebook. So, how badly do you want it?

I think there's room for both where you could just be the business guy. The best thing about being an engineer is the way that people think about things and their process for thinking about them. So I think it's good for every business guy to be able to code.

How did you come up with the idea for AppSumo?

AppSumo came from the number one problem every single person in the world has, and every single business has: how to get customers. My thought was, "I was pretty decent at Mint.com and I gained customers doing marketing and business development. What if I could make that a business in and of itself?" With Gambit we were doing payments for companies, and every company was like, "Dude, I don't need more payment solutions, I can do payments, I need more customers." So I was like, "Wow, this is a really big problem for everyone," so we kind of have a Groupon daily deal or weekly deal model, but that's just a means to an end. That's just one method of helping developers distribute their software and helping the right customers find it. So, it's trying different ideas like we did with RewardLevel.com and it's trying to find the most optimal way and the fastest ways of getting developer software out in the right people's hands.

It's about finding the right people too. There's no value if we send any company all these low-paying customers, who will never pay again or subscribe.

Did you have cofounders or were you solo?

I went solo because I had a 'challenging' experience with Gambit/Kickflip. We had three founders and everyone pulled the dog in different directions and there wasn't one person accountable; everyone thought they were worth more than they were. That just caused issues, time and time again, where I thought I was doing one thing and I was bringing so much value and the other guys were thinking otherwise.

Ultimately, maybe I'm a little arrogant; I think to run a company successfully you have to be confident in yourself. Aaron Patzer at Mint taught me that. Read Ayn Rand. The point was, I was just more interested in doing something at my own pace, in my own style, so I started AppSumo from scratch to do that. I brought on subsequent junior partners but it was something where I wanted to do it my way. I want everyone to have equity, that's a part of AppSumo; Gambit and my previous companies weren't as interested in giving everyone equity.

Do you think there's a stigma against single founders?

I don't care. All I care about is people; it's not about stigma it's just about building shit or not building shit. So I think the biggest problem is making excuses. These *wantrepreneurs* spend 80% of their time reading Hacker News and Lean Startup stuff and I think there's good nuggets in there but if you spend 80% of your time trying to make something or learning to code or learning to write or working on your ideas, you'll get a lot more fulfillment and a lot more learning through that experience.

Would you say it's more difficult to get funding as a solo founder?

I think you should worry less about funding and more about building something of value that makes revenue. The only time I didn't like doing AppSumo was when I was trying to do fundraising.

That was my next question.

Yeah, I've done it a bit and we're actually closing a little bit of funding. Funding should be this thing where you say, "I need this funding and if I put in X, I should get out Y." You should know *exactly* what you get out of that and I think most people are like, "Well I need a runway to make this work and if it works it should make us money hopefully", or, "I need money to make this idea work" and I think you don't need that stuff. We're at a point with AppSumo where, if someone else came out, they could compete with us pretty heavily, and by raising a reasonable amount of money, we're making it much more difficult for people and we can accelerate our growth that much faster. That's the value of raising money.

Was it more stressful or just time-consuming?

It was just depressing. All these people are fucking hating on our idea. I think if you work at something you're really passionate about there's no failure because you're like, "Hey, I want this product and if I'm the only customer then there's no losers." Maybe you're a lone kind of loser but I think you'll be okay, so I was just doing AppSumo; I really work on it. Everybody who works with us likes it. The customers like it, the partners like it, and I'm talking to these angels who—for five minutes—judge us and criticize us and so I'm like, "Who the fuck are you?" Frankly most of them didn't start a lot of companies. I'm not knocking on all angels, it's just so much easier to judge and criticize because I think people think of themselves as smarter when they do that versus compliment.

Maybe they judge the idea too much and should focus more on the founders?

Yeah, it's the founders. Ultimately, I think the real thing is the process; how does the person think about it? How is the person understanding? And I think where we're doing a really good job with AppSumo is understanding what our problems are, why those are our problems, and what the best solutions are. If we focus on that, I think we're doing a great job. When we launched RewardLevel.com it did okay; we kept trying to work on it, we gave it a fair amount of time and we had a goal and didn't hit the goal so we said, "Alright, let's go back, reevaluate," and now we're doing something new. Andrew Chen is our advisor and he has been helpful in getting us to think that way.

When you launched how did you get users?

Originally with AppSumo it was word of mouth and having good deals. We had certain press lined up that we already confirmed. We got some of our partners to promote it. That was a little inconsistent though, not all of them are doing that. Recently we started buying some advertising.

Any pivots along the way?

I wouldn't say pivot. We still have the same objective, right? Our objective is to help startups succeed in distributing software, to be a hub for distribution and so we're pivoting all along. It's all about, "What are the best ways to make that a reality?" So we did AppSumo by doing bundles of 10 and then we found out doing single deals worked just as well, so we're trying that. We did RewardLevel, which was taking our deals and making them into widgets people could put on their sites, and that is still doing okay but not as great as we'd like, so now we're trying more on the affiliate side to see if that is a way that we can get more growth.

Did you ever think AppSumo would fail? Any really stressful moments?

The night before we launched I was a little nervous people wouldn't buy it, but I knew I would buy it myself. I think that's the easiest test of your product or your business: *would you pay for it yourself?* And a lot of the time like you feel like, "Man, your deals are way too low, you could make way more profit." But I'd rather people really love us, and I'd rather have a price point that I would pay, I just think that's way too much for it.

I was a little nervous that people wouldn't buy it but I felt comfortable because it's at a price that I would want, we secured press, and I thought it should work. One of the disappointments is that there are so many downs and you have to be able to cope with that. Maybe once a week or every three weeks I'll start feeling like the work isn't as fun, it's depressing, or the sales are slower, and I noticed my mood goes up and down with how our sales are doing. But it's just kind of digging through it and realizing tomorrow will be better or just pushing on and eventually it gets better; try to remind yourself why you're doing it.

You don't have cofounders to drag you out of slumps right?

It's also bringing on the right people; I have a big team of people that, I don't need to just give generic answers, and I hate when people do that, but it is having people that are focused on the same mission with you. Something that has been great lately is, I've been talking to my team and I'm getting some of the best ideas for the company just by asking them. I ask them, "If you were running the company, what would you be doing differently? Am I doing anything differently than you would?" You kind of discount them, you're like, "Oh, well they're just on this part of the company, they don't think about everything." But they have really good ideas and have been helpful making the business successful.

You remember that tomorrow will be better and then you just wait and tomorrow is better. Then you talk to people and try to figure out, "What are you really sad about? What's bothering you?" Then, you try to solve that.

What is your work schedule like?

It's never 'work' but I guess a better question is, "What's a typical day?" I'm trying to instill reading, so I read for 30 minutes every day. Right now I'm focused on learning about copywriting so I read books and articles about copywriting. I'll check my email once in the morning. So I download all the emails, takes about an hour or two to respond. I have a goal list so I try to set up between three and six things per week. It's automatically open every time I open my computer and so I'm just knocking off things, or I try to. You get distracted, you read Hacker News and you have phone calls like this. I think ultimately it's, "Is this a good way to add value?" So, I love talking to customers so I do customer support. I think of better ways I can add value to the business and I think that's the way people need to be looking at things: "Am I adding the most value doing this work?" If not, you should have someone else do it or set up a system so it's done in a different way. Then I'll have dinner and then work, I may go play pool and then weekends I'll maybe do work for a few hours.

You've got to fit showers in there somewhere too.

Yeah, showers like once a week. My girlfriend works at a startup so she knows how it is. I'm not sure what else I would do with that time. In terms of enjoyment, I get the most enjoyment seeing AppSumo grow. One of my new passions is disk golf so every other day, when it's warm out, I'll go play an hour or two of disk golf and turn off my phone or just think about things.

How many hours per day would you say you're doing AppSumo?

Maybe 10 hours a day. I really think Sunday you just need to chill out, you need to go walk around, you need to go to a supermarket and just check out people or go play disk golf or escape to get your mind off things. I used to go running and I would get amazing ideas, running. Maybe I should shower more often in that case.

What's AppSumo's biggest challenge today?

Scaling our growth. We're profitable, it's fine, people like it, but it's like, "How do we take it from 50,000 people to 100,000 to a 1,000,000 people by the end of the year?"

Any advice you'd give to an undergraduate student interested in doing a startup?

I would say there are probably three things you should do: go subscribe to Hacker News; Andrew Chan, Eric Ries, go read all their blog posts. Secondly, I would reach out to people in your local area. There's always startups or entrepreneurs that you could talk to; buy them lunch, buy them presents, just get them to meet and learn about their experiences. It's like me doing this with you. I met you a few times and I'm glad to help out other people. The third would be balancing all that with trying something out. Even if, in the beginning, it's not what you are super passionate about, just the act of doing something, you'll learn. It doesn't need to be technical; it doesn't have to be something where you need to program. Sell door-to-door or mow lawns but just building something, you'll start thinking about how to set up a process where people can just submit to Wufoo for new customers, or how to track things, or how to set up a calendar. It will help you learn fundamentals, if you ever want to do a technical startup or just a regular business.

Can you talk about the time you most successfully hacked some non-computer system to your advantage?

I have a social hack. So, Dharmesh Shah from OnStartups.com, had a competition where he said, "Alright, I need you to write on my Facebook wall about why you should get this free $3,000 ticket to 37Signals master class," and I knew that there were going to be 100 to 200 submissions and people saying random stuff. I said, "Screw just hoping that I win, *I'm going to guarantee I win.*" So I went and got all these friends of mine to go like my comment because I knew I would be the only one to have 10 likes on their post. I ended up with 8 or 10 likes on my comment and I ended up winning. So that was kind of one-way. The other thing, recently, we're using Mechanical Turk to validate and set up some of our sales system. So I think that's kind of a cool way we're using some AI and people to solve problems—we could write scrapers or we could set up more complicated things where it's like, "How do you set up something that might be more effective and cheaper without coding it?" So there's a Mechanical Turk, we've started to experiment with that.

AppSumo is hiring right now—why would someone want to work there?

I think AppSumo would be good for someone who likes what we're doing. They think that our purpose of helping startups succeed and distributing the software is meaningful and interesting. I'd say, secondly, it would be good for someone who is really inexperienced, very hungry, and wants to be part of a startup, wants to put it on their resume, wants to learn from someone who has had successes. You're going to be a part of something successful; we like what we're doing and you get to learn a lot and actually won't be doing much bitch work. You will produce measurable results. Most of the people who work with me, I think, will say, "Yeah, I learned a lot with Noah during that experience."

Kevin Hale, Wufoo

Tags: coincidental, Y Combinator, profitable, designer, design-focused, major league player (Alexa top 1,000)

Overview: Wufoo started in 2006 as an online HTML form builder that allows anyone to easily and quickly create contact forms, design online surveys, handle event registrations, and process simple online payments. As Kevin describes it, "Wufoo is like a web-based version of Microsoft Access but it looks like it's designed by Fisher Price." The major value proposition is that Wufoo is very easy to use and also very powerful. Wufoo has helped people collect over $100,000,000 worth of revenue for the users and about $200,000 in payments per day. I remember Kevin Hale because he would attend every YC dinner, even though he was from a much earlier batch—I think he still showed up to every YC dinner to attend the talks. Kevin also does something interesting for the founders at the end, near Demo Day, but I won't explain the details—we'll keep that a surprise for future founders, assuming that tradition is still going.

How did you get started with entrepreneurship? You can go back as far as you can remember.

I had never really intended on becoming the lead of a company. I had zero entrepreneurial intentions coming out of college. I actually thought I was going to get my MFA and teach art to hippies; that was my goal.

It wasn't until I met Chris and Ryan, the two other founders at Wufoo, that they got me excited about ideas and some projects while I was taking a year off, trying to figure out what I wanted to do in the interim; it ended up being the project that we worked on and it took off and was really exciting. All of the business aspects and financial aspects, the interest and the management aspect, have come as a result of always being interested in trying to do the best I can at whatever I'm working on.

How did you get into design and user experience?

In college I double-majored in digital arts and modern American literature. Digital arts was this interdisciplinary degree that combined computer science, art, and music all together—basically a fine arts approach. I did interfaces for museums, designed my own musical instruments, and worked on a lot of performance pieces. I was using all these skills to create experiences and interfaces for artists, musicians, and for people who attended museums. So, in that respect I had this background and understanding, but actually a lot of the interfaces I created in college were not as user friendly. They were more about bringing curiosity and eliciting emotion wherever I could because the electronic medium was very difficult.

Spending a lot of time on those things also influenced how I decided to design software for Wufoo. I knew I wasn't interested in creating software that reminded you that you worked in a cubicle, and I thought, "let's look at some more of the emotional aspects, since we're basically doing a database app, and try to differentiate ourselves in that way."

In high school do you remember doing any design projects?

In high school I was a big TV productions nut and I did some programming and web design, but it wasn't a primary focus. Like I said, going into college, I was premed- and computer science-focused, and I ended up graduating with this weird fine arts degree and a background in writing.

In college I joined the newspaper, it was actually kind of weird. I rose up from the design angle and became editor in chief through the design track, which is sort of unorthodox for most people, but because I did design there; had worked on all the different sections of the newspaper; and had a writing background, I had a good understanding of the editorial process. When you become editor in chief you deal with lots of teams; having to deal with the ad design and concept development, meshing those two together and trying to figure out how to get things to fit, have schedules in place, and figure out how to get contributions and user content, all work together in a way that fosters community.

In that respect I had a lot of background and experience through working on the newspaper and even in high school, my background in TV production touched some of the same things; it's about understanding how to take news and content and formulate it to present it to users in an electronic medium.

Did you know anyone going into college?

I knew one or two people but the college I went to was very small. It was about the same size as my high school; it was a small, private, liberal arts college called Stetson University that was near Daytona Beach.

So you weren't looking for cofounders in college and didn't have interests in a startup?

No, nothing like that. I didn't even know Chris and Ryan were at the college. I met them during my first job outside of college. They are brothers; Chris is actually the one got me hired. He saw my portfolio background and was interested in all the web design I had done. He was doing basic database development for a research firm out of the public university here in Florida. He did web design and database applications and I also did some web design and wrote articles about covering research at the university. During all of the collaboration sessions we had to build these mini-database applications, we identified that there was a need for this kind of product, since all we did was these very tedious applications that we thought should be automated.

The idea came about very naturally because we had a problem we were complaining about and at some point realized it was an opportunity. It wasn't necessarily that we were both looking for cofounders or that we had a goal we wanted to accomplish and recognized each others' programming skills or design skills. I think it was part luck and part recognizing opportunities.

You met Chris and Ryan at your first job outside of college, what did you do there?

I was hired as a writer, primarily. I was supposed to cover research at the university, basically all sorts of PR stuff. My job was to wake up in the morning and think, "what's something that I'm interested in?" and then see if any researchers at the university were doing research on that topic. I covered stories about engineering, robotics, cancer research, anything that I was interested in. Chris' job was to help researchers at the university find electronic funding. So I also helped with that but his job was to facilitate database use, build apps, and look for funding opportunities for these researchers.

Because we were constantly looking at potential funding sources and opportunities, we heard about Y Combinator. When we saw it we thought, "that's a really exciting opportunity that we could take some of our ideas to."

And how did you find out about Y Combinator?

Y Combinator showed up in some RSS feed that I was reading. I don't know, I couldn't tell you exactly what it was.

But you heard about it and was there anything in particular that stood out about them? Did you look at other sources of funding?

No others. There weren't many other sources of funding at that time. There wasn't TechStars or anything else like that.

It sounded kind of like an internship where you get money for just submitting an idea proposal but instead of being an intern, it's like starting your own business. That sounded really exciting and it had to do with creating software and web applications, which definitely we knew we had the skills to do and we thought—it was on a whim, even if we didn't get in, it would be okay. It couldn't hurt to just apply because it didn't cost anything, all it took was some time to get setup.

We had been writing a blog called Particletree for about a year and a half before we even heard about Y Combinator and, basically, we wrote about any interesting new thing or technique we came up with, or anything we discovered about how to write web applications. We wrote experiments and case studies that ultimately showed we knew how to create stuff that people were interested in. I think at the time we had 10,000 RSS readers on that blog.

Did you pay your way through school with this project you did with Chris and Ryan?

I was really lucky. I had a full tuition scholarship when I went to Stetson. So I was actually one of the really lucky few that graduated with zero debt.

Did you party a lot or take time away from class?

No. I wasn't one of those college hippies. I spent a lot of time in the computer labs, and different museums, and a lot of time writing papers. I did a lot of creative writing, creative interface creation, and video editing work, outside of class.

In college, I found web art or Internet art to be the least interesting to me, of the tracks we were studying, because I found out it was really difficult to elicit emotions and get people interested, in a museum context. I find it really surprising that I completely changed my mind about that, now that I am doing it as work. I find a web application to be a lot more organic than any art piece I ever did in college because every change I make affects hundreds of thousands of users at the same time, once you get a significant user base.

You see the application as almost a living, breathing thing, as you make changes to it; you see how it affects other people and how it evolves, whether it's financial metrics or user metrics. It's really interesting to see that dynamic interaction with the users, so especially on the things that we do that aren't necessarily just product-focused or business-focused, you see a lot of people appreciate the little design touches that we add in to make things either easier for users or an overall better user experience.

You could have gone down the path of being an artist. Was the immediate feedback what drew you in?

Yeah. I think it's because, as a designer, I came in at the founder level and I had complete editorial and design reign over how the app was going to feel and look and talk—I wrote all the copy in the early days.

Did anyone inspire you while you were in college?

In college I studied artists like Nam June Paik and the Fluxus artists. So I was studying how to create really weird experiences inside a museum setting.

What was that when you guys decided "we need to build Wufoo"?

We actually applied to Y Combinator with two ideas. We didn't pitch Wufoo as an online form builder, we actually pitched it as a content manager that had two sides to it. The idea was you could both input data from the back end and from the front end, we called them "reversible forms" at that point, and we had to really thank Paul Graham during the interview process because he said "that's really confusing, just call it a form builder."

We were really lucky that we ended up going that track; it helped differentiate us out there because the market for form builders and the way that software was defined. It was a huge opening for us because the experiences there were really poor, unlike if we had tried to approach it as being another content manager or another database application builder. I think we would have been lost in that whole vertical.

You met your cofounders at work. Was it just serendipitous that you met or were you assigned to work on a same project?

Chris was the one that interviewed me at the university for the job. So he's the one that actually got me hired. We hit it off really well. We didn't decide to do a project together for a while, he was still learning a lot and we became friends in the meantime.

Here's an interesting story. I think Everquest 2 was coming out during that time and they decided to do this forum thing dedicated to Everquest 2.

So they built this mini website and forum community area to talk about Everquest 2 and it didn't take off because people didn't end up liking it when it finally came out. But I helped them during that process with some of the design stuff and later on we ended up going to South by Southwest together. I was very interested in going and I told them about it and they both came along with me. My parents had a house in Austin so we had free lodging. We saw a session by Jason Fried called "How to do big things with small teams" and after that we were like, "There's no reason their team is any different from the three of us or anybody else that was in that room." We felt really inspired, like we could do what these other people were doing. We just had to put our minds to it.

One of the big things that Jason Fried talked about was: they created this blog first and they generated an audience and once they got that audience, then they released an app and were able to release it to this trusted users that they had established relationships with so it wasn't starting from scratch. So we said "alright, we'll start a blog and we'll just write about everything that we learn about how to create software; then when we finally build this thing we'll hopefully have an audience" and so that's why we did Particletree. It was after South by Southwest and about a year and a half after getting into Y Combinator and building it, we were able to announce Wufoo to the 20,000 blog subscribers that we had cultivated.

Nowadays, Y Combinator people go in with finished products or things that have already launched or have user bases. At the time we didn't even have a prototype, right? We hadn't written a single line of code at that point. All we had was the fact that we had done Particletree and we had had all these ideas; it showed that we were technically capable; we definitely had a design sense; and that we knew how to work well together.

If you didn't have this blog would Y Combinator still have talked to you?

Probably not. The reason Paul picked us out there as one of the final interviews, he said, was because he had been an avid reader of Particletree, for a while.

If we came with no prototype *and* we had never done Particletree, there would be nothing to prove that we would have been able to do it. At the time our other batchmates were ex-Microsoft employees, ex-Oracle employees, people that graduated from MIT, Stanford, and we were three guys coming out of Tampa, Florida.

Particletree helped us when we launched Wufoo; it helped us get into Y Combinator; it helped us understand how to write software a lot better. So, I highly recommend it. I think my advice to anybody that's interested in entrepreneurship or trying to get something to happen is, have some place where you're publishing your ideas and thoughts and experiments. That way, it helps you get better and also establishes a community to help you get recognized by other people that are like-minded.

You kind of took the approach of building interest before building the product; some people take the opposite approach where they'll just build whatever and then go out and try to find people.

One story that we tell people, is that when we launched, we launched on TechCrunch and gave them an exclusive. We had some bad server configuration at the time and it immediately crashed from the traffic, and while we were figuring it out, obviously, all these comments were showing up on TechCrunch; people were sort of making fun of the issue.

But, I'd say, seven comments in, one of our users who had been beta testing and was a reader of Particletree, immediately chimed in and goes, "Hey, you know what, I've been following these guys for a really long time and I was beta testing their stuff and they're really, really awesome, so give them the benefit of the doubt, I'm sure they're just ironing some things out." It turned the tide on the conversation right there on our launch day and that has to do with us establishing really good relationships with our readers and users right from the get go.

Tell me about your fundraising experience. Was that positive, negative, stressful, time consuming?

Well, Y Combinator was pretty straightforward. It was stressful in terms of going through the application, and going out and doing the interviews, because you don't have a lot of time to make your case. Nowadays, I think it's like two minutes long. We had 10 minutes because they interviewed a lot fewer teams. But we still felt like it flew by.

After Y Combinator, we did really well on demo day. There was a lot of interest in our product based on the demo we had shown there, so we interviewed with everyone that was interested. Tons of VC's, tons of angels—and I'd say we got really lucky because there were two angels that offered us funding really early on in that process. They told us to definitely go talk to other people and then come back to them, but we ended up going with them in the end. So essentially, we knew we had guaranteed funding even before most of the interviews with VCs and angels.

I think Y Combinator, now, is in a completely differently state. We were the first ever, California class and the second ever, Y Combinator class. So the Y Combinator buzz and stature of being part of that organization wasn't as beneficial as it is now, when it comes to fundraising.

We definitely knew from the start that we weren't interested in venture capital, so we weren't too stressed about having to try to secure that, as that tends to be a more tenuous process.

Also, we didn't meet too many VCs at that point that we really liked or clicked with, and with the goals we had in mind and the kind of company we wanted to run, we knew it was going to work out well. But I have to say, we really owe the most to Y Combinator. If we hadn't gone through that program it would have taken us forever to get our angel funding afterwards, if we had gotten any at all.

Did you do anything to prepare for the YC interview? Can you offer any advice there?

Being one of the oldest alumni in the Y Combinator group, we are always referred to—speaking with different potential YC groups—and they always ask things like, how to prepare for the interviews. I have to say, there's no way to prepare for them because you have no idea what they're going to ask or how it's going to go.

I feel like the three of them are very unpredictable; what they'll latch on to with your application varies heavily and the best thing to do is get comfortable with your idea and your application. Have a lot of confidence in your ability to execute the ideas, potential, etc.

I think everyone's interview is different and so they might call you in there and say, "we hate your idea and we've got to come up with a new one here on the spot, but we really like you guys" and they might argue about something that they don't ultimately care about because they're just trying to see how much you push back.

I think you can't prepare for it, other than to just be determined to start a company and do whatever you have to do to show off your determination, your intellect, and that you're just really nice people, which shouldn't be hard to do. Y Combinator loves to fund people that they would like to hang out with.

Is the $150K from Yuri Milner a good or bad thing?

Wow, it would be a great thing. We wouldn't even have to do another round of angel funding if that was available. The thing is, we never took more money after our angel round. That convertible note would have remained a convertible note because we've never done a series A venture capital round. So, for us, it would have been awesome because we only raised $100,000. That would have been more than we ever needed and we were able to get to profitability just off of that. It's great for the communities. I guess for other investors it might be more difficult, depending on the aspirations of the founders.

I've always been of the mindset that company founders should do whatever they can to do as much as possible with as little money as possible. At our stage now, we have so much more leverage if we ever decided we wanted to take a series A round. Once a week we have VCs calling us up asking to meet with us or saying, "If you guys ever need funding please do contact us first." It's at the point where we're turning people down all the time. We had one VC that we met, just at the recommendation of one of our existing angel investors, as a courtesy, and he was like, "Oh god, I'm so glad I was able to get a meeting with you; I feel like it's harder to get a meeting with you, than with the founder of Wikileaks."

How did you guys spread the word about Wufoo? Sending the hand-written cards is a well-known tactic, now, but what other things helped you?

In the beginning we had Particletree, so we were able to use that leverage. Also, right before we got into Y Combinator, we knew we were going to try to start a business and build this software upfront. So, two months before we had even applied to Y Combinator we decided that we were going to start a web design/web development magazine called Treehouse. The reason we decided to do this was because Particletree had gotten Slashdot coverage twice within two months, and at that time we had a lot of traffic; we figured we could convert small percentages and do some kind of money, based on this content.

We could probably make enough money for us to work on the side to build the software. What ended up happening was Chris kept his job while Ryan and I quit our jobs and Chris split his paycheck with the two of us while we started building out Treehouse. So, Ryan built this digital download system so that people could pay for the magazine and get a digital download. I worked on the design and editorial side, and we worked on a publication schedule where it would just take a week and a half to build up the magazine, to create 100 pages of content, and then we could spend other weeks designing and building software.

Two months into all this, we got accepted into Y Combinator but we had this readership base that was pulled from Particletree. We wrote our first lines of code for Wufoo in January 2006 and then we had this interface prototype. We knew it was crucial to get the user experience for the form builder right initially, to figure out how the flow was going to work, and whether it was going to work or not. By early February, we had a prototype working and we were like, "this is really, really cool, this feels right."

But it wasn't hooked up to a database and you couldn't save or do anything yet and we thought, "maybe we can just leverage this; maybe we'll do an interface demo launch." So we had a teaser screen that said, "this is going to be Wufoo; you can play with the live demo", and people could play around and get an idea for how the whole thing was going to work. When you tried to save your form it said, "thanks for trying out this interface demo, if you want to learn more about the service sign up for the mailing list or we'll let you know when we launch." So about 7,000 people subscribed to be notified about the launch of Wufoo, just with the interface demo, and I think we had over 100,000 people try out that interface demo within three months.

It's really cool even though we didn't have the working software, we were able to leverage what we did have built up to that point to generate marketing, buzz etc. At that point we had very low conversion rate from TechCrunch users and it wasn't indicative of who our paid users were going to be in the future, which we didn't know until later. At the time, we had all these people visiting the website and trying it out, but we found out that no one was paying for it and we had really low conversions and didn't understand why. We thought maybe our business model was incorrect but it ended up being just the audience and the links that we were starting from. Early adopter tech users were not an appropriate way to measure whether the app was going to be successful or not.

It sounds like you guys had a great launch. What happened after July to continue your growth?

We had 100,000 people try out the interface demo. So they didn't become users. On launch 5,000-7,000 users signed up for the service and then afterwards we actually didn't spend any money on marketing for the first four years of Wufoo. It was completely word-of-mouth.

The way Wufoo is designed, it's a freemium model; on the free plans if you click an entry, it takes you to a confirmation message but it says, "Powered by Wufoo." So, whenever the free accounts are collecting data, it says that the form was "Powered by Wufoo" and we got referrals through that.

The only other thing we ever did was focus on remarkable customer support; that led to a lot of word-of-mouth about the quality of the product and the experience. From that point on, everything was just people talking about how unique the experience was, how easy it was, and how much they enjoyed using the service. It was software that was described as really fun to use, even though it's a database app that helps you create replacements for paper forms.

Would you say that the emphasis that you guys placed on

customer service is the reason you were able to grow as quickly as you did?

I think it was. I don't know how significant it was, but it was the only thing we did. Everyone in our company has to do customer support and so the way we approached it was, every single problem or issue or request that someone had, we said, "you have to look at it as an opportunity to turn someone into a fan." Just the fact that we would respond to people within two-to-five minutes of them sending their question or issue, people were constantly saying, "wow, that was really fast."

I believed it wholeheartedly but I don't think we have direct metrics on it. Those were really the only things we did: the free forms that said, "Powered by Wufoo" and really good customer support. We have this cancellation service—for people who are deleting their Wufoo account—and it asks whether they would be interested in using Wufoo again. We still have around a 90% satisfaction rating, where people who are deleting accounts still say, "I would use Wufoo again in the future."

You're in that class of companies that actually takes their design and usability very seriously. So it also seems like that gets some of the credit. Maybe the product is actually just so good that people want to tell other people?

I think it helps to stand out. There's this really great quote, I can't remember who says it, that says that "advertising is the price you pay for not creating a remarkable experience." So it's one of those things where, if you have to spend a lot of research or resources on marketing, it's because the product doesn't speak for itself.

Last year was one of the first years that we actually started doing more traditional advertising and marketing and we found out the conversions on regular display advertising were really poor and that the only good returns on investment we saw, were through re-targeting. Re-targeting is this ability where, when someone visits your website, you're able to show certain text ads to them when they go to other websites, based on key word, search engine advertising that we did.

I think we tried to do a fair share of speaking and interviews and conferences and such, but we don't find large conversion rates coming from those either. So usually it's our users telling other users.

I've noticed, anecdotally, that you, WePay, and Hipmunk are big on ad re-targeting.

It's effective so that's why we like it.

I think someone needs to figure out a way to not do re-

targeting if you already have an account somewhere. I have a Wepay and Wufoo account, but I still get ads from you guys.

I think the things you can tweak on that. I think Chris, who does our advertising, is going to see if there's a way to make changes on that.

Did you ever do any other big changes or pivots?

Payment forms is a big feature that we have at Wufoo and that's something we even didn't think about when we launched the service. It's one of those things that our users ask us about, constantly. People are asking for payment integration like crazy; let's just see what we can do to make it happen, and our payment integration is something that we're really proud of—it's this really easy way of assigning prices to different choices in the form fields, and a significant driver of revenue for us. Interesting fact: Wufoo has helped people collect over $100,000,000 worth of revenue for the users and we process probably about $200,000 in payments—in transactions—every single day. So Wufoo helps generate a lot of significant revenue for our users.

Did you ever think Wufoo would fail or did you ever get really stressed for some reason?

We never got to the point where we thought the thing was going to fail, we didn't launch Wufoo until we had billing systems set up and were charging for prices. We always had paid plans on Wufoo, we never started out with free plans. From day, one we started making a little bit of money and we knew that based on the growth curve.

So nine months after launch, we finally were profitable and able to make money to cover our living expenses and knew that we wouldn't have to go get other jobs. Once you become a profitable company, you find out that it smooths over a whole lot of issues and problems and answers a lot of questions. So it's a lot harder now for us to have huge problems or issues, because we know that things are going to be okay at the financial level.

Our darkest day was probably a couple of years ago: we were having all these problems with our backup system. None of us are server administration guys so we hired this third party to manage that for us and they were just not really doing a good job on the back end and at some point, some cascading failure occurred and we ended up losing some of the file attachments for a very small percentage of our users, like 0.01%. For us, being a database application, we saw data loss as the worst thing we could possibly do. We had to go through this process of finding all these users, trying to figure out what data was actually lost, and then contacting them. We spent 12 to 18 hours handwriting apology emails to every single one of the users that were affected and it was still thousands of users that were affected. We figured that that was going to blow things up.

We figured that we were going to have a huge amount of criticism out there. I had to credit our fantastic support up to that point and how we decided to handle it, because we informed users as soon as we realized it, before they even realized that the data was gone, and we didn't have a single complaint, not a single "Wufoo sucks", or "I'm canceling" blog post written. We didn't lose a single paid client as a result of the experience and we've been really grateful ever since.

Now afterwards, obviously, we got rid of that server company and moved over to Rackspace and completely changed their architecture and all that stuff; we pumped a lot more money into the back-end stuff, even though we were willing to pump in money beforehand with the other team. I really thought that we were going to take a huge hit from that experience; I thought, "that's the worst thing we could possibly do", and I felt we were going to lose a lot of face and a lot of reputation points on that, but we came out stronger than ever. It was as if our users appreciated us even more and they knew that we would do whatever it takes to make things right for them.

You hit profitability nine months in. Was there anything in particular that helped you get to that point?

I can say look at our revenue curve and I can't say that there's any one feature that we implemented that affected the revenue. For the first four years of Wufoo, we worked steadily on building new features and working on the product constantly to get it to a mature state; I can't say that any one feature made anything jump, significantly.

I think everything helps a little bit along the way. The only thing that ever affected revenues or changed the slope of that curve was, we did raise prices a couple of years ago on our two lowest plans, and that's the only phase where we raised plan prices by $5 and that jumped our revenues up, considerably. So chalk one up for the business guys for doing one little tweak there and actually making a difference, as opposed to writing a thousand lines of code.

I've heard complaints about building billing systems. What was that experience like?

We had to spend two months writing the whole billing system up; Chargify and those services didn't exist at that point. So, if we wanted to have recurrent billing we had to write it ourselves and do all the logic. Chris is the one who wrote all that and it took a lot of time, but I have to say it was worth it that we did that early and launched with those capabilities, because I think looking at the revenue curve, we see that launching early and collecting money as soon as possible, helps increase your revenues. There's not too much else that does. I'm really, really glad that we launched when we did and we launched with prices attached to our service and product.

How did you guys split up the work? Has it changed?

I did all the marketing and the copy and all the interface design on the app. Ryan is the database expert so he handled a lot of the infrastructure to figure out how that's all set and built; he's also a whiz on front-end design, so he handled a lot of the JavaScript fanciness.

Chris focused on metrics, customer support, and he's a PHP programmer also. He's one of those guys that has a high level of integrity and you can rely on him to do whatever it is that you ask him to do. So Chris had a lot of bitch programming work, unfortunately, so he did things like a login system, the billing systems, writing out the payments integration; stuff nobody wants to work on but is extremely important and needs to work really, really well.

So all of us had our own work but we all did a little bit of marketing too; in order to release any feature, we always required that documentation be written. We split customer support between the three of us in the early days and now it's set up so that Ryan is in charge of the development team and he leads two other developers; they work on PHP and JavaScript. I still do all the interface design in the product but a lot of the marketing design work is now handled by another designer that we hired. In support, we have three guys: one lead on customer support and two others. Chris still does programming and feature implementation but he also does a lot of analytics in terms of business metrics and advertising and other marketing needs.

What was the schedule like in the early days? Has it changed over time?

During Y Combinator we were probably working 18 to 20 hours a day, it was nonstop. We only had four or five weeks to build the prototype and demo to pitch to people. So we never worked harder than we did during that period in Y Combinator. Afterwards, we probably were pulling around 12 to 16 hours, and now we have this four-day work week. It's a much better work-life balance now, just due to the fact that we have scale and we know we're in this for the long run so it's important that everyone is taking care of themselves. We make sure that we partition off work from life and family and rent issues and social issues.

What is the biggest challenge today at Wufoo?

I'd say exposure. We love our product and think it's really mature and great; so right now, we know that if everyone in the United States knew about Wufoo, we'd have a much larger user base. So our goal is to get the word out there as much as possible. We're doing our best to increase PR, increase exposure, get people using us. Part of that is working with integration into other apps. We're on the third version of our API and getting people to integrate with us on their own—we have over 30 applications that are now integrated with Wufoo. I think we can also do better in showing off case studies and examples of Wufoo. Wufoo is a really powerful, interesting, and useful app, so let's show people how to maximize its usage so they see its benefits—that's our biggest focus, marketing and relations and increasing exposure for our app.

What's the culture like at Wufoo?

It's really laid back. It is a company of friends, everyone hangs out and it's very, very close knit. It's mostly self-managed; you have to figure out how to motivate yourself. There's a lot of this fun aspect to the company that's about being friendly and also being respectful of everyone.

I guess the biggest cultural part is based on a support-driven design philosophy. Since everyone in the company has to do customer support, a lot of things are done in terms of looking at the software development to make sure that features are developed with the customer in mind, but also making sure everyone takes care of themselves so that when you're doing customer support you're in the correct mindset; you realize that these users make your livelihood possible. So a part of that support-driven design approach is everyone doing customer support but also everyone taking the time to thank the people that pay their paycheck.

We're trying to do something really interesting and fun but we also need to be humble about the achievements that we had because we know that everything is based on this foundation that we're trying to do what's right for the customer. As a result, any arguments or issues or any sort of disagreements that ever come up, no one ever takes anything personally, because everyone knows what we're trying to do was ultimately right for users. So it's a really interesting culture.

Wufoo reminds me of Zappos' customer-oriented culture, I went to a talk they gave at Startup School '09.

Yeah, I actually didn't go to that one, but that culture and community is excellent. Another person that we were inspired by is the founder of Kayak.com. All their developers and programmers do support there and they have this big red phone in the middle of their office and whenever it rings one of the developers has to answer it; the basic idea is that once you have a programmer answer that phone a number of times, they'll eventually write some code to prevent that issue from coming up again. He has some really awesome ideas of how customer support should be done by the people who are most empowered to fix the problems, reducing that distance between the ability to solve the problem permanently and answer the problem when it comes up.

Have you ever had trouble motivating people? Any productivity problems or anything like that? If so, how do you fix them?

Yeah, we actually did tons of little experiments. We read a lot of psychology research about management—we're huge research nuts, the three founders, and it has to do with our backgrounds. So when we went to hire our first guy we knew, "okay, there's a right way to do this" and there's got to be stuff that science has shown on what's the proper way to set this up. So we play with financial incentives, we play with social incentives, we try to figure out *what are the issues that cause people to lose productivity and lose motivation.*

One of the first things we read about was this idea of *social loafing,* where, when people come together they tend to be a lot less productive because they spend time socially interacting with each other; it's one of the reasons why we don't have a central office.

We know that we need some organization so people have to come together and figure out what needs to done but *to actually get those things accomplished, they need to be left alone.*

We also play with all these weird incentives. So every year our company has its company trip. We've done snowboarding, we've done a Mediterranean cruise, we've done a resort in Costa Rica. We know that you can't push people to always do this *crunching period* where you're having people work 60 hours a week, because whatever happens is eventually that period has to stop, and there's productivity loss and the area of that productivity loss is actually greater than the productivity you gain from doing the crunching period.

So we have this work-life balance put in place and that's why we have four-day workweeks and we say, "make sure you manage your time appropriately and take the days off when you need and get enough sleep." But before we have a company vacation where we know we're going to get 10 days off, we will do one crunch period because we know the recovery rate where everyone is able to recover during that company trip. During this crunch period, we try to make it interesting in a lot of different respects: when it was just the three founders we had really aggressive schedules and then whoever got the least number of things accomplished on their aggressive schedule during that crunch period, became the trip bitch on the company trip and they would have to carry people's bags or do all the reservation stuff or drive people around if anything needed to be done or go get drinks and food.

So there's this social pressure to make that crunch period interesting; now that we have 10 people, we've actually changed it to the gauntlet model. That crunch period is now two teams against each other. This year it was the founders versus the first-time hires. So we had "A team" versus "B team"; we had this really friendly competition and at the end of it, kind of a hack-a-thon. The teams presented what they worked on and how they made Wufoo better or whatever features that they implemented.

I'm happy to say that *the founders won*. The gauntlet period—we destroyed them, we built like 15 new support apps during that period. So it was a wash. I think they're really motivated to beat us next year, but I don't think they have *any idea* what they're in for.

We've also done a thing called, king for a day. It's actually for a weekend, but one person gets to tell people whatever they want to do in the company. So if there are any mingling issues or any wish-list items that they didn't want to do, they got to tell everyone else to work on those issues and features. It's a nice way of being able to be management for the day and it's done over a two-day period.

Anytime that we need to do big push we always try to think, "What is something we can do to make it interesting or something that somebody might want to talk about or share with other people." So, for example, when we had our API contest we called someone to do a custom-forged battle-axe that we gave away; we had this huge outpouring of entries because of it. A lot of that had to do with the word of mouth that came out of the bragging rights of winning a *giant, medieval battle-axe just by programming code.*
Do you have any tips for hiring? I think some people might get to that point in their startup and find it difficult. Do you have a process in place for that?

A large part of it is personality. The big thing to look for is self-discipline; usually you can't measure that in an interview. With almost all of our major hires, we had to do a test project. So we had our two developers work on a side project for us. They didn't know that we were going to hire them as a result of it but they did a really good job—they were already working another job, they were doing this in their spare time, and they spent so many hours on it and did such a good job that we offered them jobs as a result.

For our design hire, we had our experienced staff work with him on a redesign for a three-week project to see whether it would be a good fit or not.

For our support people, we really got lucky on that front. Wufoo has a really good audience and our blog does pretty well, so we just announced the support position was up for grabs on the blog and we had over 150 submissions in two days and these were people from all over the world. We actually had to close it early because we knew we couldn't even get through all the applications in time.

We didn't look too hard at resumes; we looked at writing samples and what they wrote about; then we had personal interviews. I feel like we got really lucky to have such a great audience for the work that we do. It's the right sort of audience, lots of web designers and web developers use Wufoo; they are technical and they're the kind of people that we need, so we were able to tap into that very easily. They're really enthusiastic because I think they see the personality of the company and the personality of the app and as a result they're very attracted to it.

What causes you to say, "I want to talk to this person"?

One of the four people we hired came with really fantastic questions. She had a good resume, it was a standard resume, but when we went through the interview process, we got to the point where we asked them "do you have any questions?" and we noticed that no other person that we had interviewed up to that point had asked. They were like, "no, everything seemed really straightforward", and she asked these really in-depth, probing questions that either she was curious about or because she had done research on our backgrounds. That showed me that this is someone who took time, they care but also have a way of looking at the world to try to figure out, *is there something deeper I can know about this*?

I'd say hearing the questions that people ask is a really big indicator for us. Demeanor is a big part of it but, then again, we had to work with people for several weeks in order to get a feel for whether they were self-motivated enough to be able to do work on the schedule that we want them to do, because the four days we have people work is an aggressive four days where people need to get things accomplished—it's basically just compressing 40 hours into four days.

I think also that seeing like people go through the decision process, seeing that they make good decisions on their own or they're able to make the right assumptions to make those decisions—that's important. It doesn't really work, from a management standpoint, to have to be the one that everyone always filters everything through, in order to do any kind of action; that slows down the person who's doing management, especially for three founders, because we all still work and write code. We're still the center behind but we don't want to have to answer every single problem; we want to see who's able to make decisions on their own without a lot of supervision.

Can you provide any advice for undergrads who want to do a startup?

I don't feel like it's ever bad for anyone non-technical to learn how to program because it's going to score you points when you need to find a technical founder. From my experience, when I hear someone that is purely non-technical or has no technical background I already discount anything that they're going to say by like 75%, because I feel like they lack a lot of experience or understanding of how a technical startup is going to work or be managed. People who are in a technical startup, there's this creation process and those kind of creative people are motivated by very, very different things and they require very different management styles.

I definitely recommend people work in a crappy job. Work in a job for a large company. I say a lot of reasons that we change how we decided to do our management or the reason we did research before we making startup decisions about the business was because we had worked for the government and we hated every bureaucratic process there. We were like, "there's got to be a better way of growing the company than however this is going to be run".

During Y Combinator we worked really hard because we knew what we were fighting for; we knew that we never wanted to work in a cubicle ever again and, as a result, you try to make decisions that prevent you from going back to that—it makes you a lot 'hungrier' to do things. I feel like college students—who have never had a job but they have all this computer science background—who go and found startups, often don't realize the kind of companies that they're on the fast track to creating, because they don't have the experience to know that these are bad paths to go down. They think that this is going to be some fun or interesting experience and that they'll just go and do something else afterwards; that's not the way to look at it. It never gets more fun in the real world; it never gets better than you being in charge of your own destiny.

Can you talk about the time you most successfully hacked a non-computer system to your advantage?

We came to this realization that a rice cooker is essentially a pressure cooker and you can cook more things than just rice inside of them. It sounds really weird and lame.

Did you guys cook anything else in there besides rice?

Yeah, we cooked steak, stews, roast chicken, meatloaf; all kinds of vegetables.

Maybe I should get one of those.

You can make Ramen a lot quicker in a rice cooker than you can waiting for it to boil on the stove and it's all going to come out right. Pasta too.

That's a pretty good food hack, actually. I didn't think about this.

Yeah, you just pop that sucker in there and it's going to cook, especially those fancy fuzzy logic Japanese cookers, they all figure out how to time anything that you throw in there, but yeah, macaroni and cheese. The other thing is: it has that warm setting so it automatically pops up and then it just keeps it for as long as you need it.

I don't even have a microwave. I should get one of these.

Try a rice cooker. I mean, rice is awesome but of all the things you can cook with, it is pretty good. I think now they have these cookbooks for other things you can cook with a rice cooker, but at the time we just did our own stuff. It was the only cooking appliance we brought with us when we came to do Y Combinator.

Unfortunately, Wufoo isn't hiring right now—but can you tell us why you aren't, despite your profitability? Why would someone want to work at Wufoo, in the event that you decide to hire in the near future?

We did just hire another support person to add to our team. But we're really slow to hire anybody. It's really awesome to come work for us, if we ever are in the hiring mood. We have profit-sharing which is based off this performance review multiplied by a percentage of your salary base and based on your responsibilities, whether you're a manager or not. That profit-sharing happens three times a year and Wufoo is a very profitable company; our revenues grow month-over-month and we also have the annual

10-day company trip and we go to places all over the world. This year we're going to take everyone to stay at this medieval castle in England.

You have to still do customer support on whatever your customer support shift is while we're out there, but that's like one or two days out of your week. We also have automatic raises; every six months that you're with Wufoo you get a 3% raise, automatically. So it's kind of this loyalty incentive and also, unlimited paid time off. We don't track how much time you take off or how many vacation days you have. So long as you get your work done, you have people covering the stuff that you need to do, people take many weeks off. We already give the entire week for Thanksgiving off and we give the entire month of December off.

It's a 4.5-day work week we'll have one meeting a week on the Friday. So if you like to get things done and like not being interrupted you get to work from home and you get equipment for us and we pay for your iPhone or if you don't have an iPhone we buy you an iPhone and pay for it.

So when you guys are hiring people need to apply for Wufoo?
Yeah. You have to be quick too.

John Devor, Little App Factory

Tags: self-funded, programmer, profitable, Y Combinator (previous company: Divvyshot), design-focused

Overview: Little App Factory was started in 2003 to create consumer-grade media apps. They've created numerous popular applications including iRip, RipIt, and Tagalicious. In 2009, John Devor received a letter from Apple and Steve Jobs asking Little App Factory to change the name of iPodRip and eventually the name was changed to iRip. My first encounter with John was when I first stopped by the Palo Alto Hacker House, back when Sam Odio was still living there running Divvyshot, and John was the only guy in the house, sitting in this corner room really late at night, and hacking away on some app in XCode. I stayed in touch with John ever since and he's been someone who I could go to for advice on a lot of different things—I remember reaching out to John several times for advice about college, specifically.

How did you get started with entrepreneurship?

It started at the University of Virginia, back in 2006. As a freshman, I was doing the norm: heavy drinking, partying, all that college stuff. It was fun, but I knew I wanted something more. As an example, I remember being at a fraternity party one evening, looking around at everyone else and thinking to myself "Wow, this is pretty fucking lame. I want to do more with my life and I don't want to be that guy who remembers these days as the best of my life." This epiphany motivated me to find something new in my life. Soon afterwards, I answered a flyer on the wall for an entrepreneurship and coding fraternity called Eta Lambda Chi. and it was actually started by Sam Odio and Omar Bohsali.

So Sam and Omar, they had just started posting flyers. They got together and they decided to start this fraternity and they were looking for another founding member and I saw one of their flyers, it was pretty cheesy, something like 'Do you want to change the world? Join our Frat' and it also had this really interesting website that was a series of puzzles wrapped in HTML or MX records of a server. So I did this online puzzle and found out who the frat was and then contacted them and told them a little bit about myself and what I had done in school and they thought I was a good fit and then from there we just started coding. I basically lost track of my normal routine and was at Sam's apartment—Sam graciously donated his apartment for the frat, and I was there until 3:000 or 4:00 AM multiple times per week. That's really when I learned how to actually use a computer, learned how to use terminal and UNIX, how to run a server and all that. Basically I learned that really quickly just dicking around with my friends in the frat and just working on small projects, so that's how I got into it.

I wouldn't call it a fraternity; I'd call it a club I guess. It had a fraternity name and I guess it was a fraternity but this was fall of sophomore year that's when I really got into it and yeah my social life went down—well it didn't go down, it changed, I'll put it at that.

Did you code and build apps before you joined this fraternity?

Yeah, I'd been coding I had been doing Mac programming since roughly eighth grade. Well I started off doing calculator programming in probably 6th or 7th grade, just making stupid programs in the calculator and my brother taught me and then after that I started doing desktop programming pretty extensively in high school, just doing small contract work. I really got interested in the Mac because it was just far better in terms of design, not the Mac itself but the programs that people wrote for it were a little better quality and so I started to focus on design and user experience quite a bit.

Did you build any apps in this fraternity?

Yeah, we built one app which is kind of funny, we called it Six Starts and it never really saw the light of day, but there was one week during winter break where Omar and I, I think we coded 110 hours or something like that in one week. It was an all out sprint and I will never forget it. If you have Safari or Google Chrome or I think maybe even Firefox has it now—Safari has I think nine start icons for your most frequently used websites, we basically made that before anyone had done it and we called it Six Starts because there were six start icons for your most frequently viewed web sites. I won't say anyone stole the idea. I think it was the obvious progression of the idea, but it was just kind of funny to see it roll out in Google Chrome a year later.

I can think of at least two large companies who should pay you a couple of million dollars at this point.

I wish.

What kind of classes did you take in college? What was the experience like?

Yeah. It was kind of funny. Freshman year in college, I was getting straight A's or almost straight A's, had a great GPA and I was really into college and then my life kind of got flipped upside down where I threw myself fully into this business coding fraternity—I went from straight A's to straight C's. I'd never gotten a C ever, not even in high school but I got straight C's and that was kind of the point at which I realized this is what I wanted to do, like I don't necessarily give a shit about the courses.

Some of them were interesting, but I was enjoying coding, I was enjoying the guys that I was working with, and grades didn't really matter that much to me at all. It was the spring semester of my sophomore year I got straight Cs. The next fall semester during junior year, I got halfway through this semester and I had this one paper in some history class. I just couldn't write it. And I was fully invested, actually at that point I had a project that was making money while iRip was out in the open—it was making money, and I just couldn't do the paper and at that point I had been calling my parents and relatives for advice on whether I should stay in school or not and everyone was giving me a different answer.

My brother was saying "yeah get the hell out, you have started to make a little bit of money," and my parents were telling me to do the exact opposite. I had no idea what I wanted. Yeah, I wanted to make my parents happy, but at the same time I thought I had a really good opportunity and that turned out to be true. I think what I took away from it was school is always there: you can always go back, and it's a good problem to not have to go back, but at the same time school is really fun. If you are there for fun, have a great time. Also study, but don't forget to enjoy yourself. For me I was just doing really well and decided that school wasn't for me so I took a year off and helped Sam start Divvyshot. I can talk about that briefly.

My following junior semester, Sam and I had this idea for a photo sharing website called Divvyshot that would enhance the photo sharing experience because currently it kind of sucks. You have all these photos. I just went on a big trip myself and would like to do be able to share these photos with a group of people easily, and I'd also like to get their photos in return. Doing that's a fairly complicated process these days especially with high quality photos: you have services like Flicker and Facebook but they don't quite get there. Facebook is getting better. So Sam and I, we started this photo sharing site, went out and applied for Y

Combinator funding after applying, and after making a pretty dorky demo video of the prototype we then flew out there, got interviewed, got accepted and then the day after Christmas we packed up by all our stuff and drove out to California. And then we started the Hacker House in California which became a big dude fest as I'm sure you know—is it still alive?

It's alive and well actually. There are a lot of hacker houses now. It's like Fight Club.

That's great. So there, halfway through Y Combinator, I realized I was running two businesses at the same time. I was trying to do a startup and also to run the iRip business—I realized that I had a profitable product on one hand and a startup on the other, and I had to let go of something. So I let go of Divvyshot, said farewell to Sam and then focused solely on iRip.

I returned to school for just a little while actually, after realizing that my friends were still at school having a great time, and I wasn't drinking as much, which was terrible. I returned to school. I got straight C's again that fall semester and dropped out again the next semester but more importantly, I "finished up" with my classmates. We had a good time and lots of fun, but I bought a company from another guy who went to another school in Virginia. This company was called Frat Music and that was the coolest company I have had the pleasure of working with, but also one of the most chaotic companies. Basically, Frat Music is a music website for college kids or for people who like to party—and generally speaking fraternities have a very good selection of music—so we just mashed the two together as "Frats and music." People came to love it and we realized from the startup that it was a terrible idea.

Doing any business in the music industry is a terrible idea. That's something that took me a long time to realize. Once I have a business going on I like to keep it going and any roadblock that stands in the way I try to beat down, but dealing with the record labels is not something you want to spend your time doing: it's a very unpleasant business, especially when you are just waiting to get sued any moment. If you're looking for a fun time I definitely recommend starting a music website and giving away awesome music for free: you will get a lot of hits, but you may get sued at any moment.

What happened to Frat Music?

I sold it to one of one of the partners in it and it's still alive right now and still running at FratMusic.fm, but it's different now. I had to withdraw: at one point we contacted some lawyers who were pretty well known in the industry. These are some of the guys who golfed with the heads of Sony Records and BMG. They basically told us "the music industry is just waiting to sue you and they already know about you, they are just waiting for you to get big enough and then they will sue you," which sucked because on the one hand you do want to pay these artists for the music, but on the other hand for a small company it's impossible to do because you can only get contracts if you have a few million dollars sitting around ready to be spent on lawyer fees, which obviously we couldn't do. Long story short, I withdrew because of the risk involved.

It was the coolest business because we were kind of like mini-celebrities on campus: Frat Music was well known in all these colleges around the country. It was getting 50,000 hits every day, and then it was just growing rapidly. At UVA, everyone knew about it and we would walk around campus with our Frat Music shirts and everyone would be like "Oh my God! Those are the Frat Music guys." It was a fun startup.

What are your thoughts on Grooveshark?

I actually ran into one of the original Grooveshark investors the other day in San Francisco. I love Grooveshark and I use it every day, and I know those guys want to pay the artists. Everyone agrees that artists should get reimbursed, but—and I think the music industry will come to realize this—you cannot really charge for music in the way that it's getting charged for right now. You cannot really stop something from being free on the Internet. All in all I am surprised that Grooveshark is still around considering what the music industry has pledged to do to them. I think it's a great product and I would love it if it had a price or subscription service that allowed me to have the same access to all the music.

So was Sam Odio a bad influence on you?

Yes and no. If you talk to my mom, definitely. If you ask me, he is really a great guy and he is probably one of the most serial entrepreneurs that I know personally. Him and Omar Bohsali are two interesting people.

Was it pretty tough to leave Divvyshot? I imagine that had to be kind of stressful.

Oh yeah, that was very stressful. I had committed to Sam, I transferred my whole life, I got into Y Combinator which is the crème de la crème of seed funding. Well, it wasn't that necessarily. It was just that I committed to Sam so much that it kind of tore me. It took me a long time to finally realize that it was better for him and better for me to withdraw from the company. And Divvyshot went on to be sold to Facebook, and Sam did a great thing with it. So I am proud of him, and I think he did an awesome job. It worked out for everyone.

So when you were early on and you were doing iRip, what was the motivation there?

Should I give the true answer? The true answer is I had just broken up with an ex-girlfriend and I needed something in my life, so coding kind of filled that gap. I threw myself into this project head over heels, which probably is not the best thing to do if you have just broken up, but it's a very good way to get your mind off of an ex-girlfriend, a good project that you are excited about.

Did you know anyone going to UVA?

I knew nobody going into it. I usually worked more outside of the University: like the club that I did participate in, Eta Lambda Chi, wasn't really affiliated with UVA at all. What I intended to do, and I guess this is probably the fault of my high school programming days, but I went to a high school that didn't have any computer science program, so I naturally went to the Internet and just had a lot of digital friends that I worked with. That kind of carried over to college. I did work pretty hard in my CS classes, but I did more networking outside of the university, online, than I did at the university. I mean everything: IRC, forums, AIM, Skype.

Do you have any specific advice for people in school looking for cofounders?

Yeah. I would say work with several people and don't pick the first person only; work with a lot of people. I think it's kind of like dating, the more experience you have with other people, the more you understand other people as well as yourself, and how compatible you are with what kinds of personalities. Your cofounder basically fills a gap that you have in yourself, or at least I think so, and so you need to know yourself pretty well to be able to find the right person.

Every Internet venture or Internet startup whether you are a coder or a business guy has a community out there. You just have to go find the community. For me it was Mac programming, and there was, six, seven years ago there was a small Mac developer community relative to what it is today. I found that and just started participating and gaining a reputation there. That's what I would recommend: find your community and just get involved.

Did anyone inspire you in college?

I think Sam and Omar inspired me quite a bit in various ways. Other people that inspired me include a couple of guys: freshman year I worked on this CS project. Basically, we built a GPS tracking unit that allowed my buddy to jump into his car and drive all round campus, and through a GPS unit attached to a radio transmitter feeding data into another radio transmitter attached to a car battery attached to a Macintosh with a script running, we created a system that allowed us to watch this guy drive his car around campus on a Google map. It was really cool, but it was just how hard we worked to get that project going, and to see the final results appear was really cool. Those two guys inspired me to work really hard.

So you're a Mac guy, are you a Steve Jobs fan?

I'm a fanboy, but I don't think Steve is the fan of me. I got a letter of from Steve once. Basically our product—which is now called iRip—was formally called iPodRip and the original product had been around since 2003. So the name had been in use for a long time at that point, and I received a cease and letter from Apple's legal representatives about the name, about having iPod in the name. I was pretty distressed because I felt that we were not really harming them in any sense. We had been using that name for so long that if you go to Google and you type iPodRip, we are the first results that comes up. Long story short, I wrote Steve an email asking for forgiveness and asking for an exception to the trademark rules or whatever and he wrote me back.

I wrote this really long letter of me pouring my heart out in this full page letter, and Steve writes back two lines which were, "change your app's name, not that big a deal, -Steve" and then below that was "sent from my iPhone." I was kind of picturing him writing that while he was going to the bathroom or something like that, just to amuse himself, but in all seriousness I was pretty honored to get a response from him at all. I ended up showing that email to a bunch of people who were all pretty amazed at that. One of them happened to be in the tech industry, in the tech media, and asked if he could publish it and I said yes—which I don't know if it was the best idea, but it got us a lot of press and Steve doesn't like me anymore.

Did you ever think about raising any money for The Little App Factory?

No, I have been very lucky that we have always been cash positive but we have never needed any additional funding.

How does a student coming out of college live in California cheaply?

I would say live with other people but don't overdo it. With Y Combinator, those three months are already fairly stressful, but at the same time, I wouldn't take the $3,000 or however much they give each founder and sacrifice your sanity because of it.

It's tough: if you don't have enough savings built up I honestly don't know what the right answer is. Those three months are incredibly important and you need a good workspace in a quiet environment with minimal distractions. I have no good answer for that.

How long did it take to build iRip, your most popular Mac software?

I didn't write the original iRip. That was written way back in 2003 by my cofounder Matt Peterson. Basically he let it languish to the point where it wasn't doing any significant amount of business, but the name still had a little bit of value to him. He basically proposed to me that we would be partners in this venture. He would give me the name for the application if I was willing to rewrite the app and to start reselling it. I said I'd do it, not expecting to get so much out of it, but it turned out to be a really good decision and the rest is history.

I would write the app, Matt would test it and he would come back to me with bugs. I would rewrite it, and he would test it some more. We had a very good symbiotic relationship between us, and I think that's actually something—if you are a freshman in college or if you are whatever, if you are thinking about doing a business, I would say that the most important thing to me was having someone there that was almost like a father figure; someone who even when I was depressed either about my ex-girlfriend or just slammed with homework, or just having typical college-age angst or whatever about life, there was a guy there who would pick me up and dust me off and who would basically get me going. Matt was really useful. When you run into a lot of bugs in your project and you are disgruntled, or you have three midterms coming up, having someone there to keep check is extremely important. I think he was also one of the people that really inspired me.

What do you do when you go through motivational or productivity problems?

I always like the metaphor where in football the guy throwing the ball has a lead blocker. You basically need a lead blocker, someone who is going to take the hits for you time and time again, and I was lucky enough to find one of those guys very early on. I met Matt sophomore year of high school and we worked for seven or eight years, but yeah when you are doing too well and you are not feeling so hot, I don't know, take time off. Don't burn yourself out.

I feel like everyone I worked with especially in Eta Lambda Chi experienced different degrees of burnout, but burnout is something real and very serious. I had it myself, where I couldn't look at a computer for several months. I would be wary of that.

What happens when you can't look at the computer? Do you just go do other stuff?

Yeah, that's what I would do. I would try to dabble here and there with small projects to get back into it, but that seems to work as well. It's kind of a good way to test the waters and to see if you are ready to dive in again.

I've actually seen many of your products advertised on YouTube when I watch Starcraft 2 casting. I think you guys at one point sponsored a Starcraft tournament. How do you guys achieve growth? What tactics do you guys use to get the word out and sell the products?

We use a variety of avenues; advertising is huge for us. We spend $250,000 in Google ads every year. Most of it is word of mouth: people hear about us or they go to an Apple store and the Apple person working at the counter will tell them about our products.

We use lots of tactics: advertising, special promotions, working with software promotion sites specifically, sponsoring a Starcraft tournament or sponsoring Daring Fireball.

Did you have any big pivots with either The Little App Factory or Divvyshot?

The Little App Factory grew fairly naturally given the growth of its biggest product, iRip. The next biggest product, RipIt, was an acquisition. That was pretty stable in terms of what we expected to get from it: it blew away our expectation in terms of profit.

Frat Music is a good example of something that got turned on its head time and time again. It was a company where we were grappling with school challenges every day, but also trying to create what we could in the limited amount of time. We had to build the iPhone clients, and we realized that it would actually take months of full-time work to actually do it how we wanted it. We would end up scrapping a lot of things and just focusing on what we could control given our limited resources, and I think that's also an important thing, to actually understand, especially in school that you don't have a lot of time. Being scrappy and ready to fail are very important things. Don't be persistent for the sake of persistence: acknowledge when you are about to fail and just let it go. Don't exhaust your energy working on projects that have no future.

Did you ever think any of these products would fail?

Yeah. Frat Music again was a great example of that. That was pretty much a constant headache—I was always thinking "oh shit, I am going to get sued tomorrow," or waiting for that cease and desist letter.

As for the other companies, I think I was in a nice position. I wrote iRip and once it was released I knew it was successful.

And the fact that it actually made more than a thousand dollars to me was a miracle. Once I had that first sale, that was a success, and I think there is something to be said for that. The measure of success and failure for a college student is completely different from someone who has actually run a business before. If it's your first venture, just making twenty bucks is a success. When it happened to me, the whole day I was jumping up and down—I'll never forget that day, it was crazy.

What advice would you give to a student who is thinking about doing a startup but they're not sure where to begin?

If you are interested in computer science, finding cool computer science people, people that know computer science and that you also want to hang out with regardless of their knowledge, is very hard because in the field of computer science there are a lot of—I won't say nerds, but you want to hang around fun people, or your type of people. Find people that you like and enjoy and people that you will learn from. You will learn so much more than you will from professors.

Should non-technical people learn how to program?

I would say you should learn how to code, and I think everyone should know how to code. It's not that hard and it obviously depends on what your idea is. But even if you don't intend to write the products yourself, just knowing how to code even just a little bit is very valuable in terms of finding your tech cofounder and being able to understand what it means to actually write a piece of software. It'll help to understand the effort that they have to put into their portion of the company. Having no knowledge of the tech side is a good recipe for disaster.

Suhail Doshi, Mixpanel

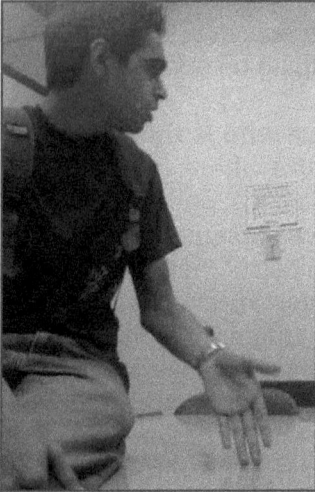

Tags: programmer, designer, undergrad founder, dropout, funded, cofounder search, design-focused, hiring, Y Combinator

Overview: Mixpanel launched after they went through Y Combinator in the Summer of 2009 as a way to easily track how users interact and engage on websites in real-time—they now track over 1.5 billion actions per month and provide analysis for sites such as Quora, BitTorrent, Posterous, and Ubisoft. Mixpanel has raised $500,000 from investors such as Max Levchin (PayPal, Slide) and Michael Birch (Bebo).

You guys are like Google Analytics except you're real time, right?

We don't track any page views, we just track actionable behavior—so we track what people actually do on a website because page views are effectively a dying metric.

How did you get started with entrepreneurship?

I was really into hacking when I was back in high school and found sketchy ways to sort of make money. One summer I made $50,000 in three or four weeks doing something.

How were you making $50,000?

The summer during senior year in high school, what ended up happening was that I was trying to find a job: work at Walgreens, work at CVS, something. I applied to five places. I have never dressed better for an interview other than the time when I went to Walgreens, and I still didn't get the job there. Anyway, my mom got mad at me, and she was like, "You're not even trying to get a job." And my dad was like, "Yeah, he is trying." So in an effort to prove my mother wrong, I decided that I would make money this summer. I thought, "Fine, I'm not going to find a job but I'm going to make money." So I started doing a bunch of web design. I'd participate in contests and drew up two logos for people—I made $60 and then this opportunity came along where I did something a little bit more sketchy on the blackhat side, but I ended up making $50,000 in three or four weeks. So that was pretty awesome.

Can you talk about what you did?

I prefer not to for now. I wasn't stealing money from anyone, but it was spammy. I never got in trouble for it or caught for it but I'll wait for the place to die first. So when it dies then I'll be more public about it.

But what happened is I made $50 in three weeks, made another $5,000 a few months later, something that, and it was crazy. What I learned was that it was really easy to make money if you wanted to. Hackers, they kind of figured it out, you can make money if you really wan to. But what I really felt was, "Okay, great, I can make a bunch of money." As a result, money became less attractive to me instantly. It was just like, I would refresh my monitor and I would see oh, "I made $50 in a second." So that novelty sort of wore off after a certain amount of time. What I thought was more challenging was making money legitimately. I wanted to build something that could generate revenue but in a legitimate way.

I was 17 years old when this was happening. After that summer, I was in college and I started doing a few projects. I think one week, I think what really sent the signal to me was seeing Kevin Rose on Businessweek. They were like "Oh, this young entrepreneur is worth $60 million," and I was like, "wow, if that guy can do it, I could do it." I started doing a few projects—this was back when personalization of RSS was more of a novel ideal: the idea of figuring out what content you'd be interested in and then showing you that content using RSS. I would curate what feeds that I would scrape stories from, and then I would show it. It had a tag cloud and there was AJAX, it was the whole web 2.0 thing. Whatever.

It was the first major attempt to build a project or a startup and ironically that was called Mixpanel, so that's where the name for this current company came from. It was because of that name lying around. I learned a few things: one was, another company came out and they raised $5 million to do the same thing. That was crushing for me because I was *one person* doing it in college. So it was demotivating, but I later learned that you shouldn't let that demotivate you. Another thing I learned is that people don't really enjoy reading that much—they like to read headlines, but unless it's a very valuable article, they won't really read a bunch of content pushed at them. And people generally find stories through something like Facebook or through their friends, word of mouth.

So doing this RSS personalization thing probably was not the best idea. That was the first project.

The second project was something called Outquib, which is closer to what Quora is today actually. We wanted it to be the Wikipedia of opinions, and this time I found a cofounder. You could do Coke versus Pepsi and there could be a debate on which one is better. We were going after political stuff in the beginning as a vertical, but we didn't execute very well, and we were in Mashable and all that, but then OpenSocial happened, which is Google's answer to Facebook apps. We sort of ditched that, and I learned at that point that you should actually stick with things. We didn't stick with it for very long, but also the product was completely wrong. Everything I could possibly have done was incorrect in that product, and so OpenSocial happened and we built applications on OpenSocial because we thought it would be like the Facebook platform.

We thought we could build huge Facebook app companies like Slide and RockYou. It was a gold rush, so we all rushed and I built an application called The Verb that would let you send events to your friends. You could pick an icon, you could pick a basketball and say "Oh, I want to play basketball with you." People just picked a nice drawn icon, and you could send it to your friend. It was really viral: it got 800,000 app installs on Hi5, it was on Myspace and it was everywhere. What I learned was that it was very difficult to monetize. It turned out that we had a lot of Philippine users, and they made me 1/20th the amount of money that the US users would have made me, or something like that.

Did this get acquired by Slide? I know you worked at Slide before, was this how you got in?

No. Slide almost acquired it but eventually they said, "No, we don't want to do that." Some blogs picked it up: Hi5 did a press release about it and published install numbers without me knowing. But this was my foray into Slide. I built all these apps—I knew OpenSocial better than most of the Slide devs. I was fairly well known on OpenSocial because I had done a lot of work: I built a framework that people started using for all kinds of stuff. People use this JavaScript framework that I wrote that handled a lot of the OpenSocial BS. Slide ended up hiring me as an intern, and that's how I got into Slide.

How old were you when you did this JS framework and worked on the Verb Facebook application?

It was right before I was 21 because I remember getting kicked out of a bar once. That was at Slide. I wasn't even drinking.

At that point I didn't even like drinking at all.

How did you meet your cofounder for Outquib?

It was just a friend in school. It turned out that I had made a Facebook status update, and then he saw it, and he knew that I was a coder so he reached out. He asked "Oh, do you like to do the startup stuff?" and it took off from there.

What kind of classes did you take in college?

My major was computer engineering; I started out in electrical engineering (EE). I've been coding since 8th grade. I didn't want to do computer science because I felt like it would be boring. I wanted to learn something else, even if I sucked at it. So I did EE, but it turned out EE was hard for me because I was just not into it. In the end, I did computer engineering: it was a hybrid of CS and EE.

Classes I liked were classes that taught me something lower-level about computers, like how they work basically: circuits, gates, and so on.

Classes that I hated were the ones I weren't good at which I think is why most people hate those classes. I hated classes that were more like "learn how to be a team" and "go build this thing as a team" and they give you all this—you have to do UML diagrams and you have to do a proposal and you have to put all this stuff together that doesn't actually matter when you go build a project with a team, and we certainly don't do that for Mixpanel. We had to draw UML diagrams, you'd have to describe X, Y and Z, and it was just a lot of busy work. I think they're called capstone classes at some universities. Those were ridiculously annoying. They just don't provide much value.

Did you know anyone going into college?

Yeah, I knew a few people, but most of my friends went elsewhere. I didn't really know that many people.

Did you know you wanted to do a startup? In the back of your mind were you trying to find a cofounder?

I think from the moment I entered school I was doing tons of projects and trying to start a company. I've always been trying to find a cofounder. The first year I didn't care to find cofounders; I was just doing stuff on my own. The second year, I felt that I should find a cofounder after Slide—actually the first two years I didn't feel like I needed to find a cofounder, it just sort of happened. After Slide I tried to find a cofounder, but what I realized was that my school—I went to Arizona State—it's not exactly the most entrepreneurial school in the world nor ambitious nor known for ambitious students. Because of that I had a hard time finding a cofounder, and one day I realized that when I was building the current Mixpanel I was trying to find a cofounder and just sort of gave up.

I was just like, "I don't care, I'm going to build it, people will see it and if they think it's cool they'll join. If not, that's fine too, I'm not going to waste my time any more." I was initially trying to build a gaming company right before Zynga got big, probably before the whole Mafia Wars thing got huge. It was six months before it all went big. I was trying to build a gaming company. I was trying to get my friend who does some artwork to join me, I was trying to get other friends to join me, and it was just impossible so I gave up on that project because I found that I wasn't passionate enough about games and I couldn't really find a cofounder from it. And then I decided to do Mixpanel instead.

Did you work on anything else outside of class besides these projects? Did you play any sports?

No sports. Well, I was doing a break dancing club. I joined a B-boy club that was three hours; it was 2 days a week, three hours. So I did that, probably played some basketball and not a lot of clubs. I joined some volunteer groups, something called Step or something like that. But it was just to meet new people, mostly.

Some students might be looking for cofounders. Should you be intentional there or should you let serendipity happen?

I would say it's best to just not look for people. I think serendipity is a little bit better. You'll just waste your time trying to find people, and you'll never build what you end up building and then you'll lose all the motivation for it.

Instead it makes more sense to just build immediately while you have that passion and interest—just build it as soon as you can and then people will find you. At the end of the day you'll go out, you'll meet people; you'll show them your crazy idea. It will probably look like crap, it will be something that someone, it will make someone else passionate about it. It's tough to get people on board your crazy idea especially when it's *your idea* it's difficult. When they see it, it's a little bit better.

How did you pay your way through school?

Well, I went in state so I went free. I had a scholarship.

Did you take time away from classes? Did you party much?

I feel like I had probably the least valuable college experience ever. Anything related to college, I missed out on. I really enjoyed coding—I wasn't into drinking at that point. I definitely didn't party it up or anything. I sort of regained that after college, but I didn't do any of that during college.

What was happening right when you graduated college? What were you doing? Did you want to do a startup?

I never graduated. I dropped out. Tim and I both dropped out the same year.

So how did you and Tim meet and why drop out?

Tim and I, we met in a discrete math class and there's all these kids—I was doing Mixpanel and I was like "Hey guys, we should do something. We're all programmers we could build a business doing these cool projects." And all the guys were like, "Yeah, okay," but Tim was actually the only person that was like "Yeah, let's do it, when do you want to meet?" He was the only person that had an action item and said, "When do you want to meet to talk about this?" And so that's how I met Tim.

Unfortunately Tim and I never started anything, and he ended up going to do study abroad later in Singapore. But we met again in a class later, and then I brought him on later after I had already written lots of the Mixpanel code. I had been working on it for four or five months, and then he joined.

Why drop out?

We joined Y Combinator and we ended up raising $500,000 from Max Levchin and Michael Birch. Max is PayPal, Birch is Bebo, and we actually dropped out because Y Combinator demo day was August 24th and school was starting August 20th, so we just said, "well we'll just take a semester off, it's worth it." Then we raised money and we said, "Well, we're obviously never going back."

You can defer your scholarship and you can take a leave of absence. I think they give you two-year minimum for a leave of absence. I'm pretty sure I lost my scholarship. I know Tim has lost his and he had a national merit scholarship actually, so he lost that. I think I'm still on leave of absence because of my mom: she wants me to have the ability to go back to school. She really wants me to go back to school, kind of like your parents, so she has made me take leave of absences for as long as possible. I think you can do four semesters or something like that.

I remember, I talked to Max Levchin and I asked him—this was back when I was a sophomore—and I asked him why he went back. He said his grandmother on her deathbed said she wants him to graduate. So yeah, it seems the parents are fond of that.

Max's grandmother actually wanted him to get a PhD. His grandmother really wanted him to get a PhD because that was crazy: sort of a very crazy achievement I guess.

Do you have any specific advice to students who are applying to places like Y Combinator?

These days in YC if you want to get in, you have to have something built. You have to *prove* that you can execute, you have to *prove* your commitment and part of that means maybe you build something and you drop out and then you apply to YC. Certainly harder to get in now, but it's really just about proving that you can build, execute, and commit. If that doesn't get you in then you need traction.

I have friends that applied to YC and I'll find myself telling them the weirdest things like "Wear a t-shirt of an early Y Combinator company to the interview." I don't even know if it helps; it probably doesn't even matter, but I remember Paul Graham—that was the first thing he commented on. He was like, "Oh, you guys know thesixtyone?" I guess it helped us stand out a little bit.

Yeah, we have a bit of a crazy YC story on how we got in. We met Garry Tan, he's one of the cofounders of Posterous. Garry was helpful. We reached out to him, he helped us with our app, reviewed it and then he also met with us and helped us refine our pitch to PG, although I don't think that really mattered that much.

But we had to go take the Cal-Train from San Francisco down to Mountain View, and Garry was on the train. He was like "Oh, I'm going to go on the train too to see my girlfriend." So we were going on the train and Garry goes "You know, wouldn't be cool if I just added Mixpanel on the train and so you guys have data when you showed up to YC?" We said "Yeah, that'd be cool." So Garry busts out his USB Wi-Fi dongle, plugs it into his computer, integrates Mixpanel on the train, and pushes it live to all of Posterous. We get to the YC interview and we go "Oh, by the way, Posterous integrated us" and the data just showed up in real time. That was big because then they were huddling around the monitor and looking at Posterous data that had just happened and that had impact. So we owe Garry a lot for getting us into YC.

How did you guys meet Garry?

I think I just randomly cold-emailed him to use Mixpanel once, and then he may have replied back. And we talked on IM or something like that, or just exchanged email after a while.

Was there anyone while you were in college who inspired you?

Yeah. In the beginning, before Slide, I was just self-motivated. I think seeing Kevin Rose on Businessweek made me think, "Oh, I really want to do that." But then after, what really motivated me was Slide. It was Max who was really inspirational for me, because he worked so hard and busted his ass to do all this stuff, and he had a crazy work ethic, and that's what it took to build a company. Seeing what everyone did at Slide and like, "Wow, these people are just like me"—I think all of that together was very inspirational. Slide was probably the best thing that I ever did before I started a company; it was absolutely necessary. I would recommend to somebody that they intern somewhere before starting a company.

I totally agree by the way. I started out at TokBox, that was my first Silicon Valley experience and that taught me quite a lot. How did you guys get the idea to do Mixpanel?

When I worked at Slide I learned a lot: learned about the product, learned a lot about engineering. But the thing I learned at Slide was, one big piece was that they did all these metrics, and RockYou did metrics, Zynga did metrics, all these guys in the space were doing metrics. It was crazy; they were all building up this in house system. It was very obvious that "Hey, everyone is doing X, if I built Y, then would they just do Y?" We just built the platform or service so that they could do that. It was very common among startups. Initially I started building a gaming company but then I became disinterested. I was pretty apathetic about the whole thing. I couldn't stay up until 3:00AM building a gaming company. I would just stay up till midnight and then I'd go to sleep and I felt like if I was just staying up until midnight and going to sleep, I wasn't going to win; I wasn't going to be number one in gaming.

So what I wanted to do is to learn how to scale. I wanted to learn how to scale tons of data. I wanted to really learn that. I thought that would be useful, and then I was like, "Well, this is a good project. What better way to do it than to do analytics: get everyone's data, then scale it." I was great at the Slide, I have this interest to scale, and then every day I would stay up till 3:00 or 4:00 AM, wake up late to go school at 8:00 or 9:00 AM, and I was like "Wow, if I'm staying up until 3:00 AM I can win this." So I just kept doing it. That's sort of how the idea took off: it was scaling and Slide.

Tell me what your experience was like raising money. Was that positive or negative?

That experience sucked, and I'm still in that process. It's a lot better now but it still sucks. It's still very taxing.

When we went to raise before, we were six months after the recession which meant that it was very hard to raise from anybody because they were being super cautious. Sequoia did this "RIP" slide thing. It was challenging, and so it sucked because you just got a lot of "no's." We were two kids from ASU, never done a company, had never worked anywhere really interesting. We had nothing going for us other than that we were in YC.

So raising sucked; we almost died actually. We were probably a week from just dying, thinking "Oh guess we're going to go back to school." I was like, "Tim, if you ever want to build anything, build it now. We might not be alive in the next month, so just build it now." And we actually ended up raising from Max Levchin and Michael Birch at the last second, and that saved us. We were like, "Oh, we finally did it, we raised." But raising was just taxing because you end up talking to VC's who have a million reasons why your idea sucks, won't work, and then you talk to angels who won't invest in you until some other angel invests in you. You have this chicken and egg problem.

Sequoia's leaked RIP slides happened October 2008, and we were in the same YC class which was Summer 2009, so the summer right after. People may forget but it was actually kind of a challenging economical environment.

Yeah. I think the companies that raised—you had to be pretty decent if you raised. I think we were more lucky than decent.

Do you think the 150K from Yuri Milner is good or bad?

It's hard to say. I think it's great because—I think it's good in the sense that it makes it easier to start a company and produce innovation. I think it's bad in that it makes people think that it's easy to start a company and raise money, and it create this false perception of what it actually takes to start a company. There are stories where people were doing anything to get it to work, and have this strong commitment, sweat, blood and tears. It's like the AirBNB story. It's not inspirational to be like "Hey, I started my company and I just got $150,000 for doing basically nothing." I got into YC, that was it and YC is not like—it's not hard to get into YC necessarily. It just makes people think that it's just so easy to raise $150,000 and build a huge business. It's *extremely hard,* and people should realize that. I think that piece is not good, because it makes people forget what it takes.

Did you guys have advisors in Mixpanel?

We never had any advisors although I showed Max the first version of Mixpanel ever, and his user ID is 15 or something on the site. And that was when I was still in school. We weren't even in YC at that point. Max was always helpful: he said "Mixpanel wouldn't scale" and stuff like that and he was right in the beginning. But we never got any formal advisors necessarily. Max became a formal advisor later on when we ended up raising money from him.

How long did it take to build your first beta?

Started November 2008 and released something that someone could sign up for and use a few months later in January 2009. That's basically what I showed Max.

How did you get the word out?

I didn't really get the word out. Initially I was just building. I just knew a bunch of other app developers from OpenSocial and started asking them if they wanted to use it. Later on, we got the word out by doing all kinds of crazy things. We created fake personas on websites and said "Mixpanel is awesome" back in the early days. We had created a Twitter account that automatically followed people—we followed who'd like Eric Ries. We would follow everyone that was following Eric Ries automatically, using a bot that would get us our first really leads to use our service, and then we just started publishing blog posts and trying to get them on Hacker News and stuff like that. Or I would just go out and just massively email tons and tons of people and be like "Hey, do you want to use this?"

Fake personas totally work by the way. We did it, Reddit did it, Hacker News did it, I think a lot of people do that.

I have a fake persona I use, but I won't say his name.

Are you the fake Steve Jobs?

No.

Did you guys ever do any big pivots in Mixpanel?

The biggest pivot was trying to go from not real-time to real-time. That was it. The core idea has always stayed the same.

Any points where you thought Mixpanel would fail or where you really had stressful moments?

Yeah. It happened two weeks ago. It happens a lot. Basically when you're doing real-time data analysis, the problem is that you have to pre-compute everything. You have to do it all right when the data comes which means that if you don't scale the rate at which the data is coming in you start to get backlogged. You just have data that's piling up over time and so we definitely had scenarios where we were not real time, we had 24 hour, 48 hour, 72 hour delays for two weeks, and there are definitely points in times where the scaling problems were so bad that I would just *lay on the ground* and think *"How I'm I going to scale this? How I'm I going to do this?"* And the thing is, if you can't, you die.

I remember the delays in Mixpanel's early days.

Yeah, things like that still happen even today, but they're less severe. We have a better handle on it obviously, but there was definitely days where things just got really, really bad, and if you can't scale you just lose.

Did revenue ever take off? How did you cause that to happen?

Yeah. It was after Y Combinator and after we raised half a million but those two events were totally unrelated. It wasn't because of those things that we started making more money to be clear. It's hard to say *why it happened* but it just started happening.

We learned one really important lesson and that was that "no" doesn't mean "no", it just means "not yet." So what that means in this context is that you might ask "Hey, Justin.TV, do you want to use Mixpanel?" And they might ignore you, and then they say "no," or they're trying to be polite about it but they say, "no, we're not interested." It's very clear, and that is obviously really disheartening. You're thinking, "Nobody wants to use my stupid site—no one wants to use this thing that I've been working 18 hours a day on for the past six or eight months. This sucks, my work is useless." But what it really meant was that if you just wait a little while, it turns out that if you wait, sometimes "no" turns into "yes," and with Justin.TV, they were like "no" 5 times and then six months later they'd say "yes" and then they spend $1,500 a month with us.

And so that's what we noticed. We noticed that we just keep building products, keep moving, get the word out, getting people to hear about us more than just one time. *You have to hear about that name several times* and then it'll be like, "Oh, maybe I'll sign up now, I want to see what the hell this thing is about." And then you sign up and you start using it, and you like it. And then these people turn into paying customers, so revenue just took off because we just waited; we were just persistent about it. We just stayed alive.

Did you guys do any other marketing like hire PR, anything like to help growth?

No. We used a few viral strategies that I'm not willing to talk about yet. We did a lot of guest blog posting to get the word out. We just write crazy in-depth metrics in all these posts to try to meet readers in our industry and that worked really well in terms of getting customers it was like "Oh yeah, I should track that," and then they would go sign up with Mixpanel because we obviously would talk about what we could track.

How do you split the work up?

We try to put people in charge of what they're best at. I think if you try to run things as a dictatorship—well, we don't like to run things as a democracy. Things as a democracy fail very hard.

There's too much contention and you never get to a conclusion.
Maybe it's a benevolent dictatorship?

Yeah, it's also benevolent dictatorship. I think we structured it nicely. What we try to do is, if you're really good at X, then you become the dictator of X. So if you're the most badass person at MySQL, I could argue with you all day—even if I'm CEO, I could argue with you all day about what we should do in terms of MySQL—but at the end of the day I'm going to submit to you because you're the person that is in charge of it. What we do is we try to piece that off. I'm in charge of product and engineering, more marketing and sales type stuff. I'm in charge of a lot of things, trying to dish it off. We have guys that like a full-time support guy, who is in charge of support. Tim is in charge of front-end engineering, fully in charge of doing that. We have another guy Avery, he's in charge of the back-end stuff. I can argue with Avery, but at the end of the day he's building it and he knows it really well, so he gets the final say, even if I'm running the company.

You guys are among the group of companies who make a priority on design and experience. Was that planned from the beginning or did you decide to add it in later as an afterthought?

I did a lot of things when I was younger like those logo contests during that one summer and I learned a lot about design. I've always just felt that it's very important to have very good UI and UX. I definitely used to be more of an engineering person but these days I'm more of a product person and I just think those things matter. I think I brought that into Mixpanel.

What's the work schedule like? Has it changed from the early days?

Yeah, it's changed significantly. What it used to be was: we would wake up and sleep at 3:00 AM, and that was an 18-hour workday. We did that every day for the first 10 months of Mixpanel. Things changed when we raised money, moved to San Francisco, and got an office. It's a little bit more of a balanced schedule because you realize that you're not running a sprint—maybe the first six to eight months, you have to—but we realized later you're in a marathon and so part of that is, one thing I disagreed about the way Slide worked was that those guys would stay up till like forever. The whole gaming industry operates like this: they'd stay up forever and keep working nonstop. But it doesn't matter, you can stay up all the time that you want, but if you don't have a good strategy, you will lose inevitably to someone that—even if I stay up for 12 hours and you stay up for 18 hours and if I have a better strategy, I will still win. We try to focus on goals and strategy and try to live on a more balanced work-life. That means like 10, 12, 14-hour days, it just depends.

Sometimes it's on and off. Maybe one day of the weekend we try to say "you can work on anything that you want." Even if I said, "Hey, we should not build this product," you can still build that product on the weekend to prove me wrong or prove anybody else wrong.

What's your biggest challenge today?

Our biggest challenges are probably recruiting and keeping pace with the amount of data that we get. Scaling has become less of a challenge, now it's more like recruiting and finding the right people to help build products. Our biggest bottleneck is we just have so much to do but not enough people to do it.

What's the culture at Mixpanel like?

We're a real-time analytics company so what we want to do is be real-time on all ends. So that doesn't mean just data analysis is real-time and it's up and we're never backlogged—that's a big piece but it's not the only piece. The main piece is that *everything* feels real-time. If customer support is slow, then we as a company do not seem *real-time*. Even if our data analysis is real-time, you just don't appear to be real-time. You seem sluggish and slow so everything end to end is real-time. So support is real-time, the analysis is real-time, the website feels real-time; it feels fast. It feels like everything is updated constantly. Even when we hire people, we try to make offers to those people as fast as we can— faster than any other company would. We try to make everything just feel like we're a real-time culture.

Let's say an undergraduate student knows they want to do a startup but they're not quite sure of what or how. What advice would you give to them?

I would say work somewhere or intern somewhere before you do it and that will give you the best idea of what it's like to work on a team. Intern at a startup; don't intern at IBM. It will give you an idea of what's it like both emotionally and technically, and it will give you the right amount of knowledge to know what it's like to do with your company, and it will give you the network also. The biggest thing I got out of Slide was the network of people.

If they're non-technical, should they learn how to program?

If you're a technology focused startup, yes.

Can you talk about the time you most successfully hacked a non-computer system to your advantage?

Last summer I managed to get an internship at Slide, but a month after accepting the offer I decided that I wanted more hourly pay before I even started at Slide. I was able to convince the recruiter that I had numerous offers still outstanding from companies like RockYou and Zynga and that I had in-depth OpenSocial experience that was deserving of a $10 an hour raise. Luckily I was able to get it and the pay was very good that summer. I guess I was able to figure out how to get more money, more of an hourly salary, even after I had accepted the offer and before I even started.

Why would someone want to work at Mixpanel?

If you want to work at a company that is small and you want to actually make an impact. It's harder to make an impact at like 20 or 30 people, let alone if you're a thousand people. Facebook tries hard, but at the end of the day it's just more difficult. Basically, if you want ownership over having built something very successful in the beginning of something that's actually growing and improving, then we're the right place to join. The other part is for engineers that are interested in scaling and doing really hard technical problems in terms of hard engineering problems. We definitely have no shortage of those.

What's your development stack? You guys deal with tons of data in real-time so I'm personally curious.

We do primarily Python, Django, Git, and we use every data store on the planet like Redis. Not Casandra though. We use Mongo and MySQL, Memcached, and all those cool new SQL things. We're more of a bleeding-edge type of company, so it's kind of fun.

Evan Reas, LikeALittle

Tags: Y Combinator, businessperson, hiring, side project, iterate quickly

Overview: LikeALittle started in 2010 to allow people—primarily college students—to anonymously connect and interact with people nearby. LikeALittle went through Y Combinator in 2010 and has goals to become the next big social network. When they wrote an ad for hiring in December 2010, they had over 20 million page views in less than six weeks since launching. A contributor at TechCrunch wrote that "LikeALittle kind of reminds me another social network that blew up on campus." I ended up using Evan's favorite non-computer hack—which he mentions at the end of this interview—to land an interview with Foursquare's Dennis Crowley for this book. If you want to get a meeting with anyone you want, I'm convinced you can use his method to do it.

Take me back to when you first got started with entrepreneurship.

Growing up I did a lot of the stuff that most other kids did. I had the lemonade stand and traded baseball cards; I think I liked the reward factor in saying, "I bought this for $5 and sold for $10." I really liked like major results and achievements. When I was 12, I started investing in the stock market too—I think I started with a few hundred dollars, something like that, and made a little bit of money over a year. That was my big foray into stocks.

When I was 16 or 17 I convinced my parents to give me $10,000 to invest for them; two weeks later I lost $8,000 of it. I put it in all these ridiculously risky stocks. I was really confident, lost 80% of it, and was at $2,000. For the next few months, every week my dad would say, "So how is the portfolio doing?" and I would say, "Oh, good, very good," and I was totally lost and didn't know what to do but was determined to figure it out.

I studied the market relentlessly to try and figure out an algorithm to gain money back; I got back up to $10,000 within the year so finally, I could tell my dad, "yeah, we're at $11,000, we're good, we have a 10% return so far." So, I didn't tell them that I actually lost most of it, initially, but that experience ended up teaching me so much that I actually took the $10K to about $200,000, over the next couple of years.

It was cool to see companies grow, watch their stocks go up, and monitor all that through simple technologies. Watching that growth and understanding what things had led to it made me really want to start my own company. So, my first real startup experience was in college. I was a junior and was asked if I wanted to help start a biotech company.

I worked with a couple of Johns Hopkins scientists. I was involved from day one and we helped launch this VC-funded company; the experience of taking it from this small office with nothing in it to a real company, was awesome. Afterwards, I realized that biotech was not my thing; it takes way too long to actually see results and I'm very impatient and want to see results quickly, so I decided I wanted to come out to the Valley to do my own thing, and that was where my inspiration started.

So your earliest experience was at 12?

That was when I started investing; in addition I did do a little lemonade stand, and the baseball cards, and I actually made gems. I used to cut gems from rough minerals and sell them.

How did you cut the gems?

I actually went to mines to find them and I bought these tools to cut them. I was really horrible at it, but my relatives bought them because they knew I worked hard on them.

What kinds of classes were you taking?

I went to this tiny little liberal arts school in Ohio, called Ohio Wesleyan, which I chose because it was on some top ten list for creating entrepreneurs. The university was about 2,000 kids, so I knew my entire school. I took some entrepreneurship classes, but I majored in economics. I didn't really challenge myself as much as I could have in undergrad; I was more interested in doing other random stuff. I was still investing, and doing a lot of random startup and leadership stuff. I was student body treasurer, captain of the ultimate frisbee team, things like that. But even with all that, I wanted to get a 4.0 because I considered it a challenge and because I am extremely competitive and never wanted anyone to have a higher GPA than me. So, I took easy classes to make sure I could get a 4.0 and, at the same time, do stuff I actually cared about.

As I mentioned, within the economics department there were a couple of classes that focused on entrepreneurship, where you actually had projects where you would build and start selling something, things I thought were quite interesting. Most of those classes were really intimate—10 students or so—and I really enjoyed them because in addition to learning from the class, you were learning from your peers.

Did you know anyone going into college?

No. I grew up in Wisconsin and went to Ohio because I thought it would be a big change. Wisconsin seemed like this very small place you never get out of. I thought Ohio was this crazy, far away place, when in actuality it was only a seven-hour drive. But I liked the fact that I was still close enough that I could go home if I needed to.

How did you meet people outside of class?

Mostly activities. I got into ultimate frisbee really quickly and met people on the team. The other big clubs where I met a lot of people were, fraternities, investing club, and student government.

When professors randomly paired us up with people to do projects, I met some other people but, generally, if they just told us to go pair up, we would just work with friends. There were very few times where I met new people through class.

Do you have any specific advice on how to find cofounders? It seems like you were pretty active with lots of different things, were you looking for cofounders through all of that?

I didn't look for cofounders much in undergrad. When I was in grad school at Stanford, even though I was in the business school there, I spent probably 50% of my time in other schools: computer science, engineering, and design. I like being around people that have different ways of thinking about things, that's more interesting to me than just being around the same group of people all the time.

So, any class I could take at a different school, where there were a lot of group projects, was fantastic. I would take CS courses where you're hooked up with other CS people and do projects together; you really learn how to work well with other people that way. I had the same experience when I took classes in the design school. Just engaging in different disciplines and doing projects with people who have different backgrounds and interests really teaches you how to work with diverse people. That skill set and knowledge is really helpful when you start a company and, in fact, I ended up doing a few projects later on with people I met through classes in other departments.

It's not artificial to introduce that kind of diversity as long as you are legitimately getting to know people, seeing how you work together, and gauging each other's value.

I also like to throw parties. It's kind of funny because I don't really like huge parties that much. I don't throw bashes, but I do like to throw small gatherings where people really get to know each other. I generally invite five or ten friends and have each of them invite two or three of their friends that I don't know, who *they* think are really interesting. So those kinds of champagne parties or dinner parties where you can meet people in a very small, intimate setting are a good way to get to know people as well.

Which is more important: making a concerted effort to find cofounders or letting serendipity run its course?

I think trying to force things to happen in a certain way, doesn't work. Trying to meet or get in with specific people that you think can help you do something is ridiculous. If you're interested in meeting people, you have to be genuinely interested in people. Be interested *because* they have different value sets, different backgrounds and perspectives than you do; don't let differences be a limiting factor.

One of the guys that I worked with on a design school project is now the cofounder of Pulse, a really popular iPad application. He and I started a company together a couple of summers ago, just because we wanted to try some different projects. We made this iPhone app that was really exciting but a terrible app; it didn't work at all. But the experience was really good, to learn how to work with people from different disciplines. So, I think it's all about always being genuine. Just be interested in people, not motivated by what you think they can do for you, because people always see through that.

How did you pay your way through school?

It was mostly just the investing that I did. I don't think I had any jobs in school.

Did you know you wanted to do another startup right when you graduated college?

I knew I wanted to come to Silicon Valley but I wasn't sure if I wanted to go to business school right away or to do a startup. I knew I wanted to go to Stanford or Harvard. A lot of people told me I probably wouldn't get into those business schools right out of undergrad, so I thought, "Okay, if I can get into business school then I'll do that and then start a company, otherwise I'll just start something right away."

When you were in school, was there anyone that particularly inspired or influenced you?

Good question. Warren Buffett has always been a big influence, just from the investment stuff, which is interesting because he doesn't really help much on the entrepreneurial side. Other than him, it's actually athletes that inspire me most. So, I was influenced, both by people that I played with that I just thought were awesome for how hard they tried and how motivated they were, and by people like Michael Jordan. I love reading and watching and hearing about inspirational athletes because I think there's a lot that can be learned from them.

How did the idea for LikeALittle come about? I remember having this same idea before I started my last startup—I wanted to flirt with girls in the same lecture hall as me. Of course, it'd be too easy to just walk up to them and introduce myself.

As soon as I graduated from business school I started a company called ProFounder with two cofounders, Jessica Jackley who had started Kiva before, and Dana Mauriello. While doing that, I met my current cofounders for LikeaLittle, Shubham and Prasanna. They had left Microsoft, came to Stanford, and used to hang out there because they were trying to start a company. A mutual friend introduced us and after a month or two we decided to join forces.

So we started ProFounder. I worked there for about six months and then it moved on to L.A and I didn't want to go to L.A; I decided I wanted to stay in Silicon Valley and do some consumer Internet things. So, Shubham, Prasanna and I came back to Palo Alto, lived together in a one-bedroom apartment with no furniture, slept on the floor, subsisted off of rice, and tried a bunch of stuff until we caught something that worked.

This was January 2010. For several months we just brainstormed; it wasn't until October that we actually came up with LikeaLittle. We had probably tried 10 ideas before that and they all failed miserably. So, in October 2010, we created a first edition of LikeaLittle.

You said you went through nine or ten other projects before LikeaLittle. What were they?

One of them was a personalized news startup where you would take your Twitter and Facebook and stream the information; try to create, kind of, an interest strap so you could then find the top 100 articles every day that you should be reading. In theory it's great, in practice people didn't really care about it that much.

So we made an iPad app and an iPhone app for that, which went okay; we sold around 10,000 copies but it just wasn't taking off. What else did we do? We did one where we would track your credit card purchases and give you little points for every place that you went within your local area, and we did a social network for your five most trustworthy friends, trying to create this "most trustworthy social network in the U.S." We had all these really interesting ideas that all got some sort of traction, but none of them really ever took off.

Did you guys all focus on the same project or did you split up and do multiple projects at once?

With almost all of these ideas, we were all working on the same project. There were a couple of times where there was a bit of overlap, where something would be doing okay and one person would focus on keeping that going while the rest of us would try another project to see if it would be better. Generally, though, we would put all our energy into one project.

You're in the Winter 2011 YC batch. Had you raised money before YC?

No. We've been working together for almost a year, but before YC we had not done any fundraising. We were bootstrapping the entire time; we were living in a one-bedroom apartment our entire time together and then for a two month period, they lost their visas, so we had to go and live in India together. So we lived with my cofounder's family in India and were doing the startup from there. It was interesting, the power would go out all the time and our users were in America so we had to be on U.S. time; all kinds of crazy stuff was happening.

But, in India there were no expenses. The family would make us food and we'd stay with them; we literally had a zero dollar burn rate in India. So that was pretty fantastic; we kind of had an infinite runway. We've basically spent the entire year living off of rice and beans and sleeping on the floor, together.

That sounds pretty much like Y Combinator.

Exactly! Been going through it for the last year.

Is the $150K from Yuri Milner a good or bad thing? You're one of the companies that will receive these new terms.

I think it's great as long as the drive and desire for other YC founders doesn't go down, and I think PG is good enough at picking the people so the drive doesn't go down. It should actually be a good thing because it will just extend their runway on entrepreneurs; so no matter what happens their drive is going to be huge. I think it's going to be a very, very positive thing.

It seems you were able to operate at a very low burn rate. Any advice for students who might move straight out of college to do a startup instead of grad school?

I think you just have to know your priorities. Our priority is our company. Period. So we don't go out much and we do whatever we need to succeed and to win. We work until 6:00AM because we know that while our competition is asleep we can get ahead. We eat rice and beans. You can figure out how to live on pretty much anything, I've learned. Then you have stories like Airbnb, which sold cereal to make enough money part time. I think if you're determined enough there's definitely a way to figure out what you have to do and to live off a very small amount of money for an extremely long time.

How long did it take you guys to build your beta and how did you get users at first? You moved around on projects, and I've heard some people talk about "the only thing worse than failure is mediocrity," so how did you know when to move on?

So this, as I mentioned, was the ninth or tenth project that we'd tried over the past few months. When we came up with the idea, we decided to spend one day coding it, which we did, and then one more day marketing it around Stanford, just see whether it took off or not. We figured if it didn't we could go back to a different project.

When we decided to try, it was a very small little thing, and it just took off from there. It helps that I know a lot of people at Stanford right now. When I told them about the site I asked them to start using it, compliment people around them, and share it on Facebook. We put up flyers and chalked the streets ourselves.

How have you maintained your growth?

I think we're at close to 500 schools now. There was a big drop in traffic during winter break, in December, when nobody was at school. So, we're just trying to get back to where we were before the break; everybody is back at school now, trying to use the site again, and we have lots of schools on our waiting list, so we're just trying to figure out how to scale it quickly. A lot of the people just come from Facebook and from people talking about the site.

They're either putting it on their Facebook and other friends and family at different schools see it, or they'll just tell their friends about it at school on Twitter or something. It has been purely viral growth, and people talking about it. There have been no marketing expenses or costs, so far.

So you've noticed that usage correlates with students being in school?

Yeah. Right now, weekends are a little bit lower usage because people are out partying and hanging out; they're not in front of their computers and can't post quickly, and our mobile web app is not very good at the moment. We just submitted an iPhone app so we think that will help usage actually go up on the weekends, but right now, the highest usage is definitely when people are bored in class or in their dorms or the library, things like that.

Were there any moments for you guys where you started to worry that it wouldn't work?

The number one thing for us is making sure that the three of us are going to stay together no matter what and that we see this business through. So team dynamics have never been a problem as far as sticking together and making sure we're going to figure something out. On a daily or weekly basis, we have crazy stuff that happens, whether the servers go down, or we lose a bunch of data, or somebody spams the site on some specific page, or something like that.

You wake up and TechCrunch wrote about you and you didn't want them to and you have to figure out what to do with that. So there are a lot of things that come up and just figuring out how to fix them is always front and center. I think there are tons of those 'blood pressure moments' you mentioned that happen all the time; it's just about how we solve them, what's the best we can do with them? Because every problem has a solution, you just have to think creatively.

Have you started making revenue?

Not yet. We thought maybe we could make money some day doing one of the ten things on our list. Since we're in the hyper local, mobile-location space, there's a lot you can do because you know where somebody is, where they like to be, and things like that. There are lots of advertising opportunities, but we haven't really started with that, we're really just focusing on making our product.

How do you guys split the work up?

Generally, someone will jump on whatever needs to get done and get it done. Every few days we'll figure out what are the big priorities, what needs to be done, and who's going to focus on them. I'm not a programmer so anything that requires programming I leave up to my two partners—they are just fantastic and they take care of it. I do a lot of the fundraising, marketing, and community stuff to make sure relationships with schools are going well. We have campus reps and we do our business development and partnerships through them.

We have this running joke that nobody ever knows what day it is at LikeALittle. Everybody who works at the company is constantly working, to include a couple of interns who live at the house. We have this house where everybody lives and works. So you wake up, jump on email, start working, work until you're on break and then go take a quick walk, come back in, we might have lunch together, keep working, etc. We're pretty much working all day, every day, and taking breaks whenever we need them; whenever it will increase productivity.

What is your biggest challenge right now?

The biggest challenge is just making sure we have high-quality growth. Whereas we could open to every single school tomorrow, I think that would be a mistake because the number one thing that we focus on is positivity and high-quality posts and users. So we don't want a million users who aren't going to put up genuine posts, or are going to be negative; just making sure that we're opening as fast as we can go but also keeping the experience quality as high as possible, is the challenge.

How do you deal with the spam that shows up on LikeALittle?

We have a couple of things that we do—it's a lot of community-powered stuff so the community has devoted to deal with the posts; any person can delete any post that's a part of the community their site is on. We have algorithms that filter out spam and negative stuff right away. We also have a bunch of moderators that volunteer to help go through the site and get rid of any spam or negative posts, so we're doing a bunch of that.

What's the culture like at LikeALittle?

I think we really focus on, what we call, a 'hacker culture;' that sounds cliché, but we want everybody to be a hacker regardless of whether they're programmers or not. What we mean by that is: just find a way to get something done quickly. If it's not the prettiest way or the cleanest way, that's okay because we can fix it later, but if we need to get something fixed right now, then we'd better have a way to do it.

So, we do break stuff sometimes. We don't use the cleanest code at all times. We don't make sure that everything is perfect because it's all about moving fast.

What did you write the site in? Do you unit test?

We're using Ruby on Rails right now. The way we test our code is by pushing it and seeing what users yell at. So we don't really do any of that stuff yet. At some point, I'm sure we'll have to do that, but right now it's like, "Code it up, push it out and if it's broken we'll fix it."

What advice would you give an undergraduate who's thinking about doing a startup?

Be sure that you want to do a startup, knowing it has crazy emotional ups and downs, and it's 24/7. You're going to think about it all the time. If you're sure those factors are ok with you, the only thing to do, is do it, right? When you start something, you learn the most just by doing it. There's nothing else that can compare to users calling up at 3:00AM to tell you something is broken; you learn what you need to do incredibly fast. Just go ahead and start.

What do think, so far, of Y Combinator?

The people are fantastic. I think for us the most powerful thing is just the network of people—really smart people who are willing to help each other out on anything. So when we need feedback, we send them thoughts and questions about what they like. We needed a quick design done a couple of days ago and didn't have a designer to create it for us so I just emailed the batch and somebody designed a button for us in an hour.

I think the ability to be on call with all these awesome people who are doing awesome stuff and being able to call them for help any time you need it, is just invaluable.

You guys have drastically improved you UI design and experience. I remember your first version and it was pretty rough. Design in general seems to be a problem for many early-stage startups.

I think the Valley is putting more value on designers, which is great. They're learning design skills and at least have a basic eye for design. I think that PG and the other folks at YC, they've brought in Garry Tan from Posterous to be the resident designer. I think that's really smart.

Can you talk about the time you most successfully hacked some non-computer system to your advantage?

I'm very confident that I can get access to anybody in the world and get in front of him or her. So one guy, specifically, that is now an investor in our company—an advisor and investor—I sent him 12 emails. Every single month I would send him an email and give an update and say, "Hey, here is what we're doing, here is what is going on, we'd love to hear your thoughts, whenever. You're just an awesome guy so we want to get in front of you."

I think I did this for six or seven months, then after that I was like, "Okay, I'm going to send you an email every single day for the next month and if you don't respond, fine, but I'm going to keep sending them to you until you respond. If you tell me to stop, I'll stop, but I think you'd be really helpful, here's why." So every single day at the same time I would send him an email that said, "Here is what's going on, let's chat, talk to you tomorrow."

I think it was after six or seven of those emails he finally said, "Okay, let's go grab coffee." So we grabbed coffee; he was an awesome guy. I told him he was awesome and it turned out that he would be an advisor and an investor in the company as well as an awesome mentor. So I think it's all about perseverance, persistence, being able to keep pushing and getting things done.

Why would someone want to work at LikeALittle?

We are building the next great company. My cofounders are some of the best hackers in the world—one of them was the top student at IIT-Delhi, the top university in India, and the world physics Olympiad gold medalist. The other was ranked #1 in India at TopCoder, was youngest ever Google code jam world finalist, twice, and ACM world finalist, twice. We are putting together the best imaginable team because that is what it takes to win. We want people who are the best in the world at what they do.

Dave Paola, Djangy

Tags: programmer, anti-school, undergrad founder, self-funded, profitable (previous company: ThatHigh.com)

Overview: Djangy started in 2010 as a Python cloud host with the goal of instant deployment: single command under 10 seconds an app is hosted online instantly with no customization required. Djangy also offers instant scaling in addition to instant deployment. I remember seeing Dave Paola while I was at UIUC, although we didn't start hanging out as much until he moved to California and I heard that he was interested in startups. Dave started ThatHigh.com before Djangy and that web site paid his living expenses while he focused on doing his next startup.

If you were trying to explain what you do to somebody, would it be safe to say you're the Heroku for Django?

That sounds accurate enough.

Okay. Can you tell me about the earliest entrepreneurial experiences, going back as far as you can remember?

The first time I did anything entrepreneurial was in 7th grade, maybe earlier, 6th grade; and, I don't know if you remember this or not, but in middle school, Warheads—those really sweet, really sour candies—were pretty popular. People used to eat them for lunch at our school; the black cherry ones were always the most sought after, the most in demand. So, my mom would take me to Marc's, a grocery store in northeastern Ohio, and for $5 I would get a big bin of Warheads, go back to school with 30 or so of them, and sell them for $0.50 each, or to the highest bidder. It helped me pay for my lunch everyday and then some. That's the earliest hack-type thing I can remember.

In high school I fixed computers. It's almost stereotypical, but I was charging $50 to $75 an hour and, as long as I did good, high-quality work and I didn't make people feel stupid or act in a typically nerdy manner, it was a good way to develop social business skills as well.

I was also in a band in high school. We didn't make a bunch of money but, looking back, there were a lot of good lessons there in marketing, being creative under pressure, and performing, because we played a lot more shows than the average high school band probably does. We played once a week, at least, and then the weekends, sophomore through senior years. I was the lead guitarist and singer.

Again, that's not something we made a lot of money from, but it was definitely a good introduction to working in a very close, tight group where you don't have to talk but can sort of predict what's going to happen; even if people make mistakes you can recover very gracefully through mere eye contact.

How did you transition into college? What was college life like for you?

I actually got in quite a bit of trouble my senior year of high school. I was arrested in front of my peers the day before graduation, senior year, and I was barred from graduation and expelled. I didn't get my diploma until January, which is the maximum allowable time to withhold it—180 days in the State of Ohio.

I was put under house arrest; I had 250 hours of community service and was on probation. So, I had quite a summer. I had to go to summer school once I was off house arrest; needless to say it was not the best summer to have after you graduate high school. I was scheduled to come out to Illinois for freshman year registration on July 4th weekend, and I wasn't sure if they would let me in without a diploma. I had no idea what was going on. So I came out and it turned out there were some nice folks who still thought I was worth admitting so they let me in under conduct and academic probation.

So that's how I began college and, I think I might even hold the record—I should look it up—for completing college while on academic probation every single semester, even the first one. I needed a bit of a release, so I partied the entire time. I had a great freshman year because of it; I had a 1.68 GPA or something, and subsequently got kicked out. But this actually runs deeper than you may think.

My family, very much values academics—at least they tried to raise me that way and they were raised that way. My Mom was the valedictorian of her high school class and for me to very publicly be kicked out of high school was crushing. It felt, for them, like a huge, huge failure, and then to make things even worse, I didn't do any work my freshman year and actually got kicked out of college. I'll never forget the day the dismissal letter arrived. Ever.

Pretty epic failures, two years in a row—letting everybody down around me. I was pretty depressed, actually. After I got dismissed from UIUC my freshman year, I went to Kent State; people know about Kent State mainly because of the shootings in the '70s. So I went to Kent State for a year and I remember being in the basement lounge of one of the dorms and kind of realizing my life had gone to shit. I had gotten into this great school and gotten kicked out and I had thrown away all these opportunities, and I remember thinking to myself, "Well I still enjoy hacking; I still like building things; I still like software and I'm not an idiot; not much about me has changed." I realized I had nowhere to go but up. Around the same time I read Steve Jobs' Stanford commencement speech, about the similar realizations he'd had.

Simultaneously, I had learned to play poker and I completely sucked but started to learn the game and skills involved in reading people, bluffing, and taking chances, so I basically wrote a readmission petition to Illinois. At the very end I said something like, "Listen, I have no idea what the future holds, no idea what I'm going to do with my life, but I know that I'm going to do something big and if you want me to be an alumnus from Illinois, then let me back in." And they did, which was pretty cool. **You're not the first founder who has spoken about illegal or 'morally questionable' things. Even outside of this book, I have spoken to very successful Silicon Valley startup founders who say they should have been handcuffed and taken away by police for some of the computer crimes they committed. Not to justify their actions, but I wonder if hackers can take it to extremes sometimes when they're 'beating the system.' One founder in this book has mentioned making money in questionable ways when they were younger. I have spoken to a couple of founders who didn't even go to class for a while—I do the same thing. I have a pretty negative view on public education, and I remember this being a major source of frustration from a very young age—I've always had really good grades, but I questioned the usefulness of what I was learning. I've heard stories of founders who paid other students to do their homework or get the attendance points, but I'm too lazy to do that. I'd rather just take a 5% hit to my grade on attendance and not show up when I know I'd be**

wasting my time if I did go to class. I've done some 'questionable' things in my childhood, although I wasn't arrested, I definitely got into some trouble with the school when it came to their network security.

One other thing I did was, in the 7th grade with the money I made from the Warheads, I didn't like doing my math homework so I actually paid this guy a dollar every day to do my math homework. Actually, that had far reaching effects because in 7th grade we were doing advanced algebra or geometry—that's when you're supposed to learn a unit circle, right?

One half and pie and whatever, so I never memorized those formulas. Throughout physics and chemistry and calculus in college, I never could remember these very fundamental things about math, which significantly contributed to my horrific performance in those subjects!

To say that I got in trouble senior year just does not do it justice. The amount of stuff I did meant I had no other project my entire senior year of high school. Somebody who saw me, someone who didn't like me very much, turned me in. But it was quite an experience because they didn't just handle it internally; they decided to bring the police in because they were completely incompetent. The day before graduation, my band mates were going to the Guitar Center in Cleveland and they were going to pick me up on their way; I figured I'd just shoot over to the high school to pick up my cap and gown for the day after, so I showed up, gave them my name, and they told me I had to go see the Principal to get my cap and gown.

I figured I had forgotten to turn in a library book or something. So I went into his office and said, "Hey, I'm Dave Paola, I'm supposed to pick up my cap and gown here." He said, "What's your name?" I said, "Dave Paola" and then he said, "Oh, hold on," and walked out. When he came back in he was like, "Dave, come with me." So I walked into his personal office and there were probably 15 people sitting in a semi-circle around his big oak desk with one empty chair in the middle, for me. There was a cop in the corner and the Superintendent was there, and it was a big deal and he said to me, "David I don't know anybody in the history of this school district who has been in as much trouble as you are now." Needless to say, my friends had already gone to Guitar Center and they came back and it was a big cluster fuck of a day. I was on the front page of the paper.

I was interested enough in software and the way computers worked. This was just more interesting to me and, I hadn't even thought about the consequences one bit; it seemed so easy, and it was. The people running the network were probably in their 50s—I'm sure they're very smart people, but to grow up around that technology and to have a deep understanding of it while the people who were in charge were so comparatively incompetent, it's kind of easy to skew the consequences in your mind a little bit; especially, if you've never failed or gotten in trouble. I was a pretty straight-edged kid; I didn't drink, I didn't smoke, I didn't do anything bad. I went to church every week. **I think the reason things like that happen—and it's a stigma in society—is because school can be boring and what they teach isn't interesting, depending on what you're studying and what stage you're at in school. I just remember distinctly being frustrated with high school, but when I went to UIUC and started taking engineering classes, it was completely different. The material was challenging and the professors expected you to hustle. There was still some expectation of rote memorization, which frustrated me a little bit, but at least the assignments were actually about learning technically challenging things and pulling all-nighters to get it done instilled the proper work ethic.**

Especially when it comes to things like math; here's how you do math and algebra: you take X and Y and you divide, to get to X you divide the other side by X and then you... It's a procedure they teach you. It's not education, it's training. You're taught an algorithm, you're not taught what math is, you're not taught the meaning behind it; so I was never exposed to anything like that. I'm sure most people aren't either.

I guess the point I want people to take away from all that is, actually, it has nothing to do with a hacker mentality, it has to do with failing. I haven't yet experienced failure on a really large, professional level, but on a personal level I absolutely have, at least twice. I disappointed everybody around me and it sucked, a lot, but I do remember halfway through that year at Kent having that stark realization; everything changed. I was like, "Holy shit, there's no pressure anymore, I can do whatever I want," and I didn't die.

So let's talk about your move to college. When you went to Illinois and even Kent, did you know anybody?

No. I'm from Canton, Ohio and I didn't know anybody in Illinois. My parents dropped me off and I was 700 miles from anybody I knew. I got very lucky, though. I made a lot of friends very quickly my freshman year because I lived in Carr Hall and had a really awesome RA.

Did you know you wanted to do a startup in college? Were you looking for cofounders?

I'm not sure I actively thought about looking for cofounders, but I definitely wanted to do a startup, absolutely. Actually, the summer I was under house arrest I discovered Paul Graham's essays, and the one that struck home for me was, his essay on *Why Nerds Are Unpopular*.

Same here. It was the first essay I read as I moved to a different high school in the middle of sophomore year.

That was the first time I'd ever even thought about high school from that perspective, from an outside point of view. I was very much caught in the bubble at the time so, of course, I absorbed the rest of his essays and knew instantly that I identified with almost all of them.

Did you do any clubs or groups or anything else outside of class at UIUC?

Yeah, but not freshman year. It's not useful for me to treat college as one unit of time, because there were three discrete periods: freshman year, Kent State, and then UIUC afterwards. UIUC afterwards was by far—in terms of skills and my professional aspirations—the most useful unit of time. So I joined ACM because of its reputation; there's a different mentality at ACM.

When I got back to UIUC, all of the friends that I had had freshman year, had all gone different directions. They each had their own groups of friends, and I had been gone long enough that we weren't really close anymore; basically, I didn't have any friends again. It was like the beginning of freshman year again, so I joined ACM and basically hung out there all the time and forced myself into the organization, which was awesome. ACM has its advantages and its disadvantages, depending on how you look at it. In terms of the hackers in ACM, if you are a good hacker or at least compared to people around you then you'll be respected.

As far as disadvantages, it's very much a little bubble, but I suppose any community is like that. It was valuable for me because I learned a lot and met tons of cool people. I surrounded myself with folks who knew a lot more about everything than I did and I absorbed as much of it as I could.

I think I got lucky when it came to meeting smart hackers because one thing ACM does effectively, is network. It is a very valuable network, in and of itself, but it's also very exclusive. So, if you are a part of a group like ACM, it's likely that if you nurse the friendships you make there, you can find a cofounder. If you're not involved in a group like that, I have no idea how to do it, because that's how I learned.

Did you take time away from class to relax and party—do things most college students do?

After I got back in I literally spent all of my time in ACM until my senior year. So, there was a period of about two and a half years where I did nothing but hang in the ACM office. It was like an incubation period for me; I learned a great deal about different technologies; how to hack really well; how to build things effectively and efficiently. I learned how to write really good code; it's also what gave me an even healthier lack of respect for class, learning things in the classroom environment and how ineffective that can be. So no, I was not wild after I got back in.

If I had to do homework, I would do it there, but that's only because I was always there anyway. In ACM it's very much, "Oh god, I have to do this MP—a Machine Problem which is the homework computer science students have to do—I'm going to put it off until an hour before it's due and hammer it out then." I can't even tell you how many times I did that and, looking back, I can't believe I got it done. For the most part, I had nothing to do outside of class work. Someone would want to write a file system, and they would do that. Or, I'd want to write a music player because another one sucked. So we'd spend a weekend doing it. It was very much project after project and then hanging out. One time we built primitive logic gates out of LEGO bricks, for example.

What happened right when you were graduating? Did you know you wanted to do a startup?

Well, I knew I didn't want to get a job. Everybody around me was getting jobs and I knew that I didn't want to work 9 to 5 but I didn't really have any ideas. I started a website called ThatHigh.com. I honestly can't even remember where the idea came from. I was never a stoner; I still don't consider myself a stoner at all. But it did seem like a good niche to me; there was nothing out there that was as good as it could be for stoners to entertain themselves on the Internet. I had always had this thought in my head that this was a niche that was not being capitalized upon, and I was positive that I could build something to take advantage of it but I was too lazy, I had other things to work on, it wasn't really a priority at all. Then, in February, one of my friends suggested the same idea I'd had for a long time, except he had a good idea for a name. He said we should call it That High and we could make it like FMyLife and I thought, "Holy shit, that's a fantastic idea."

I bought the domain name, and there was a period of two or three days where I didn't do anything else. I was at Café Kopi in Champaign and I got a phone call, a voicemail, somebody wanting

209

to buy the domain name I had just registered three days ago. It was somebody in New York City, and I don't remember how much he was willing to offer. In retrospect, maybe I should have called him back, maybe not. But I knew at that point that we had to make a choice to either try to sell the domain name because there was something there, or just build it.

So three of us: me, my good friend, and my girlfriend at the time, spent one night building the site. We hosted it on App Engine, which is Google's infrastructure, basically because we wanted to do it as quickly as possible and not have to worry about being system admins; we just wanted to be able to deploy it. We'd seen Heroku and didn't want to use Ruby on Rails; we're primarily Python hackers so we used App Engine. We launched it, sort of in parallel with graduation. So that was February and there was a big spike from College Humor, and from then on it became a pet project of mine. The amount of hours I have put into That High is absolutely staggering.

I got around 20,000 visitors in a day from College Humor and that was, by far, the most visited thing I ever built in my life, and the code was pretty horrible so I spent a lot of time re-factoring and caching things and making it scale well on App Engine. I redesigned it and put some ads on there and the whole time, making money off it was very much built into the model. That's the only reason I was doing it. I have no passion for that niche, again, but it was something that was easy. It was very time consuming but not that technically challenging. I learned a lot from it but there was nothing unique or original about building the site. So that had a very slow organic growth period; I started out making no money and we had spikes along the way and each traffic spike would land us higher than before, but not much higher—no pun intended!

But it was a very slow process and I've been building it up for almost a year. It pays my rent now. So, I had that to rely on. I knew I didn't want to get a job right out of college; I had a steady, passive income stream that I didn't have to devote time to, and I could work on whatever I wanted to. I also knew that San Francisco/Silicon Valley was the place to be. So I sold everything I owned until I could fit my life into a backpack, and drove across the country.

That drive is brutal, by the way—I've done it a few times without taking any rest.

I made it with one of my good friends from freshman year. We took a scenic route. We went up through Montana and South Dakota, around Seattle and came down the coast, camping the whole time. It was awesome.

How did you meet your cofounders for ThatHigh.com? You said there were two other guys that built it with you?

My friend Stoyan, who I met through ACM, and my girlfriend at the time, Mo. They were both also very active in ACM.

So when you were graduating, what was going through your head?

My graduation was far more emotional than I expected. One of my best friends committed suicide that December, so I was very emotional, and then I broke up with my girlfriend and that was also very emotional because it was a pretty serious relationship and I basically wanted to get the fuck away from everything— everything I knew, everybody I knew. I just wanted some time for myself; that's what was going through my head.

So my good friend and I made the trip; we had a fantastic time. That's one of the best trips I've ever taken in my life, actually. We started out with a bunch of food, supplies, and whiskey, and we'd drive as far as we could each day for 10 to 12 hours and then stop someplace, camp, drink, smoke hookah and cigars, and eat over the fire; we did that for a week all over the country.

Did anyone inspire you in college?

I suppose you could say Paul Graham, although that's too cliché. I'm not sure he inspired so much as I could identify a lot with what he had written.

I can't name a specific individual, but I know that right now, the time we're in now, historically speaking, is incredible. We're at a point where it's like the renaissance meets the industrial revolution, when it comes to software, right? And that's still very much my philosophy, but I don't think there's anybody in particular. I'm mostly inspired by the fact that some seemingly normal people create these hugely successful software projects that end up making them millions of dollars.

How did the idea for Djangy come to you?

After starting ThatHigh.com I realized the ways App Engine isn't so great. I mean, everyone has their own perspectives, but there are some design things. With App Engine, you have to use their code so you have to sort of rip out parts of Django or parts of whatever framework you're using, and get Google's code to interact with their data store. Anyway there are some things that I didn't like about working with App Engine; there was some friction, basically, and I had used Heroku way back when they launched publicly, were in beta, when they had their online code editor and all that. So I'd used that and then I'd used it again later; I had messed around with Rails a little bit; we had an ACM project where I learned it, and I remember it just being incredibly awesome to use, especially after we'd already tried to host Rails ourselves at the time, which was horrible. This was in 2006/2007 and, at the time, everything around Ruby was very slow. It was by far the slowest interpretive language out there. So the idea for Djangy is much older than when we began. It started when I wrote ThatHigh.com on App Engine. But I didn't do anything about it until I got out to San Francisco; I was out here for three months before I even decided to work on it.

I remember, I picked you up at the train station at one point and I don't know if you were even working on anything during that time.

I wasn't. I was just nurturing ThatHigh.com. When I got out here, ThatHigh.com was making around $700 a month. Since then, I've built it to where it's making more than that. But I started Djangy because I did feel that I was atrophying a bit. I had nothing to work on; I knew I had to work on something. I had to pick a project; I had to build something valuable out of my time.

Did you have cofounders when you started Djangy?

No. I was living in the Mission at the time, I was subleasing from somebody and I spent two days building a prototype. It was really, really horrible. It was quite a hack, but I wanted to see how difficult it would be to build this, and I know nothing about hosting, I know nothing about infrastructure or being a hosting company. Certainly, I know nothing about being a system administrator, or, I didn't at the time, so I spent two days hacking the prototype and it worked. It was horrible, but it worked; at the time I had purchased a $1 template and I had a SQLite database to collect email addresses. I registered the domain name and somebody found the site and posted it on Hacker News and it got something like 1,500 to 2,000 email address sign-ups in 24 hours.

I had to make a decision. I thought, "This is something that has mass; should I continue building it or should I do something else?" So I put the word out, I might even have put it on Facebook, I said, "I'm going to be building a Python cloud host, is anybody interested in helping me?" And I had two people respond, Sameer was one of them. One of my other friends also wanted to work on it but he was still a student and logistically it would have been really difficult. So, Sameer and I started working on it in August.

Sameer was working in Mountain View at another startup founded by UIUC alumni, but he was looking to get out of it. He was unhappy living in Mountain View and was looking at different cities across America to move to. He was looking for a change, basically, so when I asked him, he responded and said, "Let's meet and have a talk about it." We met up and talked about the architecture and the business strategy, and we started working on it a couple of days later. It was a very fast process, probably less than a week from prototype to beginning to build with a cofounder.

Did you think about raising money at this point?

We didn't give any thought to it at all. We had no idea what we were doing and still have no idea what we're doing, which I think is something that is not stressed enough. I think a lot of people who start companies have no freaking clue what they're doing. We had no strategy in that respect. We know GitHub focused on revenue and that, I always thought, was a better idea than trying to flip a company because that was much riskier and I didn't have a lot of money. I had no savings. I was living off of ThatHigh.com and Sameer was living off of savings; we knew we had to focus on revenue because we didn't want to be a company with no value. We wanted to have paying customers so we could eat. So yeah, we built the company over the course of five, six months.

Within the past month and a half we have looked at investment options. We've met with quite a few investors but we've never actually asked for investments, and we started this before Heroku announced that they were acquired, and the fact that they were acquired changed a lot. For example, when I was at home for Thanksgiving, I was trying to explain to my relatives what Djangy is, which is really difficult to someone who is not familiar with the industry at all. The reaction I got from them was sort of, "Ah, yeah. Whatever." Maybe I just did a poor job of explaining it. But it's so far removed from what my family is educated about. It was very much, "Oh, there's Dave, working on his little experiments," and then when Heroku announced they were being bought for $200 milllon, I went back home again and all of a sudden mine was a very legitimate project! All of a sudden, it was no longer just, "He's working on his pet project," it was, "He's working on a company." It was interesting to see their reactions change.

As Heroku was acquired, a whole host of competitors popped up for different languages and frameworks. PHP has two or three of them now. Python is by far the one that has the most competition now, though, and we were first, I think. So we still have lots of people signed up waiting for their beta invitation. I think we have close to 700 users; very few of them are paying customers at this point. But we've basically decided we don't want investment, we don't want to hire people. At this point, up until we get investment, it's still very much an experiment. It's still in beta; if we stopped now nobody would really care.

Did you guys have any big pivots or changes since founding Djangy?

Not really. Not the actual product. The architecture has definitely had some pivots; it had two complete rewrites.

We started out using Apache with mod_wsgi to run everything, and that's a very monolithic-type system. We were actually running into problems with Apache handling all the different applications and we found some bugs in mod_wsgi pertaining to security; log files were kept open, for example, before forking, and anytime you forked, any application had all access to log files across the entire system.

Were there any points where you guys thought this was going to fail, or where your blood pressure went up?

Early on it was stressful because—and this is a good example of how getting there first isn't always the best, doesn't always mean you'll win—we got there first in terms of the Python community and Eldarion was much more respected. Obviously, it still is. They have credibility; they have a history. I know we don't have a history, nobody has heard of us in the Python community. But while it was definitely a little stressful, it was certainly nothing I lost sleep over.

Have you thought about revenue?

We haven't been pushing that. For the past month and a half we've been really, really focusing on what we are doing, answering questions like, "Are we going to try to flip the company? Are we going to try to get bought, or are we going to build slowly like GitHub?" The only strategy that's going to work now, because there are so many competitors, is to get as many users as you can and flip the company if you want to be successful, and when I say successful, I mean building a very, very profitable company. So Heroku's valuation, I don't know much about how they were valued, but I know that they're the only ones; they were first in this space.

It can be attractive to join a larger company in a very competitive space.

Yeah, of course it is. And because we haven't taken any investment, I have no savings, right? This website is like my lifeblood. It would be nice to have a little more money.

How do you guys split the work?

One of the biggest time sinks—and this is something we're still struggling with—is customer support. As we've grown—we have almost 700 users now—support is the biggest, unexpected task and it's to the point now where we get so many support emails there's no way we can answer them all. It's just impossible, logistically, without having more help or finding some kind of technical solution. We've been looking into building a community around Djangy and having users help themselves and each other. But, in the meantime, we've been alternating days where one person has to interrupt their work whenever a support email comes in and answer it while the other person continues to focus on coding and then we handle business end things as they come in, like taxes, incorporating, faxing things. Then, at the end of the day, we talk about big-picture stuff. We talk about our overall strategy, what our philosophy is, etc.

What about culture?

Culture? God, I don't know. There's no time. To say that we have a culture would not be accurate. We're also two very, very different people. For example, Sameer is not a big party person. I enjoy partying a lot. I don't mean to say he's not fun to be around, he's awesome and funny and smart and all that. We're just different people.

What is your biggest challenge today?

Prioritizing. Figuring out what exactly is the most important thing to work on, right now, because there are so many tasks. There's a mountain of work with something like this: support, fixing bugs that come in, figuring out which features people want versus which features people think they want and figuring out how to sort of meld the two together to something that's going to be successful or worthwhile, especially since there are only two of us, it's all the more important that we don't waste any time.

There are all sorts of things. I constantly think about the user experience, the flow, and how things are designed, what the website looks like, what it feels like to interact through Git, how fast it is, what the text output is. When you're dealing with hackers who use Git everyday it matters what the Git output looks like. So, thinking about that while trying to think about a way to migrate all of our databases from MySQL to PostgreSQL with no downtime is a difficult problem and it requires lots of context switching.

Have you and Sameer had any motivational challenges? Do you ever hit a productivity brick wall?

Over time, we started to work from each other's apartments. We spent about half the time working independently, each of us at our own places, and half the time working together. Whenever we hit productivity problems, just getting back together and working in the same space almost always solved it—I think that's pretty much it.

If a student were interested in doing a startup, what advice would you give them?

Start looking for a cofounder now, and try to identify different groups of people that you identify most with, and that share your philosophy about life in general, what you want out of life. Focus on those kinds of deeper questions, rather than, "How do we make a lot of money?"

I'd also say: get really, really good at building things and try to develop a breadth of skills. One of the most valuable things about working with Sameer is his breadth of knowledge is staggering and that has been very valuable for me; ACM was very much the same thing.

I could walk into the ACM office and people at one end of the room were talking about why MySQL sucks versus PostgreSQL, while other folks would be building touch-table music boxes. One end of the room is talking about filesystems, the other end is talking about graphic design; someone is doing some video editing and other people are working with all sorts of different programming languages, right? We used to have talks about all these really archaic, very unpopular languages, like Prolog and Ada, which was always interesting.

Overall, I'd say surround yourself with people who are smarter than you.

Should non-technical students learn to program if they want to do a technical startup?

That's a hard question for me to answer because I'm a technical person but the average, really good hacker, doesn't want to work with a business person, especially just starting out. It's not necessarily the other person's fault, but from the hacker perspective, the businessperson has no idea how to build software and, so, will always be ineffective at judging how long something will take or how much work it is. From the business person's perspective, the hacker has very little—at least I had very little—understanding of how companies are run, how you incorporate, what it means to be a corporation, how taxes work, what it's like to hire people, what it's like to fire people, how to nurture a culture, etc. So I don't know how to comment on that. It seems easier to learn about business stuff when it comes along than to learn how to hack when you need to build your product.

Can you talk about the time you most successfully hacked some non-computer system to your advantage?

In college, someone was selling donuts in ACM for a fundraiser at $6 for half a dozen. I ended up buying four or five boxes and reselling them for twice the price. I made a wild profit and it took, I don't know, 15 minutes to quadruple my money. I had beer money for the next week.

Knowing what you know now, is there anything you'd go back and tell your younger self?

Yeah, a lot. The biggest thing I would say, is don't worry about failing, it's okay to fail. I think a lot of people still live their lives in this constant grip that failure has. There's this fear that most people have and they don't realize they have it, about failing; about disappointing people or not achieving what they want to achieve. It's a pressure that most people can't really articulate; it was very much there for me, and it's gone now. I know what it's like to fail in very specific ways, in very big ways, and it's not as bad as people make it out to be; it just takes time to realize that.

Sam Odio, Divvyshot

Tags: acquired (Facebook), Y Combinator, anti-school, school worker, programmer, iterate slowly, design-focused

Overview: Divvyshot was created to make group photo sharing easy. After going through Y Combinator in 2009, Divvyshot was acquired by Facebook in April 2010. Just before it was acquired, Divvyshot had 40,000 active and loyal users.

How did you get started with entrepreneurship? Can you recall your earliest experience?

It was definitely my brother Daniel who is 9 years older than me. He was into entrepreneurship—he sold candy bars on the bus ride to school and was always doing stuff like that. I would always emulate him growing up. We lived around DC and so July 4th was a big deal. Everybody was going to Washington DC to see the fireworks, and he would sell sodas to the crowds and make a couple of hundred dollars over the course of the night which when you're 12 years old is an insane amount of money. Of course after he went to college I started doing the same thing.

I started building computers when I was 13 years old, and I was always interested in hardware. My brother saw that and when I was 17 he sat me down and said "Sam, I'm going to show you how to incorporate a business." And so in an afternoon we incorporated my first business. I got into computer repair and I just spent the next year passing out fliers while I was in high school, trying to convince people to pay me 60 bucks an hour just to fix their computers, which for me was good money. I saw the Geek Squad charging $70 and I thought, "I can definitely charge less and deliver a better service."

What was college like?

I actually got deferred and then rejected from every college I applied to, so I ended up going to this school called Longwood University in Farmville, Virginia—like the game, Farmville. It was crazy. There aren't very many computers there, so I found somebody to take over the business in Northern Virginia, and then I started advertising online. This was in 2003: I would advertise through Google Adwords for the DC Metro area and then I realized "Hey, I could do this nationally."

I started advertising nationally and whenever I got a new job in a new major city, I would find a computer technician using Craigslist. Then I'd start targeting that city. In this way I grew city by city and expanded the presence of this computer repair company; eventually we were fixing computers in a dozen cities. That was my first year of college and it was pretty rough for me getting rejected from every school I applied to. It was a really tough experience.

I ended up at Longwood deciding that I still wanted to go to the University of Virginia. In high school, when I learned I had gotten deferred, I decided, "I'm going to do everything I can to get into UVA." So I made a website called "chance-for-odio.com" which basically said "you should let me into your school," and I sent it to the dean of admissions a framed photo that I'd taken. It's still online at http://odio.com/colleges/uva/

Later at Longwood I got a 4.0 so I made a new site "sure-bet-on-odio.com." Eventually I was able to get in but it wasn't an easy experience. It was definitely tough.

So I'm trying to really hard to get into UVA because that's the school I've always wanted to attend, since I was 12, and at the same time I'm running this computer repair business where I was probably making the equivalent of minimum wage. It was a complete failure because 10 people would call me and nine of them would want advice over the phone—and maybe I would get one job and the tech would go on-site and fix the computer. I wasn't good at sales. It was tough because I'd make $40 from that job and would have to spend most of that on advertising.

I remember getting a call at 3:00 AM. I was hanging out at my friend's dorm room, we were just drinking and talking, and it was a computer problem and they wanted help. That's when I had the realization: "I've got to do something else. This is not going to work for me."

At the same time Longwood was actually giving me a really hard time for running a business out of my dorm room. I ran it to pay for school and they were actually making me shut it down. I refused to but they were basically threatening to kick me out of the school if I didn't shut down this business. They suggested actually that I shut it down and I work out of their cafeteria for $5.15/hour. I did the math and I realized: there are not enough hours in the day for me to work at that rate and still go to class unless I didn't sleep.

I thought, "There's no way I'm doing that." I knew I had to do something else though because this computer repair business wasn't working out. That's when I read about the Iraq dinar in the Wall Street Journal. I ended up founding a business around that article. That article paid for pretty much my entire life for the next few years. It paid all of my college tuition; my living expenses; it paid for Divvyshot; it paid for everything. I think that shows that you never know where you'll get your next idea from. I'm probably going to have the Wall Street Journal for the rest of my life.

It all came from that one article. I think the article was written in 2004. I read it and it was about people exchanging the Iraqi dinar. I thought, "Hmm, that's just something that I could do." I could trade the dinar but at the time I had only $500, so I tried to convince everybody I knew to loan me another $500 to start this business. To buy enough dinars to be able to resell them you have to buy them in bulk. That means spending about $900 in dinars. If you bought anything less than that then you wouldn't really be able to make money when you resold them in the US.

So finally I convinced my roommate Jeff. Everybody thought I was crazy like, "What the hell is this," right? I convinced my roommate Jeff to go in with me. We threw up a website, spent a hundred dollars on Google AdWords and bought some dinars. Then I actually had to leave school for summer vacation.

I left on vacation and within the first week we had sold the inventory that we had purchased four times over and that's when I realized that we might be onto something. Before that everybody including myself thought it was just a crazy idea that would never work.

As soon as I built the site and as soon as that happened I realized, "Hey, there might be something going on here," and that's actually where I developed what I call the 'see if it sticks' model. It's basically where you just throw something out there and see if catches on. So in an afternoon we built the site and then we were all of a sudden overwhelmed with orders and that's when we realized, "This is something we've got to build up."

We had to turn off AdWords so that we could spend the rest of the month filling orders that were already placed. It kind of went from there. That was pretty much what I spent the rest of my college undergraduate years doing—trading dinars.

Interesting story, we actually shut the site down six months after we started it. We decided that the opportunity was gone, nobody else wanted this, the market was saturated, whatever. This was in 2004 and since we made the decision to shut the company down, the company had grossed 99% of its revenue. When I shut it down, I didn't turn off the site. The site was $10 a month to keep online so I thought, "I'll just leave it up."

We just shut everything else down. We turned off our phone number, we stopped advertising, and so on but I kept getting orders until finally I decided to start it back up and I decided I'd get a little bit more serious about it and that's when things took off. With dinars, maybe six months after I'd gotten started, my competitor got started. They executed well. They're currently doing over $300 million a year in revenue today and the only reason we're not in that position is because we just weren't serious about it.

This happened to me a few times with a few different companies. So now I still think it's important to just throw something online and see if it takes off but spend a week building it up even if it's just a landing page. Spend an afternoon building out a landing page, put it online, turn on Google Adwords and see if anything comes out of it. But once you make the decision that it's a good idea then you have to throw yourself into it for at least two years to turn it into anything.

That's probably the most important thing I learned from that experience—that you need to spend at least 2 years on something to really turn it into anything. I took that two-year lesson from the dinars business and I applied it towards Divvyshot which was my next startup. I told myself in 2008 that I would spend at least 2 years on Divvyshot before giving up and so I started Divvyshot in 2008, got into Y Combinator, launched on TechCrunch in May 2009.

We released a thousand alpha accounts, they went within a couple of hours but nobody came back. Nobody used the product. At the same time I was trying to raise money. This was right after Y Combinator ended and I just couldn't raise money. No investor was interested. So I spent basically the next six months working on the product and finally I decided I would have to hire people to work with me; this was too much for me to do by myself.

At the time people were basically telling me to shut Divvyshot down. I could see in people's faces they didn't believe in Divvyshot and it was a really demoralizing experience. It was definitely what PG calls the trough of sorrow. You do your initial launch and then nobody uses your product and you try to figure out how to fix this. Luckily though I was kind of prepared for that.

I knew there was going to be a tough start. I would give myself two years in that position without any positive external feedback and I would continue working on the product, and if nothing happened after 2 years maybe I'd shut it down.

So at the end of the first year things aren't going well. That's when I remember this lesson and I decide, "Okay, I'm going to need to hire somebody else." I take basically everything I have and invest it into Divvyshot to hire a designer and a developer, and I tell them, "Listen, I have enough money to pay your salaries for six months." There were three of us, me, Paul Carduner, and Michael Yuan.

We have six months to basically turn this into something that users love. It was a six-month sprint. After six months we did everything we could and then we re-launched the site and launched our iPhone app. We went from 1,000 users to 10,000 users in the course of a week. That was pretty huge for me. I remember it was actually Christmas Eve when we hit the 10,000-user mark and that was huge because I think getting from no users to 10,000 users is pretty hard, sometimes impossible. Once you've got 10,000 users it's much easier to get to 100,000; and the same from 100,000 to 1 million.

I think it was December 2009 when we were at 40,000 by the time we sold to Facebook in early 2010.

How did you jump from 1K to 40K users so fast?

The iPhone app was a large part of that. We launched the iPhone app and then we got a lot of positive press about the Divvyshot launch. Michael completely redesigned the product and then Paul built it out, it was essentially completely a new site and the press loved it. Ultimately a majority of the fans came from the iPhone app. We were featured in the app store and that was huge for us.

A friend of yours mentioned that you started a business fraternity?

I sat down with my friend Omar Bohasali and we came up with a list of everything we thought hackers would want: huge monitors, projectors, comfortable chairs, nice desks, etc. We just went out and bought it all, and we converted my apartment into a hacker house, as a way of attracting these guys. And so that's how we found John Devor. John and I ended up moving out to California and we started another one. The hacker house on Poe Street was our second iteration.

The weird thing about the Charlottesville place was that I lived there but nobody else did, and so it was kind of weird that people would be working at all times and I'd be walking around in my bathrobe or whatever. It's better that either everybody lives there or nobody lives there. I remember one night at 3:00 AM, I brought a bunch of girls back to my place and there were five dudes hacking in my living room. It was just awkward for them.

What was the work schedule like in the early days?

So when I was doing Y Combinator, I really, really wanted Divvyshot to be successful. Actually, I was a little obsessed. It was almost a little unhealthy: so what happened is that I was at the hacker house, I would fall asleep at 1:00 or 2:00 AM after coding all day and then I'd wake up at 7:00 or 8:00 AM. That's unusual because I usually need at least 8 hours, but I couldn't sleep. My mind was so active; I was always thinking about what I needed to be doing. I felt compelled to get up and go to my desk. You could draw a triangle between my desk, the bathroom and me and it felt like I wouldn't leave that area for days.

It was just because it was so important to me. It was crazy how much I wanted this. That was a little insane and that was kind of how Divvyshot got started. Then I tried to slow down a little bit after Y Combinator. I kind of got into a routine and then when I brought Paul and Michael on we had office space and that ended up working out pretty well. It was a little bit less crazy than in the hacker house. Still long hours but Paul and Michael were both great. I think the three of just got along really well.

Were there any points where it was particularly stressful or you thought Divvyshot would fail?

I thought it was going to fail the whole time. The thing that's really hard as an entrepreneur is you have to piece apart whether or not you're just insane or whether or not you've got a genius idea. I still don't know the answer to that, and I think most entrepreneurs don't know how to do that either. When you're in a job it's different: you have a boss that's telling you whether or not you're doing a good job.

My girlfriend was telling me to shut down Divvyshot around a month before I sold it. Literally a month before the acquisition she was telling me that it was basically worth nothing. Most of my friends had no idea whether or not Divvyshot was going to go anywhere. I didn't have any idea as to what it was going to become.

If an undergraduate student came to you today and asked for advice on how to start a startup, what would you tell that person?

I would tell him that nobody knows what they're talking about. Anybody who gives you advice: they've been thinking about whatever you've thinking about for about a sum total of five minutes. So take whatever they tell you with a grain of salt.

I'd also make sure they understand the trough of sorrow. That's the only thing that got me through Divvyshot was being prepared for the trough of sorrow. This is basically a theory by Paul Graham that after your launch there's a period—it can be 2 months or 2 years—where your startup won't get traction. This will be one of the hardest times for you and your startup because you won't be getting much positive reinforcement from your users.

The final piece of advice I'd give would be something to the effect of: build a company that's profitable. Build a company that's going to make money and this is actually advice that the former CEO of Snapfish gave me.

Photo sharing is a really hard industry to be in. It's extremely hard to monetize. For your first startup, if you can build something that actually has a business model you're going to be much better off. Whenever somebody is pulling out a credit card, you want to be involved in that in some way. There are plenty of ways you can make that process easier and they're all monetizable. If you're doing something around that then you're golden.

Did you ever struggle with productivity or have motivation problems?

Not really because I had hit brick walls with my previous projects and I just told myself I wasn't going to make the same mistake again. I just refused to entertain the idea. Back in early 2004 I had started a wiki service similar to PBwiki and Jotspot (which was founded a few months earlier but I hadn't heard about). I thought that was a good idea, but I ended up not executing. I worked on it for a couple days a month and then let the project go stale. I wasn't serious and I was out-executed by my competitors. That happened to the first 3 companies I started, and each time I got a little bit better.

I've always felt that I've had to act on ideas. My problem was not whether or not I had an idea; it was just sticking with it. I told myself with Divvyshot that I was just going to focus on the execution.

What was your best non-computer hack?

Hacking school. I did the minimum amount of work required to get the grades I wanted. I mean, at the same time I was running these businesses and all I really wanted was a B average, so I hacked school to get a B average in about 4 hours a day. If I got all A's then I probably worked too hard and I wasn't using my time efficiently.

First, I crammed for all tests 12-24 hours before. The way I saw it, a typical test was one hour. It shouldn't take me much more than 12 hours to learn one hour's worth of material; if it took me more than 24 hours to learn the material than I wasn't studying the right stuff.

So usually, the night before a test, I'd sit down with 3 things: a bunch of caffeine pills, a few sheets of paper, and all of my notes/course material. I'd then try to figure out exactly what was going to be on it. I'd use clues from the professor and the material to create a "'cheat sheet' that was a few pages long. Usually it was pretty easy, the professors were unintentionally obvious at hinting at what would be on the test and I got good a picking up on that. Then I'd spend the rest of the night studying that cheat sheet.

I also was very active in class. Time spent in class was a sunk cost, so I tried to spend it as efficiently as possible. My goal was to spend no time outside of class on school (other than cramming before a test). I'd either be doing work for another class or I'd be extremely active in discussion. I'd try to learn as much about the material as possible so that I wouldn't have to spend time studying later. I always tried to avoid that feeling of being lost in class, the feeling where you have no idea what the professor is saying. That's the point when you get in trouble and the best way to avoid it is to ask a lot of questions.

Finally, I procrastinated on everything. This was actually great for me because it'd force me to work efficiently. Eventually I learned how to procrastinate until a few hours before something was due and then just get it done. It wouldn't be great, but it'd be good enough.

Some people feel like this approach meant that I wouldn't learn the material and that school would somehow be a waste. To that I have two points: the first is that most of what I learn is outside of school. For most professions little of what you do after school involves course material. Of the stuff I learned in school, most of it was how to work with others and manage my workload. My second point is that by being extremely active in discussions I actually would often gain a better grasp of the concepts in class than my peers.

Justin Kan, Justin.TV

Tags: Y Combinator, VC funded, businessperson, school worker, Ivy League, major league player (#1 live video site, Alexa top 500), hiring

Overview: Justin.TV was founded in 2006 and originally started out as calendar software in Y Combinator. Justin.TV has since raised $7 million in venture capital and is now the single largest live video site online with over 40 million users a month and nearly half a million channels broadcasting live video. Most recently, they launched a new product called Socialcam: a mobile app that lets anyone easily share video from their phone.

How did you get started with entrepreneurship? You can go back as far as you can remember.

It started off in 2004 when two college friends of mine and I were thinking about ways that we could try something new. We were seniors in college and we didn't really have anything to do. We thought this was the perfect time to try to start a business, and we had this idea for this calendar. Everyone had seen Gmail and that was new in 2004, and my friend said someone should make a calendar like this. We started working on what we called Kiko; it's like Microsoft Outlook but online. After a couple of months we had a prototype and that's when somebody told us about Y Combinator.

Y Combinator was new at the time, so it wasn't something that everybody knew about. At the same time, I was a senior at Yale and they didn't have a big startup scene or anything like that. People didn't really know much about startups. We were amazed that somebody would actually give money to companies to get funded or to get them off the ground. We didn't really understand how that entire economy worked. We applied to Y Combinator and went up to Cambridge for an interview. I think this is documented on my blog, but I remember they said, "you guys look promising but your idea sucks." So we went up there and talked to Paul and they accepted us; that's how we got started. We spent a year and a half working on Kiko and eventually that failed so then we started Justin.TV and it's been four and a half years since then.

Do you remember doing anything when you were younger in middle school or high school building stuff or selling stuff?

A friend and I wrote this program called Gravity Simulator. It was this 3D physics program written in Visual Basic, which is the worst for any sort of graphic manipulation. We were taking this class at this community center about programming, so we started working on this app. We'd been taking the class for a couple of years. It was one of those things where you could just show up during these certain hours and this dude who worked at Microsoft—who was kind of a mentor of ours early on—would just teach kids how to program whatever they wanted. That was pretty awesome. It was our first exposure to programming, and I've never been a very strong programmer to be honest. I've never been the guy who's carrying the team in that respect.

The gravity project basically simulated the universe and it was like a little 3D physics model. You could create these planetary bodies and then put in initial mass and velocity and it would run the gravity simulation of what would happen. You would try to get these orbits going on and try to make stable planetary solar systems that would have actual orbits.

Of course in practice that never really worked well, but it was actually pretty good considering we were high school students. We thought about how we could monetize it or sell it. I remember meeting with a lawyer and thinking about setting up a company, but nothing never really came of that except that we were kind of exposed to programming and the joys of creating something. That was probably the first thing, I think.

Do you remember how you got interested in computers or technology?

It was probably through playing computer games. I always loved playing video games and I grew up with Colonization. I remember in that same class we tried to make some other games but obviously nothing ever really worked out. I feel like there are lots of kids today that are starting their startups at 18 and they are really competent, but that wasn't me. I didn't really understand anything about businesses or actually writing software that other people would use for a long time. I made small things: I think I wrote a Dungeons and Dragons dice program, but nothing really big.

What kind of classes did you take in college? What were your favorites and least favorites?

In college I was a physics and philosophy major. I was pretty good at getting decent grades, but I don't think I was very good at taking advantage and really learning much about the topics. Yale is a liberal arts school; it's much more about trying to give people a well-rounded education, but I've always been one of the types of people who—I've got to live it, and with academic subjects it's kind of hard for you to do that. So I feel that most of my interest in startups and technologies really came after the fact, after graduating, and wasn't really assisted in any way by my college experience. The good thing about college was that we were able to have a lot of time to network, and I met my cofounders there.

Did you go into Yale knowing anyone as a freshman?

Emmett, one of my cofounders at Justin.TV and I have known each other since the seventh grade and we went there together. I wanted to go across the country because it was more of an adventure. I think I was going to go to the University of Washington because I'm from Seattle and my dad just retired from there, but I wanted to try something new.

Did you do anything outside of class in college?

In college I played rugby for a year. That was fun. That was probably the best thing I did. Other than that, I was in the Asian student organization for a year or two. I was also in the Yale Entrepreneurial Society and we applied to their business plan competition, and that gave me a really stilted view on entrepreneurship because we had to write a business plan. I'm not saying that you shouldn't plan, but for me, I look back on our original Kiko business plan and we didn't know anything, right? You have to learn the industry by being in it, not by writing about it.

How did you meet your cofounders?

One of my cofounders I knew from back home, and then he went to Yale with me. The other, Michael, was one of my college friends and he was a very good salesperson. He didn't join us on our calendar business, but we had talked to him while I was doing that and he was always listening and interested. Eventually when we started Justin.TV he was convinced to come out and start it with us. With Kyle, we emailed the MIT CS list because we needed someone to do some hardware for us because with the original Justin.TV show we wanted to build a physical piece of hardware to broadcast.

So you met Michael from the dorms?

Yeah, from the dorms.

How did you pay your way through school?

I worked in the summer at a law firm. It wasn't really anything glamorous; I was basically a file clerk. I guess it did tell me that I never wanted to do that again.

Did you take time away from class to party, go streaking in the quad, etc. or was it mostly academics?

I was that guy who was running—actually I did that. I definitely had a lot of fun. I spent most of my college years having fun and I did party a lot. I feel like my experience was largely social and I'm lucky because I was able to make a lot of great friends there. I think that was probably the thing I gained the most from college: it was really the friends that I came out with and could rely on for various things.

It seems like it's between letting serendipity happen where you don't look for cofounders but you sort of bump into them or it's the opposite approach where you're actively looking for cofounders.

I think that the best thing to do is go places where there's a lot of smart people, and I think my key to like being a little more—I don't like to say that I've been successful because I think there's still a long way to go, but to get to where I have been, the thing I've primarily done is find the smartest people possible and stand next to those people. It's like the old saying, "You want to be the worst musician in every band you play."

Did the idea for Kiko come up as a business plan competition? Was it just something you guys wanted to build personally?

No, it wasn't something we wanted to build personally and that I think was a big problem actually, because it's a lot easier rather to build something where you can be one of the early customers because it reduces the feedback iteration cycle. For us, we had thought that it would be a cool thing and something that would be needed, which turns out to be true. Millions of people use Google calendar. We just didn't execute very well.

We didn't really understand the space strategically because nobody actually wants calendar without email. We didn't know what we were building, which turned out to be a big problem.

For Justin.TV, how did that idea come about then? What was that point where you said, "I want to start streaming my life to a bunch of people on the Internet?"

We were winding up Kiko and we didn't know what we wanted to do next. We were pitching Paul Graham on another idea where we let people publish their blogs to print: you could make a magazine of your blog, and he thought that nobody would use that. He asked us what other ideas we had and I'd been talking about this idea for Justin.TV, which would be this new form of reality TV show entertainment, and then he said, "Okay, that sounds interesting. You guys are passionate about it." That was kind of like incredulous that anyone would actually give us money to do that. But we walked out of there with a check for $50,000 and that's how Justin.TV started. After we had raised money, we recruited Kyle and Michael so I knew I pretty much had to do it at that point.

What kind of technology was inside of this camera you were carrying around?

It was basically a computer that streamed video from a camera over 3G. Basically you can do that from your iPhone now, but I was carrying around a 25 pound backpack. That became obsolete pretty quickly.

How long did that take to build?

It took us six months: we started in October and we launched it in March.

How did you spread the word at first?

We put it on TechCrunch. It's a pretty easy story, right? We got picked up on local news like CBS news, and then it was a newspaper story because we knew this reporter for the SF Chronicle, and then it got picked up by the Today Show and G4TV and a bunch of other things. So in the first three weeks, it exploded.

Did you do anymore fundraising after that first check?

We raised $250,000 our angel round right before we launched.

What was fundraising like? Was that a positive or negative experience?

It was pretty positive considering what we were pitching in retrospect. I think we got a really good deal. We got investors like Mike Maples and Paul Buchheit. Later, we raised a few rounds of VC. The hardest part of the process was when we actually had to raise in 2008, and we raised right before the market crashed, but it was on the way and it was definitely a lot harder. I'd say the angel round and our first VC round was a lot easier. Michael, my cofounder who is the CEO of the company, he was the one who did and still does the fundraising.

The 150K from Yuri Milner that recently started happening, do you think that's a good or bad thing for founders?

I think it's really great for founders; I think every single person took it except for one, maybe someone who already was going to raise a bigger round anyways. I definitely don't think there's anything bad about that for founders. I think that it's questionable as far as whether that's a sustainable model, because Milner's not getting Paul Graham prices for that money. But at the end of the day if they're investing $500 million in Facebook, it's not that much money. You're only talking about $12 million a year.

Didn't you guys sell Kiko at one point? Were you able to use that able to help you cover living expenses in California?

Kind of—we still live extremely poor. After we sold Kiko, after taxes we had to pay an asset sale, so it was double taxed and it wasn't that much money. We just put it in the bank and didn't think about it. We basically lived off that $50,000 for six months. We were four people to a two-bedroom and we were not spending any money.

Any advisors when you were fundraising?

Sam Altman helped us a lot. He's probably the primary one. Paul Graham helped us too.

How did you continue to get growth on Justin.TV? Have you done anything to promote it?

I think it's just kind of viral by nature. Really, the hard part for us is learning to scale the product. We were not very experienced engineers at the outset of this, and even though I think we have extremely talented and smart people, we've learned through the past four years how to scale. It was really focusing on the technical side for a long time and making sure we got that right.

Did you ever make any big pivots?

When we started off this show it was like a reality TV show, and we pivoted to a platform approach. When we launched, a month later we got a response but nobody was launching and we got two pieces of feedback. People were like, "You're extremely boring, how can I do something like this myself?" So that's why we thought, "Maybe people want to broadcast stuff. We should allow them to do that."

Was it ever frustrating? You had this camera attached to yourself 24/7 streaming everything you were doing. I don't know how long you did that but was there a point where you said, "I've got to figure something else out"?

Yeah. That was about a month in. We were trying to do whatever it took to get traffic and we couldn't really hack it as a content creator. We weren't really experienced in content creation.

Were there any panic moments? Did you ever think Justin.TV might fail?

Yeah. That happens every week. That's a natural part of a startup, and startups are totally bipolar. There was a great article on Tim Ferris' blog about how to capitalize on the bipolar nature of startups. When you're in growth mode, you should be out selling and fundraising and recruiting. When you get to the trending downwards mode, you should be doing budgets and more conservative stuff. When you're in the low, low point where everything is going wrong you should be doing nothing. You should just go and find moral support from your friends and don't make any major decisions.

I thought that was really insightful because I've always heard about the bipolar nature of startups. Every three months I'll be like, "Oh my god, things are horrible," and then a month later I'm riding high because we're about to release something awesome. And then we release it and it doesn't get as much traction as we wanted, and then we feel bad again and then it starts picking up, and then everything is great. And really figuring out how to cope with that and to harness it is a very important part of running your own company.

It's interesting you bring that up. I suspect that some of the founders I haven't heard from who I wanted to interview may be going through this phase, and that's why they probably don't want to be interviewed right now. Actually, I spoke to one founder who told me that explicitly—he said he wasn't ready for an interview because things were really stressful. You always wonder if there's some secret trick that people use but I did read that article and really liked it.

I like the idea that you would do different things at different times.

Was there a point where you noticed revenue increasing? If so, what might have caused that?

What happens is that when we start measuring a stat, and we say, "This is important," it always goes up. We've done that for several stats including growth, number of broadcasters, revenue. Someone told me once "You can't manage what you don't measure," and that is definitely true.

How do you split the work up? What's the work schedule like at Justin.TV?

When we started off, everybody was working around the clock. Some people were on the 'wake up at 5:00 PM, go to sleep at 5:00 AM' schedule. Over time we've normalized it. People are generally in the office 10:00 AM to 6:00 or 7:00 PM, five days a week—it's not crazy here. We just did a product sprint to release Socialcam where we were working overtime but that's something you only pull out of the bag once every couple of years. For us, we've got 26 employees at the company. It's more of a real company now; people are assigned jobs. With the founders, we're still all the management at the company, we have a few other executives but we're most of the management and so we often rotate jobs just because of what the company needs.

Six months ago, Kyle—who is one of my cofounders—was really focused on our product direction because that was what we needed, and I was really focused on general management because we were pretty bad at management in the past. As that has evolved, as we've grown over six months he'll focus on something else, and I'm focused more on Socialcam. People have different responsibilities and those get passed around.

What's a typical day like for you?

I spend all my time in email, on my to-do list, using Workflowy, in the calendar on Yammer, and in Google Docs. My job is glorified product manager. I help figure out specs; who should be working on what; trying to remove barriers for people to be productive. I also come up with the PR plans; the strategic plans for where the product is going, who we should be talking to with. I'm also working on how we get more customer feedback from our new apps and dig into the stats.

It's kind of a mixed bag, and that's the way I like it. I'm more of an ideas guy than I am an operator. I'm pretty bad at operating something over time and making sure something gets done consistently. I'm probably better at finding creative solutions to various things or coming with a short term plan that's going to drive towards a specific goal and so that's kind of the role that I play at the company.

What's the biggest challenge today for Justin.TV?

We've gotten the business to a certain point and it's pretty good, but our goal was always to kind of create a business that's really, really big and so we are working on trying to figure out how we get our business to be a billion dollar business.

What's the culture of Justin.TV like?

I read an article that I thought was really good on Hacker News that said, "Culture is your values plus your dysfunctions," and I think that that definitely describes the culture at Justin.TV.

We're not perfect but we want to make it a great place for engineers to work. And we want to actually enjoy work. Those people should be working on the product.

I would say the dysfunctions are: we're a very opinionated group of people and often times, it's the place where people love to debate everything. There's a lot of what we like to call Yale arguments. It's the type of argument people have at Yale where both sides don't know anything about the actual given topic but they still feel inclined to debate it. So I think we do a little bit of that.

I think there are very good aspects and some things that are probably not as good but I want to be perfectly honest about it. **Ever have motivational problems where it's hard to get work done or you just hit a productivity brick wall and if so, how do you get around that?**

I think it's important to have a balanced life. We just did a sprint, so that's why it's on my mind so much but in general people want to do other things and we try to make this a fun place to work, right? We're all going on a company vacation to Hawaii in a month, the entire team for a week.

That was something that we wanted to do because everybody has been working really hard and we feel like we've accomplished a lot in the past year. Balance is super important otherwise even the most passionate people burn out and it's very easy especially for smart and motivated people to burn out because they're willing to do the work of multiple people all the time. I've definitely experienced that before at Justin.TV and Kiko and it's really important that you know your own strengths and you know your own limits.

Any tips for hiring? Is there something that tells you someone is a good candidate or a bad candidate?

Every technical person needs to answer a technical problem before they can have an interview. Only people who are motivated to work in your company and enjoy programming are going to bother doing that, right? You can also distinguish people who are good programmers from bad or mediocre programmers by using code challenges.

You should also go with your gut. If we had listened to our gut in every case I don't think we'd ever have been wrong. Another important thing is you should definitely fire fast because everybody is going to make mistakes and it's not good for the employee or you to employ somebody who is not doing a good job. It's definitely not good for the team.

If you could give a single piece of advice to an undergrad,

what would it be? Maybe they're non-technical and they want to do a technical startup, what advice would you offer?

Just start out doing something. The first version of Groupon was a WordPress blog; you don't need to be a super hacker to make that happen. You can start a business online with very limited knowledge, you just have to approach it scientifically and really discover what people want by iteration. You can teach yourself enough to learn how to program, like I did. When I started Kiko I taught myself everything from scratch, and I still consider myself a shitty programmer and I wouldn't hire myself as a programmer. But I always say if you're not a better developer than I am, I'm the low bar for developing, like the low, low bar.

So just get started and start trying to do something. My brother is in the same position right now actually. He's playing around with his own stuff. He's not a developer but I think he's interested in the web and it's exciting to see that you can get things done, you have to build simple things and get started without being a great coder.

Why would someone want to work at Justin.TV?

I think we're doing revolutionary stuff in video that touches a lot of people. For someone who is smart and motivated I think it's a really fun place to work. Obviously I'm not objective in any way on that and you should get independent verification but I think if you do the research you'll find out people really enjoy working here and they feel like they have the opportunity to learn a lot here.

Ashvin Kumar, Blippy

hvin Kumar
founder, Blippy.com

Tags: programmer, coincidental, hiring, side project, VC funded, iterate quickly, design-focused

Overview: Blippy started in 2009 as a place where you can share what you're buying with your friends and see what everyone else is buying. Blippy has raised $12 million and as of 2010, users on the service are sharing over $500,000 in purchases every day. I met Ashvin through Bill Clerico at WePay and learned firsthand what it feels like to be humiliated in just about any sport. Ashvin and his cofounder Chris rapidly iterated through several ideas before coming up with Blippy and when I first saw the prototype I wasn't sure whether people would actually enter their credit cards or not, but today it doesn't seem like such a strange thing to do.

When did you get started with entrepreneurship?

I was messing around with computers from very early on. First bubble in the late '90's—there just weren't enough programmers in the Valley—I was getting paid pretty healthy amounts of money, for a high school kid, to write java applets. So that was my first taste of how the Valley operated and how there was such a need and demand for people who knew how to develop products. That got me really excited and set the tone for what I wanted to study and what I wanted to do after I graduated.

I didn't even know Java before I started; I only knew Basic and I knew some C programming that I taught myself for fun and they said that they needed something better. They were like, "do you know Java?" and I was like, "yeah". The shit is so easy to learn from a book and so when they said they needed xyz, I just went out and bought a couple of Java books, figured it out, got paid. Make the money son.

How did you get into computers?

It was games, for me. I played Multi-User Dungeons (MUDs) growing up and the first thing I ever compiled was open source MUD; that was like the first thing I started messing around with and that was pretty much how I learned C, but I quickly got over that and wanted to write other stuff, other than just MUDs.

When you were at Stanford, what kind of classes were you taking?

Once I got to college I was pretty confident that I wanted to do computer science. I like broad educations and so it was either computer science or—there's a major at Stanford called Symbolic Systems, which is a combination of computer science, psychology, philosophy, and linguistics. It's very cognitive, almost like applied cognitive science, that's probably the best way to think about it. So I considered doing that, but as soon as I went to my first psychology class I just couldn't sit through the whole lecture so I scrapped that idea and ended up just focusing on computer science and I minored in linguistics. So I really enjoy cognitive science.

What were you favorite and least favorite classes?

I didn't like psychology; I just found it to be super fuzzy. It didn't feel like enough of a science to me, at least at the level I was at. I was taking Psychology 101 and, I'm sure it gets very scientific as you spend more time, but the first class was just so dumbed down, I couldn't take it. Whereas linguistics to me was always— and this might be a function of how they teach at Stanford—like math with words, which was awesome. I ended up spending a lot of time taking linguistic classes and computer science classes.

Did you do any startups or projects on the side while at Stanford?

No. There just wasn't enough time for it. Most of my time outside of class was spent doing something related to soccer because I played soccer at Stanford, so we had travel and practice, which is a huge time commitment.

Did you go into Stanford knowing anyone?

Stanford is right across the street from my high school so I knew some kids from my high school. But for the most part, my early social circle was everybody—when you're playing on the soccer team the season starts prior to school starting, so I was there 2 months before classes started and the guys I generally hung out with were my freshman class and my soccer team. So that was kind of my social circle, it was pretty much most of the college actually.

237

I had a hard time keeping up with school because the commitment to soccer was so high. A lot of the guys from the team are out playing pro right now; it's a very serious commitment. So I ended up not playing my senior year because I had to graduate. I played through my junior year and then decided to call it quits so that I actually could finish up my course load.

So at Stanford, you weren't actively looking for cofounders or thinking about startups?

Not at all. When I was there I very much was not thinking about what I was going to do after Stanford; it was very much *in the moment*. It was all about what classes I was taking that quarter and then most of my time was spent figuring out how to get better at soccer.

Did you take time away from class to relax?

I think you go through your freshman year and you kind of try to figure out what's fun for you and what's not. During my freshman year we'd go to parties, but I realized pretty quickly that wasn't my scene. I ended up not doing a lot of that stuff; I wasn't a heavy partier. As I developed a close group of friends we would just hang out together. There were a couple of guys that were also doing computer science, but for the most part they were doing all sorts of different things.

Did you have a lot of jobs in college? What happened towards your senior year as you were graduating?

The summer after my freshman year I needed to find a job that would keep me on campus and give me flexibility to train because they're intent on you training pretty hard over the summer and if you get a 9 to 5 job, it really affects your ability to get better at soccer over the summer. So, I found a job at a lab on campus, doing bioinformatics stuff and I could do it on my own time. I split time and did that for a few hours a day and the other part of the day I'd come out to the field, train, run some soccer camps, that kind of stuff. So it was a summer that was split between programming Java in this bioinformatics lab and training; that was my first summer.

My second summer, I thought I'd do something different. I was the technical web guy for a team of guys that went to Botswana to a refugee camp to do some teaching. I ended up teaching basic computers, and for the people that knew computers already, I taught Quick Basic just as a way to introduce them to some notion of applied programming. So I ended up doing that for about a month then I came back and I trained the rest of the time.

At the end of my junior year, after I quit playing soccer, I felt like I needed a big company experience and so I did an internship at Amazon for a few months; that was my first experience figuring out, "alright what do I want to do when I graduate? Maybe I want to go to a big company." So I went to Amazon for a few months, which was awesome, they treated us really well, got paid great, had a lot of fun. It's one of those environments where you get pushed pretty hard but if you make a mistake nobody gives a shit; it's not a big deal. You can still have a good time, still party; you take it as seriously as you want to. You can take it seriously two days out of the week and the other three days have fun. So that was the experience at Amazon, but I realized I didn't really want to do that on a full-time basis. They offered me a full-time job but I declined without even knowing what I wanted to do after that. I had no idea what I wanted to do; I just knew I didn't want to do the corporate thing.

Halfway through my senior year, I said, "let me find a startup to go to", and that's when I started poking around trying to find something interesting. I didn't know what; I wanted to work at a startup; I just wanted to work on a great team.

Around the time that you graduated, what were you doing?

I had a lot more time after I quit soccer; I had a ton of time, way too much time. I remember working on a bunch of small little projects during my junior and senior years. I had this deep fascination—and I still do—with sports betting, and I basically downloaded a ton of data and sliced and diced sports information, particularly in baseball, to see if I could come up with patterns I could eventually use for betting purposes. I wanted to take the analysis, I did the bioinformatics type of analysis, or the financial analysis, and applied that to sports betting, because the amount of data in sports is so rich and it was fun to slice and dice the data. I think I hacked that together in Java or Perl.

My senior year, on my way to graduating, I was trying to figure out what I wanted to do so I met a bunch of small teams; I actually spent a couple of months working at a hedge fund in San Francisco, did that for 2 or 3 months. I was trying to figure out what was exciting to me. At the same time I was meeting a few small startups and just getting a sense for what they were doing and what I found exiting. So that's how I ended up finding my first opportunity—they were friends of friends and I ended up accepting a job well before I graduated and I went there once or twice a week before I graduated and then once I graduated I went full time.

How did the idea of Blippy come about? Did you work on any projects leading up to it?

We had a ton of side projects before Blippy happened. We had between 15 and 20 projects that we did, some of which we never even released the code, it's just sitting there today. For the most part they were all consumer Internet projects that we felt that we could get users for, really quickly, for some reason or another. We felt like we could quickly find out if they were interesting or not.

Our focus was to get users *cheaply*. I think what we realized was, it's really hard to build a product that gets users, especially when you have no money. It's really easy to think about awesome communities online but it's much harder to actually build those from the ground up because of the chicken and egg problem of creating a community or marketplace. Pretty much all of our ideas were around *how do you solve that chicken and egg problem?*

So most of our applications were built around some type of pre-existing channel that was growing; as Twitter grew, we would grow as well, or as Facebook grew, we would grow as well.

I don't know if this is you or not but I thought there was one app that did so well that it got banned from Twitter.

Yeah, I forget what it's called now but it went ridiculously viral, it got banned but we just repackaged it out as Fun140 and made it not as aggressive. Now Fun140 is in the top two or three hundred apps on Twitter with 1.1 or 1.2 million followers.

We were pretty fortunate in that the first project we did was Userfly, and that actually gave us some recurrent revenue. That was enough to basically pay for our servers and barely cover the cost of all our other projects. So we didn't have to worry about money too much. I don't think there was any way we could have survived for a numbers of years, based on the money Userfly was making, but it gave us enough to survive for a year.

Userfly, is that the usability app you guys built?

Yeah, that's the usability app.

Okay and so that gave you some money and then what were you doing after that?

Then as other things started making us some money, we started working on some other stuff. So we were working on GreetBeatz, which was a pretty fun product.

I've used it, it's great. I sent a GreetBeat to Paul Graham and Jessica Livingston once.

Yeah, but it didn't grow like we wanted it to, so we maintained it for a while and kind of gave it up. It was an awesome product. Thinking back now, if we had some money we probably could have made it grow a lot faster. We could have seen it through, but we had no money so we couldn't subsidize stuff, it was really tough to actually grow that marketplace without money.

We always hoped that the fact that music is so viral, that that would be enough to drive us free users, that somebody would have such a great experience they'd share that song with their friends and their friends would come and buy shit for their friends. But the numbers didn't really work out. It sort of worked like that but not enough to keep the growth at a rate where it was where it was always growing. Now if we had some money then, we might have had a chance to learn that faster but it took us a few months to figure that out. Then we did Fun140, which basically shot off like a rocket. We were one of the first developers on the Twitter platform. This is as Twitter was starting to kick into high gear and everybody started to use it and as the first developers on the platform we really had the opportunity to figure out—before everybody else—what worked and what didn't work; we optimized the hell out of it. Just for volume usage, some nights we were picking up 25 or 50 thousand followers, when we were at super viral.

Did you know that it was going to explode?

We didn't know it was going to be like *that*. But it's not that hard to be viral on Twitter. It's just a question of *what's the endgame* and that can be not as interesting. You make some money in advertising but it's not like a valuable product or anything.

What happened after Fun140?

After Fun140 we worked on a few different things; Blippy was kind of a combination of a bunch of different learning experiences. Blippy was just one in the next in line of project ideas that we had that we wanted to pursue. Fun140 was helpful because it made us pretty confident that we didn't want to build the viral product but build the business around a viral product because just getting a lot of users and having a lot of volume is not enough to build the business. That's especially true when the users are not having high-quality interactions with the product; you're not really adding that much value into their lives. But it's really fun to build.

We got a lot of advice from people saying *building a small business is just as hard as building a big business* and so if you're going to do one or the other you might as well build the big business. So then the question was, where do we want to spend our time? And we decided that we wanted to spend our time building something that was a much more valuable business.

I remember when I first heard about the idea of Blippy, I think it was called Blippify back then, it was so out there and crazy.

Now it's not as crazy because you keep hearing about it and I've used it and it kind of grows on you, but at first it was such a weird idea. How did you guys come up with it?

I think it's one of those ideas where you say, "it's so crazy that it just might work." I think academically, the idea was very sound. Twitter had shown there was a lot of value in making information public and building it on an open platform. We also noticed that if you can unlock a new type of data set and make that public to the world or unlock a data set for other people to use and see and explore, you're really adding a lot of value in the world. We kind of looked at *what are the types of data sets that have not been shared with the world yet?* Facebook is a good example for photos where photos were always kind of locked up and Facebook unlocked people's photos and made people want to share their photos in a public way and that did wonders for their company. We looked at that and said, "okay well, the things that people are buying, the places where people spend money has not been unlocked at all." Most of this information is kind of buried behind your bank or in your email like the information is out there and available but it's just so fragmented that nobody has done anything to pull it out, let alone pull it out in a social way.

So Twitter was very much our inspiration in saying, "can we do the same thing for this type of information that Twitter has done with people's thoughts?" Twitter made it really easy to get people's thoughts from their heads onto the Internet and we thought, "alright, let's make it real easy for people to share where they're spending their money and the things that they are buying and let's just share it in a really simple way on the Internet for anybody to be able to access."

So you weren't necessarily scratching your own itch, you used Twitter as a source of inspiration?

Yeah, our thought was not, "oh wouldn't it be cool if I could use this" or anything like that. We weren't building it for ourselves per se. We weren't scratching our own itch with this product. We approached it in a pretty academic way.

So it was you and Chris, your cofounder, early on?

Yeah. So Chris and I, we built the initial prototype in a week or something. We built that pretty quickly. We didn't have a way to get people's bank information so we just wrote a Mint.com scraper so we'd get your Mint username and password; it would login to mint, grab your transactions and then share them with your friends on Blippify, as it was called back then.

How did you and Chris meet?

Chris was a good friend from college but I really got to know him well the summer that I was working at Amazon. We were roommates and he was working at Microsoft.

What was your experience with raising money?

We always wanted to bootstrap. When we first started we had this idea that we wanted to be like 37Signals. We wanted to build a lifestyle business. That goal quickly changed. That's not really what we wanted to do after a while. That's how we started and that's why we looked for businesses where we could kind of start small and just slowly build and build and have a nice lifestyle income, so that's what we told everybody when we were getting started.

In the process of building ideas and sharing with people, we met a partner at Charles River Ventures (CRV). This was in January of 2009 and he actually said they had a spare office at CRV and that he'd be happy for us to move in there for free and just work on projects and get some free lunch and free office space. For him it was just fun to see what kind of stuff we were working on because we told him we were working on a new idea every couple of weeks.

We were pretty clear with him that we weren't planning on raising money and he was like, "that's fine, it's cool for me, regardless." So we moved in to CRV and spent almost a year there, met a lot of new people and built a great relationship with that partner. As we were working on projects and as our goals changed, he saw how we operated and liked the way we operated and thought about products, and he made it clear to us, saying, "whenever you guys are ready if you guys want a raise, no questions asked like we're ready to write a check." So fundraising was never that complicated because we'd spent a lot of time building relationships very early on. We always knew that whenever we had something that we were excited about we could go raise for it the next day. And that's what ended up happening with Blippy; we had Blippy, we got excited about it, we decided it was time to raise, and the check was there.

We shared our ideas with everybody, anybody that would listen to us we shared our ideas with, and that was always really helpful to us.

Do you have any tips for living cheaply in Silicon Valley, as recent college graduates?

I moved in with my parents and Chris moved in with his girlfriend. So we did everything we could to live cheaply. The thing that made it work for us was the fact that we were fortunate enough to build something that made some money early on. We didn't make a lot of money but enough so that if the shit really hit the fan we had enough to get by. We had an infinite runway, basically.

How long did it take to build the first beta for Blippy? How did you spread the word?

The product itself probably took a week or two—we were basically scraping Mint and adding some basic social networking features. For the beta we just told our friends. It was a super interesting product because nobody had unlocked that information before, so there was a lot of excitement around sharing it. The first ten people were the hardest to convince to use the product, but after that it was easy.

Have you guys had any pivots?

We're always looking to pivot to something that makes more sense. When we first started we didn't know how this information was going to be used and so we weren't sure, are people going to use this to share stuff they're buying? Are they going to use it for expense reporting? We even have some non-profits out there that are just using it as a way to stay financially transparent with their constituents.

We wanted to build a generic platform where this could be used in any number of ways and then we would kind of foster the use cases that we thought were the most interesting. Since then we've geared the product more towards subjective information about products, so it has been more about the product reviews and recommendations. That's the kind of pivot that we are in right now, but to this day we're still looking around for novel uses of the platform and as we find them we try and encourage them.

It's almost like Yelp for everything else.

Yeah, you could think about it that way.

Did you ever think Blippy would fail or did stress levels go up?

For Blippy as a company it has been pretty smooth. I think our most stressful time was when we did not have financing, we didn't have a product that people used, we had 15 to 20 projects and few of them were kind of working. But at that stage, all we were really fuelled by was the hope of the next project. And I think those were stressful times.

Now it's a different type of stress, now it's like we've got a product in Blippy, an idea and framework for moving forward and a lot of money to spend time doing it. So it's a different type of stress but it doesn't compare to the stress of basically living with your parents, where you don't have enough money, and you're struggling to find an idea that you can get excited about, that people are going to use.

I remember there was one point where someone wrote about you guys and they said there were a couple of credit cards that got leaked out? Was that difficult to deal with?

That was a pretty bad time for us in the short run. Security was always a major concern for us, we always knew that it was really important to be super secure but we still operate really fast. We write code and we push it, and one time we pushed the code and it exposed this bug for the course of about 12 hours before we fixed it and it ended up biting us in the ass. So at the end of the day we learned to basically develop in a much more defensive manner than before. But as far as how it affected the business, it was really bad in the short run but I think it taught us lessons for the long run.

Was there a point where you guys started to notice revenue taking off?

No, we have no revenue on Blippy. We're still very much in the mode of getting users and still trying to build the product that users are going to really want but we're not thinking about money.

How did you split the work early on and how has that changed?

If there was ever any non-technical stuff, I used to take it. Very early on there wasn't that much non-technical stuff so Chris and I basically split the technical work pretty evenly but as there were more and more non-technical things, whether it was customer development or we wanted to run our ideas by people, I started to take that on more and more. That's how it is today, I do much less technical stuff than Chris does but if Chris needs my help for something, I jump in and help out.

What's the work schedule like? Has it changed?

It actually hasn't changed too much. We have worked pretty much every day since May 2008.

How many hours per day do you work?

It's all we do, we just work. Obviously it's fun, there's not much else in our schedules. Chris and I both live 10 minutes from the office.

How are you so good at basketball if you do nothing but Blippy?

Those skills are learned when you're young! *(Laughs)*

How did Blippy sustain its growth after its initial wave of press?

Press helped a lot, and now we don't market it as much in the press, we kind of let the product grow by itself. We've got a fairly organic community that uses the product and we get more and more users every day so we just try and make sure that the users that are coming in have great experiences and then we encourage them to tell their friends. That's how the product has grown so far.

Have you focused on the viral aspect or have you just focused on product?

We built a lot of viral stuff before and I think the best products are going to grow regardless of whether you build viral shit into them or not. So our goal is to build a product that's going to grow regardless of whether we build in viral hooks or not, that means building a product that has value for people.

What's Blippy's biggest challenge today?

We're still trying to find product market fit. For most consumers in other companies that are not named Twitter and Facebook, it's a struggle to find product market fit, and we're still doing that. You can't be satisfied providing value for a very small niche of people, which is sort of where we're at today. It's a small group of people that get value from our product. We're trying to find a broad audience to get value for the product. So that's the biggest challenge. That's not different than most consumer Internet companies, that's what everybody has to do.

How would you describe the culture at Blippy? How would you describe it to somebody?

It's a good question. I was thinking about this myself the other day because I wanted to have a more formal way of saying it. But, I think the culture is primarily a reflection of the founders. I would say that Blippy is a super fun place to work but at the same time we probably work a lot, but we try and have fun doing it.

As it relates to everyone else, I think we're trying to build the best product possible. But as it relates to what it's like to work here at Blippy I would say it's a fun place to work but that we work our butts off.

Have you ever hit a productivity brick wall?

Everybody deals with productivity brick walls and motivational issues. I think especially as you iterate, looking for product market fit, that's not an easy thing because you're going to end up working on stuff for 2 to 3 weeks at a time—even more— that you just end up throwing away. I think for anybody to work on something for months at a time and then just remove it or throw it away is a very difficult thing to get used to. That obviously leads to motivational issues right? But that's what working on a startup is like; you spend a year doing something, you realize it's the wrong thing and you've got to pivot away from it and do something else and you basically throw a year's worth of work away. Not everybody is going to deal with that in a positive way.

It seems like you've attracted smart engineers and designers, is there something you're doing specifically to find them? Is there something you're looking for when you start interviewing people?

Yeah, if we like you we'll hire you. It's as much about personality as it is about technical skills. I think technical skills are pretty straightforward to learn and so I think if you have like a base level of technical competency you can learn the skills fairly simply. But from the attitude standpoint and from a culture standpoint, I think those are things that *you've just got to have*. You've got to be a good person, you've got to be self motivated, you've got to have curiosity, I think those things are much more important.

Do you have any advice for a student interested in doing a startup?

I think it's actually really valuable to join a start up or join any company for at least a small period of time to understand what it's like. I think that makes a really big difference. And then once you understand the space that you're passionate about and you have some type of direction to it, it's valuable.

One thing that Chris and I did that was not extremely positive, in hindsight, was that we worked on a bunch of ideas across a random amount of spaces. We were trying to do a little bit of everything. I think we were very fortunate that we found something we were excited about as opposed to starting with a general space that we thought was interesting, say, "I'm really interested in e-commerce" or "I'm really interested in group collaborations software"; so, starting a space that you're excited about and then really iterating within that space. I think you get the best ideas when you have at least some semblance of direction.

Do non-technical people need to learn to program?

I always find it strange when a technical person wants to do a non-technical startup or when a non-technical person wants to do a technical startup. It's great for a non-technical person to work at a startup but depending on their appetite they should probably just look to start a non-technical startup. So Groupon is a great example, you don't need to have any type of product skills to build a massive business. Groupon started on a blog or something. So for a non-technical person they should just iterate in the fields that they could be really good, themselves.

You and Chris were rejected from Y Combinator at one point weren't you?

This was like the second project we did; we built one project just to learn Rails. It was something like a weird messaging system. Then we were like, "oh shit, Y Combinator application is coming up" and we applied to Y Combinator with some random idea and we got the interview. We ended up not wanting to build what we applied with. We built something and that wasn't really a good idea either, but people kept telling us, "Paul Graham doesn't care too much about the idea, he's more interested in a team" so we were like, "we'll just let the application be a showcase of our abilities; we know the idea is not that good." We went in there, presented the idea, presented the team and then we got an email from Paul Graham, he was like, "Yo, this idea is not that good" and then he rejected us. That was fine. That was good for us, we were happy to be rejected. It's not the first time in my life that I've been rejected.

I don't care and I don't think anybody else should care either. That's why I hate stories like that; it's like get over it.
Yeah, it's not something to take personally.

Yeah, we don't take it personally whatsoever and I love Y Combinator. I wish they'd accepted us but yeah, shit happens like that, it's not a big deal.
Can you talk about the time you most successfully hacked some non-computer system to your advantage?

Oh yeah, I remember what I put on my application. This is pretty lame but if you write a postcard or a letter and you're sending it to someone else in your town and you just don't put a stamp on it but put the return address as the person, it just gets a "return to sender" for the person. That's what we put on there.
Why do I still use stamps?

I don't think it works to send across the country, but if it's within a small area it's okay. Most of these things get funneled to like some central location in your area and then go out again.
Knowing everything you know now is there anything you would tell your younger self?

I heard Brad Garlinghouse give some advice, which I thought was really good. He basically said, "Look at your career not as a sprint but like a marathon." Personally I'm always looking for the fast way to success—well, not as something I would think of like that, but we can do it now, it can happen right now, we can do it this way it's going to happen like tomorrow and I think that's the wrong way to think about building great products. Great products take time, they grow organically.
So maybe thinking about longer term success in companies?

Yeah and also with your own personal career too—it takes time, building the skill sets accordingly. I saw a great documentary last week called Waiting for Superman. There's this one scene in it, just a random scene but it resonated with me, about this guy—it's about the public school system and teachers—who was an awesome teacher and he's the type of teacher that everybody wants in the United States. He's super motivated, at a certain time he was young he knew he wanted to be a teacher that was his passion so he went to school to be a teacher and he said he came out of school and regardless of how good he was, his first two or three years as a teacher, he was no better than average even though he had met all the best, he wanted to succeed, he was passionate about it, he worked his ass off, he prepared; but it took him 2 or 3 years before he said that he started to learn his craft a little bit. By year 3, year 4, year 5, he said, "*I was good*, I was getting better and by year 5 I was a master teacher", and so I think that really resonates with me because, regardless of how much you want to work hard and regardless of how passionate you are, it *takes time* to be the best, and you just have to keep working at it.

None of these things happen overnight.

That's probably one of the key things that I hope the book communicates because people read these stories about entrepreneurs in these magazines and newspapers and the media glamorizes it and they make it look like it's easy but it's really not. I hope I don't discourage people but I think that's the core theme out of most of the interviews.

Yeah, it's a long process.

Blippy is hiring right now—why would someone want to go work there?

Apart from all the clichés of why you want to work at a startup, we have very high goals for what we're working on; we're very ambitious in our approach too. So I think people that are looking to work on projects that are game changers would be attracted by the stuff we're working on. I think in the way we think about products and the types of things we try and do—as we talked about earlier—when Blippy first came out it was very, very audacious. I think that's the way we think about products here. That takes a certain type of person to feel passionate about that challenge.

Is there something about people that makes you say "I want to talk to this person"?

It's hard to judge from a resume, frankly. But I like people with personality. When I get a resume I look more at the non-technical stuff than the technical stuff they've done. So it's great you have a computer science degree, blah, blah, blah, you know how to program, fine, everybody knows how to do that. I actually look at the other things; so let me see what they minored in, or what aspects of their personality are super fascinating?

You don't make them play basketball do you? *(Laughs)*

No, that's a bonus I guess. But I like to see what else they're passionate about. I think that tells a lot about a person, a lot about their curiosity.

Jake Mintz, Bump

Tags: Y Combinator, VC funded, programmer, hiring, dropout

Overview: Bump makes it easy for anyone to use their phone to interact with the real world—exchanging contact information, for example, is done by simply bumping two phones together. Bump can also allow users to share other data, such as photos, apps, and music. Bump launched in 2008, went through Y Combinator, raised $20 million from investors and since launching has been downloaded over 27 million times with over 8 million active monthly users.

How did you get started with entrepreneurship?

My grandfather is an entrepreneur and I always wanted to follow in his footsteps. I went to college in the Bay Area because I wanted to be around all the tech startups. When I graduated with my electrical engineering degree I didn't feel ready to start my own company and there weren't a lot of really interesting startup jobs in 2004.

So, I went and worked for Texas Instruments for a few years, learned sales, marketing, business development; decided after a few years that I wanted to start my own company, and ended up going to business school, which isn't a traditional route. But when I looked at it I thought, "I have three options: I could try and start a company part time while still working; I could just quit and try to start a company; or I could go to business school, be surrounded by like-minded people, and have a lot of resources at my disposal." I went that third route and it has been everything I had hoped for.

I went to the University of Chicago's Booth School of Business. There were hundreds of people in each graduating class but very few of them were serious about entrepreneurship—those of us that were, had a good, small, tight-knit group. Dave had the idea for Bump a couple of weeks into business school; it came out of the frustration we were having at meeting hundreds of people and trading business cards; it seemed like such an archaic way to exchange information. Why are we still handing around pieces of dead tree or typing phone numbers manually in the 21st century?

So, we spent a few months building a prototype. It was me and Dave—we both have technical backgrounds but weren't doing the development—and Andy, who was a colleague of Dave's for two years before he went to business school. We built a proof-of-concept and put it on the App Store to see if anyone cared. People loved it, which gave us the confidence to drop out of business school and work on it full time.

Did you do any side projects while you were in school?

Yeah, when I was starting high school, back in the days of PHP3, I taught myself web development and built a few projects for fun. I was really into cars and built an aftermarket-part review site, kind of like Amazon reviews, but just a central database for all the aftermarket parts. I built a computer hardware-review site and I did some reviews with my brother. I built a couple more projects in college; I was always building stuff; always loved to build stuff.

I stopped doing paid web development sophomore year because I wasn't getting good grades. I studied electrical engineering because I wanted to learn something new and thought it would be really difficult to teach myself. I loved it, but didn't have the same passion for building side projects as I did with programming.

What were your favorite and least favorite classes?

We had this course called Mechatronics that was basically a class that integrated everything we had learned in all our other engineering classes. The final project was to build a robot that could compete in some kind of competition. For our class, it was a wild west shoot out where two robots would start back-to-back, walk three feet away from each other, turn around and shoot ping pongs at each other.

That was awesome. I mean, getting to build that, to program that, was the highlight of college for me. It was above and beyond our senior project. It was really fun and kind of lighthearted, right? You don't have to build these things that are super serious, so it brought back a lot of that fun that I hadn't felt in a while.

My least favorite classes were probably my engineering classes that were closer to physics, like semiconductor device physics.

Do you have any advice on how to meet cofounders in school?

My current situation is interesting, in that, Andy—the technical founder—was a friend of Dave's; I didn't know him originally. Dave and I were both in Chicago, but Andy was out in Sunnyvale; it wasn't until we launched Bump that we actually met face-to-face even though, by that time, we had been working together for six months.

I actually think there's an analogy between finding cofounders and finding marriage partners. Not that I've been married, so maybe I don't know what I'm talking about, but I think a lot of people take it way, way too lightly and are really stressed about starting and building something, so they just take anyone but it's very much a case of the tortoise and the hare, right? One of the most important decisions you make is whom you're going to work with.

You can't change that decision very quickly or easily so finding someone who complements you, finding someone you have a great working relationship with is tough, but critical. Rather than just finding someone that seems to have the right skill set on paper, work with someone for a while; build something together; get into a situation where there's some conflict and see how you guys resolve it. If after all that you think, "Oh my God, we can build something amazing together," then go out and do it.

There are so many ways a startup can fail due to misalignment between the founders; it could be something as simple as level of commitment, right? If one person wants to build the next Google and the other wants to get to a million dollars as quickly as possible, you are in for a world of hurt when your company's worth "enough" so that person can get two million dollars—that happens all the time. So, make sure you believe in that same vision; make sure you want the same outcome; make sure you can work together and don't just rush into it.

Did you have a job or do any consulting when you were in college?

I did consulting for the first year and a half—from 2000 to 2001—and made a ton of money doing web design and development but that contributed to my not doing well in school. Ultimately I had to decide whether to work and make a lot of money right then, or actually attend the classes I was spending a lot of money on and try and learn something and get a degree. I was fortunate enough to be in a situation where I didn't need to work so, a year and a half or so in, I decided to focus just on school.

I worked my ass off in engineering—it felt like I was working a lot harder and longer than any of my close friends. But college, for me, was also about growing as a person and growing in all those cliché ways that you think of. On a daily basis I don't really use most of what I learned by studying electrical engineering, but every day I *do* have to talk to a partner, interview someone, or talk to someone on the team, and If I hadn't grown through college, I don't know if I'd be the type of person that could do all that stuff.

Did anyone in college inspire you?

Absolutely. There were lots of people I found really inspirational. My grandfather is one of the most inspirational people in my life; he's one of my mentors and the most successful entrepreneur in my family. But it's hard to think back and pinpoint a specific person. I think more than by individuals, I was inspired by the atmosphere and the culture of Silicon Valley—that a couple of people with an idea and a lot of hard work build these companies out of nothing—and it's this beautiful amazing thing that doesn't happen in very many places and it's very hard to do, but easier in Silicon Valley than anywhere else.

Growing up in Alaska in the late '90's when the Internet boom started and moving here and being in the middle of it and realizing that it's real—that it's normal people doing these things, had a huge impact on me. It made following my dream and starting a tech company seem like a real possibility.

I read Paul Graham's essays. I thought they were really powerful. I've read a lot of books, like Founders at Work, that made the idea of starting a company really accessible and highlighted the contrasts between what working at a startup versus working at a big company would be like.

In big companies, everything's slow; no one has any responsibility or accountability; no one is willing to try something new or do anything innovative and you think, "God there's got to be something better than this!" Then you read about these startups and think, "Oh my god, these people are just doing it, this is awesome, I want to do that." So, that literature kind of keeps the dream alive.

How would you describe your experience at Y Combinator?

I don't know if we ever told Paul this, but we applied for the most random reasons, ever. Dave and I wanted to come out to the Bay Area and were looking for ways to subsidize our summer. We didn't know a ton about Y Combinator; I'd read a few of Paul's essays but Dave and Andy weren't that familiar.

Both Dave and I had friends who had gone through Y Combinator a year and a half before we did, and we thought there might be an opportunity there for us. Unlike a lot of founders, we first started digging into it without knowing too much about it. None of us had accounts on Hacker News; we weren't reading TechCrunch every day. I don't even know how we first found out about it, but every once in a while we sit back and reflect on how we were so lucky because I don't think we'd be where we are today, and having as much fun as we are having, if we hadn't been a part of YC.

Paul's mentorship was probably the most important thing about YC, early on. There are two distinct moments I can remember where he made it really, really clear that we weren't thinking big enough. Even in our interview we started off as you typically do with a demo and Jessica and Paul and Trevor were Bumping each other and then Paul kind of puts his head in his hands and closes his eyes and goes, "Now how do we make this *bigger than Google*?" And the fact that he was even asking that question blew us away. So that was the first moment.

The second, was realizing, "He's thinking about this seriously, why aren't we thinking about this seriously? Why does he think our business can be bigger than we've ever considered?" And so that kind of straightened us out and then I think the second or third time we met with him, we were weighing all these different features and had all these different partner opportunities to integrate into Bump, and he said something simple like, "Why can't you just Bump *anything*?" We were like, "Huh?"

We had kind of talked about how you should be able to Bump anything but we weren't really doing anything about it—how do we eventually get to this world where, forget about phones and all these other things and just think about what would you want to Bump. What would you want to do if you could Bump anything? And that was really inspiring for us. So, Paul is awesome.

The network of other companies has also been very valuable to us. There are a million things we ended up doing for the first time that we had no experience in and that specialized information helps you to make less mistakes or be more effective, like fundraising or hiring people; these are things we'd never done before and so to be able to go talk to a few other successful companies and learn from their mistakes and their successes, hopefully it helped us avoid mistakes, grow the company faster, all that kind of stuff.

Another thing was, the dinners—the combination of seeing everyone else working their asses off and not wanting to fall behind; we didn't want to be the only ones not getting things done. The speakers were great too, there's so much mythology in the Valley and so many peoples' stories are sanitized and it makes you think the guys really succeeded, did everything right and it was just perfect the entire time. But when you get these guys in— and I remember one example, Max Levchin from PayPal and he told real horror stories from when PayPal was being built. These stories made it clear that successful founders *aren't perfect*; they made mistakes but recovered from them. It's about not giving up, not about being perfect. You learn that in order to be successful you can't be afraid of making mistakes; you have to make a lot of mistakes and you have to fail a lot to find the right thing. And if you're afraid of failing, then you'll never get anything done and you'll die either from not being creative and innovative enough or from indecision; so hearing these stories just took away a lot of—it made it okay to fail and to try things, because everyone else did and that's how you build a great product.

The last thing that was so helpful was fundraising. Having never done it before, not being from Silicon Valley, not having worked at a startup, it was so helpful to get Paul's and other founders' introductions to investors because with people like investors and partners and employees, the way you're introduced to them is important.

Have you experienced any particularly stressful moments in Bump?

We had some scaling nightmares, the worst of which was probably when, towards the end of YC, we heard we might be in an Apple commercial and then one random Monday, a month and a half later, all of a sudden our servers started going crazy. At the rate our traffic was growing we would be done in less than 48 hours and there was no way that we'd be able to get the servers back up.

We had scaling plans that would take weeks to implement, not days. So we sent out a plea: "Someone help us; this is our stack, this is our problem." We emailed it to the YC founders list and Alex Polvi from Cloudkick responded within 15 minutes. We jumped on the phone with him to give him more details. I think that night he and another one of the guys at Cloudkick came over to our office, sat down, and were surgically helping us optimize all of our biggest problems; if they hadn't come over I don't know what we would have done.

We lived through that and if not for their help we would have been down for weeks. So that was looking into the mouth of disaster and just barely being saved by the generosity of Alex, donating his time.

What's your usage and growth like? How did you get users besides being in Apple commercials?

We just found out recently from Apple that we are the number eight most-downloaded app ever in the U.S.; number three most-downloaded app ever in Japan. In the U.S., Facebook is number one, Skype is number nine, Pandora and Google are also ahead of us. A bunch of name brand apps are next to us on the list. It's crazy. How did we get these downloads?

We haven't done any serious marketing. We've done a little bit of PR and most of our first several thousand downloads were probably due to good PR. But the thing that really drives our growth in terms of downloads is very, very simple: Bump only works with two people and our existing users are incentivized to get their friends to download Bump; it's not an economic incentive or anything like that, it's people saying, "I want to give you a photo and I think Bump is the easiest or coolest way of doing it," and some people just want to show off the technology because it's fun and magical, then they get you to download this free app from iTunes; it takes less than a minute, and then you Bump.

When we had a chance to step back and try to figure out what was driving our growth, something really stood out: if you measure the amount of time between when someone opens Bump for the first time and when they Bump for the first time, for the vast majority of our users it's less than 15 minutes. I think there's a lot of opportunity for other apps, not to copy it, but to take away a very powerful lesson: build apps to use with other people because if it's valuable to me and it's valuable to my friend then I'm going to share it with them and I think we're seeing a lot of apps doing very clever things recently, leveraging the address book as a starting point for the network. I know of several apps that gained millions of downloads in their first several months by doing that.

What was the investing process like for you? Was it positive or negative?

We've done three rounds since Y Combinator. A couple weeks after demo day we raised a couple of hundred thousand dollars as a bridge from some angels, led by Ron Conway. Our goal for that money was to start hiring more people but have time to find the right partner for our series A. That was in August of 2009. By October or November we had closed a $3 million round with Sequoia. Just recently, at the end of December 2010 we raised another $16.5 million, led by Andreessen Horowitz.

The process of getting investors has been really, really positive. But I think there are a lot of big misconceptions. For instance, a lot of people spend a lot of time on a business plan. Or, they think they can get great investors with no track record, no team, and just an idea. I think building something, releasing it, and showing some proof that people value it, would much better serve those people. Build something that tests your most fundamental assumptions and be able to show numbers. We had a couple of strong debates with Sequoia where one of the partners would say, "Well, I think you're totally wrong with this assumption," and I'd go back and say, "You have a great point but I can show in the data and bring up the slides that, at least for the last nine months, my assumption holds true;" having data rather than just ideas is really, really powerful.

Also, every product changes a lot. Every idea evolves, everyone's market changes, and so if you can do a lot of that meandering with the product *before* you raise money, you'll be able to get investors who—when they invest—are believers in something that's closer to what ends up being the actual product. If you have to do a huge pivot, maybe that investor is not the best investor for you anymore. Paul says, "Build something people want." I'm a big believer in that. Build it and test it before you raise money; anyone can do that these days.

Another big misconception is: a lot of people focus on valuation and are confused about what the dynamics of a round actually are. I've only raised 2 rounds from venture capitalists, so, small sample aside, maybe this isn't how it works for everyone. But honestly, valuation never really comes up. There are two numbers: how much money you want to raise and how much of the company they want to own. For series A, from a name brand investor, with only one major investor, they're going to want anywhere from 20 to 35% of the company; they'd much prefer to be on the high end of that range and—if you're building and in the company for the long-haul—you want to get as much money as you can rationalize because no matter how much you raise, it ends up being the same amount of dilution. So people worry a lot about valuation but valuation is a result, not really part of the equation.

Is Bump generating revenue?

We're not making money right now. There's a framework or a model in the Valley, popularized initially by Reid Hoffman, I think, where you first focus on getting users, get them engaged, and then monetize them. We think this is really smart because if you monetize too early, you can end up optimizing for a local maxima because now your product decisions are being driven around that revenue source and there could be with a slightly different product and a slightly different revenue model, a much bigger revenue source, that you never even got a chance to see because you limited the scope of the product up front.

So, we're definitely in the camp of: first, building a really important engagement product, and once we think we're on that trajectory then we can start thinking about monetizing it. Not to say that we haven't spent a lot of time thinking about how we could monetize it, and most of those ideas revolve around, whether we are facilitating connections and interactions between a user and a brand or a consumer and a merchant, that's a very valuable connection link and people are willing to pay for it.

We want to make sure that we have the product and the user experience right. I'm much more worried about that than I am about monetizing it, eventually. There are a million different models for monetizing the right product, so we're not putting a lot of time and effort into it.

Have there been periods where you lose motivation? How do you deal with that or power through it?

I think it's really important to have multiple founders. I can't imagine doing this by myself. There have been so many days where it's such an emotional roller coaster and something will happen and make you think that the sky is falling, that it's the end of the world, that there's no way you're going to recover from this mistake or this rejection or whatever challenge you're facing; with the three of us, there's always someone who's still positive and optimistic and can pull the other one or the other two out of the nosedive.

Can you talk about the time you most successfully hacked some non-computer system to your advantage?

That was one that Dave answered and his response was, either in college or in graduate school and it was when online poker sites were really taking off and they were serving out huge incentives to acquire users. He and his friends found this loophole where they could basically sign up, cash out, sign up, and cash out. They got a couple of thousand dollars for free and then went on a ski trip. It was totally legal, just found the loophole in their system.

You're hiring aggressively at this stage. How do you approach that as a cofounder? Is there anything you worry about when you hire people?

There are a lot of hard things about starting a company and one thing people talk about a lot is building your team. You have to hire well, you can't compromise, you can't lower your standards; you hear all that and you nod and smile and then when you go out and actually try and do it you're like, "Oh my god, hiring a great team is so difficult," and it's absolutely the most important thing you do.

If you are only going to do one thing well, it has to be that because everything else relies upon it. And hiring is still tough for us. A pretty common way of hiring your first few employees is either through your school or your work network. So, if you got your CS degree at Stanford or you worked at Google or Facebook or something, you have these amazing talent pools where people are already vetted, you know what they're like to work with, you know how talented they are, and all you have to do is sell them on the new opportunity and convince them to come over. Unfortunately, the three of us that founded Bump are a bunch of double E's and none of us had a strong Silicon Valley work network to jumpstart things.

Hiring is incredibly difficult but our intern program has been one of the things that have been most successful. 15% of the current team were interns last summer. It's great because you get a chance to bring on people that you think have high potential and watch how they perform. At the end of the summer if you love having them work there and they love working with you, it's a no-brainer and it takes away a lot of the other risk factors you have with hiring someone completely from a blind resume.

Bill Clerico, WePay

Tags: Y Combinator, programmer, profitable, hiring, VC funded, design-focused, undergrad founder

Overview: WePay was founded in 2008 to help groups collect money online. WePay makes it very easy to keep track of the complex situations where multiple people owe each other money, and they allow people to send payments directly through their service. WePay received its seed funding from Y Combinator, went on to raise $9 million, has over 25,000 users sending bills each week on the web site, and processes over $2 million in payment volume per month. WePay most recently hired Rasmus Lerdorf—the creator of the PHP programming language—to join their team. I first met Bill Clerico when I flew to YC for early interviews: both our startups were rejected from TechStars, but I believe we both had exploding termsheets from other investors. I've stayed in touch with Bill ever since and I started using WePay as soon as they had a beta ready; it made splitting bills with my roommates a lot easier.

Can you talk about how you first got started with entrepreneurship?

I always knew I wanted to start a company but I was never really sure what that meant, or how I would do it. I started out selling flowers for my Boy Scout troop, stuff like that. I was involved in a bunch of different organizations and I liked to lead them; I liked working with people, I liked doing things, but I never really did commercial, for-profit projects.

In college, Rich and I started a small company that sold taxi advertising; that was our start in business and we really liked it. We really liked working together, and we knew we wanted to do work together long term, but that particular business didn't work out.

At the time, we were both interning in New York City and the opportunity presented itself. We sold some ads and got by that summer but we basically only broke even, it never really went anywhere, and we decided we didn't want to pursue that.

I also started a business plan competition in college with a couple of other students. That was interesting because it got me some exposure to the startup and venture capital world. I really identified with the guys in that group—they seemed like they were having lots of fun, there was really high energy, they were making money; it seemed like where I wanted to be with my career. So we started this competition in order to increase the profile of entrepreneurship at Boston College, which I think we succeeded in doing. Now the business plan competition is in its fifth or sixth year and they are getting 50 or 60 plan submissions. So it has been a success. Personally, it helped me meet a bunch of people who have since become my investors and mentors.

After school, I sold out and became an investment banker for a year, which was a little speed bump on the way to becoming an entrepreneur, but I am still glad I did it; I learned a lot. I did that until I realized I would never really be happy in that kind of career. Once you admit that to yourself it becomes really easy to start a company because you know what's going to make you happy.

What kinds of classes did you take in college and what was your experience like?

I was a computer science major, so I took a bunch of CS classes but I took business classes as well—I didn't want to be purely technical. I took a class called Undergrad Tech Trek West which was pretty cool; it's a bunch of seniors and it's structured like an MBA class where you do case studies on companies—we actually went out as a class and visited the companies and met their executives in California over spring break. So that was super interesting and really piqued my interest in startups.

One of my classmates in that class, Tyler Gaffney, ended up working with us at WePay and Professor Gallagher, who teaches the class, now brings his students to visit WePay. So it has come full circle; we were in the class and now we're in the case studies, which is pretty cool.

Other than that, I spent some time running a Red Cross Disaster Action Team in college. Monday nights we were on call and, if there were disasters in the Massachusetts Bay area—house fires, floods, etc.—we would respond and assist with mass care, housing people, and mental health counseling. That was my biggest extracurricular.

Oh, I was also my college mascot—the Eagle—so I was pretty involved in different sports and school events. There was actually an article in the Wall Street Journal entitled: 'From Boston College Mascot to Venture-backed CEO.'

Did you know you wanted to do a startup and were you actively looking for cofounders in college?

I knew I wanted to do a startup but I didn't really know what that meant, so we were always thinking about different ideas and working on different projects, but we were never really that serious about it. We thought we were being serious about it at the time, but looking back on it, we just weren't doing the right things.

Can you give any advice on finding cofounders as a student?

Start with your friends and people in your CS classes; people who have similar interests. I think the best way to see if someone could be a good cofounder is just to work together, hack on different projects. It's really hard to know how people function until you've worked with them. Rich and I started that taxi business together so we knew what it was like to work together. So, when we started WePay it was easy in that sense, kind of a no-brainer.

How did you meet your cofounder, Rich Aberman?

We had the same scholarship to BC. It's called the Presidential Scholarship and we met while interviewing for it, actually before freshman year, and we then ended up being roommates throughout college. Rich is from Florida and I am from New Jersey; it was just luck that we bumped into each other so early on. That scholarship paid our tuition.

Did you take time off of class to relax?

I definitely worked hard in school but I also had a lot of fun—we did our fair share of partying. We'd also go skiing or go to Red Sox games all the time. My friends from college are some of my best friends.

Did anyone in school inspire you?

I think Professor John Gallagher—who taught the Tech Trek class—really opened my eyes to Silicon Valley and inspired me. Just working with different alumni for the business plan competition was also really important. It was inspiring to see what they had done with their careers; they were definitely people I wanted to emulate.

How did the idea for WePay come about? Why group payments?

It grew out of a problem that Rich and I had. Throughout college we lived with roommates, had a big group of friends, and were always doing stuff and planning trips; Rich and I always ended up being the guys planning or organizing and there just wasn't a good tool to collect and manage money. So we decided to build it.

You did early interviews for Y Combinator; do you have any advice for people trying to raise money from programs like those?

I think for Y Combinator, in particular, it helps to be technical; it helps to be tough and come across as an entrepreneur that's really dedicated to an idea and is going to see it through. I think it helps to have a pretty good sense of your product and market. So, if you don't have a working product, have some kind of demo or way to show you've tested the idea in the market, and that customers are willing to use and pay for it. The more proof you can assemble ahead of time, the better, and it really increases your chances a lot with the accelerators. The good news is that there are a ton of these accelerators now, so there are lots of opportunities for people to get money and work on really cool ideas.

Do you think the $150K from Yuri Milner is a good or bad thing?

$150K on an uncapped convertible note is awesome, no one can deny that. Whether or not it's good for the ecosystem, I think, remains to be determined. I think there's a lot of competition among startups now, for resources, talent, office space, all that. Keeping bad companies in business is not necessarily good for the system as a whole because they suck up talent, occupy office space, and make everything more expensive for everyone else.

I think if it increases the successful companies coming out of YC, then it's definitely a positive thing. If it ends up just funding zombie companies, that's a bad thing, but only time will tell. I definitely think the quality of companies coming out of Y Combinator continues to increase every year. It will probably be a good thing, but there's definitely a danger of just keeping bad companies alive.

You raised more money after Y Combinator, what was that experience like?

We raised a series A and a series B after Y Combinator. It was stressful but also kind of fun. You come out of YC, you've got a product, you've got some users, and now it's time to go sell it to the world and take a chance at the big time. It's cool to make your way up and down Sandhill Road, meet with the guys that have funded all the great Internet companies, and argue with them about your ideas and your business. It's challenging but exhilarating.

I did most of the fundraising by myself while Rich continued to focus on the product with Eric, our first employee.

Do you have any advice for living cheaply in California, coming out of school?

We stayed super cheap. We didn't live in Mountain View or Palo Alto because it was too expensive. We lived in Milpitas, which is South East Bay; it's definitely a lot less expensive. We all lived together in a 4-bedroom house and cooked for ourselves, we would go to Costco and get burgers and whatever else we could get for cheap. It's definitely doable, I think it's good; it keeps you focused. When you have money, it takes time to spend. When you have no money, there's not much to do besides work.

I remember you guys were living with Apigy and Dailybooth, and it seemed like a pretty lean operation. Let's talk about growth, how did you get your early users?

Rich did a really good job, early on, in reaching out to users. Our first users were some fraternities at Stanford and then, just friends from our YC class. I think you guys [Jared Tame and his roommates] are actually probably some of our first users, so we had friends and then different groups we had reached out to, to get feedback. We would do stuff like have them over to our house for barbecues and host poker games, anything that got people using it and providing feedback; once you get that feedback it starts to grow. So, we did a pretty good job on Facebook, early on, just getting our friends to like our fan page and contribute to the discussion, which kept everyone posted about what we were up to.

Did you have any big pivots?

No, not really. We've always been pretty focused on building a consumer tool to collect money. We've definitely changed our design a bunch and we've changed certain ways our product works, but the basic strategy has been the same.

What about points where things got really stressful or you thought WePay would fail?

I think, as startup founders, it's always stressful and very emotional, regardless. It's always like the best day or week of our life, or the worst day or week of our life, depending on the day.

Before we raised our series A it was definitely speculative, whether or not this was a viable business, because building a payments products is hard. We were very inexperienced when it comes to what payments were, and payments is a tough business. There are compliance, risk, fraud, security, there's a lot of big issues. So a lot of investors were uneasy about funding a payments company, backed by two 23-year-old guys, without much experience in payments.

So, that was definitely stressful, but I think once we got over that hump and proved that, hey, we've got a product that works and this could be a business, that was a big step forward for us. We also were able to address a lot of their concerns as we had more time to operate.

So you guys have done your fair share of hacks when it comes to addressing some of those challenges that come with a payments company?

We definitely have done things over the course of our company history that are basically hacks to get ahead and get by.

YC helps out a lot. It's good to be able to hack systems to your advantage because as a startup your biggest advantage is that you may have to play by the rules, but you can be a lot faster and more aggressive with them than big companies can.

Was there a point where you guys started to notice the revenue taking off?

Our revenue grows every month. I don't think there was ever a moment in time where it started going off the chart, but it's consistently growing month-to-month.

I think a big inflection point for us was when we redesigned our product, three or four months after Y Combinator, after we hired Khang; that was a big turning point. Our product became a lot easier to use, we weren't forcing people to use it anymore, they actually enjoyed using it. So that was a big turning point for us.

You guys have focused on design, and not every tech startup in the Valley makes that a priority. Did you decide to make that a priority from the start?

Yeah, our big advantage over PayPal and other payment companies is our UI and how easy-to-use and intuitive it is. We think about it every day and how to make it better, and we do a lot of testing. We have certain metrics that we measure around user engagement, transaction volume, conversion rate, all that good stuff, so we are always testing, improving our UI and seeing how it performs against these metrics. So yeah, we've maybe gotten six or seven homepages in the last four or five months. We iterate pretty quickly.

How do you guys split up the work? Has it changed over time?

Early on, it was a pretty natural division. I have a CS degree and Eric, our first employee, is technical, so the two of us wrote code and Rich worked on marketing and tried to get users. That was the basic division. I am still very involved with product and marketing, but now I focus more on sales, business development, financing, operations and compliance. Rich focuses most of his time on product and marketing.

What was the work schedule like, in the early days? Has that changed since then?

During Y Combinator it was definitely seven days a week. We didn't have air conditioning in our house and it gets really hot in Milpitas. So, we would basically sleep during the day and then work all night because you couldn't really be awake during the day, it was just too hot. We would sleep from 10:00 AM to 6:00 PM or so, and then wake up and work until, like, 9:00 AM the following morning and go back to sleep.

Our YC dinners were usually breakfast for us because we would wake up, go to YC, eat breakfast and then go back home and work all night because it was so hot. We had a thermometer and sometimes it was 114 degrees in our living room. It was ridiculously hot.

After you guys launched, how did you continue to get users?

We got a bunch of press and buzz, which definitely helped. Rich does a really good job of writing blog posts and content and engaging the community; Hacker News, Digg, Reddit, TechCrunch, Mashable, etc. pick those up. That has been a really effective channel for creating good content and syndicating it, and we also do some search engine optimization, some pay-per-click advertising. We just launched a referral program last week that we are pretty excited about—we are basically paying our users to refer new users.

That kind of reminds me of the early PayPal days.

Yeah, exactly. It's a bit old school but it works pretty well. Our customer satisfaction rate is around 99%, so why not? If your customers are happy with your product, why not encourage them to share with their friends? That has been pretty effective for us.

How do you handle hiring? It's tough for many startups.

Yeah, it's hard. What we did earlier on, that I am glad we did, was sit down as a team and figure out what our values and culture were and from that we made a list of things to use as hiring criteria—we wanted to hire people that had those values and would fit in well with us, because there are all kinds of cultures, right? The culture at Twitter is much different than Google or Facebook. So you want to make sure that you know what you are looking for and that you are thoughtful about it, and then you go find those kinds of people.

We have a hiring process. People apply, we look at their resumes, we do a phone review, if we like them they come in and meet with one person, if that person likes them then we have them meet with other people. It's a pretty standard hiring process but I spend a lot of time recruiting. I would say I probably spend half of every day recruiting because it's a contact sport. You've got to contact a ton of applicants, you've got to screen a bunch of them, you've got to be really tough in the interview process. It's painful when you spend all this time finding an applicant, screening, and then finally you get to the end and they're not quite there—they're close but not there, and it's tough to say no because then you have to start all over and do it again. It's painful but it's critical if you are going to put together a high-caliber team.

Is that your biggest challenge today, recruiting?

I don't know if it's our biggest challenge. I think our biggest challenge is scaling customer acquisition. You get to a certain point where, you could have a front page article in the New York Times every day, and you are still not going to grow because if you want 20% growth this month, that's a lot harder than 50% growth, six months ago, right? We are just so much bigger now. So our biggest challenge is: how do we continue to scale all these customer acquisition channels? But recruiting is definitely time-consuming and challenging as well.

What is WePay's culture like?

I think the culture at WePay is fast-paced, we're very much a family; we all really like each other and look out for each other, and yet, we are very competitive, not against each other but as a company. We are out to win.

But, we do have a lot of fun as well. So it's a work hard, play hard culture. We also have a thing where everyone at the company has a chance to plan a social event, on a rotating basis. We do two per month; we have quarterly company off-sites, and hang out a lot after work. So, it's a pretty cool culture. Pretty diverse too, it's not just 24-year-old guys, we have older people, younger people, men, women; it's a good, diverse culture.

Do you guys ever burn out?

We have not really had any problems with burnout. Basically, the way we've set up our week is that we all work about 12 hours per day, Monday to Friday then we all take the weekends off.

There are some companies where people are in the office 15 or 16 hours every day. But our belief is that it's really hard to be productive for that long and you end up just screwing around and wasting time. So, we come in, work very hard, very solid days and then on weekends we all go home and hang out with our families and friends, it's a good mix of work hard, play hard.

Did you have advisors, were they helpful?

We had investors. We don't really have any advisors, but our investors serve as advisors and they have definitely been helpful. Max Levchin is one of our investors and has given us advice on payments and fraud; Ron Conway and David Lee and those guys have been really helpful with advising on business development and marketing. Our VCs, Peter Bell from Highland, has been a great help with general management, building a company, culture, hiring, sales; David Hornik from August Capital has greatly helped with consumer Internet and business development introductions; and Mark Goines who is on our board, was on the board of Mint and knows a ton about marketing, financial services and consumer Internet.

We definitely put together a good team that's there to help us out for sure, because we are young, first-time entrepreneurs, and these guys have deep rolodexes, deep relationships, and lots of knowledge. So they have been super helpful.

If an undergraduate came to you today and asked what you would do if you were in his shoes, what would you say?

I would probably advise them to go work at a startup and just get a feel for it or, if they are interested in a specific industry, I would tell them to go learn about that industry, what problems people have, what people are willing to spend money on, the vocabulary, etc.

I actually think getting experience in sales is really helpful. If I were to redo my career, instead of working in investment banking I would have gotten a sales job because, so much of what I do is related to selling candidates on joining the company, selling investors, and selling customers. Having that ability, that tenacity, and the grit that comes with being a good salesperson, is critical. Sales are what the company is all about at the end of the day— sales bring in the revenue, and without revenue you are not a company. So, I think it's incredibly valuable to have that experience.

If you're non-technical and it's a technical startup, what do you do?

That's tough. You have to think about where you can add the most value. If you are a smart, analytical, quantitative person, you can learn to code. If you think you could be a good coder, then it might be a good path. But, if you are pretty convinced that you are never going to be a good coder, then I wouldn't waste time learning the code, I would become a good sales person or go learn a ton about the industry or go figure out ways to get customers.

There's really no silver bullet, you have to think about what you want to do and how you can add the most value towards that goal and go do that.

Can you talk about the time you most successfully hacked some non-computer system to your advantage?

The one I put on my YC application was kind of funny. We had an apartment in Boston before we moved; it was on the border, between the cities of Boston and Brookline. Literally, the border was right outside our front door. I had my car and parking in Boston was just horrible; it costs a fortune. If you want to rent a spot to park your car it's $1,000 a month or something like that. So what we did, was, for a week I recorded the times that different meter maids came by: what time the Boston meter maid came by, what time the Brookline meter maid came by, and, instead of paying the meter, I would just shuffle the car back and forth between Boston and Brookline. So, it would be parked all the time but always just outside the jurisdiction of the meter maid.

The Boston meter maid would come and see my car illegally parked, but it was in Brookline. So they couldn't write me a ticket and then, after they left, I would move it back to Boston and it would be illegally parked but the Brookline meter maid couldn't write me a ticket. So I just shuffled, I never paid for parking. I got like two parking tickets over the course of three months, which is way less than paying the meters and paying for spots.

It seems like you've put a lot of effort into the recruiting process—when you get an application, what makes you say, "I want to talk to this person"?

We like people that are kind of go-getters. Not only do they have to get the culture, they have to be go-getters because there's not a lot of structure here; there is not a lot of, do A, B, and C, and you will get D. It's very much, "okay, this is the mission, we are going to build a great product and then we are going to get the people to use it, how can we advance that mission?" and we want people that can take that mission and go turn it into actionable tasks and do valuable things without having their hands held every step of the way. We will train people, we will help people, we give a lot of resources, but there's not always going to be very explicit instructions. We want people that can think outside the box, that are self-motivated.

Ryan Amos, DailyBooth

Tags: dropout, Y Combinator, school worker, undergrad founder, hiring, VC funded, major league player (Alexa top 5,000)

Overview: DailyBooth launched in 2009 and is described as the "Twitter for pictures." DailyBooth differentiates itself from other services such as Instagram and Path as being a front-facing camera experience where most users take pictures of themselves, whereas users on other services are taking pictures of things, or using the back-facing camera. Having gone through Y Combinator in the Summer of 2009 and raised $7 million afterwards, its users have snapped more than 14 million photos on the site. While Ashton Kutcher, Demi Moore, and several high-profile YouTube celebrities are now "boothing," DailyBooth is a startup that came close to failure in its early days.

How did you get into entrepreneurship? Where did this all start for you?

I started making money when I was 12 or 13. I had a little online, it was kind of like an FTP server that people would pay for access to and download stuff. I never had a job when I was growing up because that helped for a while, and then I started getting into programming. When I did get interested in programming I started to make money -- I started doing some consulting. This was when I was 14 or so: I started building websites and I started making money that way. When I was 16, I created the first image-hosting website that I'm aware of with a friend. We had 50,000 members and people were actually paying for image hosting for eBay stuff. We were basically the first to do it that way, and then we sold it my senior year of high school. From there, I went on to college and through college I never really had a job. I was just consulting and building websites and selling them and making money that way. I have had one real job in my life, which was an internship after my freshman year of college, which paid for nothing really. That's the only thing that I've actually done outside of doing entrepreneurial stuff.

What kinds of classes did you take?

I went to Ohio State. I was going to the computer science and engineering program there and I was taking the typical classes. The classes that I was least interested in were calculus and statistics, and obviously the classes that I was actually interested in were the CS classes. But even those were sometimes quite boring because all the stuff that we were getting taught was stuff that I already knew so it wasn't that interesting.

Did you work on any startups or projects in college?

The summer before I went to college there was a website that was being sold that was making a lot of money and the guy had to sell it pretty quickly. I took a $10,000 loan to try to buy this website from him but it fell through. So I had $10,000 in the bank and I could either pay my loan back automatically and pay a little bit of interest, or I could have time to build my own projects and that's what I did.

I saw a website on SitePoint.com that allowed people to embed music videos into their MySpace pages and it was getting quite a bit of traction. It was getting ridiculous amounts of views and making a ton of money and got sold on SitePoint for $200,000. When I saw that I was like, "that'd be easy for me to make."

So I tried to create that same exact website and I realized that after I launched it, I wasn't getting any traction. I ended up turning it into a turnkey software solution and then that made me quite a bit of money for around 6 months, and I was probably making $5,000 to $10,000 a month. It was reverse engineered based on Yahoo's music video site, so Yahoo sent us cease and desist letters. I had to shut that down, but then I ended up selling it shortly before I went into YC.

Did you know anyone going into Ohio State?

I did not know anyone that went to the exact same school, as I actually went to a branch of Ohio State the first year having applied so late. So I did not know anyone that I went with. I wasn't actually thinking of doing a startup at this stage. I was more like just paying the bills by doing consulting and stuff like that, not necessarily an actual startup, and I was not looking for cofounders.

Did you take time to relax in school or was it a grind?

There were definitely times where you had to just sit back and relax a little bit. I went to Ohio State and it's a very big football school. During the football season, there is no time to be consistently grinding.

You dropped out to do DailyBooth, so you never graduated?

I was consulting and I was doing my own things, my own projects, but I never actually did graduate. When we launched DailyBooth I had two quarters left in school, and we got traction pretty quickly. Having applied to YC I had to make the decision: either drop out or give up this opportunity.

How did the idea for Dailybooth come about?

Jon Wheatley and I met from when I bought a website off of him, a couple of years ago. That's how we initially met, and after I bought that from him we kind of stayed in touch and we'd always talk about our own projects and what we were working on, stuff like that. We would bounce ideas off each other and he would hire me from time to time for stuff that he wanted done.

Jon had the idea of DailyBooth about a year prior to us launching and he hired someone else. Basically he saw a YouTube video go viral where some guy took a picture of himself everyday for 3 years and Jon wanted to do that for himself but he knew he didn't have the discipline to do it himself. So he wanted to build a tool to make it easier to be able to do that, but when we launched it, it kind of changed into more of a social communication through photos.

What was the website you bought off Jon on SitePoint?

It was BannerManage.com. Basically, a first generation Adify is what I've heard it called. I wanted to use it but it didn't have everything I wanted in it. So I knew that without buying it I wasn't going to be able to get the features that I wanted. I decided to buy it, build the features I wanted into it and then continue. It was software that was licensed, and then I would just continue to license it. But I eventually just didn't have time to do it, so I added a few features and sold it.

What was your fundraising experience like?

We actually launched Dailybooth prior to applying, but we applied to YC and then we applied to TechStars and one other venture program. We got interviews for each one, but we decided to go with YC. The site was taking off and I was paying for the servers and stuff off my credit card, so we were both out of money and we weren't going to be able to make money right away. That was the best option, to try to get some investment.

Jon threw the idea around and I looked into it a bit more and I thought YC could be a huge help. That's why I didn't expect even to be able to get an interview: because of the fact that we aren't MIT grads; we are not the typical Stanford student. We applied to YC with only hopes of getting investment.

I can't say that it was negative because everyone that we applied for we got an interview for. We were definitely nervous. We had no idea what to expect. I guess the only thing that I would say is just make sure that you understand your products and the vision of what you're going to be doing. Also, the earlier you launch the better. Even launching before applying is probably best.

Is the 150K from Yuri Milner a good or bad thing?

I don't know, I'm torn on it. It's good for this session because they didn't know in advance and they had those few months where they were already working their asses off. But future companies, I don't know. If they have $150,000 guaranteed to them, they might not work nearly as hard as all the classes before. However, it could end up meaning higher quality people actually apply for YC. It could end up being really good.

How long did it take you to build the first beta for DailyBooth? Were you the only person building it?

I built it over my Christmas break in 2008 and then we tweaked all the bugs and finalized some smaller features in January and then launched in the middle of February. We didn't really promote it. We launched it and literally had a thousand members the first day. It took off pretty quickly, but that was also due to someone we became friends with while we were building that. She was a YouTuber who created videos that other YouTubers were interested in, and eventually it just grew from there. We didn't really have the marketing or anything because it ended up growing pretty quickly.

Did you ever have any big pivots or change of plans?

The only thing that we did prior to launch was Jon's original idea was just to take a picture everyday, but then he added the following system. We added the follow system and then we added picture comments a week before we launched it, just because Jon thought it would be a cool idea. It ended up being probably the one thing that has made us into the social platform of communication through photos. It's because of the picture comments.

People might not realize this, but you had celebrities on the site fairly early on, like Ashton Kutcher. How did that happen?

Ashton Kutcher and Demi Moore both joined around the time that we were raising our money just because we were being talked about through the investors, and Ashton was around someone at some point where we were brought up a couple of times. The celebrities that we had were more of YouTube celebrities as opposed to everyday TV or movie celebrities.

Initially we did not reach out to the YouTube celebrities. It was more that their other YouTube friends were getting on—the people that had a lot of subscribers as well. It's kind of a natural fit for them because they broadcasted themselves through video, but to broadcast through a picture is an easier way, and they don't have to edit anything or whatever. It was kind of natural for them to hop on and spread the word.

Did you ever think Dailybooth would fail? Or was there a point where things got really stressful?

Definitely. There were times when we had no money left—literally, even during YC. We barely had money left to be able to even pay our rent. We were in the unfortunate situation where Jon got turned around when he tried to come to the United States for YC because he lives in the UK. So we were paying two rents in two different places and as a result we were going through money quicker than a lot of other YC startups. The only other really big stress problems were scaling issues because of our growth.

How do you survive in California as a dropout student with no income?

I don't really have any specific advice other than spend the money wisely. I was sleeping on a foam thing that was like 2 inches thick for the whole YC session. We literally spent no money. I didn't have a bed. I didn't have anything. I was sleeping on the floor. Other than watching what you spend your money on, that's all the advice I can give on that.

How did you guys split up the work?

Well, Jon is not an engineer, so I did all the engineering. Jon worked with some designers that we were contracting out as well as product features and the spec.

During YC I got up probably around 4:00PM and then I would work till about 9:00AM to noon and go to bed for a couple of hours and then get up to do it again. I worked literally nonstop other than the few hours that I went to go maybe to the grocery store or something like that.

Did you guys work weekends and holidays too?

Yeah.

Has the schedule changed since you guys started out?

Yes and no. I don't work nearly as much on the weekends but I definitely still work on the weekends. My sleep schedule is a little bit better now, but two weeks ago, I was getting up at 4:00AM and working till 7:00PM. It's not unheard of for me to have crazy hours.

How did you sustain your growth?

The only thing that we really did was we added different things that users already were asking for. Like when they took their DailyBooth picture, it would Tweet automatically for them and stuff like that. It was really growing by word of mouth as opposed to using advertising.

What is your biggest challenge today?

Right now, it's hiring engineers. Other than that our growth is still good and we're still going well. But just hiring other good engineers is the most difficult thing for us.

Have you had any problems with scaling?

We did during YC. I had never scaled anything to that extent, especially something that has a social graph, that's not typically easy to scale. That was definitely a challenge, but as we got it under control with all the different data stores out there that are available now. It's become a little bit easier.

There are now 7 people working at DailyBooth. What's the culture like?

We're all friends. We don't try to take everything too seriously. We just try to have fun and to get work done. I typically like to lead by example where I'll build shit, and hopefully everyone else follows as opposed to someone telling them to get work done.

We've kind of fallen behind on being open and telling the users what's going on and everything. But we're trying to improve on that, to tell them what we're working on and how we're doing that. Community is very important—we notice that people really enjoy the community stuff and actually feeling like they're a part of something.

Have you had any problems with staying motivated and productive?

Hitting the brick wall with productivity happened most during fundraising, but it's not been that much of an issue. At least for myself, the people using the product that I build drive me. That is exciting, and they get excited over it. That drives me day-to-day to build something cooler or more exciting for users to use.

With the fundraising, because Jon was in the UK, I had to go out and I was the only engineer at that time; we had to fundraise and I was the only one here to do it. So development halted for a couple of weeks. Luckily, our fundraising process was fast. But yeah, engineering stuff kind of stopped for a little bit, not completely but it did stop a little bit.

If Jon were in the US, he would have been the one that went out to do the fundraising. He's much better at pitching the vision and just talking to people in general. I'm much more of an introverted person. He's more extroverted than I am.

What were the most beneficial aspects of Y Combinator for you guys?

For us it was the money and the connections that we made through the people that we met at the YC classes. Our class, the people that we knew there, and then just the connections we had with getting investors. I was from Ohio, I had no connections to investors out in the Valley and Jon was from the UK and that's probably even worse. So, that was the biggest thing for us is the connections and then the community that YC has.

The speakers were helpful, particularly their horror stories of what they did and what happened in their startups. Those were more helpful because they tell a story that's passionate and they're telling you something that gets your adrenaline rushing, as much adrenaline as there probably was during the time that it happened. That's the most beneficial thing. The only other talks were about fundraising and stuff, and I found that those fundraising talks were more towards Series A as opposed to seed investments. I found the way that seed funding worked to be completely different than what series A is. So I didn't really see the Series A funding talk as beneficial.

How did you find Series A fundraising to be different from seed funding?

From what I know the seed funding is more—our main seed investor was Ron Conway and he doesn't care as much about our valuation as a lot of other seed investors or angel investors do. Working with him was like completely opposite of what a lot of people said during YC. He was completely open: they told us things and those things actually happened. They asked who we were talking to and they were completely open with everything, and because of that we were completely open to them.

The difference is that if you're raising a Series A, you shouldn't necessary talk about everyone that you're talking to, or at least that's what the people said during the dinners. You're just talking to another VC. I think with a lot of angel investors it is because the angel investors in the Valley talk to one another, anyways. They want to know whether or not you tell them.

Hiring is difficult, and you mentioned that before. Do you have any advice for hiring?

For us, the one thing that I can say that shows a bad candidate is someone that doesn't use the product before they come in for an interview. So, someone that doesn't really understand what the product is and they just come and say "yeah,

I kind of looked at it," but they didn't register for an account. People that don't do that, we basically are saying "no" to because they don't even care. As for finding good people, I have no idea because we haven't really figured that out yet.

Let's say a student wants to drop out like you have done and do a startup. What advice would you offer them?

The one thing that I would say that we were not capable of doing is or that we didn't even try to do is basically finding a mentor or finding someone that actually knows or has gone through the process. A lot of people are open to helping out if you're not wasting too much of their time. Finding those people and asking the right questions at the right times and not wasting their time but asking important questions is probably the one thing that I would say is the most useful.

Andrew Hsu, Airy Labs

Tags: programmer, hiring, funded, VC funded, dropout, design-focused, solo founder

Overview: Airy Labs is changing the way kids learn by building social games for kids. By making learning fun, Andrew hopes to teach academic courses and broader life skills that can't be found in traditional schools. Andrew's educational background includes receiving 3 B.S. degrees in neurobiology, biochemistry, and chemistry at 16 years old. Andrew dropped out of the Stanford Ph.D. program to start Airy Labs at 19 years old and was accepted as one of Peter Thiel's 20 Under 20 Fellows.

School is a very interesting topic to me; it's something I talk about with all founders interviewed for Startups Open Sourced. How did you progress from K through 12?

Sure. So I'm originally from Seattle, where I went to public elementary school up until 4th grade and I was 7 years old at that point. I skipped a few grades by then and I was in some more advanced math classes, as well as the gifted program. The story there is: in 4th grade, my parents and teachers discovered I was so far ahead that I was making trouble and getting distracted. My parents finally made the incredibly wise decision to homeschool me. My homeschooling experience was done right because first off, we had my private teachers who my parents hired, my parents also taught me, and I also learned by myself. I did online virtual school type of curricula. Washington State has a very high concentration of homeschooling families, so we attended a co-op in this mega church called Legacy School.

A lot of the teachers also happened to be parents, and some of them were college professors. The classes were segregated by ability rather than by age, which is great. All of my classmates were much older than me, but I was at the right intellectual level. I was homeschooled from ages 7 to 11. When I was 10, I decided I wanted to become a biologist and run my own lab. I convinced a professor at the University of Washington to let me work in his microbiology lab for a year. While I was in that lab, I entered a project into the Washington State Science & Engineering Fair, and I won the grand prize there. I eventually went to the Intel International Science & Engineering Fair—this is when the Sarr scare was happening, so China and Taiwan didn't show up.

Eventually, I applied to the University of Washington and a lot of other colleges, but the others insisted that freshman live in dorms the first year and my mother said "no" to that. From 12 to 16 years-old (2003-2007), I got three degrees: neurobiology, biochemistry, and chemistry, and I also minored in math. After that in 2007, I knew I wanted to start a business but I didn't know what the timing was. So I ended up going to Stanford and studied neurobiology. I didn't go to M.I.T. because—and I am trying to choose my words carefully because I don't want to offend anyone—I felt like people were a little bit more friendly at Stanford and it's in Silicon Valley. I didn't want to deal with the Boston weather. When I interviewed at M.I.T. I was wearing a winter coat, and it was still extremely cold there.

At Stanford, I was doing my neuroscience Ph.D. and I just left in January of 2011 to incorporate my company, which happened in April. We just raised some seed funding, so that's the quick overview. The reason I dropped out was because I felt I had enough education as it was; I knew the timing was right to do a startup. I was happy to get out of there after 3 years because the time it takes to complete a Ph.D. is about 6.5 years. Whatever I did, I knew I wanted to be sure it had a major impact on the world. I wanted to build products that people would immediately use.

To me, the most impressive thing is how quickly you completed school. You were done with high school at 11. What's your secret? Was it the homeschooling?

A lot of people ask me this. When I started college, I was really young so I received a lot of media attention. I received an offer from a publisher in China to write a memoir autobiography when I was 12, which won the national children's book award and they all ask this same question. To be honest, I don't have a complete answer. I think genetics play a small role. I'm naturally smart and I have the ability to absorb information pretty quickly just by reading. But that only counts for a small part. I've read a lot of self-help books, but there are a lot of rigorous and diligent systems that I make sure I follow in order to get things done.

At the end of every day, you measure yourself by your productivity and how much you get done. There are systems to ensure I stay productive.

Do you have any particular daily habits that you use or do you have a favorite book?

I'm trying to setup systems right now to maximize productivity, and the major part of that is goal setting. Most people just don't know how to do proper goal setting. It's important to plan for the next day what you want to get done.

What is proper goal setting? Most people when they set goals, if they want to learn a scripting language like Lua, they'll say "I want to learn Lua today." But proper goal setting is about using numbers, quantities, and times. Be as specific as you can, and set very specific goals for every single day. What are you trying to accomplish by the end of the day? Do it the night before. At the end of the day, it's okay if you don't accomplish all of your goals—that might even be good; it means you might be setting a high bar for yourself.

At the end of every day, review your productivity for the day. Then you set your goals for the next day. That's the cycle and the ritual I've built up over time. I think it's psychologically very effective because it gives you a specific set of things to do and it sets up a structure for doing them. There are a lot of myths people believe about planning about how it stifles creativity and innovation: they think it creates too much rigor, so you can't be imaginative. That's a false dichotomy.

So every day, do you basically wake up and say "last night I told myself I have to do these three things" and then you figure out at the end of the day what works?

Yeah, the core of setting goals and getting those goals done works for me, and I've told people about it and it works for them. I'm trying to use the same strategy in the company because it's a tremendous tactic to be successful.

Do you use software to do the goal setting?

I use Google Docs.

How do you deal with distractions though? I think a lot of people set goals and they want to be productive, but then distractions get in the way: you have TV, Starcraft, games, all of that stuff.

I'm running a game company. I love games—I played so many games in college it was ridiculous. I could have had much better grades if I didn't play games. My time is very limited now, so I play them every once in a while. I don't own a TV, but I watch stuff on Hulu occasionally.

But when you set specific goals, you just know what you need to do. It affects your psychology. You're less prone to be distracted. I'm pretty athletic, so I enjoy all types of things—sports, computer games, hanging out with friends. I don't have a magical way of dealing with all of it, but I just set goals for myself and I try very hard to strive to complete those goals. The goals I set for myself are slightly unrealistic because it helps me push the envelope and be more productive.

For distractions, I just try to deal with them as they come. For e-mails, I try to respond to them immediately. I read an article by the person who started Slideshare, and she always replies to e-mails on the spot because if you don't, you are taking up more mental capacity to read once and then again later.

Do you think the public school system is broken in any way? You were homeschooled; do you think there's anything that public schools can learn from that model?

I have very strong views on the education system. I've done non-profit stuff my whole life, but one I'm currently setting up is to create a series of public charter schools around the world starting in northern or southern California. They'd use the mechanics of games, technology, and neuroscience to transform the curriculum. More people are talking about "how do we revamp the industrial age educational model" and what I saw at the Legacy School co-op was an important split according to skill, not age. The caveat is there needs to be proper socialization. This wasn't a problem for me because I was athletic from a young age, so that worked to my advantage, but a lot of parents aren't cognizant of this. Parents want to homeschool their kids for the wrong reasons, like they don't want their kids to learn about evolution; that's terrible.

Here's where I see an ideal school heading, hopefully in the next 5 years or so. The actual physical size of the school will shrink. The types of spaces present will become areas where kids need to socialize—for example the gym. There's going to be a blend of physical schooling and online virtual schools. This will help democratize education because kids will be able to get the best education from the best teachers around the world. This is similar to what Mega Study is doing in Korea. The teacher's role transforms from a one-way faucet of information into a manager and curator education. At some point, they'll use newer technology—think iPads—to track analytics. The parents will also have access to the analytics to see how the kids progress. There are companies working on this right now, but this is where it's headed. I think technological tracking of educational analytics and advancement plus the use of powerful gaming mechanics to make it engaging is what I see the ideal future of the school becoming.

Do you think the Khan Academy is the right model?

I think the videos are a little bit archaic. I think there will be an evolution into a much richer multimedia experience. Beyond video, there will be games and interactive experiences.

Is this the gap you're filling in with your startup?

Yes. My mission is to change the world by changing education. I love games and I think it's how education will be transformed.

You've mentioned neuroscience several times now—is there a reason why you're interested in neuroscience rather than computer science or computer engineering?

From a young age, I knew I wanted to do stuff related to science in the future. I was going to be a biochemistry major in college but halfway through, my grandfather developed Alzheimer's Disease and that peaked my interest in how the brain works. I am very interested in lower-level molecular and cellular neurobiology and higher-level cognitive science and psychology. Even though I'm leaving my Ph.D. program, I'm not leaving science in any way. I'm mostly using the principles of neuroscience and technology to make learning more fun and effective.

When you took your ACT at 11 and scored so high, were there any tricks you used to study? Did you have any game mechanics that helped you, or did you pick up a prep book?

I took the practice tests, like the Kaplan test prep. There actually are tricks to figure out for the questions. For every standardized question, there's a trick to answering them and Kaplan has figured that out. It's more of a process, which is why I don't think it's an effective test method. Apparently from the test studies they've not found anything better.

I recently read an article about studying how people might focus on memorization, while others will link it to existing knowledge. What approach did you take?

This gets interesting because there's some application to neuroscience here. There's a principle called the "binding principle" which states if you're trying to learn new information, your brain retains it if you have a previous cognitive schema or memory to bind the new information to. Let's use kids an example: let's say you're about to teach your kids a new lesson, have them create an advanced organizer. This organizer is a diagram or set of diagrams of what the student already knows about this topic. As you teach them the new information, they can think about it in the context of what they already know and they can make mental links to their existing knowledge. It increases learning effectiveness significantly.

I didn't completely understand recursion until I knew about stack memory. Once I understood stack memory, I realized that recursion was just an implementation of stack memory and it made sense mentally to me. I didn't always study like that—if I took more time, I probably would have understood a lot more. There are some interesting techniques to memorize if I have to do that.

Flash cards are very effective for memorization.

Spanish should have been called "Advanced Flash Cards." I want to ask you about when you decided you wanted to do a startup?

I knew I wanted to do a startup at some point. At Stanford, I kept thinking about doing a startup so I took a summer class there through the Graduate School of Business.

When you decided to drop out, did you think you could finish it? Why the sudden urge to drop out?

I was halfway through, I had about 3 more years. I had to decide: do I want to spend 3 years doing the Ph.D. or doing a startup? And the decision was easy for me at that point.

You did the Peter Thiel 20 Under 20 program; did you apply before you dropped out? And can you give an overview of how the program works?

I applied before I dropped out. The program is giving entrepreneurs $100,000 if they're under 20 years old and they have to drop out of school and do a startup. They flew out 45 people to the Clarium Capital offices and we interviewed there. Eventually 24 people were selected, so they went over the original 20. Some people are choosing to start the program later in the year depending on whether they do a summer internship first.

They are as hands-on or hands-off as you want; they have a strong network of mentors. The people network is extremely powerful, and that's one of my goals in life is to surround myself with the best people in the world. They've been making a lot of introductions and creating a lot of connections. I've been really impressed; everyone in the program will stay in touch.

I think most of the Peter Thiel Fellows don't actually need college because they're all driven, smart, and motivated. I think it's a great program overall.

What was the interview process like? When I did Y Combinator, we met once per week and there was pressure to get stuff done. It had its advantages.

The program just started, so things might change, but we're all friends now so we all organize events to go to. People aren't required to move to the Bay area, but they're strongly recommended to do that. If we want to meet up, I'll call them up. But there's nothing formal where we meet each week at a set time.

What's the name of your startup and what are you building?

The startup is called Airy Labs and we make social learning games for young children. The idea is that educational games mostly suck and we want to make them fun. I see games as these enormous opportunities for learning because games are simply abstract rules based on new systems. We want to make massively popular games that tens of millions of kids will play and the parents will actually support it. We're trying to align the parents' and children's interests.

Most games we're setting up now are learning agnostic. I think we can teach anything with games, and we'll start off with math, English, biology, and memory training. Some parents have e-mailed asking about anti-bullying conflict resolution type of games. A leader from a youth golf organization e-mailed and there's a lot of etiquette that we can teach there, for example.

We want to be the Zynga of games, but on the long-term act more like Disney where we have a strong brand that parents trust and kids love using. I want to build a larger scale business around making learning fun.

We talked about a comparison: it feels like you are Khan Academy except instead of videos, you use games to teach.

I see our games as being very consumer-focused. The problem with most educational games is they go to schools and try to impose the system on kids through the school system. We'd rather make massively popular games that kids will be gossiping about on the playground. The parents will pay for it, but they'll pay for these things anyway: things the kids nag them to buy, and things that benefit their kids' education.

How many games are working on now? What language are you using to build this? How will the games look and feel?

We're in the prototyping stage right now. We'll aim to release something within 6 months. Those decisions are still up in the air, but right now we're starting with Corona SDK (Lua). This was a fairly impulsive decision, so it might change.

Mostly, we're trying to encourage social pressure to play and learn. That's the social part that is exciting. We'll have 2d or 3d vector graphics as part of it, we want to have a high bar visually.

Do you have any cofounders?

I'm the founder but I have a founding tech team. I'm an Entrepreneur in Residence at StartX (the AOL building on Page Mill Road). It's a great accelerator and we'll probably have to move soon because we're hiring now. There are 6 full-time people here now, and we have several interns. Hopefully we'll have about 10 full-time employees by the end of the summer. It was a bit scary leaving the Ph.D. program, but it seems to be coming together now.

How will you get your early users? Will you approach schools?

The first thousand users will be easy to market to neurotic moms who want to increase their children's IQ. After that, the major drive of growth is going to be word of mouth between kids. We'll use online and offline advertising to reach those kids and then we'll build in mechanisms into the games to encourage kids to talk about the games. This is how social games work, so we're recreating that.

You said it was scary to drop out, since you have dropped out have there been any low points?

The fundraising was stressful up until the end because I was doing it alone. It eventually got finished, but there's enormous trust placed in me because they invest in me. Now that it's done, I have to deliver and not screw things up. That's my next goal: not screwing things up! I have to pay back that trust.

There were people who turned me down, and my personal opinion is I don't think it's a smart decision. You just ignore that and move on.

What's your work schedule like?

I'm more of a night person. When I was doing fundraising, I'd stay up until 4 or 5 AM. That's bad for your health—I was really into athletics and participated in the sleep lab at Stanford, which is another topic, but it's important to get lots of sleep. Generally, I work late into the night. On average, I work around 18 hours per day.

Is it true that a person who needs 8 hours per sleep can do 5 hours and work well on that?

It's not healthy at all. You can't perform at a top level unless you get adequate sleep. In my case, I would be more productive if I got more sleep so I need to fix that.

What's your biggest challenge right now?

The single most challenging thing is hiring good designers. I have an opinion that great designers are very rare. There are lots of mediocre designers, but finding the top designers is difficult.

Why would someone want to work with your startup?

We're looking for frontend iOS developers—hardcore Objective-C developers. We're looking for a Chief Creative Officer, UI/UX designers, and strong engineers.

It's not a hard sell to convince people to join the company; our mission is changing the world by changing education. We're building a huge company and have an important mission. This is going to be a multi-billion dollar company, we have the top investors, and we're going to change how the next generation learns. Our impact will be felt for the rest of history.

Can you talk about the time you most successfully hacked some non-computer system to your advantage?

In 4th grade, my teacher had a table full of cool prizes that every kid would dream of: kites, paper airplanes, rubber bands, all types of raffle prize stuff. Every time we did well on a math quiz or some test, we'd get these yellow construction paper with a printed peanut on it. You'd write your name on the back and if you collect enough of them you could buy prizes. I had lots of peanuts, and there was a fossil that I really wanted. There was no way I'd get that many, so I cheated. I stole yellow construction paper while my teacher was gone; I snuck back in while everyone was out for recess. I used scissors to cut them into the peanut shape and used a black Sharpie to forge the peanut graphic. The fatal mistake is I wrote my name on the back of them. The peanut cash register had a code on it, and only one student knew it. I found out this code and I got the prize, but I eventually got caught because I had my name on the back.

I don't know why I didn't just steal the fossil. I went through all of the trouble. I think I felt like I was creating value and contributing, this might just be rationalization.

Ooshma Garg, Gobble

Tags: businessperson, undergrad founder, hiring, side-project, self-funded, coincidental, iterate quickly, solo founder, design-focused, VC funded

Overview: Gobble started in 2010 as an online marketplace for home-cooked meals from local chefs. Gobble's mission is to give everyone access to fresh, homemade meals and enable anyone to easily become a chef. Since starting, Gobble has raised over $1 million and handles over 500 orders per month in the Bay Area.

Can you remember the first time you did something entrepreneurial? What was that like?

I think I have been entrepreneurial my whole life but only realized that I was, and what the word 'entrepreneur' meant, when I came to college at Stanford. I did what most kids do—had lemonade stands and trade shows with neighborhood kids where we would value and trade our Beanie Babies. Learning about sales and marketing in business was something I enjoyed doing from a young age and that gave way to an even more entrepreneurial personality in high school. My best friend got involved in and led many existing organizations in the school. She was head of the school newspaper and student body president. I liked to start new organizations in school. For example, I founded a Model UN team when I realized people had no forum to learn about or discuss global news, events, or issues. I got the school's headmistress to fund the team, found a faculty sponsor, and worked with other chapters to help start my own. I followed the same process with a few things in high school—clubs were kind of my training; like I was building mini-startups. A large part of Model UN was debate. I think debate skills also influenced my ability to sell, get jobs, and start climbing the professional ladder at a young age.

After starting Model UN, I asked our high school to let me use the gym every Sunday and started a dance class for local community members to come learn different kinds of dance. I would teach them Salsa, Indian dances, and Hip-hop, and then we would hold performances at all the local churches and temples. I also organized the first, overnight dance fundraiser at my school and was a Girl Scout for 12 years.

Now that I look back, a lot of things I did were dance-related. For my Gold Award project in Girl Scouting, I took the idea of teaching classes and applied it to a mini-summer camp model, where third and fourth-graders came and learned about different cultures through dance classes. Then, we went back out to the community and they explained what they had learned and performed at local nursing homes. I learned ballroom, Latin, and Indian dance on my own, and used that to help people of all ages explore other cultures and learn more about the world.

Tell me about college. Did you do any startups or projects at Stanford?

My parents are both in medicine and I developed an affinity for science at a young age; I was strong, academically, in middle and high school science. I entered college thinking I would get my pre-med requirements out of the way in case I wanted to follow in my parents' footsteps, but learned that I was more interested in problem solving than I was adept at memorizing information. So, during my sophomore year, I decided to major in bio-mechanical engineering because I liked building things with my hands and doing problem sets instead of writing papers or answering test questions.

My initial involvement in startups actually came about, accidentally. I was late and rushing to class, and I passed a woman manning a booth at a career fair on campus. She stopped me and asked if she could show me a demo of her company's product. Begrudgingly, I agreed. She had a product that lets you send a voice text message from one phone to another. So, if I were going to be late for this interview, I would pick up my phone and say, "I'm running late. I'll call you at 5." Then you would get a text indicating that Ooshma sent you a voice message. It initially had a niche use case for people that didn't want to call and talk, but were too busy to send a text message.

So, she showed me her demo and said, "We need interns, do you have a resume or contact information?" I gave it to her thinking nothing of it. And then she called and invited me to see their offices for an interview; the fact that I decided to go and interview, changed my life. I met the CEO, Nikhyl Singhal, and his startup, SayNow, which I worked for five years ago when there were only four people, was just acquired by Google this month! It was really neat to see their success and to work at a startup that grew to become something great that another company can incorporate and use effectively now.

That summer I could have volunteered with an orphanage in India or tried to get a job on Wall Street. Instead, I decided to work at a startup because I would have a ton of responsibility, and it was a time-sensitive opportunity that would be completely different the following year, as they would no longer be such a small, close-knit team. The last thing the CEO said to me—which I tell people that come in to interview for Gobble now—was that he wanted me to come into his company and "break glass." He said, "We don't need someone in here who is going to tiptoe around and try to do things perfectly or ask for directions, we want someone who isn't afraid to try things out, make a mess, and get stuff done."

When you were taking classes at Stanford, what were your favorites and least favorites?

My favorite class of all time was actually machine shop because it was so hands-on and I had never welded anything together before! Our first project was to make a magnifying glass and learning about the tricky aspects of machining, such as developing the contour of the glass piece in the magnifying glass, was fascinating; I loved the independence of the planning stages, and building something new with my own hands. My least favorite classes were the huge, lecture hall classes. I remember bio core being such a pain because everything seemed so impersonal and everyone was just a number, and so competitive, doing anything to beat the curve; that wasn't fun.

Did you know anyone going into school?

I didn't know anyone from my hometown. I had met people at Stanford's admit weekend and stayed in touch so I had one or two friends that I had just met, that actually became my best friends throughout college. In fact, the person I met at admit weekend before I even attended Stanford is still my closest friend to this day.

Were you actively looking for cofounders in school?

I never thought to myself, "I'm going to start a company now." I just started a company when I saw the need. So my attitude at Stanford was, "I want to meet and get to know as many people as I can because everyone here is wonderful and I don't want to miss out on meeting a very talented, intelligent person." But I wasn't searching, at least until after I decided to start my company, my junior year. As a junior, I was starting a company in addition to attending school, which was incredibly difficult. Looking back, I'm really glad I took the full course load my first two years because it was easier for me to finish my major and take the absolute minimum course load during my last two years.

Were you involved in any other extracurricular activities at Stanford?

The most important extracurricular activity for me was Stanford Women in Business, a network of 400 smart and very savvy women; I led the group for a year and that gave me a lot of exposure to great people at Stanford, but also a broad alumni network of companies that wanted to interact with us.

Were you working on your startup right when you graduated?

Yes. I essentially lived with my boyfriend during my senior year of college and I turned my dorm room into an office; we even hid the key outside the room so when I wasn't there, people working on the company had access at all times. We lofted the bed and crammed four desks, chairs, and lamps into a 100 - 150 square foot room!

When I graduated, I moved out of my dorm room into a real office on California Avenue, to continue running my company.

Did anyone inspire you while you were in school? It seems like you were pretty active in a lot of different areas.

Stanford has a lecture series called ETL – Entrepreneurial Thought Leader seminar. I remember one talk in particular, by Jen-Hsun Huang, who is founder and CEO of NVIDIA. He was really unique in that he is one of probably a handful of CEOs that started something, kept it going for decades, and remained CEO of the company. His story and the genuine love and fulfillment he found running this company, possibly for the rest of his life, was very inspiring. In fact, he just built a new building at Stanford this year and that seminar now takes place in his building, so all entrepreneurial centers are housed in the Jen-Hsun Huang Technology Center.

How did the idea of Gobble come about?

Put simply, I was hungry. I realized that there is no easy access to healthy, but delicious meal options in the world, especially for people who don't have families or for families with two working parents that are too busy to cook. So, that was the genesis of the idea and, literally the day after I had the idea, I started asking friends if I could organize a trial meal for them or find a chef to cook dinner for them, to see if matching local chefs to people and companies would work out.

As soon as a couple friends said yes, I started posting on Craigslist and got a flood of responses from interested chefs, so the business was started in about 24 hours.

When we first met, you were working on Anapata and Gobble was just a side project for you, right?

I started Anapata my junior year of college out of the business need wherein big companies wanted to recruit specific talent from colleges but there was no online network or database of these students and their resumes. I developed a site that would give companies access to these groups of talent at different universities around the country.

Anapata became an enterprise-focused startup, which I didn't understand or anticipate when I started the company; it also ended up becoming a startup with, what I call, a 'low ceiling.' It wasn't a billion-dollar idea, at least not in the form that I had imagined it. In retrospect, I consider Anapata my startup boot camp. It taught me a ton about how to structure an idea, build and run a company, and about what I loved and was good at. It's also what led me to Gobble, which I seriously consider to be my 'soulmate company.'

When you've had many different experiences, some bad, some good, and some that just didn't feel right, it makes you deeply appreciate it when the right one comes along; whereas you may not have recognized it otherwise. That's sort of how I see what happened in my life; I tried Gobble out while we were getting modest acquisition offers for Anapata and once Gobble took off I knew the stars were aligning and the timing was right to sell my first company and transition to Gobble, which I think will take me to the next level and create an impact that is, hopefully, worldwide.

So you sold Anapata?

I did, in October of 2010. We sold Anapata to a mid-sized company in the legal world. When Anapata took off, there was a company with a fleet of recruiting and productivity tools for law firms that wanted to use Anapata's software and brand to supplement its current suite of tools. It's now in great hands; I consulted with the firm for a few months initially, post acquisition; now I'm an advisor and board member for the company.

Did you have any cofounders at Anapata or Gobble?

I didn't have a cofounder for Anapata. I looked for one for quite some time. Perhaps it was because we were all students or someone else would have had to jump ship for my very specific idea, and that's something I learned—the idea that I had was not something everyone could relate to or become passionate about. Gobble has a very different story, simply because the idea is a very basic one that appeals to so many people. That has helped immensely with recruiting our team and investors.

We're only six months old now. We're building a fantastic team with technical talent from consumer companies and marketplace-based companies that have done well in the past. With regards to founding the company, I'm the founder. It just happened and I found people to come onboard that are just as driven to help me grow and achieve the vision. The key team members have significant ownership in the company and we treat everyone like partners, whether it's the office manager or the CTO.

Did you bootstrap both startups?

I used my savings to fund Anapata, initially. I bootstrapped it for almost three years, which was, in a sense, crazy because I was the only full-time employee during that time. I did everything from hiring contractors, design firms, outsourcing to India and the Philippines, and recruiting interns, to hiring part-time workers; we were a hodgepodge of employees, which contributed to our slower growth, I think, because in order to have rocket ship growth in a company you need a lot of people with their full hearts in the game.

So, I didn't bootstrap Gobble. I guess I started the company with those initial sales to startup customers. They ended up subscribing and we were actually making profits within one month, so after the first month I paid myself and another person. We had enough to cover our food and rent and everything was great. That continued, and after two months we started raising money and received over $1.2 million in funding. Now, we have offices, salaries, whiteboards, and a few board games too.

Can you summarize your fundraising experience?

We were very lucky because I had experience in the trenches via my previous company and was somewhat connected already in Silicon Valley. I also had very generous friends who supported me and introduced me to angel investors who, upon hearing the vision, seeing our initial results and looking at our business model, introduced us to more investors. We just kept 'climbing the ladder' in Silicon Valley to find the right investors and within a couple months, had a great syndicate of people and a nice cushion to take us to over a year of full-speed operations.

How long did it take you to build the beta?

Two months? Maybe less. Probably four weeks. The reason I can't give you a straight answer is that we can never decide when it's done; we can always make our product better, always add an extra feature or scrap it and redo it. So, even though we have something released, we're still trying to build our beta every day.

Did you ever have to make any major changes with Gobble?

We're at a critical point now—we've built the initial marketplace where people can post and buy food. We've learned that, actually, people are more interested in creating sort of a food playlist, like a Netflix queue. So you might say you need Gobble meals for lunch every Monday, Wednesday and Friday; you tag all the food, put it in your 'playlist' and we just bring it to you over those days.

We're making a drastic change to our product and product offering right now so the question is: "Do we rebuild the whole system or just build on top of our existing beta infrastructure?" I've learned that everyone's first version of something is always thrown out at some point because you learn so much from your customers that you ultimately have to rebuild a cleaner and more robust product from scratch. So, I'm comfortable with that idea but the question is when do we do it? It's really cool.

And then, competitors are actually popping up every other day. In the last week, I've gotten emails alerts about four competitors and another four or five the week before. Previously, our competitors were matching chefs to consumers, but there was no marketplace to feature the chef's food or meals. Recently, we've gotten emails from three different kinds of startups that list meals from chefs, just like Gobble. So, we're trying to stay ahead of the game and, as far as we can see, no one else has thought of our exact strategy yet.

How did you get the word out at first?

We're still planning that. Right now, very few people know about the company and I think that's important for new entrepreneurs — you don't have to send the word out on the day you release your website. Your website could be live for a month before you get the word out or have a launch day which, in a sense, is the case for us.

I've tried to be very thoughtful about how we're getting the word out so, for instance, one of our investors is connecting us to Wolfgang Puck—a chef with one of the biggest empires to the food industry with multiple restaurants, a show on the Food Network, magazine articles, you name it; so we're connecting with him to see how we can get the word out in the food community. We're also trying to connect with Rachael Ray, Oprah's magazine, and a few other places that cater to our target market, which is families, working parents, and professionals, and with some cooks and chefs as well.

So, we haven't gotten the word out yet because I want to connect with the right people and organize our 'word-out day' to make a big splash in the right places. I think startups should be very thoughtful in thinking beyond the technology world and launching in channels that specifically target their audience.

Were there any moments you thought Gobble was going to fail, or just got really nervous about something?

Yeah. I lose sleep every day over Gobble and that's a founder's job: to carry the worry so nobody else has to. It's no surprise that founders get gray hair before everybody else—every time I get that email about a new competitor my blood starts boiling. That's just one example of what makes me worry and want to run faster.

One of my friends told me that as a startup founder and entrepreneur, basically, you want to cry at least once a day but that's not the whole story because we absolutely love what we're doing. It's just like you said, we're constantly in the trenches and founders have a huge responsibility. So the worry is constant. I never think we're moving fast enough, but it's our challenge to balance progress with the health and happiness of the team, while ardently trying to make our startup the best product and service in our industry.

Did you say that you had customers, before the site was built?

Yes. I wanted to test out the real-world logistics and the viability of the idea before building a site because our company has an interplay between real-world and online activity, similar to Webkinz, where you sell a toy in the store and then you can build a life for that toy on their website. In those kinds of cases, you have to see if people are really going to buy a stuffed animal in a store and then type a code online to interact with their toy, before you build the whole virtual world that the toy lives in.

Our challenge was: many people can build a basic marketplace website, like Craigslist, or pay for one to be built, but are chefs really going to drive to somebody's house, deliver food that's warm, on time, and desirable enough for customers to order it again? That's why we worked to find customers before we built the website—to see if our idea was even viable.

I think it helped me with fundraising when investors heard that I actually went to the chefs' houses and watched them cook and then sat in the delivery drivers' cars and watched them carry food to companies. We actually delivered the wrong number of meals to one place and I even spilled a meal on myself when I was walking across the street. What do you do when you're delivering food to a venture capital firm and some parts of those meals are missing? That experience really instructed my thought process in managing failure modes; setting up the best practices for chefs on our website and understanding the full spectrum of what we would have to control online so that everything would work in reality, for the consumer experience. It helped us make a better product and get better investors because they knew that I wasn't just hypothesizing.

So for the VC that didn't get his lunch that day—what do you do in a situation like that?

We carefully made an extra meal by taking a little bit from all the other meals. That was *very* stressful. Now, we ask all chefs to make an extra meal; if all the meals survive the delivery, then the delivery driver can keep a meal and that's a bonus.

The extra meal has come in handy a lot because spills continue to happen. The bonus meal is a huge incentive for the driver. It's worth so much more than the meal costs because the food is so delicious and it's home cooked and now there's a big difference between the value people see in working as a delivery driver for us versus for somebody else who might give them a few more tip dollars, so we're applying these sorts of incentives to other parts of the company. Tony Hsieh talks about 'wow moments' that are non-monetary but great, goodwill-creating incentives or practices for employees and customers. Just yesterday, we brainstormed on how to create more 'wow moments' at Gobble.

What's the work schedule like?

Regardless of whether we're at work or not, I'm constantly thinking about Gobble. I used to work constantly, and whether I was home or not I was always checking my phone and on-call, working until I felt tired and needed a break. That's not really sustainable. Just recently, Alex Schorsch, who is the Lead Engineer on our team, suggested that we routinely take every Saturday off. We tried out his idea and the results have been incredible; I love it. I still came to the office last Saturday, just for an hour, but the fact that everyone knows they don't *have* to come is amazing for happiness and productivity. I went out to dinner with some friends and was actually able to sit in my house for two hours—just hanging out on my couch, not working and not sleeping.

So our Saturdays off tradition is really refreshing for everyone; everyone is happier and multiple times more productive during the week. We also provide lunch and dinner everyday and people stay through dinner at the company and go home anywhere from 9:00 PM to 2:00 AM, depending upon their schedule, but the idea is that everyone knows what they need to do and when they need to do it by. So there's no guilt in going home at 9:00 or 10:00 PM during the week, even 8:00 PM if you're on track. In general, my friends and I have very different scheduling and working philosophies for our startups, and I'm not sure yet what style will end up being the best for us.

We also have no-meeting-Wednesdays that we might turn into Pajama Wednesdays, since there are no meetings, and we might as well be comfortable. One thing I want to adopt from—it's either Square or Wufoo—is, they spend all Friday afternoon writing letters to their customers which is part of that 'wow moment' or goodwill idea. The whole team sits down and writes letters to their customers. I want to dedicate a piece of each week to doing the same thing because our business is just like theirs, very people-focused.

In the early days everyone has to do three or four peoples' jobs. So what's funny is actually the only two full-time employees right now are Alex and myself, and Alex does all the back-end engineering and I do all the front-end engineering and business, so we'll make to-do lists and laugh because everyday his to-do list is summarized as, "Build website" and my to-do list was summarized as, "Get money." More recently, mine has been, "Get talent." And currently, it's "Get users." That's how I see my job. But in the early days we've just been splitting up work by looking at what's immediately ahead of us, and matching that to our skill sets or availability.

But, we're quickly hiring and even by next week we'll have four full-time employees. So, instead of making a list of tasks, your job transforms into making a particular metric as high as possible. I really like that because you can structure your own tasks and have the autonomy to define your own job, so long as you are working to better your metric.

Have you ever hit a productivity brick wall or had motivational problems?

Most of the time when someone isn't motivated to work, it's not because their job or the purpose of the company isn't inspiring, it's because they've been working too much. They've worked three days straight, they haven't done their laundry, they haven't eaten much food; they've just been killing themselves. Really, the solution is for them to rest and it's really important when you see someone that looks that tired, to immediately send them home. It doesn't matter if there is a huge deadline. I think if someone is that tired and not motivated and you can see it in their face, it affects the whole team. They're going to be with you for the long haul. So I think it's really important to be aware of everyone's personal health because they'll appreciate it and, at the end of the day, be much more productive than they would have been if you ask them to stay.

I've heard horror stories from people that actually work with Gobble now about working somewhere else previously, where the CEO or founder would just hand them a Redbull when they looked tired. That's one way of doing it but you don't want someone to resent you or think you don't care about their personal health. So honestly, instituting something like Saturdays off, as a rule, motivates people a ton because they get to plan personal things, and there's absolutely no shame in having hobbies and projects outside of work.

I've been interviewing engineers recently, in fact, who tell me about their hobbies in almost a self-deprecating way. They say, "I just want to make sure it's not a problem that I'm taking this chemistry refresher course," because they like science or, "Because I want to do this sailing competition next year and I kind of want to sail." I would like to encourage hobbies. Hobbies work a different part of the brain and make people more creative.

What advice would you give to someone in a similar position in college interested in doing a startup?

I loved the fact that I started a company while I was in school. If you think you're an entrepreneur, I would say—if at all possible—to start a company during college. You have a great network of professors around you and the fact that you're a student will carry you so far in your startup. People don't even recognize the value of starting up while you're a student, until its gone; you get free tickets to big events and amazing CEOs meet with you *because* you're a student. Once you're not a student, you're just somebody else who wants to meet them.

My advice would be to just start something—identify a need that you personally notice; it doesn't have to be the biggest need because you just need the experience of starting a company. So don't wait for the perfect idea, just start something and that will teach you so much. Then, you might build that small idea into a bigger one, or from your experiences, you'll think of a bigger idea much sooner than you would have otherwise.

Can you talk about the time you most successfully hacked some non-computer system to your advantage?

It's difficult for me to name one time because I think an entrepreneur's and a founder's job is to constantly hack non-computer systems. When you're building a startup you are constantly hacking the world and figuring out, "How do I get free food today? How do I get free furniture? How do I get access to a conference? How do I meet with the speaker?"

I think I'm reasonably good at hacking things. For instance, we can't get parking permits in Palo Alto and a lot of our team members have been getting tickets because you have to change your parking spot every two hours and we forget because we're knee-deep in our work. There's a building nearby with lots of empty parking spots and no one checks parking; we've been tracking it for a while and now we all park our cars there, that's hacking a system.

Another example is finding out that one restaurant gives such big lunch specials that it can actually feed two employees. We now ask the restaurant to separate the food into two boxes so everybody's employee lunch only costs us $4 or $5; they love the food and it's a perfect portion. I try to hire people who think like that, who think, "How can I get this done in a scrappy, resourceful startup way?" There are a lot of people that don't have that mindset; they don't go out of their way to find an unconventional or hacky solution to a problem. You want someone that thinks scrappy, especially at the outset of the company, someone who can hack the system.

I think our job is to constantly hack systems. YouTube gets a lot of people to publish their own videos and then influenced the creation of Vevo that allows for copyrighted content to be streamed online, which wasn't possible before. So, even with Gobble, it's very, very difficult for home chefs to have their own businesses and officially cook for other people, and currently, we're hacking that system and figuring out the easiest way possible for these great home cooks to sell their delicious meals and, hopefully, officially become chefs.

You've done two startups as a solo founder, one of which was bootstrapped for three years. Do you think solo founders are at any particular disadvantage or do you feel like it's a stigma? Was it challenging to raise money in that position?

Actually, because of that stigma, I went in to fundraise and I told people that I was the founder but that there were actually three of us. So they would ask how many of us started Gobble, and I'd say, "Three of us: myself and two other engineers." They'd say, "Okay, are they full time?" And they weren't, they had other jobs. They were working with me part time until we got funding. The best investors would correct me and say, "So there's really one of you—it's you." And I'd say, "Yes, it's me." They'd respond,

"Alright, I'm in!" And then they'd write me a check for $50K or $100K.

So, yes, I think there's some stigma, but I truly believe that if you have an idea, that you shouldn't wait for a cofounder or stop yourself for any reason from realizing your vision. If you just go out there and do it, then people will invest no matter many founders there are.

Hiten Shah, KISSmetrics

Tags: businessperson, school worker, undergrad founder, hiring, profitable, VC funded, iterate quickly

Overview: KISSmetrics was started in 2008 to offer analytics tracking to help customers understand their users' behavior. Some of the metrics provided might be: average revenue per user, lifetime value of a customer, and this data can be tied to web activity as well as things that might happen on the back-end, such as product upgrades. KISSmetrics powers sites such as Zappos, GitHub, SlideShare, Etsy, and more.

Can you recall your earliest experience of doing something entrepreneurial?

When I was between the ages of six and eight years old, my father began to promote the idea with me. He had always told me that you should work for yourself; I don't know if he ever used the word 'entrepreneur', but he basically meant that you want to do businesses, or be the type of person that doesn't have to work for anyone else. You should not be in a situation where you put in a certain number of hours and the money you make is based solely on the number of hours you're putting in.

In middle school I just started working on a lot of different, random things; I was always trying to sell things. There isn't a specific story that I have about middle school, but when I was in high school and I started driving, things started to get interesting.

I had always wanted to fix up my car because that was the craze back then, especially in Southern California where I grew up, so one of my friends and I started a business selling car parts. The whole idea of that business was just to make money so we didn't have to pay for those improvements on our cars. We never made it profitable, but we made it profitable enough that we didn't have to spend money improving our own cars.

Once you got to college, did you do anything else outside of class?

Yeah. I always tried to make money in college so I started several college-based businesses, whether it was selling things to my friends or just finding opportunities to make money with the frat system. Most of the stuff I did was offline so there were a few scenarios where I had helped the frats throw parties. That was a very interesting experience: I actually made money on it and the frats had fun having parties.

One key lesson I would say I learned is that there is much more to college than just partying and actually going to class and learning that way. I would encourage college students to think about business opportunities where they can make money while they are in college—not by getting a job, but by creating a business out of nothing. One way is to do it based on an unmet need that college students around them might have.

What kind of classes did you take in college?

I actually ended up creating my own major. I took economics, sociology, and business classes, and as a result I had a diverse group of people that I hung out with. For me, I think the most interesting part of college was actually the people, more than the classes. That being said, without actually going to college, I wouldn't have had that experience.

Going into college, did you know lots of people?

Actually, freshman year I didn't, but one of my really good friends from high school who was a year behind me, ended up coming up to the same college the following year. I didn't really know many people going into college, but I made a lot of friends while I was in college.

Were you actively looking for cofounders and thinking about startups?

Actually, not at that time. I went to UC Berkeley and there is no entrepreneur community there that I was able to find, or maybe I wasn't even looking for it. Most of the stuff I did was very offline oriented; I was trying to literally do whatever I could to make a profit on the college students. I would say that I didn't really focus on startups while I was there. I actually got into it, somewhat by accident, after I graduated college.

Did you take time away from class to relax?

For me, college was pretty busy. I was always trying to find new opportunities. Again, I was taught from a young age that you shouldn't ever have to work for anyone so, whatever I did— whether it was college or pre-college—it was all about working for myself, not getting a regular job like most people have. That was really my motivation for everything.

Were you able to go through school without working for anybody else?

Yeah, absolutely. In my whole life I've only had one job and it was an internship in high school that paid $15 an hour to learn more about technology at a medical devices company.

What was going through your mind as you were graduating?

I actually didn't know exactly what I was going to do when I got out of college, simply because I didn't really think of it like that. I wasn't going to go get an MBA or go to law school or anything like that. That wasn't my plan at all.

When I got out of college I began a consulting company with a friend, actually, the brother of my now-wife. He's about four years younger than I am, so, he was just out of high school. At the time, he was doing search engine optimization and Internet marketing for a client who was paying him about $3,500 a month. I basically joined him and we ended up doing a bunch of consulting for people that also wanted search engine optimization; that turned into a lot of other things over time.

So actually, the story goes, my cofounder Neil and I were working on consulting stuff and we realized that we always wanted to build web-based products, build more scalable revenue. So we started investing a majority of the profits we made, back into trying to learn how to build product for the web. I'd say we've probably hired close to 100 web designers, developers, and development agencies, and probably tried close to 20 different web-based businesses that all failed, from a hosting company to a podcast advertising network. Eventually, we created our first software service product called Crazy Egg that creates heatmaps of where people are clicking on a page. The plans on the site only go up to $99 a month.

That company is still running; that was the one that worked out, of all the different endeavors we tried over about three years. We launched this product at the end of 2005, after working on our consulting company for two to three years and trying lots of different ideas. I'd say the thing that we realized is that if we were on the Internet and were pretty good at marketing, we should probably be building web-based products. So, we dumped all our profits into trying to learn things that we didn't understand or didn't know at the time. Neither of us were technical; we don't know how to program or design, but we are very good at marketing. I'm not a developer but I can fake it because I was taught by the people that worked out really well, out of those one hundred people we hired, several of them are still working with us today.

I was taught a lot about engineering and development along the way, and I realized that my cofounder had the passion for sales and marketing and I had a passion for building great products on the web, and that's something that came out of those consulting days, trying to build these products, and trying to learn things we didn't know.

For better or worse, the way we learned was by actually spending money and trying to create these types of products on the web. That's how we grew our company and that's how we learned how to do things. In fact, I would say that's how we learned how to do everything we know, because we didn't have any of this knowledge prior to starting in the industry.

I noticed a few other founders followed a similar path. They came out of college with one project that seemed to bring them revenue and gave them runway to build their next startup. Blippy, for example, created several profitable apps before they came up with what is now Blippy. Did you guys think, *let's just build a ton of stuff and if something works out we'll focus on that one*?

Yeah, somewhat. A bit of a difference for us is that, they are engineers so they could build the stuff themselves. We had to support revenue by doing consulting and then build products on the side, so to speak, and I would say we waited too long before we actually made the leap to go full force into one of our products, because we had to keep making money the only way we knew how, which was consulting. The thing about a consulting business is, it's a services business; you're still working for someone, it's all your customers and it's not as scalable. So, it actually took us longer than it should have to get out of that.

How did the idea for KISSmetrics come to you? Why track users?

We actually were doing CrazyEgg at the time. While we were building that product, we realized there was a big opportunity to build more products, to sort of build a second version of our product. That's what led to KISSmetrics. We started looking around and decided to raise funding for it because we saw it as a much bigger opportunity than Crazy Egg.

You started this with Neil, your cofounder. How did you meet him?

We met because I was dating his sister. I'm now married to her.

Was raising money a positive or negative experience?

It has been a very positive experience. It has a lot to do with who you raise money from, as to what kind of experience you're going to have.

We actually tried raising money for Crazy Egg, back in the day, and wasted a lot of time trying to do that. It wasn't necessarily a negative experience, but it wasn't as positive as our last experience raising money because KISSmetrics actually worked and we did raise money.

We've raised two rounds now, so I would say that KISSmetrics was easier for us because we had already built relationships and, actually, already pitched some of the same people that ended up funding us. So yeah, I'd say Crazy Egg was a little bit rougher because we didn't really know what we were getting into. KISSmetrics was a lot more straightforward; it was easier. That being said, it's never easy to raise money. There's always a negotiation and there's always something going on. Even if you're a serial entrepreneur, there are always things you've got to overcome.

It seems like most people choose one of two approaches to fundraising. It's kind of the James Lindenbaum school of thought, which is basically, decide that you don't know the investors but you're going to close in a month and you're going to get everybody to either get on board or just not do it at all. Whereas, people like Ashvin Kumar prefer to take time to get to know the investors, build relationships with them, and after several rounds maybe raise a round with them. I'm not sure if one approach is better than the other. You took time to build up relationships with VCs—do you recommend that approach in general?

Absolutely. That's the way to do it. If you can get to know them, you're going to have a better time in general after they fund you, and that's what you're looking to do.

Did you have advisors?

Definitely. We've had a lot of advisors along the way, both prior to raising money, and now, directly advising the company.

How long did that first beta take to build? How did you get the word out?

This is much more of a common practice now, but we did it almost six years ago with CrazyEgg and it wasn't really popular at that time. Basically, we put up a splash page and gave some idea of what we were working on. I don't want to say we were the first, but we might have been one of the first to do it about six years ago, where you just put up a page and collect email addresses. To be honest, it has actually gotten much easier to do this, just because of the way that the Internet has been going in general; it's easier to put up a page, easier to collect these email addresses and see some sort of growth right from the beginning, because you have five, ten, twenty, thirty thousand email addresses before you even put the actual product out there. So, I'd say that's a practice we use regularly, and will continue to.

Did you ever have any pivots?

Yeah. We pivoted two times on the product, just based on the type of customer that we were aiming for. Right now, we're actually in the middle, not of pivoting per se, but of expanding our product and feature set.

Were there any stressful moments? Did you ever think KISSmetrics would fail?

Sure. With KISSmetrics, we haven't really had too many of those problems, but with Crazy Egg we were basically one of the first large scale web apps using Ruby on Rails and, as a result, there were a lot of scalability issues we had to get over. Rails wasn't multi-threaded at the time so there were probably a good six months where we really stressed out about just keeping the servers up.

The struggle for uptime actually led to something really good. Back then, we had a couple of folks working on the product and a certain piece of it wasn't working well, which eventually led to us finding our current KISSmetrics CTO. He ended up taking over the whole CrazyEgg project, at the time, and making it successful. He's now our CTO at KISSmetrics and to be honest, I don't know how—being non-technical—we could have built these products without him

On the one hand, you guys had users, which is good; on the other hand, you had scale issues, which is bad. Did you ever have any other problems with the team, money, or product?

I'd say in the consulting company we had a lot of highs and lows, just because we'd be funding some of our products, like CrazyEgg, as part of the consulting company. Even prior to that we did a lot of experiments around trying different businesses. We tried almost 20 of them.

We had two additional partners in the consulting company; neither of them ended up being partners in our latest ventures. So, we've already dealt with a lot of those things, but to be completely honest about it, there is a new challenge every day when it comes to your team and—whether you want to call it managing a team or working with the team—as you grow and try to expand the team, if you haven't done it before there's always new stuff that comes up and surprises or challenges you. I'd say I deal with those kinds of challenges on a regular basis. You just have to get through it and not let it get you down.

How do you know when to move on to the next project? You said you worked on 20 projects before this. Is there a point where you think, "I'm bored with this" or "we've spent too much time on this, it's time to cut our losses"?

I used to be really bad about that. I've gotten much better at that, thanks to the concept of 'lean startups' that Eric Ries put out. His principles help you fail faster and help you get a much clearer indication of when something is not working.

I've always hunted for a process or any kind of data I could get on how to build better products, products that people want to buy. Running into Eric Ries, reading his stuff, and really trying to apply it has helped us build things that people actually want; it gives us a good framework for knowing when to call it quits.

Did revenue start to take off at a particular point?

At one point with CrazyEgg, actually, we saw revenue taking off. It's kind of an interesting story, we actually removed the free plan on the product and doubled our revenue in the first 30 days of doing that, so we thought we knew something at that point because that happened, but at the end of the day, I'm not really sure how smart of a move it was. We recently did some analysis and found it was a smart move, in the short run. We saw that 25% of our sign ups were actually coming from users that had been using the system for free, the last three to five years, and we got rid of this free plan about two years ago.

Those are just insights that we have now, and we have a better process for doing things than when we first created Crazy Egg. So based on what I know now, I think that kind of information is sort of stale at this point and I don't think I'd do that again. But, while that did lead to a lot of growth in terms of revenue, our daily sign ups dropped by about 90%.

How do you split the work up?

Neil focuses on sales and marketing. He's the one making sure that our marketing including our blog is doing well and that we're closing sales, stuff like that. I focus more on product and engineering. Basically, over time, we learned what each of us really liked, and individually focus on those things. Our schedules haven't changed. We're always working.

What happens after you get written about by the blogs? How do you sustain traffic?

When it comes to search engine advertising, marketing, promotions—you name it, we probably do it. We know how to do it all and we push forward on every possible front there.

The important thing is we measure everything. So, over time the channels change and stuff like that, but at the end of the day, it's all about measuring. We can find channels to be effective if we measure and optimize the traffic coming from them, know how much that traffic is costing us, and how much we're making off of it. For us, it's a measurement thing; that's why we like to try anything and everything.

What's your biggest challenge right now?

We've gotten a lot more serious about hiring lately with KISSmetrics so I'd say a challenge, as well as something that I'm excited about, is hiring; really trying to find people that are going to be a good cultural fit for our business and help us grow.

What's your culture like?

I wouldn't say we're as customer service-oriented as someone like Zappos because I don't know if anyone can be at this point, but we definitely try to be. I actually try to answer as many support emails as I can, personally.

We don't have an office yet; we'll have the office sometime this year. We're going to have an open floor plan. For us, it's all about people that want to try new things, test different ideas. We're also all about measuring everything that is going to affect the business and the bottom line, and letting anyone's ideas flourish.

I think that people are going to feel a culture of empowerment with us. What that means is that people should feel like they can speak up about anything, at any time no matter what their role in the company is. If they don't like something I say, they should be able to speak up and not feel like they'll get shot down or yelled at by me or anyone else on the team.

At the same time, we're focused on areas where people can improve skill sets around engineering and product, things like that. We look for people that want to improve over time, want to make themselves better, hone their skills, and learn new things. All those things are really important to us. So, I'd say we have a culture of empowerment. We empower you to grow into whoever you want to be, develop whatever skill sets you want to have. At the same time, we focus on providing an environment where people feel like—for lack of a better word—there is no boss.

Do you ever have motivational problems?

We found some solutions to these kinds of issues and ended up building our own product management tool so we could try to solve our problems, ourselves. The reason we built our own product management tool was because the engineers and designers were getting inundated with product requests and things like that, so we decided to actually implement a system that made it so that they didn't feel so bombarded all the time; so they knew why they were working on what they were working on.

We do a lot of that kind of stuff. If an engineer has a lot of repeated tasks, for example, we'll try to find a way so that a non-engineer can also help with that, or build tools so that non-engineers feel empowered to take control over something and make changes, directly. There's a lot of that in our company and our business—a lot of those tools become inspiration for things that we build for our customers.

Do you have a hiring process?

We try to make sure that as many people on the team, as possible, interview people that are considering joining our team. That has been a very useful tactic for us.

What kind of advice would you offer to students interested in startups?

Do something would be my first answer, and what I mean by that is: don't just sit on your ass and think that solutions are going to come to you. Depending on your likelihood of being successful, let's say programming, ask yourself, are you someone that can sit in front of the computer pretty much all day and program? Are you someone that's not like that? I think knowing yourself will help you get the answers to that.

The best pieces of advice I have is, first, to use lean startup principles and customer development, there's a lot that can be done without writing a single line of code. Second, whether you're an engineer or a non-engineer, you need to learn how to talk to customers and to build things that they want; be able to validate your ideas as quickly as possible so you don't fail 20 times like I did. If you do fail, then, you do it in a very compressed amount of time, not years, more like months, if not days or weeks.

There are a lot of ways you can build things today without having to actually code a single line. You can throw out landing pages to validate ideas and things like that. I don't think there's ever been a time when, *fake it till you make it,* has rung more true.

Can you talk about the time you most successfully hacked some non-computer system to your advantage?

Love that question, I've never heard it before. I'd say the best one is—and I'll say it because I still do it but plan to stop sooner or later: I don't put my license plate on my car. The free tollway isn't the reason I do it, because I actually do pay for the tollways, it's just, if you have a newer car—within the last three to five years—it's very hard for cops to tell that it's not just a new car thing. So, I can get away with that. Additionally, I have heard that by having the license plates, you are putting yourself in a more suspicious position, although I call bullshit on that.

The main reason I do it is to become immune to those red light tickets. I don't blow through red lights or anything, but I definitely am an aggressive driver. I've been trying to get better since I have a kid now.

I think Sam Altman is the reason that question shows up on the Y Combinator application and, coincidentally, he does the same thing. He drives a Nissan Skyline and you won't find any plates on his car. How do you know whether someone is the right or wrong person to hire?

I like that non-computer hack question. To be honest, what I look for is how they contact us. If they actually get through our job listing page which is KISSmetrics.com/jobs then you'll see at the bottom, there's a call to action. So one filter is, did they actually read it and decide to email us? Because it's not necessarily the most prominent thing on that page.

That's one thing. Second thing is, when they do email us, how much research did they do? I say that because, at least right now, we are actually relatively vague on the site about who we are and what we're all about. So you would actually have to dig to really find out more about us by doing some Google searches, etc., and it's kind of purposeful right now, but that's going to change soon.

When we do change, it will obviously be much easier to learn more about us, but right now, that's sort of a filter; like, do they mention my cofounder Neil when they email us? Do they even mention my name? Things like that. Do they know little things about us that you would only know if you did your research or did your homework? And it's not hard, because both of us and others on our team are very visible online.

Ryan Junee, Omnisio

Tags: Y Combinator, programmer, businessperson, acquired (YouTube)

Overview: Omnisio started in 2007 to create a platform that made it easy for people to create rich and compelling presentations and eventually offered a set of tools to enhance and mark up videos, such as adding annotations and slides to video presentations. After Omnisio went through the Y Combinator Spring 2008 class, YouTube acquired them for $15 million nearly 6 months later. Ryan Junee has moved on to create another startup that is briefly discussed, but in this interview I focus on the early days and Omnisio's transition to YouTube.

Was there a difference between Omnisio and YouTube?

YouTube was basically the place that you would go and put your videos online to show to people. What we would do is later take a video that you'd uploaded on YouTube and then add a layer on top of it. You could add annotations, which are pretty prevalent on YouTube now—those text bubbles that pop up. You could do other things, like tag certain moments in the video, and an outline of the video would be generated so that you could quickly jump to certain points. Related to that, you could upload a PowerPoint slide deck and have that sitting next to the video. You could tag the times in the video where the slide changes occurred so that anyone watching the video could see the slides flip along next to it, which is a feature that a lot of people seem to like—that unfortunately never made it to YouTube.

You're currently doing another startup, what is that?

It's in a completely different space, but what I'm working on now with my cofounder is a new type of personalized shopping engine. It's a new way of looking at online commerce where instead of you having to go and search hundreds of stores and thousands of products every day, we learn what you like and then we alert you when something we think you'll like goes on sale or arrives new in a store. It's a new type of push-based ecommerce rather than the traditional search-driven approach.

I'm a big fan of Starcraft 2 and I like nerdy shirts, so you are guys basically telling me where to get really good deals on nerdy shirts online?

Yes. If a special comes up on a site—for example a nerdy shirt that we think you're going to like—we'll send you an email or you can log into our site and see that item displayed. Basically, we're trying to bring the impulse buying aspect of offline shopping to online shopping. If you go into a mall and walk around, you'll see stuff that you like and think, "That's cool, I'm going to buy it." We're putting a bunch of stuff in front of you that we think you'll like, that's just gone on sale, or that's just arrived.

Can you tell me how entrepreneurship got started for you?

At a philosophical level it's something I've always wanted to do. I think that if you are an entrepreneur, you're an entrepreneur because you don't really have a choice; it's what you have to do. As you know, it's an incredibly difficult thing to be doing; it's pretty risky, but most entrepreneurs I know who are doing it, they do it because they just can't really stand working for someone else. That's always been the case for me.

I'm originally from Australia and went to the University of Sydney for my undergrad. I received two degrees: computer engineering and commerce, which is like a business degree. I then came to Stanford to do my Masters in electrical engineering, and at the time that I was at Stanford, I was also working at a startup that my friend had founded. I was the first non-founding employee there. It was in the network security space, and that gave me a good insight into how startups actually work.

They raised a whole bunch of money from VC's, hired a whole bunch of people, but unfortunately ended up failing. It was a good experience to see a company go from zero to 70 people then back to zero again. After I'd been working for them for a few years, I decided that it was finally time to make the jump and to do my own thing. I left that startup and found my 2 cofounders for Omnisio, who are friends that I knew from Australia. One of them was already out here, and I convinced the other one to move out here because I think Silicon Valley is obviously the best place to do a startup, especially in the tech space. Once we were all out here we started working on Omnisio full time. We decided, "Let's put in an application for Y Combinator," which I'd heard about, and I was a regular reader of Hacker News and all that stuff. We decided to apply, and got in.

Did you do any other groups or clubs in college?

I spent a lot of time TA-ing in college. It's probably what took up most of my time. I was a TA for computer science and I taught 12 different subjects during my time there over a whole range of things. I loved doing that.

Did you know anyone when you moved to the US to go to Stanford?

Some friends founded the startup that I was working for at the time that was called Sensory Networks. They are Australians, but two of them had gone to Stanford a couple of years earlier. They were telling me about it, saying how great it was, and saying that I should definitely apply. I applied and I ended up getting accepted into the electrical engineering PhD program. I told the founders, "I got accepted, what do you think? Should I go to it or should I keep working with you guys on the startup?" And they basically said, "If you don't accept it we're going to fire you and make you go."

That was a big part of the decision of me coming to Stanford, having such a strong recommendation from them. I moved to the US, didn't really know anyone, but there's a whole lot of international students in the grad program at Stanford. No one knows anyone really, and pretty quickly I met a lot of people. One of the first classes that I took when I arrived was one called Technology Venture Formation. It was actually in the Management Science and Engineering School. That course was essentially about putting together a business plan, learning how to raise VC funding, learning how to do marketing, acquire customers and all these kinds of things. You work in a team of 4 to put together a real business plan and at the end of the quarter you pitch your plan to a panel of real VCs. It was their feedback on whether they would fund you or not that determined your grade. I took that in the first quarter that I was at Stanford, and that made me realize that Silicon Valley was an awesome place for doing startups, with access to all these amazing resources.

That pretty much changed the trajectory for the rest of my degree program at Stanford. I started taking a whole bunch of other classes in technology strategy, marketing, fundraising and all these sorts of things in addition to my core electrical engineering classes. I pursued the same dual track that I did for my undergrad, but with much more of an entrepreneurship focus and I was actually learning from real experts in the field.

Did you try to find cofounders while you were at Stanford?

It was always a background process that I thought about. As I met people I'd always mentally take note, "This is a person I could start a company with one day." I didn't find many of them because I have a pretty high bar for who I'm going to work with on a cofounder level, but I did find a few. And obviously when I was really getting close to the point of starting Omnisio, I really started thinking, "Okay, of all the people I've met, who would be the absolute best people to work with," and so Simon and Julian who were my cofounders were those people.

Simon became the CTO of Omnisio. He's a really good developer that I'd known back at Sydney University, and also he worked for Sensory Networks, the startup that I worked for. He was over here also studying at Stanford so it was a good set of coincidences. And then Julian was our designer. He's just an excellent graphic designer who also happens to write code. I knew Julian from Sydney, and he also worked at Sensory Networks. He wasn't over here so I had to fly back to Sydney and convince him to move out to the US. He did move over to the US but he moved to New York because he thought that was a better scene. I then had to fly over to New York and convince him to move over to the Valley, so I eventually got him here.

How did you pay your way through school?

Australian universities are pretty good because there's a student loan system that the government runs. Firstly, the government picks up a large part of tuition, and secondly the part that you owe you gets an interest-free loan from the government. So it was easy.

Stanford is another story. It's much harder to fund your studies here in the US, and essentially what I had to do was to take out a massive loan that I started paying back once I graduated, and that was one of the things that really pushed me over the edge of leaving the startup I was working for to start my own: when I looked at my budget and saw, "Okay, I've got this huge debt that I'm paying back. At the rate I'm paying it back, it's going to take me X number of years. I don't really want to be paying back debt for this long. I need to do something drastic." That was a big part of the decision to leave, to go start my own thing, and fortunately circumstances turned out well for me and we ended up selling Omnisio to Google. I ended up paying all that back, and it felt really good to go from negative net worth to positive. That was one of the biggest changes financially that I've had so far.

Did you take time to relax in school?

My first few quarters were all about working hard, and gradually over time it became more about just enjoying the experience at Stanford. We definitely threw our fair share of parties. I started taking some less-demanding courses towards the end there, but I'm sure I got the full well-rounded Stanford experience.

In college, was there anyone in particular who inspired you?

There were a whole lot of folks through the courses that I took and through the speakers that they brought in. I went to talks from Jeff Bezos, Elon Musk, and Bill Gates. I heard from all these amazing speakers that they brought in to talk about their experiences that I just wouldn't have had access to in Australia at all. Even in the US it's hard to get access to that caliber of people. Being at Stanford and going to those events and those classes opened a lot of doors in terms of learning directly from the people who've done it.

Right as you were graduating, what was going through your mind?

I knew I wanted to do a startup. I was actually already working part time for the startup Sensory Networks while I was finishing up at Stanford. Pretty much once I graduated, I just moved to being full time with that startup. It was fun because the startup was headquartered in Australia, but we had an office here in Palo Alto. Initially I was the only person there, but it grew to about 5 people. It was a very small company, and being a generalist I got to do a lot of different things, but it still wasn't my own startup. I eventually left and did my own, it was a good transition.

How did the idea of Omnisio come up; what was that moment?

The initial idea came up when I was reading a copy of Business 2.0 Magazine, which unfortunately, they don't publish anymore. It was a really good magazine back in its day. I was just reading an article about a salsa-dancing teacher who had succeeded in putting some videos online of his classes, and he was charging something like $9 per video to watch them or something like that and he was saying how great it was that the Internet allowed him to make all this extra money. I started thinking, "Well, how could we scale that up and make a generalized platform to allow anyone who has expertise in some domain to put lessons online and make money from them in a really simple way—but also in a compelling way—for the viewer with a rich multimedia experience?" That's how I came up with the original idea.

I had a bunch of other ideas I was considering at the time, and I went to Simon who I was pitching to be my cofounder. I said, "Here's a few ideas I'm thinking about. Which one do you like the best?" We went through them, and the original idea for Omnisio was the one he liked the best. We decided to just go with that and start mocking up some screens and building some prototypes. Through the course of doing that, I sent some of the ideas back to my friend Julian who was still in Sydney, and he started getting excited about the idea and started working on some mockups which we noticed were much better than anything that we had put together. We decided to go full-force on recruiting him to be part of the team.

How did you meet your cofounders?

I knew Simon back at Sydney University. He was a year below me in the engineering program, and he eventually ended up working at Sensory Networks in Sydney after I had already left to come to the US. He did the same thing that I did: he left to come over to Stanford and do his Masters in electrical engineering. He was over here, and I knew he was a great engineer, so I started talking to him and going with him to some entrepreneurial events on campus. I was trying to seed the idea of doing a startup with him—his original plan was to go back to Australia after he graduated. I said, "Hey let's just work on this thing, you can do it part time while you're finishing up at Stanford. If we can't raise money and turn it into a company then fine, you go back to Australia, but it might end up being successful." Obviously that was the case and we ended up doing some great things at Omnisio and at YouTube—opportunities that we probably wouldn't have had in Australia.

My cofounder Julian is also from Sydney: I didn't know him at university, but he was a good friend of one of the founders of Sensory Networks. I met him socially, then he joined Sensory Networks as a designer/developer, so I saw his work through that. And every time I went back to visit Sydney I would hang out with him and we became friends.

What was your fundraising process like?

We never fundraised for Omnisio because we ended up selling. But after Y Combinator's demo day, where we pitched Omnisio, we did have a whole bunch of angels that were interested in funding us. We went through the usual process of meeting with them and pitching and trying to close deals, but in parallel Google had seen us at Y Combinator and also through introductions from friends, so we were spending just as much time going to Google and YouTube's offices and pitching various folks there on what we were doing.

The acquisition process took several months from first meeting to closing the deal. I pretty much spent all my time on that, talking to product and engineering folks, or their M&A team, or to my lawyer, and so forth. During that time Julian and Simon kept coding and adding features to the sites so that we kept it moving forward, because you've always got to think that a deal is more than likely going to fall through. We didn't want to be stuck if that happened, so we kept pushing the product forward that whole time.

What was that process like when Google approached you? What did you guys talk about?

Some friends of mine had done a Y Combinator company a year earlier that was acquired by Google called Zenter. I was talking to them about what we were doing with Omnisio and they said, "It sounds cool, do you want us to show a demo around to some folks at Google?" I thought, "Yeah, why not, it doesn't hurt to have them seeing what we are doing."

We went in and showed it to some teams at Google and at YouTube. We eventually ended up giving a demo to Chad and Steve, the founders of YouTube. They seemed to like it and at that point we were introduced to Google's M&A team and started talking with them. That kicked off a few months of negotiations of term sheets and contracts and so on, with lots of lawyers before we finally closed a deal.

So you were the one who talked to Google through that?

Yeah, I talked to Google for the most part. When we had to go in and give demos and show what we had done I'd bring the whole team. It was good to have the whole team represented to answer technical questions or explain the UI and so forth. But when it came down to just the nuts and bolts of negotiating the term sheets and talking with lawyers, I was the primary point of contact and I would just make sure that Jules and Simon were happy with the high level terms that we agreed on.

Was it stressful at all for you? It seems like it was a little bit time consuming—it was 4 months, although I think that's considered normal. Were there any books or anything that you read on the topic to help you do those negotiations?

The biggest thing that helped us is that I brought on Chris Sacca as an advisor. Once we had reached a point where Chad and Steve wanted to meet with us, I knew that there was something serious going on. Chris Sacca had come to speak at one of the YC dinners: he was a former Google exec who had worked on M&A deals from Google's side in the past, and I called him up and said, "Hey, I've got a meeting with Chad and Steve at YouTube tomorrow, I think they want to acquire us, what should I do?" He became quite involved and was very helpful in the process.

I ended up bringing him on as an advisor and giving him some equity in the company, and he was really useful in all my negotiation conversations. He knew how these things were done, so it just really streamlined a lot of things.

As far as stressful moments, there was a time when it didn't look like we were going to reach agreement on terms and we were prepared to walk away from the deal. That was a pretty stressful moment: feeling like you had something and then it's gone. But luckily we reached agreement in the end.

When I negotiated our sale to Loopt, I remember that being in a position where you are willing to walk away is one of the best things you can have in a negotiation.

I think as a general negotiation tactic you've got to have an alternative to a negotiated outcome. And that alternative may be to just continue doing what you're doing today. But you have to be willing to accept 'no agreement' as a possible outcome of a negotiation. It definitely helped having that mentality.

Also some good advice that I got from Chris Sacca early on about general acquisition philosophy, he told me, "Talk with your team, come up with a price, and a set of terms before you start your negotiations: what's the minimum that you'll accept?" And we had that discussion with the team saying, "Okay, this is the absolute minimum. If we can't get to this level then we're just going to keep working on the company." And so having that set and agreed upon before we actually started the negotiations was very useful, otherwise you can be seduced in the negotiations and think, "Oh well, it's not that bad, maybe we should just take this deal." But if you have made that decision beforehand when the emotions aren't as strong, you can feel more confident in your decision when you're in the heat of a negotiation.

We were told the same thing from our advisors. As 3 students out of school, we had never done this before, we had no idea what we were doing and so we worked with investors outside of YC who understood the terms and could explain to us how cap tables worked and help us understand all that stuff so that we knew whether we were getting a good deal or not. I think having the advisors was a really good thing in hindsight.

I totally agree. Initially I thought that lawyers would fill that role of advisors, but having gone through it and working with Chris and then working with our lawyers I realized that's not the case. Lawyers are concerned with minimizing the downside risk and so they don't push for things that could maximize the upside. You really need some guys on your side that will help you optimize the upside. Chris Sacca was one. I also had a really good tax guy; he helped suggest some ways of structuring the deal that would minimize our personal tax liability, whereas our corporate lawyers never even mentioned it because they were focused simply on minimizing risk. You really need advisors who are thinking of taking those acceptable risks and pushing for the best possible deal.

What advice would you give to someone applying for Y Combinator, or any accelerator for that matter?

We had a prototype to show, they always like to see running code as an example of the fact you can build stuff. That probably helped.

Were you nervous doing the interview?

I guess we were, but it was over so quickly that you don't really have time to think. You have a flurry of questions and then you are out. It was more like just a fun adventure—all three of us flying to Boston for the first time and crashing at a hotel room together, and then walking over to find the Y Combinator office in the pouring rain and going to pitch these guys, it was a memorable experience. I guess there were probably nerves in there as well, but it was just fun and exciting.

How long did the Omnisio beta take to build?

We started working on it full time in October. I think the Y Combinator interviews were around November. We'd probably only been working on it full time for maybe a month, and then by the time YC's program actually started we had developed it further.

I think a generalization I'd make is that is it's good to have external deadlines when you're really early on building a startup. I asked a friend of mine, Noah Kagan, who was running a conference if he wanted us to put his conference videos online synced with the PowerPoint slides. Basically we went to this conference not having a real product or anything yet and said, "Hey, we want to put your videos online," He was like "Yeah cool, that's good." I was sitting there with my video camera filming the talks while Julian was running around to the presenters asking them for copies of their PowerPoint slides, and Simon was sitting there with his laptop coding up the actual product that we would need to put this online. It was totally fly by the seats of our pants, and we ended up getting the videos online with the slides and got sort of a good reception, and so we started doing that for a few more other events including Y Combinator's Startup School, which was a really popular one because it got picked up on Hacker News. It got us most of our initial users.

I remember watching the Startup School videos on Omnisio. That's how I got drawn to the website and I really liked how you guys had the slides at the bottom. Nobody else was doing this at the time but you navigate the videos using the slides that the presenter used and that was very cool.

Yeah, it was definitely our most popular feature that has not really been replicated anywhere since. Unfortunately we never got that launched on YouTube, there's still an opportunity for someone to do it.

Did you ever worry Omnisio would fail? Did something ever stress you out in the startup?

I guess the main thing was just trying to figure out how we were going to survive, because by the time we got acquired I was already on credit card debt and Jules and Simon were probably in a similar situation. We had to raise money or something. Fortunately we were in discussions with a bunch of angel investors after the YC demo day. There was a pretty good chance we would have raised money if we didn't sell, but you can never take that for granted.

That was the most stressful time, trying to figure out, "Okay we need to do something to get some cash here." Other than that, I think it was actually a surprisingly easier ride, definitely an outlier in the sense of less than a year from starting the company to being acquired by Google. I'm expecting a lot more rough patches next time around.

How did you guys split the work between the 3 of you?

We had our roles, but fundamentally we're all developers and when you're starting a web-based startup all there is to do is develop stuff. We all sat together coding, but we each had our specializations. Simon was the CTO; he worked on the most difficult parts of the code base—like the whole event management system within our client. Julian, being a good designer, did all our UI. He's good in Photoshop, coming up with the visual designs and so on, but because he is also a developer he can take that visual design, chop it up into HTML, CSS, write the Ruby code, etc. And then I pretty much just did everything else, whatever else needed to be done.

What was the schedule like? Did it change over time?

It was pretty hectic. Jules and I lived together, so when we were awake we pretty much sat in our little home office there coding. We purposely lived down in Atherton, which is a really boring but very affluent area of the peninsula, and because there's nothing to do we ended up staying home coding. It was a conscious decision to do that versus moving up to the city where there would be a lot of distractions and options to go out and have fun, and it was an advantage to be in a boring area. Simon was actually still finishing up his degree at Stanford, so he was living on campus down the road from us. Because he was part time it depended on whether he had assignments or exams to study for or whatever. His time commitment fluctuated, but once he finished at Stanford, he went full time with us.

You've since left YouTube and have started another startup. Can you explain a little bit more what you're working on there?

I left Google over a year ago. I'm full time on this. I've spent the last year prototyping and brainstorming ideas with my now cofounder, and we had gone through a bunch of different ideas, but this is the one we decided to really focus on. We've been working on it full time for the last few months. We just closed our seed funding, we have a prototype built and we're still testing it with our close friends at the moment, before we start rolling it out to a bigger audience.

The name is Inporia. We haven't launched yet but essentially it's a new way of looking at e-commerce. We realized that there are so many changes going on across online stores each day. Just to give you an example looking at one store: we looked at Nordstrom, and saw that there's literally hundreds if not a thousand changes to their product catalogue everyday, and those could be things like prices dropping, new items being added, etc. As a user you can't afford to spend time on all these stores everyday noticing these changes.

We found from market research that customers are worried that they are missing out on sales for products that they love and would have made a purchase if they had known about them. Our essential goal is to figure out what you want to know about, to scan all the online stores every few hours, and to notice those changes. We want to get those to you as quickly as we can, but we'll filter them so that you only get the signal and not the noise; you only get the things that you care about. "This item has just gone on sale and we think you'll like it. Here it is for 50% off, do you want to buy it?" and that sort of thing.

Is this a different cofounder at Inporia?

Yes. Julian and Simon are both still at Google. We had an earn-out period obviously after the acquisition. I decided to leave money on the table when I left to start something new, but they're still there.

My cofounder now is a guy named Max Skibinsky and he's another serial entrepreneur. He had a company in the Facebook game space that he sold last year to Playdom. We both have come from this background of having a small early stage success, a bit of money in the bank and no immediate need to go out and fundraise or take a job. We could afford to spend time thinking about exactly what it is we wanted to do next, who we should raise money from, and all that kind of stuff.

Would you consider the challenge with Inporia to be more technical or market-oriented?

There is a lot of technology we want to build in the sense of the machine learning in order to really show you stuff that's highly relevant. As you probably know from things like the Netflix challenge, to get something that's highly relevant is actually really hard. Once we are up and running as a full-fledged company, that's where we'll be spending most of our engineering hours. Right now it's just a matter of building the basic minimum viable product (MVP), to show off the concept and to figure out our strategy for acquiring users, hopefully making use of what Max has learned from his Facebook gaming days using viral channels and so on. But I think that the biggest challenge initially is going to be the user acquisition, as it is for most consumer web startups

Where did you get the idea for Inporia?

We spent a lot of time brainstorming a whole lot of ideas. I was really interested in the e-commerce space and I felt like it was due for a renaissance. Basically e-commerce has been fairly stagnant for the last 10 or 15 years, there wasn't a whole lot of innovation until maybe 2 years ago when we started seeing some new models like Gilt Groupe and Groupon and the recent subscription-based commerce models like ShoeDazzle. There's a resurgence of innovation in e-commerce happening, and I have been thinking about that for about 12 months as well, trying to figure out what would be interesting to do in that space.

I ran some of surveys on Mechanical Turk listing out a bunch of problem statements that I saw or felt, asking people to say whether they agreed with these problem statements or not. I ranked the results and one of the highest ranking ones was, "I wish there was an easy way to find out when my favorite brands and products go on sale. I feel like there are sales that I'm missing out on." We realized we could solve this with technology, so we decided to tackle it. As we've been building it out we started thinking about other directions we can take it, building a new paradigm of e-commerce where we push stuff to you based on a model of what we know about you. Compare this to the traditional search-based model where you go and browse and search across a number of sites; I think there's something compelling there. Obviously we're probably going to change directions a few times as we build the company, but I think that the general space is interesting.

Have you ever struggled with productivity or motivation? How do you deal with that?

Definitely. It always happens. I guess the best solution is to have a cofounder. I've spent a bunch of time working on projects on my own in the past and often get to a point where I lose motivation, or not necessarily lose motivation but something else happens in your life that you end up focusing on instead, and eventually that original project fades away. Having a cofounder is important because you have this social responsibility to them to keep working hard because you know that they're working hard, or similarly if you're really motivated and positive about what you're doing and the cofounder is in a slump, you can help motivate them and it works the other way too.

When you're thinking, "Why are we doing this?" then they can come along with some ideas that will help to reinvigorate you. Definitely having that cofounder helps to balance the mood swings and the emotional roller coaster that is a startup.

I don't know if I have any other specific tips other than to keep building stuff and to put stuff in front of people, because usually having feedback from actual people—even if they're just your friends—saying that they like what you're doing is usually enough motivation for you to keep going with it.

Do you think it was a good idea that In your case you joined a startup out of school before you just created one? Do you think people should do that?

I think in my particular case it was the best way of doing it, because I was living down in Sydney. I didn't have exposure down there to anything entrepreneurship related; that's why I'm actively working so hard now to try and change that and build a startup community in Sydney.

Working for a startup that was funded by Silicon Valley VC's and then coming out here and going to Stanford and being in all these classes that were taught by entrepreneurs and Silicon Valley VC's and getting that exposure was incredibly useful for me. I think for people who are based here at Stanford or Berkeley or even other schools in the US, you probably already have a pretty good exposure to entrepreneurship, and so you might have enough of a base already to jump straight into your first startup right out of school. I guess it depends on your individual circumstances.

Can you talk about the time you most successfully hacked some non computer system to your advantage?

Well I used a computer system to help me get a reservation at The French Laundry. I was dating a girl from Australia a year or two ago, and she was coming out to visit me in San Francisco. I wanted to take her to The French Laundry—probably the best restaurant in California and certainly one of the top restaurants in the US. Because it's so highly rated, it's next to impossible to get a reservation. They take reservations exactly 2 months in advance, and so you have to call up at 10 AM when the reservation line opens and all the tables will be booked out within a few minutes. Since my girlfriend was coming to visit in only a few weeks time I couldn't take the usual approach. After doing some online research I discovered that they make one table available on Open Table, an online booking site. Of course it was sold out every night, but I figured there might be the possibility of a cancellation.

I wrote a script that checked the Open Table page every 15 minutes looking for changes. Nothing happened for a week or two, and then one day I got an email from my script saying something had changed. I quickly logged in and saw there was an opening. Not only that, it was prime time on a Friday night at 8 PM. I quickly booked it, and needless to say my girlfriend was quite impressed when I surprised her with dinner there. She also enjoyed recounting my story to her friends, explaining to them how geeks are taking over the world—she was not technical herself.

You're hiring, why would someone want to join Inporia?

I think because we're tackling a really big market: e-commerce is huge, and we're taking a fundamentally different approach to it that is a technology-based approach. If you're a hacker and you want to work on something that's going to have the chance of making a lot of money and actually affecting a lot of people, then this is a good company to be working for. We're also a team of experienced entrepreneurs who have sold companies before, so it's a good learning experience if you want to start a company yourself one day.

Alex Polvi, Cloudkick

Tags: Y Combinator, programmer, iterate quickly, profitable, acquired (Rackspace)

Overview: Cloudkick was started in 2009 to make it easy to manage cloud servers by providing detailed analytics and metrics data and notifications of downtimes. As an example, Cloudkick sends a notification to your phone as soon as your website goes down; they provide performance graphs over time; and they give you a list of servers showing everything going on along with all the metadata. Cloudkick went through Y Combinator, raised $2 million, and was later acquired by Rackspace.

How did you get started with entrepreneurship?

I'll provide some background on myself because it all ties together. I graduated in 2007 with a computer science degree from Oregon State; I was really involved with free software projects there. I worked for the Open Source Lab, a group that provides hosting for Kernel.org, Apache.org, and Mozilla.org—all the big open source projects hosted at Oregon State. That's where I got my sys admin experience which led to a role at Mozilla doing operations stuff. Along the way I did a whole bunch of other things: started a Linux users group and did all these crazy marketing campaigns for Firefox. At Mozilla, I transitioned from a sys admin, to a product manager, and eventually to the marketing team. I really wanted to do a startup at this point. If I could be a sys admin, do project management and marketing, I was pretty sure that was a recipe for trying to start something.

I met some other guys from YC and heard about their experiences; I actually had applied to YC when I was in college in 2005 and got rejected. But once I was in the network a little more, had a better idea what was going on, I left my job in August 2008 and just tried to start something; really no idea what we were going to do. I reached out to the two smartest people I know and might be crazy enough to give it a shot. We ended up putting together the application and got accepted.

Did you build anything in high school or do any type of consulting?

I did web development on the side. I thought it was such a big deal because I was making $35/hour when I was in high school. I built websites for local wineries and that sort of stuff. So it's kind of the classic company contracting/consulting thing, but more like, "Let's find some smart kid to go build our website." I was able to do it but they probably should have hired somebody more experienced.

During my freshman year in college, I had a part-time student job working at the Open Source Lab through the university. I was essentially helping with running the servers for these open source projects. One of my fondest memories of that is when I unplugged the master IRC Freenode server and ran it across campus while it was raining. I had gotten a call that, "We need you to move the server" and I'm like, "Okay, what do I do?" They said "Well, we just need minimum downtime, don't even shut it off; just unplug it, pick it up, run it to the other building, and plug it back in as fast as you can."

Was this a server on the Freenode network?

Yeah, it was a Freenode server that had the most users on it—it was like the master. We disconnected 8,000 users or something when we did that. That really started all of this and I just got lucky. From a program I started during my freshman year, I was able to convince them to give me a job even though I had no idea what I was doing.

When you were taking CS classes, which ones were you favorite and least favorite?

I got lucky and just picked computer science at the beginning and stuck with it. If you just stick with a degree, it's actually a lot less work than switching degrees.

I liked algorithms and I liked the programming languages class. I was doing contracting stuff with Mozilla at the time. One year in college I was contracting with Mozilla instead of working for the Open Source Lab and we had to do an essay in the programming languages class; you had to write about a programming language. I wrote mine on JavaScript and then my friend and Mozilla colleague, Brandon Eich (who created JavaScript) was on IRC. I messaged him and got quotes for my paper—he said all these horrible things about JavaScript. We did our presentations on our languages, so we were like, "Brandon Eich said this", and it turned out to be pretty funny.

Were you actively looking for cofounders when you were in college? Did you know you wanted to do a startup?

Yes, we actually applied to YC when I was in college—I think it was 2005. So that was sophomore, junior year and I applied with two buddies then, both super sharp programmers as well. We applied and got rejected. I'm glad I didn't drop out of school though. I think it was important to get that done. It's just a little checkbox and pretty important to get finished these days. But yeah, at the time I would have dropped out of school so it was probably for the best that I didn't get accepted.

How did you meet your cofounders? You said you applied with two other guys?

One of them, I took CS classes with. I was living in San Jose when I left Mozilla and he was living in San Jose too; he was one of the sharpest guys I knew. So we'd meet up over beers. I've known my other cofounder, Logan, since high school. He's a really solid designer so he gets the most kudos of all of this because, I just mentioned, "Hey, I was thinking about starting something up, I'm looking for someone to join" and he's like, "Yeah, let's do it", and he moved down two weeks later into the extra room in my apartment. We hadn't applied to Y Combinator and he just quit his job and came down, which was awesome. So yeah, that was really cool and then once we got accepted into YC, Dan left his job at IBM. It's a really big step when you're making good money right out of school; it's hard to walk out for the $20K.

Do you have any advice on how to go out and meet cofounders?

There are clearly people in your class that are exceptional. They stick out, right? There's no secret; there are people who are writing lots of software outside of class for fun; those are the best programmers in the world. They're sitting at home in the dorm room right now, banging away on this crazy little project that they think is really cool but it has nothing to do with their homework. Those are definitely the types of people to look out for.

How did you pay your way through school?

I got pretty lucky with all of the Mozilla stuff I was doing. I was able to buy a house in college and then I split the mortgage across my roommates in rent. I was able to get one of those variable interest rates, those horrible mortgages that they always tell you not to do but I figured I could split it with my roommates and then sell it when we were done. I had had the house for three years, lived there for three years and was able to sell it and make a little money on it, so it was pretty ideal. I got really lucky there on the timing.

Did you take time to have fun and relax in college?

Yeah, we had fun. I wasn't the craziest kid in college by any means, though we did a bunch of crazy stuff. We built a crop circle one time—have you seen the Firefox crop circle on Google Maps?

I haven't seen that—how did you build crop circles?

We used two-by-fours and a rope. Essentially, we laid out a big map with concentric circles on it and the gap between those circles was two feet. Then we had a compass, like North by Northwest sort of thing and so you just say, "Stomp from 20 feet out to 40 feet out, North to West" so you'd go stomp it out and then you mark it. So you're building it blind, but you know where you're at in the field.

We definitely partied and I had a social life, but there were people who were more hard-core than me. Bob is one of the Cloudkick marketing guys now; I met him at Oregon State throwing a snowboard competition with him. We decided it'd be really funny in the middle of May to get a bunch of snow off the mountain, put it in the middle of the quad, and then throw out an ad hoc snowboard competition. Nobody knew about it, we put posters all over campus that said, "It's going to snow, May 27th", and this was during summer.

What were you doing right as you were graduating? Did you know that you wanted to do a startup at this point?

I had a couple of opportunities for different places and I ended up at Mozilla. It kind of aligned with what I was interested in working on, plus it's a really flexible place to work; you can just come and do what you want, and at that point I wasn't ready to give up on being a sys admin. When I was graduating school, I moved to San Francisco but worked in Mountain View where I was doing product management on Firefox. I was an apprentice to the product manager for Firefox. I had sysadmin experience but wanted to try something new and they were willing to let me try. It was a really good experience.

Did anyone inspire you while you were in college?

I would say, more importantly, one of the guys that got me involved with the Open Source Labs, Scott Kveton, was a mentor. He started that lab and took me under his wing to learn sys admin stuff, so that was really helpful and he was awesome. I just saw him last weekend; he's doing his own startup up in Portland now called Urban Airship.

How did you get the idea to start Cloudkick? Were you having some server problems?

We had come up with that idea but it ended up being picked at PG's house at the first party that happens during the first week or two. We applied with something completely different. We applied with "Kiva for scholarships," it was like crowdsourced scholarships. That's what we applied to Y Combinator with and PG responded, "We like the team but we don't like the idea so come to the interview with a different idea." So then we interviewed with a different idea and got accepted but changed the idea immediately, again. What was funny about YC at that point was they told us, "You can defer your acceptance if you want because we're not sure if in March there's going to be a venture community" because it was right in the middle of the financial meltdown. So our batch only had 16 companies in it because they didn't want to accept very many people.

What they realized during our batch was that this is the *exact* time you should be investing because when you get to a company at scale that's when everything would recover. As soon as we dropped our scholarship idea, we switched to infrastructure just because that's what we knew. We had a couple of other infrastructure ideas and two others and then we ended up on Cloudkick. So Cloudkick was the fourth iteration of our Y Combinator company.

Were you trying to fail fast and iterate quickly? Do you think that's a good idea?

Yeah, it's fail fast. I think it was more just actually understanding what you know. Like, the scholarship thing is cool and altruistically very nice, but we have no idea about how the nonprofit world works or how to do any of that, whereas, we do have an advantage on infrastructure stuff because we know how that works, we know what people need, and we could use it ourselves. So iterating was more figuring out what our domain knowledge actually was. Any of the ideas could have potentially worked if we had applied enough effort. Most of the reasons startups succeed or fail are because you just try hard enough, so probably any of them could equally work out but this was the one that we felt the most confident about our ability to execute on.

Did you find that anything worked particularly well for your interview with YC?

For our Y Combinator interview it was totally using the network; totally finagling. I'd love to say we had an amazing interview and they accepted us at face value. PG might say that our team was the most recommended team in Y Combinator history, but that's because we aimed to have it that way.

How were you guys so highly recommended? Did you know some YC alum?

Well, we knew some people, yeah, and then we sold ourselves. We were shameless about asking for people to tell YC we were awesome, that sort of thing. I'm just speaking very bluntly with you. That's how we pulled it off.

I've mentioned this in another interview, but I've told people to wear a t-shirt of a company funded by YC. I remember that was the first thing they commented on. It probably has no real effect on the final decision, but maybe helps us stand out.

That stuff will help in some way—it shows that you're paying attention; you're not just a random walk-in off the street with a degree from Harvard.

After YC, you raised another round. What was that like?

We started from scratch on the product. We launched it the day before demo day like most of the companies do. Everyone does it differently but we did the classic 'Build it for the first three months, ship it before demo day, and then try to get money' approach. So we did exactly that but we had a really hard time fundraising.

We had no idea what we were doing; no idea how to raise money, and we're not necessarily that good at it. We were also in the middle of the financial crisis. Our idea, while interesting, wasn't obvious to everybody either. Who needs server-management tools? For us it was obvious and we had had good traction but it wasn't amazing. It was like we weren't clearly a winner yet so we had a hard time making money. But we wanted to raise money; we didn't want to raise $100K or $200K, we wanted to raise $3 million and go for it. So that's what we were trying to do, we were trying to raise a series A and at some point we're like, "Okay, we give up. We haven't gotten the product enough along to warrant raising $3 million so we'll just develop on $750K instead." So then we decided to go for $750K, definitely got more interest, and we ended up eventually meeting investors through Y Combinator. That was really interesting. We got tons of "No's." We got maybe 15 or 20 "No's" and we talked to way too many investors. But we finally got one that said "Yes" and we closed in August. So it took a solid—what was that, five or six months to close? That's not really a Cinderella story in the YC community.

Was that experience positive or negative then?

At first it was just straight foolishness; we had no idea what we were doing. One time, we got really close to an investor and then he literally took the term sheet away from us—like, he gave us a term sheet and then 10 minutes later he pulled it back off the table, he said, "Never mind."

It ended up working out for the best. You never know how things will go, but I really like my investors. They were super cool. Near the end, we were talking like, "If this deal does not go through we need to start doing other stuff", because we had gone from January to August on $20,000, the three of us living in Silicon Valley. We decided we just needed to start consulting and we probably would have given up, but we were starting to hit the credit card on everything and it just wasn't easy. So that part definitely got stressful but then we closed the money and it was a relief.

Do you think the $150K from Yuri Milner is a good or bad thing?

It's good for the entrepreneurs; it's good for the venture capitalists; it's not good for the angels. For companies, it gives them more time to build stuff and to get their valuation up; it's more breathing room. I think there is something to say for being scrappy and feeling that but I also think people need to be paid for their work and so you've got to be able to afford to live while you build the stuff. That's kind of a ridiculous thing for him to do, to invest in every single one of them. But the way this venture model works, you're expected to give crazy returns and so you need to do crazy things in order to get crazy returns and that's from the investors' perspective as well as from the entrepreneurship perspective.

If you're super conservative on everything you're not going to do something really crazy. Entrepreneurs got terms that they don't have to think about, this is the best thing possible. So it's good for the entrepreneurs and then it's good for the VC community because they're going to get companies that are further along. They won't see a three month-old project that shipped four days ago at Sequoia or Redpoint. They're going to see a product that, hopefully, has gotten some solid customer traction and warrants a big valuation and round of funding.

How long did the first beta of Cloudkick take to build? How did you spread the word?

We built and shipped it in a little under three months. We launched on TechCrunch when we were ready and then we did demo day and fared pretty well, from a press perspective. Whenever they did the top five companies to watch, we were generally mentioned.

Did you have any stressful moments during your early days?

There's a lot of 'leaping' that happens; like, when you're hiring your first employee, you're kind of making a leap; when you bring on an investor, you're making a leap; you actually ship something, you're making a leap, and those are always kind of queasy feelings.

Were there any points where you noticed the revenue start to take off and if so, what happened?

There was a point where you could tell the product had crossed a level of usefulness when you were talking to a potential customer; you could say it did all these things and you could sell them almost 100% of the time. That was fun and we don't know exactly when that happened but at some point it happened in 2010—and we didn't release a commercial product until February 2010. It might have been in April or May; the product really got to a certain point of usefulness. We were priced between $100 and $4,000 a month, which is small for really big guys, and a lot for small guys, right? So it was a decent sale, if we sold the $4,000 a month plan that was a pretty big deal to us, so we crossed a point where we could do that.

If we got a customer on the phone or we got a screen cast we could sell almost 100% of the time. The next phase was building a sales and marketing team around this and trying to actually scale it; that's what we were in the process of doing when we got acquired. So we never really built sales and marketing.

How did you split the work?

Dan and I are programmers; we write software and Logan does all the front-end stuff. So everything customer facing and that goes all the way down to HTML, CSS and jQuery, but also all the branding, all the copyrighting on the website, all that stuff is Logan. So, originally, Dan and I wrote all the back-end software and Logan did all the front-end work.

I think that's a killer team because making your product look really good, really professional, and also having somebody to chew on that stuff and having other guys to chew on the back-end problems, is a really good setup. Today, we've grown the team, and part of being a good entrepreneur is stepping up to the new responsibilities as they change; responsibilities change as the company grows. So, I became the CEO-type role and did a lot of stuff but Dan, who is also one of the programmers, helped do a lot of the investor fundraising stuff as well. Dan also ran an engineering team and then he also ran sales and marketing for a while. He also handled support, all different stuff. Now, Logan runs our user experience team. Dan is the product manager for one of our products. I'm the general Bay Area manager for Rackspace and Paul—who was our first employee—is our engineering manager, so all engineers report to him.

When you moved to Rackspace, did you stay separate or are you working on Rackspace stuff now?

Essentially our customer facing stuff becomes more customer facing for Rackspace. Organizationally, Rackspace is based in San Antonio and they're transitioning from a hosting company to a technology company with all this cloud stuff and we are the Bay Area presence for that. So, we are helping them build out their Bay Area operations for Rackspace.

Right now I'm in the Rackspace office in San Francisco. They're growing the team and we're still working on our products and we still build the team but we're definitely Rackers; we're part of a bigger cause now, we're running the Bay Area.

What are the hours like?

In terms of work, I feel like there's more work now because we have a startup that's fully operational, plus we have all the integration going on, so it's nearly double. But you get to a point where you can just roll with all the work that you can handle and you have to adapt to be able to do that. The work amount hasn't changed; it's just the volume of stuff to deal with that has changed. You hit limits on how much you can process; once you're there it doesn't matter if you pile more on, it's just more stuff to process.

How long was Cloudkick around before it got acquired?

We were around exactly two years after we first incorporated.

Are you glad that you guys did that?

Definitely. What happened was: we moved from a zero to X-million dollar company and now we're a very strategic part of a $4 or $5 billion company moving towards, maybe, a $40 billion company. To be part of that growth phase—while completely different than a startup—is still an amazing opportunity. Don't get me wrong, there are financial reasons for us to be here too, but there's also an opportunity to help a company which is kind of like a startup compared to its peers like Google, Amazon, and go after this market that we're very familiar with. We can do more together with Rackspace, plus we're a very strategic part of this thing out in the Bay Area and everything as well. So it's cool, and at the same time it's totally different. It's a different chapter.

Have you ever struggled with staying motivated either at Cloudkick or now at Rackspace?

Yeah. I think it's just important to take breaks. You don't realize it —you can get the guilt if you're not working then nothing is getting done, but then on the flip side, if you're not being productive nothing is being done either. So you just have to blend that balance of keeping yourself sane and working as hard as you can. That was the realization later in the life of Cloudkick that it's okay and nobody will frown upon me for taking a break. Everybody accepts that you can't work like crazy all the time.

If you knew of a student who wanted to do a startup, but wasn't sure exactly what to do, what would you tell them?

Just go for it. You're the only person holding yourself back and that's really what it comes down to. Get out of your own way.

What if you're a non-technical person and you want to do a technical startup? Should you look for a technical cofounder, should you learn how to code, what should you do there?

I don't know. I'm kind of a control freak so I would say learn how to code. If you're that early on it's better for you personally, but also it's a pretty hard sell to go to someone and say, "Go build my idea and you can be my cofounder but don't think about it, I just need you to be my programmer and build my idea." That's not how to build a company. So I would say, go learn how to program then go say, "Hey, look at this crazy thing I wrote" and then the programmer, your new cofounder will be like, "Oh, that totally sucks, I can make it better—this is cool though." You know what I mean?

That's a much better approach than just trying to come in and be like, "I'm a business guy and I know what the market is, and you build this for me." That won't work, and at the early stages, you don't need the business guy, you just need a product that actually works.

Can you talk about the time you most successfully hacked some non-computer system to your advantage?

I hacked the TED conference to meet a bunch of the cool speakers. After watching the videos online, I thought it would be cool to go to the conference, but did not have the prestige or $6,000. So I just showed up with a few signs to help get me in which read: "Just need one badge!" and "1001st smartest person in the world" (because the conference was limited to 1000 people). I ended up getting in and I shared moments with many cool people, including Robin Williams and Cameron Diaz. Steve Wozniak even zipped by on a Segway.

Jake Klamka & Wil Chung, Noteleaf

Tags: Y Combinator, programmer (Wil), cofounder search

Overview: Noteleaf was started in 2010 and went through Y Combinator in 2011 to help people prepare for meetings by pushing contact information over an existing calendar right before a meeting takes place. Right as we sold GraffitiGeo to Loopt, I moved to Mountain View and became roommates with Jake and Wil in the Mountain View. Jake and Wil didn't know each other at the time, but both were interested in startups and they eventually became cofounders.

Can you give an example of when someone would use Noteleaf? It seems like something I do all the time, so I wanted the readers to understand how you guys work specifically.

Jake: We push the right information to your phone right when you need it.

Here's a use case. I type, "Call with Jared" into my Google calendar, and, say, I'm a busy exec or whatever, I may not know who you are, and two weeks down the road I'm about to have this call or I'm about to have this meeting with you and I wonder, who is this guy? "Who is this Jared?" I'm confused, and so just as I'm going to the meeting—10 minutes before—I get a push notification on my phone.

And we basically push a whole bunch of information about you: I would get a whole profile about you out of my phone. It would have your LinkedIn info, so it would be your picture and that becomes useful if I was meeting you at a coffee shop. I could recognize you if I hadn't met you before, and it will have your email address even if I hadn't entered you into my phone book. I'd be able to email you if I was running late or anything like that. It would basically be all the information I would need to be prepared for that meeting at the right time, which is right before that meeting.

The key is that I had to do no extra work to get that. I just put, "Coffee with Jared" in my Google calendar, and we did the rest. We recognized your name, we figure out who's "Jared Tame" and not some other Jared, and then we push that information at the appropriate time.

When did you guys first start doing something you would consider entrepreneurial? You can go back as far as you can remember.

Wil: I was working at Johns Hopkins Applied Physics Lab out in Maryland and I was basically living in the suburbs, where everybody is under 18 and over 30. I was getting really bored there with what I was doing, and part of it was being intrigued with Silicon Valley because they were kind of pushing industry standards and the web. Paul Graham's essays were also influential, especially *How to Make Wealth,* because I saw a lot of people who were working and they just got stuck. They were at jobs that they didn't like, but they had mortgages or kids to pay. I already knew how to get a job. And this is something that I didn't know how to do, and it was far more challenging and I just always wanted to build something that had more widespread appeal than missiles and spacecraft. It was pretty late for me; I was 27 at the time.

Jake: The earliest memories of entrepreneurship in Silicon Valley for me came from reading Wired magazine. I used to enjoy reading Wired magazine when I was in grade school. That was my first exposure to Silicon Valley and ever since then I dreamed about it. I did some web design and online marketing and other things in high school, and then I went into physics because I was basically drawn to innovation. I went into physics thinking, "Wow, these people are studying the fundamentals of the universe. It must be the absolute most exciting and dynamic thing that I can imagine doing."

After going through physics, which I really loved learning about, going into research I found out about that physics wasn't actually so dynamic. It doesn't actually move that quickly. It's actually very step-by-step and much slower paced, and it's designed that way so that they get really accurate results. By that point I realized that Silicon Valley was the right choice after all.

When I took a closer look at startups, that's really where the innovation was happening because it was the only situation in which you could have two guys in a garage or an apartment change the world in a matter of a year.

What kind of classes were you guys taking in college? What were your favorites and least favorite?

Wil: I did electrical engineering at UIUC. I was filling a lot of the engineering electives so I also did communications systems. I didn't really like computer engineering classes, so I never went into hardware.

Jake: I did math and physics, and I ended up doing some research in high-energy particle physics—it's a collaboration of 2,000 people building this huge detector that's going to take 10 to 20 years to put online. It's incredible science; it's really interesting, but that's when I realized that smaller teams and moving faster was something I liked more.

In college, were you consciously thinking of doing startups and finding cofounders?

Wil: At the time, no. I was pure engineer: I just wanted to build stuff. So in college, I wasn't really thinking about it. When I was in college it was during the dot com startup craze, and I did hear about it but I just felt like it wasn't something that I would jump ship and go do. It just seemed like people were going crazy and when people are going crazy you know to be a little wary. It wasn't until later, when I was working in industry for a while, that I started reading about Paul Graham and his essays. For me, the tipping point was really Paul Graham's essays.

Jake: I just started reading TechCrunch way too much and at some point I was reading TechCrunch more than I was reading physics papers. That's when I realized that this is what I want to do more than research physics.

Wil: I was doing the same thing at work. I was reading RSS feeds of Joy Ito and TechCrunch instead of doing work. I also gave a presentation at work about stuff that was going on in Silicon Valley, like the new technologies were coming out, and they're like, "Wow, that's awesome." They gave me a $100 bonus and I was like, "I shouldn't be here. I should be somewhere else." I think we have similar experiences in that sense I guess.

How did you guys pay your way through school?

Jake: I worked. I did online marketing consulting during school to pay the bills.

Wil: U of I was relatively cheap compared to the other places I was going to go. It's in state, so my parents were able to cover that. My masters was at Johns Hopkins, and I was also working there, so they covered it and there was no obligation to stay afterwards. It was a pretty good deal for me.

Right as you were graduating, what were you thinking about doing?

Wil: When I graduated undergrad, it was in 2001 right after the dot com bubble. A lot of my friends were interviewing and as they were interviewing they got their jobs, and then eventually a lot of them got rescinded actually. At that point I was just like, "Damn it, somebody just give me a job doing something somewhere," and the Johns Hopkins Applied Physics Lab was the only place I ended up getting a job. Startups weren't an option or a possibility in my mind at the time.

Jake: For me it was different. I finished my masters in 2006 around the time where Google was starting to acquire some companies in the Valley, and things were starting to pick up a little bit. There was more and more activity happening in startups around that time and it got my attention.

I think you guy are really interesting because before you started Noteleaf, you guys didn't really know each other too well. You were roommates but I think you guys are one of those special cases where you didn't grow up together; you didn't really know each other too much beforehand. So how did you guys start talking about working on a startup together? How did all that come about?

Jake: The key element for me was being in Silicon Valley. I met more people who were into startups in the first week that I was here than I did in an entire year in Toronto, and it was just amazing. And that led to me to meeting Wil and to meeting you, and the rest unfolded from there.

Wil: I quit my job in 2005. That was from the lab. When I quit I didn't move immediately to Silicon Valley, but I echo Jake's sentiments. Moving here, the difference is night and day. I've been trying to do startups in Maryland, in Chicago, and in New York— it's just way better here. People sort of understand what you're talking about and the people that you meet, that whole ecosystem is here.

I moved back home, and I was working in my parents' basement for a while in Chicago just to lower the burn rate. But even though you lower the burn rate, you don't have the ecosystem to bounce ideas off people or to find cofounders for that matter. It wasn't working, so I went to Startup School 2007, and because of that, the founder of Frogmetrics at the time, Scott Brown, they saw that I had built something. They figured, "Well this guy already knows how to build something. Let's hire him," and they're like "Hey, we got into YC, want to join us?" I was thinking "Yeah, I've been trying to get into this for a while as a single founder before. I'm obviously doing something wrong, so I might as well join somebody else's startup to see what's going on." At the time you could go through YC as an early employee to the Tuesday dinners, and I met a lot of the founders. I think that gave me a sense of what it was all about, what a lot of people are like and the traits and attributes that you need to have in order to make it in the startup world. After Frogmetrics, I just moved here and ended up being roommates with you guys.

How did you hear about the hacker house? That's how you two met.

Jake: I actually saw the Palo Alto Hacker House on Hacker News. They had a room opening and I was still in Toronto at the time, and I emailed them and I actually didn't get down there in time to get that room. When I did finally make it down, here I emailed them again and was like, "Do you have anything available?" They said "No, but you can crash here for a week." So the Palo Alto Hacker House was a huge part of me getting connected into the startup scene here. I didn't know a single person in Silicon Valley when I moved down here. They put me in touch, they said "Hey, we've got a guy that used to live here and I think they've got a spare room available in the Mountain View apartment where it's all startup people as well," and we became roommates with you Jared, and that's how I met Wil, and that's how we kind of got it rolling.

Wil: I saw it on Craigslist and you had the big Y Combinator logo on it.

It was a sign.

Wil: Right, and then I found out that you were in YC and that we both went to UIUC. I figured "Well, this is a start, and it's a good place to live." So I didn't expect to be cofounders with this guy Jake until much later.

So you guys both moved in and you both were working on different ideas?

Jake: I was doing consulting for a California-based online marketing firm and working on some independent hobby projects at the same time. Over the course of a few months we became friends. I guess in March 2010 we were thinking of working on something new, and then the idea came up: "Well, if we're going to try something new, maybe we should try programming something together." We decided to give it a try, "Let's do a three week trial period and see if we work well together." We knew we had already gotten along because we were friends just hanging around the house, and that went well.

Wil: I was working on visualizing public data and after asking around I realized that there isn't exactly a market for what I was thinking about. We ended up working on the initial version of Noteleaf together just to check it out, to see how we work together really.

How did you come up with that idea?

Jake: It was just supposed to be this simple way to take notes about people you meet, and I think it was out of our own experience. We had both moved down here, we were both meeting a ton of people, and we were both convinced that we were probably going to forget a whole bunch of them and just lose track of everything. So we just thought it was a simple project, we thought, "Let's just try it and see what happens."

Wil: Yeah, I can't remember people's details for the life of me, really. So we're scratching our own itch.

Wil, you had applied to YC before right? You were a single founder for a while.

Wil: I applied to YC a total of *six times*. Once was with Jake, but that was a late application and I don't know if you want to count that. The very first time was with somebody else—a friend of mine—but that didn't work out. The other four times I applied as a single founder and didn't get in.

I applied once as a single founder and didn't get in.

Wil: With the application, once you do it multiple times you start to understand what they're asking for.

Have you noticed any patterns for what YC in particular looks for?

Wil: Besides what PG's written himself, I think one thing I noticed is that startup founders tend to make really quick decisions on things, even with incomplete information. Many times you're forced to make decisions on stuff that you either don't know anything about or you'll find out later. But the idea is that you make a decision now, you'll eventually figure it out, you'll gather the data or gather the experience, and then adjust later if you need to. When I was working on my own, a lot of times I'd agonize over stuff that didn't matter in the long run.

Jake: Having a cofounder really helps with that, and so I guess that's one thing that YC really looks for: a strong team. I remember thinking, "You can do it on your own, it's not really a big deal," but having tried do something on my own versus trying to do something with a cofounder, it's night and day. And it's a really big plus to have two different skill sets. If somebody gets stuck, there's someone else to kick you out of that and say "Let's keep moving," and vice-versa.

Wil: There are two other things. The founders are very product-oriented where they care a lot about what the users are experiencing and how they experience it. They also use the technology to support that rather than just building things that are cool but that users don't care about, or maybe they have a really shitty experience with it. The other thing is seeing the market, which is more of the business side to the product. They get a more holistic view to what it is that they're doing rather than just the market or just the technology or just the product.

Jake: The thing I would recommend most for anybody applying to YC is to just build something: launch it and apply with that. That was a huge step for us. We basically built something over the course of a month or two and then launched it. We got written up in Mashable and then we had all these users sending us email and telling us what they liked or didn't like about what we were doing. Suddenly we had statistics about what was working and what wasn't. We talked to people on the phone, we emailed people, and we just learned a ton.

Wil: You get feedback and then you think, "This is what you might want or what other people might want," but it's just a lot easier when you just throw it out there and see what other people say about it, regardless of whether it's good or bad.

Jake: That experience of actually launching something comes out in the application because not only can you say, "Hey, this is not just an idea but we actually we launched it. It's live; you can look at it. Oh, by the way, we were featured on this blog and we have this many users," Then you actually have smart things to say on the YC application because of the things you've learned. You learn that from experience, and you learn from the actual market. And it's not just something you came up with from your head.

You both know solo founders that got into Y Combinator. What separates them from the others who get rejected?

Jake: Traction. All the solo founders I've known at YC are people who have launched sites that have a lot of traffic: they're very successful websites and they have a lot of users or a lot of visitors. A lot of these questions come up when you're concerned about a solo founder: "Can they build? Can they execute?" Well, if they have a site that's really popular, then they've already demonstrated that they can. So, if somehow you can launch a site that has a ton of visitors or users and you're a solo founder, then that's the ticket.

Did anything help you when you applied to Y Combinator?

Jake: Mock interviews. We did a lot of them to the point where it was starting to seem sort of redundant that we were doing that many mock interviews—the amount that you learn and the degree to which it prepared us for the actual interview was great.

Wil: We had maybe three bullet points of things that we want to get across regardless of what they ask, and so we're going to remember to insert that in there regardless, because these are the important things that they need to know. Because this is why they should pick us. It has to be traction, our understanding of the market, things like that.

You're in the batch that receives $150K from the Start Fund. Do you guys think this is a good or a bad thing?

Wil: I think generally it's a good thing.

Jake: It's a good thing for sure. I think the best thing it has done is taking the edge off in terms of people being really worried about fundraising. I think that a lot of people are taking the approach of focusing on the product at this stage and getting that right. And PG is always telling everybody that's the right way to go about it: that you need to focus on the product first.

Wil: I think this doesn't change which startups succeed or fail because you're still judged by the market, right? Customers don't care whether you got the $150K or not. They just care whether they want to use your stuff or not, and the only two things I can see is that bad startups will probably take longer to die, or it gives them more time to play around with things until they figure out something else.

Did you ever have advisors?

Jake: Yeah. We got to know startup founders in the area, and that's another huge part of why being in Silicon Valley is awesome: there are startup founders all over the place here. We would bounce ideas off other founders before YC, and we're still doing it now. I would definitely recommend finding founders who you're inspired by and who you would like to learn more from and asking them to be an advisor for your startup.

Did you ever have any stressful moments or did you ever think Noteleaf would fail? Have you experienced the trough of sorrow yet?

Wil: Yeah it happens from time to time.

Jake: Right now we're building the product. We've got some beta testers, but we're still working towards launch. That makes us pre-trough of sorrow. But on the previous version of Noteleaf we definitely had a trough of sorrow moment because we launched it, we got on Mashable, we got lots of users, people were sending us fan mail, everything was great, and then we realized that "Hey, we actually have to build some more stuff here."

Wil: There was something wrong with the product because the retention wasn't there.

Jake: At first what we did was we tried to add things on to that previous product to increase retention, and that was tough. We went for a couple of months just trying to build a mobile version, working on stuff without much feedback from the outside world.

Wil: Fundamentally the problem was with the product and how we were attacking that particular problem. There was nothing that we could really do. In a magical world where you can read people's minds, note taking would be a breeze. But that's just not happening anytime soon.

Jake: Once we got into YC, we actually spoke with PG and we then went out and met with a bunch of users—we looked at their workflows. We were already thinking about some of these issues, of integrating with the calendar or of pushing information to people to improve our retention rate. But PG was the one that said, "You guys have got to go out and you've gotta talk to some people that should be using your software to learn. Go sit at their computers, look at what they're doing, figure this out," and we did. We went out and we spent a week visiting a bunch of people. After that, we realized that we just needed to build a new product that would center on people's existing workflow.

How do you guys split the work?

Jake: Wil is more heavily involved in building and does all the back-end code. I code, but I focus more on front-end work. I also take care of all the business stuff. It's a really good split. We have a really good balance of skills.

Wil: Where we overlap is in customer development. Anything that has to do with product, we do together.

Can you talk about the time you most successfully hacked a non-computer system to your advantage?

Jake: You helped us with this actually. As you know, we call our apartment the "Hacker House in Mountain View" and we put it up on AirBNB. We've met a ton of startup founders and developers into Mountain View because they would book to stay with us on AirBNB and sleep on our couch. Basically we bought a couch for $50, which Jared, you remember we picked up. Our hack was basically how we took a $50 Craigslist couch and turned it into this awesome way to meet a bunch of founders in Silicon

Valley and elsewhere and how that helped us get where we are at today. That was our hack.

Wil: When it comes to dates, I found that at the end where you're supposed to go in for the kiss it's always very awkward. That's because that's the first time you're trying to initiate anything. I found that you've actually got to start way in advance.

Jake: I thought the hack was supposed to be about Noteleaf? This is dating advice.

Wil: No, see you've got to warm her up first. This is a really good hack. You've got to touch her hand, touch her shoulder, whatever and work your way up to it, because if you just try to go all the way in—

That doesn't work.

Wil: It doesn't work. You've got to work her up to it, so by the time it's the end of the night and you're going for the kiss, it feels very natural. When I found that out, it was a lot better.

Jake: For our next startup, we're going into dating advice. *(Laughs)*

Amit Sudharshan, One Llama

Tags: VC funded, programmer, anti-school, undergrad founder

Overview: One Llama started in 2008 after raising $1 million to make it easy to search for radio stations online playing a song or artist that you type in. They take a unique approach to generating song recommendations algorithmically (as opposed to ranking songs manually as is the case with Pandora). I met Amit Sudharshan—who I consider to be one of the smartest engineers I've ever met—when I interned at One Llama in 2008. One Llama is one of the few startups I knew of while I attended UIUC, and I think Amit has a good perspective and message to share on the challenges of doing a startup in the Midwest where the culture can be very different than that of Silicon Valley.

Is it safe to say that One Llama is like Pandora without humans?

At the 35,000-foot level, it is. We do a lot of the same things except we use machines to do the work of the audiologists at Pandora.

Can you recall your earliest experience with entrepreneurship? Where did all of this start for you?

Remember the PlayStation mod chips that you had to solder and install in your PlayStation in order to be able to play foreign games? In high school I discovered that there was a company that developed an external mod chip that they could just plug into the outside of the machine that you didn't have to solder. I realized there was an information asymmetry where a lot of people wanted the mod chips but most people did not want to have to solder their machines. However, they also didn't have information about this source of external chips. This lasted for about six months; there was a period where I could buy these external mod chips for a lot cheaper than I was able to sell them on the premise that you couldn't solder.

The first startup at school just barely got off the ground. That was an attempt to develop technology for satellite television to help display fantasy football information, in real time, to a viewer. I was a fantasy football player and was approached by someone who asked if I could help develop the technology, so it was my first 'real startup.' We had an attorney, filed some provisionals, met with DirecTV, and even met with the NFL. As a sophomore in college, going into the NFL office at Park Avenue and sitting in front of the VP in my first big meeting, was a really important experience for me—knowing that I could handle that well, without fear. And while it ultimately didn't materialize into anything, it was a good experience.

When I was in college I was teaching tennis and, through tennis, I met the cofounder of the startup that I was talking to you about earlier. Through him, I met Rob Schultz who was a partner at Illinois Ventures and I began an internship there. I can trace how I got to where I am today through a series of connections. I think relationships are the most important thing that's been one of the most important things in my experience. You don't know where they're going to end up, but you build them because it's good.

I began as an intern at Illinois Ventures and Rob asked if I wanted to stick around for a summer and try to get One Llama off the ground. One Llama was started through research done at UIUC and so Illinois Ventures played a role in commercializing that research. At the time, my dad believed—and he probably still does—that if you want to learn business, the best place to go is General Electric and work up through the ranks, go through their training programs. I had been admitted into their IML peer internship program and when Rob asked me to stay, I gave up the internship to help found this company.

When I started the company I knew the technical cofounders quite well. There was no business leadership in place and I was only 21. But with entrepreneurs, age isn't so important; it's the ability to speak cogently and to be willing to stand up for what you believe in.

What kind of classes did you take in college?

I spent a ton of time working during school. I was always working, and I did the minimum amount of class work necessary to get by. Sometimes, I would challenge myself: I would decide that I was not going to attend classes for a semester, and just take the exams where that was feasible and see what happens. So I did that for many semesters. In fact, there was one semester where—because of that practice—a friend of mine who had a class in the same building actually visited my class to turn in my homework for me more often than I had even been to class that semester. It's about what your priorities are.

I never took a class on leadership and I never took a business class and a lot of that stuff should be read on your own and I think that people should read those books from first principles. So instead of studying economics, people should read *The Wealth of Nations*.

Business and entrepreneurship is really about leadership, it's about direction, and it's about understanding people and the psychology of how people work in order to get what you want out of them in a business relationship. So, studying people who are excellent leaders is a very good task. Reading autobiographies of really good leaders and trying to understand their thought process is extremely effective.

You did electrical engineering as an undergrad; do you think the degree was helpful for doing startups?

EE classes are helpful because they require a ton of work—far more work than I think the comparable computer science classes at UIUC do; they're really much harder.

When I got to Illinois I had a background, but I couldn't have told you how a computer worked. When I got my EE degree at UIUC I could tell you how to make a computer, how to make it run fast, and I have a physical intuition for what happens when you tell a computer to do something. So, with a self-trained programming degree, which a lot of people have, for the vast majority of tasks in this world it's perfectly reasonable to make a reasonably successful website. The tools out there are sufficiently mature that you do not need anything more than a lot of dedication, patience, a hobbyist background, and programming in order to do an effective job.

Did you know anyone going into school?

I didn't know a huge number of people at Illinois, but, my father was a professor at the university, and I grew up in Champaign. Because of that, I knew a lot more people and a lot more faculty than most people did.

Did you do anything outside of class?

I coached tennis for teenagers. I hung out with the tennis team a lot during my freshman and sophomore years.

Were you looking for cofounders in school?

I knew I wanted to do a startup and I knew I was excited about venture capital. I knew both of those things before I went to

347

college; I knew that was the outcome I wanted. I did not start looking for a technical cofounder until several found me, and from there I realized that I was being given tremendous opportunities, so I seized them.

Did you take time away from class to relax or did you focus on startups and projects?

I believe strongly in work-life balance. I made it a point in college to go out every weekend. That didn't mean that I wouldn't come back and code though. I had an immense amount of fun in college and I wouldn't trade that for anything. I think it's a just a matter of prioritizing and deciding that that's what you're going to do. I would go out until 3:00 AM, wake up at 9:00 AM, work until 10:00 PM, and then do it again.

What were you doing right as you graduated?

Graduation was kind of anticlimactic for me. I was doing my startup full time. My last year of school I forgot to take a class, so I had to wait until I was already working full time and had taken that class, to graduate. I think that if your intention is to do a startup, you should be doing it your senior year of college, and you should be in a position where you're able to work full time and go to school full time. It's a perfectly reasonable thing, working 80 hours per week is totally reasonable when you're 20.

Did anyone inspire you in school?

When I was doing my startup, Facebook was growing like crazy and YouTube—which was full of UIUC grads—had just sold for $1.7 billion or some ridiculous amount, while not being profitable. Those are the guys that inspired me.

How did the idea for One Llama come about?

Most of these ideas are not one person having a eureka moment, they are the product of a lot of people coming together and thinking about what problems need to be solved. Often times, the idea you start with isn't where you end up. But this was a technology that existed, a nascent technology that existed at UIUC that was presented to us by some professors after 20 years of research in technology. So, a lot of the credit for the idea behind the technology is theirs. Where I provided guidance and leadership was in making that something you could sell; making it something you could turn into a product.

How did you find your cofounders?

Serendipity. I had met John Wagner, the first cofounder of our company, and he introduced me to Rob Schultz from Illinois Ventures and Rob invited me to intern with them. We were presented with this technology from UIUC and we put together a technical team, for which I was amongst the cofounders, and we kicked it off. I think it was a rather unique way of starting a business, and that's how we got going.

Did you fundraise? What was that process like?

We did. We went through it a few times. I think the expectations for One Llama were to develop a human-level, acoustical learning algorithm, on a shoestring budget, in six months. We took funding that was in accordance with that. So, one of the big problems we ended up facing were unreasonable expectations for technology: the inability of our investors to truly appreciate the capabilities and capacity of the technology, so we were horribly underfunded. We went through two fundraising cycles, both of which were very interesting. The first one was with our existing and seed investor, and the second one was with an external venture capital from the I2A Fund.

Fundraising, for me, was a pretty negative experience. I think it was because we were unable to raise the amount of capital necessary to really effectively build out this tool—to take enough pressure off the research team to actually solve the problem, which is an incredibly difficult problem to solve. So we were never able to get enough interest or enough money to be able to solve that problem effectively, and it's a huge time drain. It takes about six months to really raise a round; it's very hard to make real progress, especially when you're as resource-constrained as we are, and you're working. So we'd wake up in the morning, drive into Chicago and spend three hours there, meet with tons of people, then go back to the office and work for another eight hours, and do that again the next day. It's an incredibly tiresome process and forward progress is horribly impeded during that period. I think that VC's really need to work to shelter their technical founders and their business founders from this.

How long did it take to build the beta and how did you spread the word at first?

The first beta was a dismal failure. It took us about five months. It relied on technology that had no hope of success and we didn't get out of the starting box. We had to discard the technology and the initial interface. While that was going on, my other cofounder Nikhil Pandit and I basically went into tiger team mode—we shut out the rest of the world for about three weeks and developed what ultimately became our first release, and got the word out.

We were in a variety of the technical blogs and had a huge first-day hit. We did a lot of Facebook marketing through our friends and then, ultimately, that product became the product with which we raised a second round of funding.

So you guys pivoted a couple of times?

We put up pirate flags outside the office and basically just stayed there for three weeks, working night and day. We built our own recommendation techniques and our own recommendation algorithms and built the user interface, really turned it into an effective first product. So yeah, we pivoted constantly. Startups are about dealing with the rollercoaster—sometimes you've got to pivot, sometimes you've got to stay the course; really good entrepreneurs understand when to do what.

Were there any moments where you thought One Llama would fail or where your blood pressure went up, for whatever reason?

That happened all the time. I think five years in I had developed a high blood pressure. Every day in a startup is like your last day; you don't know if you're going to be around the next day, you don't know if another competitor is going to come around with a product that just creams yours. You have no idea; every day is stressful. Ultimately, our business was not successful, and you learn a lot from that.

When we had the worst blizzard in Champaign's history, over the last 100 years, I had to have a friend with an SUV plow through four feet of snow in order to be able to restart a server; from then on, we had remote lights-out management, so we could manage servers remotely.

How did you guys split the work?

It was a team of five strong technical founders. We divided work based on expertise. We had two good researchers who really were working on the research problem, of how to make computers understand music. I was probably the chief architect, director of product development, and the person that kind of led the business operations, internally. And Nikhil was a tremendous technical cofounder. He could do anything; could write any bit of code.

We were five people and our project goal was to understand human cognition and map it to code; my job was to make sure that people knew what they were supposed to be working on and that it was the highest priority task, so I tended to be the person that helped divide up the work.

What was the work schedule like?

It was hectic all the time. It was work from 9:00 AM until 3:00 AM every night. I don't think we ever took a break and we did that for five years. But it's okay because you're doing work that's interesting. When your hobby is your work, you don't mind doing it. When you believe in something, when you believe that it's improving you, you don't mind working hard.

What is the biggest challenge for One Llama?

Making our technology work, plain and simple. Had our technology been able to achieve the capabilities that it was represented to us as having, when we got going, we would have been successful.

I don't think that the Midwestern mentality is capable of appreciating the type of environment that developers and creative technical people need to do incredibly successful things. It's something that Silicon Valley, Austin, and Boulder have really nailed, but the typical, industrialist Chicago mentality for building businesses just does not appreciate the value of technical expertise and the need to keep those people happy. So, we did not have the kind of culture that Zappos had, something I regret not being more forceful about trying to implement within One Llama.

Why do people go to California; why not stay in Chicago?

It's minus 20 degrees in Chicago right now. No joke. It's 55 degrees in San Francisco, 56 degrees in Austin, and there's skiing in Boulder. In Chicago, you have 10% unemployment; you have a general business climate that doesn't value technical success with the exception of maybe Groupon. People in Chicago value sales and business expertise over technical expertise, but in orders of magnitude, and that's not sustainable for building really, really strong technical businesses. Until that changes dramatically—you can't just be as good as San Francisco and say people should stay here. It doesn't make sense. It's just silly. You need to be a dramatically better environment whereas we're not even as good. So it doesn't surprise me that people are going out to the Valley— this is what PayPal and YouTube did. It's about where all the jobs are, and where the weather is good, and where the best technical brains are, and where the best technical brains are valued; you just don't find that here in the Midwest.

Did you ever hit any productivity brick walls?

I think throughout the period that we were kind of going through all of it. There were several moments where it was just like, "Why are we doing this? This technology is just not going to work, what's the point?"

It's funny: whenever you hit the bottom you get a little bit of hope. You get a sales call from a customer who understands the problem and wants to help you, or is still interested in purchasing your product, or you get a really favorable blog or article in a magazine, or you meet a really good contact that is going to be able to get you over the next hurdle. It seems like almost every time at One Llama, when we got to the point where it was like, "This is just not worth doing," somebody was there within a reasonable period of time that gave us that next bit of hope, and so we just kept working harder.

Did you have a process for hiring?

We were on a shoestring budget so we didn't do a lot of hiring. What we did was a lot on the business development side. On the business development side, you want to see the relationships. Ideally you want to have seen them work for you in the past or have worked for your competitors, or for someone related in the industry, and to know that they're good. Hiring a CEO was really hard for us. CEO's are incredibly expensive in the Midwest.

Only hire the best people you possibly can. Don't hire people that you have hesitancy about, and make sure that your entire team agrees that the person is really good. Have everybody on your team interview the person.

Do you have any advice for undergrads interested in doing a startup?

They should read all the time. They should familiarize themselves with the industry. They should use all of the tools. Every time something comes up they should be on it; using it. The worst thing is to see somebody who wants to be an Internet entrepreneur that doesn't have a Twitter account. How on earth are they going to figure out what shit should come next on the Internet when they're not even aware of what's happening now?

But eventually, good ideas happen. Keep meeting people and make friends. You get interested in this space, you meet the right people, and eventually a good idea will emerge.

What if it's a non-technical person wanting to do a technical startup?

Spend your time trying to meet technical cofounders. You need to go and develop a skill, whether that skill is relationships with customers, sales, legal knowledge or even getting a legal degree. If you want to become a non-technical cofounder as a businessperson, you'd better be good at something useful. You can't just be the 'idea guy.' That person is useless.

If you are a non-technical person and you don't want to learn to program but you want to start a technical company, all I can suggest is go learn a skill. Do not just get an MBA and plan on doing this. You've got to learn *how* to do something well. That does not mean, *I know business* which is a useless thing. You can't *know business*; you need to know how to *do* something. Or you need to go get a job, make a lot of money, and then invest in a bunch of technical cofounders. That's also of value.

Andres Morey, Octopart

Tags: Y Combinator, programmer, grad school founder, profitable, hiring, dropout, coincidental

Overview: Octopart is a search engine for electronic parts making it easy for engineers to find electronic components for hardware projects. All 3 founders of Octopart were in the physics Ph.D. program at UC Berkeley before they dropped out to work on Octopart full-time. The Octoparts don't know this, but they were the very first company that popped into my head when I decided to write this book, and consequently were the very first interview I did—I thought to myself, "I wonder what the Octoparts are up to these days?"

Take me back as far as you can—how did you get started with startups?

My partner Sam and I studied physics together as undergrads and then he went to CU Boulder and I went to Berkeley for grad school. A few years into our graduate programs we both decided that academia wasn't for us.

About five years ago, we were both in NYC for winter break so we got together to catch up. At the time Sam had been reading Paul's essays on startups and they had really affected him. He told me about Paul and his belief that grad students were the sorts of people that should be starting software companies. Back at Berkeley, I had just moved into a windowless office with my lab mates so the idea of a grad student-led revolution resonated with me. That night we started coming up with startup ideas.

We came up with some really bad ideas. The first idea that we took somewhat seriously was an eBay for used scientific equipment. We noticed that there was a lot of old, valuable equipment in our labs that no one was using and we thought that we could setup a marketplace to help labs exchange their old equipment. We realized pretty quickly that it was a horrible idea—too much red tape.

At the time, I was working on a calibration laser for my experiment. My experiment was a neutrino telescope at the South Pole and the device was going to be buried underneath a mile of snow so it had to work reliably at extremely low temperatures for extended periods of time. When I looked online for components to use, I realized that it was difficult to find even basic components like power supplies and relays. Once I got really frustrated looking for low-temperature capacitors so I got this idea to build a website to bring together all the information about electronic parts. I called up Sam with the idea and he liked it.

Did you have any ideas for startups in high school?

Yes and no. I didn't actively think about entrepreneurship or startups that early on, but when I look back I realize that on some level I think the idea of entrepreneurship has always appealed to me. My relatives in Latin America are mostly entrepreneurs. My dad is more of an inventor and I always admired that. When I was in junior high I was always coming up with ways to make money—we would go shovel snow to earn spending money. I also had a failed car-washing business with my cousin. I just never really made the connection between that and forming a corporate entity.

What about college—was it a big transition from high school?

I went to a boarding school for high school so college wasn't that different. I knew some people from my high school so socially I didn't feel like my experience changed all that much. The only significant difference for me was in terms of the academics. College was much more rigorous. During the summers I worked at research labs, and I also spent a year abroad. But for the most part I was pretty academically oriented; I just focused on classes.

I actually started out on an engineering track in college and then about halfway through school, realized that within the engineering department, the only class I had really enjoyed was this thermodynamics class. I had taken some physics classes here and there and one in particular, a course on relativity, really piqued my interest. I followed that up with quantum mechanics, which turned out to be my favorite class and from there, I just kind of fell in love with physics. So, I changed my major and ended up graduating with a combined engineering and physics degree. At the time, I thought I wanted to be a research scientist; that I would just work in physics for the rest of my life, so after college I enrolled in a graduate program for physics.

Was there any work-life balance during school?

I think my college experience was pretty well-rounded and my grad school experience was too. At Berkeley I would go on adventures all the time. Berkeley was a great place to go to grad school. We would take off on road trips every chance we got—down the Pacific Coast Highway, to Tahoe, camping in Yosemite. In fact, my grad school experience was probably too well-rounded. When I realized that I enjoyed reading history books more than physics papers I started thinking about leaving grad school.

In an L.A. Times interview you said you didn't have any previous programming experience; so you guys just decided to jump into it?

Basically, yeah. My only formal computer programming was an introductory C class my freshman year of college. Sam took the same class in Java.

In general, physicists don't have any hardware or software experience when they start doing research. My education was trial by fire and I learned a lot that way. I got experience using Unix by working at physics research labs and I learned a lot about hacking from the postdocs in my research group at grad school. From the beginning, I really enjoyed programming but code for a physicist is just a means to an end, so I always felt guilty that I liked it so much.

When Sam and I started working on Octopart, we knew how to write programs that worked but we didn't have any experience with basic web technologies like web servers, databases, HTTP, or HTML. We had never set up a web page and I hadn't ever heard of MySQL. That's actually what made things so exciting in the first few months. Working on Octopart was fun because we were learning how to use the technologies that powered the Internet. I would spend the day at the lab, hang out with friends, come home at night and work on Octopart for fun.

As we learned more, work on Octopart started to expand and it began to take up more and more of our time. At first, I tried to do grad school and Octopart at the same time; I really wanted to finish my degree and I was convinced that I could do it. It took a little while before I realized that it was just impossible. There was no way that I was going to be able to do both.

I never finished grad school. I dropped out to work on Octopart.

When did you decide to drop out?

We wrote the first line of Octopart code during my third year in grad school. We launched a prototype as soon as we had something ready. The prototype was awful. The logo was an octopus drawn in MS Paint and the prototype took 20 or 30 seconds to return results; we launched as soon as we had something ready, and by launch, I mean we just emailed friends and family and told them, "Hey we're working on this electronic parts search engine, here is a link." We basically did that to motivate ourselves. We knew that as soon as we got it out there and told everybody "We're working on this company," we would actually have to have something to show for ourselves. We figured, with the prototype, the more embarrassing the better—it was an incentive to make the product better.

Around that time, Y Combinator was organizing a funding cycle so we decided to apply. Sam came out to Berkeley and we filled out the application. We didn't think Octopart was very good so we weren't planning on getting Y Combinator support. We didn't even think we would get invited for an interview. But we got invited and we went out to Boston. We met Paul, Jessica, Trevor and Robert and, that night, Paul offered to fund us.

Sam made the decision to drop out of grad school before we even applied to Y Combinator. His last day at CU Boulder was actually the day before the Y Combinator interview. I was closer to graduating and I really wanted to finish my degree so I was planning on doing both Octopart and grad school.

After we got YC funding, I took off for Antarctica to deploy the calibration device for my experiment. While I was there I worked on Octopart at night and when I got back I kept doing both Octopart and grad school. But by the end I was basically going into the lab and working on Octopart, almost exclusively. It took me a while to admit that I wasn't actually doing grad school anymore. I was just doing Octopart, except that I was working on it while sitting in my windowless grad student office.

Was it your involvement with YC that finally convinced you to drop out of grad school?

At that time, Paul and Jessica would take all of the YC founders out to dinner. We met up with them at Jessica's favorite restaurant in Berkeley. We had a really nice conversation and towards the end of dinner, Paul asked me point blank if I was committed to Octopart and, I don't know, the question caught me off guard.

I told Paul that I was fully committed and he responded, "Well, as long as you're still in grad school, investors aren't going to invest in your company." I had been working on Octopart for six months already and mentally I had already gone all-in on the company. Before Paul's question I hadn't thought about how my decision to stay in grad school would cause somebody to think that I wasn't entirely committed.

The dinner with Paul and Jessica was on a Friday, I remember, and I said to myself, "Okay, this weekend, I'm going to figure out what I want to do; it's going to have to be one or the other." On Monday I went in to the lab and told my advisor that I had to drop out.

Prior to YC, who inspired you?

In college, my quantum mechanics professor really inspired me. Like most physicists, my idol was Feynman, and I wanted to be a rock-star theorist. At that point in time, the things that I found most inspiring were people within the physics community; mostly scientists.

But at the same time, it's interesting because I was in college during the first Internet bubble and I remember being jealous that there were people out there working on all these ambitious things in this new industry while I was still in school, taking classes.

Did you guys bootstrap initially?

We were physics grad students when we started working on Octopart. Our only income was our graduate student stipend, which was less than $20,000 a year. When we started coding, Sam went out and bought a desktop at a yard sale for $50 and that was Octopart's first server. He set the server up in his room at Boulder and at night, after having spent all day in the lab, we would log in and code. We actually used that machine in production until pretty recently.

When we got YC funding and they wrote us a check for $15K we didn't think we would ever need any more money. We used their investment to buy a new desktop from Dell and that was the machine we launched with. I remember wheeling our desktops into the colo facility and getting looks from the staff as if we'd shown up to the Presidential Gala wearing flip-flops.

We used a total of $5K out of YC's initial investment to launch Octopart.

Do you think the $150K offer from Yuri Milner is a good or a bad thing?

For some Y Combinator companies it makes sense. For us, the constraints imposed by YC's small initial investment were actually good because it forced us to build a really lean, resilient company. That ended up being necessary later.

On the other hand, one of the most difficult choices we faced was deciding how much money to raise after Demo Day. It was too early to know whether we should raise VC and I think our approach to fundraising reflected that hesitation. $150K would have given us some time to figure that out.

How long did it take you to build your beta and how did you spread the word?

The code we used to launch Octopart was basically written in the three months we spent with YC. For our launch, we didn't have any connections to the electronic parts industry or to the hardware hacker community so we just decided to launch Octopart cold turkey. We picked a date and submitted the announcement to TechCrunch.

Our launch got a lot of attention so we were pumped going into Demo Day. Then our investor presentation went really well so we started getting a lot of attention within Silicon Valley. That was great but our technology was still crap because we still didn't know how to code well, yet. We knew we needed help so I asked a good friend of mine from Berkeley, Harish Agarwal, if he wanted to join us. He slept on it and then dropped out of grad school the next day. He's a physicist so he had a similar coding background to us but he's also one of the smartest people I know so it was really important for us to get him on board.

After the TechCrunch write up and initial traffic, how did you get your early adopters and your early users?

After TechCrunch, hardware blogs like Make Magazine picked up our launch, so we used that to start getting feedback on the search engine. We also started going to hardware hacker meetups in the Bay Area. There was a big electronic parts industry convention in Vegas, so Harish and Sam went out there to make connections with distributors and manufacturers.

Did you guys ever really have to change directions with Octopart?

We've definitely had tweaks and minor pivots but we've never made a major pivot, at least not in the same way most companies think about it. In the beginning we wanted to build consumer-facing applications to help engineers design circuits and build hardware devices but we realized that it would be much better for us to focus on the search and data side. There are many other companies that are much better at building design software than we are, so we built an API for them to integrate Octopart into their own apps.

Do you remember when you started to notice revenue picking up?

We noticed revenue picking up about a year ago. There was a pretty clear point when the electronic parts industry came out of the recession. It was interesting for us to see this, because up until then, we didn't know how much the economy was actually affecting us. When the industry came out of recession, everyone wanted to reach engineers more aggressively so they were very interested in working with us.

Another interesting thing is how the recession actually helped us. During the recession, distributors and manufacturers were looking for new ways to find customers, so they were more willing to give a startup a chance. We built up a lot of relationships during the recession that ended up being really helpful when the economic situation changed.

Now we have partnerships with 70 distributors, including several of the largest distributors in the world. We have 450,000 unique visitors every month using the site, and we've seen Octopart t-shirts in the wild a few times. One of the most exciting milestones for me was when one of my friends from grad school told me he used Octopart on a daily basis.

Overall, were the three months during YC your most productive time period?

I think it was our most productive time period but the code that we wrote during that time is embarrassing to think about! We were writing a lot of really crappy code but we were writing so much of it we were probably still most productive overall.

It was nonstop work. The day that I dropped out of grad school, everything just hit me. The magnitude of the situation that we were in—we were broke and completely on our own—Octopart had to work or we couldn't survive. That night, I couldn't sleep so I took out my laptop and worked through the night. That set the tone for the rest of our time at YC.

Knowing everything you know now, is there anything you would go back and tell your younger self?

Our strength and our weakness is how stubborn we are. So I don't think there was anything that I could have told myself that would have made any difference.

I look back and I think I should have been exercising more; I should have taken more time to socialize, hang out with friends, and call my mom more often. But there is a reason why I didn't do those things and I don't think there's any way that I could have changed that.

What's your role at Octopart today? Has it changed from what it used to be?

Our company is still small so everybody is capable of doing everything. We sit across from each other, so we discuss all major decisions and everyone is aware of everything that is going on. Our roles are constantly evolving as we fix problems and identify new ones. Currently, Sam handles our back-end infrastructure as well as our business relationships with distributors and other partners. Harish works primarily on the search code, normalization code, and various analytics projects. I work on front-end stuff, which includes all the client-side code, and I also spend a lot of time working on our architecture. Everyone does customer service, or "fan support," as we like to call it.

What's your work schedule like, now?

I usually get to work at 9:00AM or 10:00AM and work until about 7:00PM when I go to the gym. I get some of my best coding done at night so I tend to work after dinner and often I'll code until 2:00 or 3:00 in the morning. I used to read books and magazines but now I write code instead. We moved to NYC recently and one of my favorite things about the city is that it's a 24-hour city. Sometimes I'll go out at night, come home, and work until the sun comes up. I try to take at least one day off a week but when we're close to launching something I have to work straight through.

What's your biggest challenge today?

Today, Octopart is really good if you know the model number of the part you're looking for. However, engineers doing design work usually don't have model numbers so they're looking for new components based on a set of specific design requirements. Often, the most crucial part in a design is a custom-made component made by a small manufacturer that you're not familiar with. There are tens of thousands of manufacturers, big and small, and our biggest challenge is to build relationships with all of them so we can expose their data to engineers looking for new parts.

Would you say that Octopart has a "culture"?

We're a small team so our culture is still evolving and I'm probably too close to it to even define it. However, I would say that the thing I'm proudest of is our resourcefulness. We like to get our hands dirty and solve problems, however unglamorous they are. When we were bootstrapping in the beginning we had to do things as efficiently as possible so we bought our own servers and set up the infrastructure, ourselves. When our router broke we took off for the colo, picked up a Cisco from Craigslist on the way and then spent the night on the floor of the colo learning IOS.

Would you ever hire someone that met Octopart's "cultural requirements" but was really difficult to work with?

No. Working on a startup is extremely stressful and what has kept us going has been the relationship between the founders. We genuinely enjoy working together and I can't imagine bringing somebody on board who we didn't enjoy working with.

Do you have any advice for a student thinking about doing a startup?

Personally, I found that the most difficult part about working on a startup was the idea phase. When you're searching for an idea it feels as if everything has already been done. So my advice is to just start working—on something—on anything. Even if it's cloning something that's already out there, just start coding. As soon as you start working on one startup, your brain re-orients itself and you start to see problems in the marketplace that you couldn't see before.

You're probably better qualified to answer this than most people—if somebody doesn't know how to program, what's your advice to them?

The Web is an incredible resource and everything that we learned was from reading blogs and looking at examples of code online. However, it was actually really useful for me to take an intro programming class in college, so I would still recommend that. Once you learn one programming language it's a lot easier to learn other languages. The rest is just practice.

Can you talk about the time you most successfully hacked some non-computer system to your advantage?

When I was little I fell in love with the Porsche 911 and I decided that it was going to be my first car regardless of how long I had to wait. When I was in high school my dad took pity on me and bought a 1974 Porsche 911 in salvage condition. We fixed it up and when it was ready, I took it to grad school with me. So I was 23 and my first car was a 911.

Being a grad student with a 911 was pretty cool but it turns out that it's very difficult to maintain on a grad student budget. In order to pass inspection I had to have it declared an antique. In order to afford insurance I had to figure out how the insurance company priced insurance per mile so I could work backwards to a rate that was affordable. My alternator was weak so I would park on hills in San Francisco so I could do a rolling start when the battery died. I couldn't even afford a mechanic or proper Porsche tools so when my alternator finally died, I took apart the engine to replace it. The alternator on the 1974 911 is buried deep within the engine so it was a miracle that I was able to get to it using a basic tool set. When I put the engine back together and it turned over, that was one of the happiest moments of my life.

Ricky Yean, Crowdbooster

Tags: Y Combinator, funded, businessperson, school worker, undergrad founder, hiring

Overview: CrowdBooster launched after going through Y Combinator in the Spring of 2010 and was started by 3 Stanford graduates to help companies deal with the increasing complexity of tracking their performance and metrics on social platforms such as Twitter. As businesses try to jump on board with social media—try to create engaging content, have conversations, and build relationships—Crowdbooster comes in to measure all of your social media performance, offers suggestions for the best time to run a campaign based on historical and user data, and so on.

Can you talk about your earliest experience as an entrepreneur?

I am from Los Angeles; originally, I immigrated to LA from Taiwan, so I was not really exposed to entrepreneurship at all. I was interested in computers and, from an early age, was creating websites. I ended up not really pursuing computer science, I just coded in my spare time as one of my hobbies. So, I basically was not exposed to anything like this until I got to Stanford.

At Stanford I went on a trip during spring break of my freshman year, and visited a bunch of different businesses in the Bay Area that are classified as social enterprises. I went to companies like Kiva and World of Good, and I saw the huge impact on society that businesses could have, and found that to be completely fascinating. That was when I first got interested in business, in general. From there, I got more exposure at Stanford through my involvement in an organization called Business Association of Stanford Entrepreneurial Students (BASES). I organized business plan competitions, events, went to talks and workshops and networking events, talked to entrepreneurs, and found mentors; that's how I first got exposed to all this.

I started working with David Tran during my sophomore year. A friend introduced us and we started working on the BASES website together; from there we began working on different ideas. BASES is an organization at Stanford for students interested in entrepreneurship. David Tran really wanted to learn about how he could get involved. I was pissed off about the BASES website because they had spent about $30,000 outsourcing it to a firm in India and it came back looking like shit. I said, "We could do this better", so over the summer we switched it all to a CMS, made it easy to update, taught the entire organization how to use the WordPress CMS to make the content relevant, and basically redid the whole website as our first project together.

Are you both programmers?

I'm not a programmer but David is. My other cofounder, Mark, who joined us in early 2010, is also a programmer. My skills are in organizations, working with people, leading teams, and whatever other things that you have to learn, doing a startup.

When you emigrated from Taiwan, was that particularly difficult?

Yeah it was. I think coming here it was very difficult having to learn the language and having to leave my mom. My mom is still in Taiwan; at that time there were some family issues. I grew up in a single-parent household with my dad. I would see my mom, usually just an hour or two each day—emigrating to the US made it even worse because I saw her just a few times over the 7 years or so until I went to college. So I think that really taught me to be independent.

When I moved here I moved in with a step family, so I was learning how to work with people, how to deal with a new family, how to navigate between the different individuals in the household, all the while fighting my adolescent tendencies. That was the beginning of learning how to be a 'people person'.

I started working when I was 14. I worked at roughly 7 different jobs before college. I tried all kinds of things. A lot of those experiences, I think, laid the foundation for me wanting to be an entrepreneur.

At Stanford, what kind of classes did you take? Were you doing any projects?

Initially, I was an economics major. Like many other business-oriented students at Stanford, I was pursuing investment banking or a career in management consulting. They're popular in elite universities and they are the default paths. I picked my major because it was the one I thought would best equip me to take on those careers. At that time, since I really didn't know what I was passionate about, that seemed like the right way to go. I know I was interested in business so I took a lot of classes in economics.

Later on, I think being involved in BASES and just being the organizer in the entrepreneurial ecosystem, I got a lot more interested in entrepreneurship. I did a summer internship at a VC firm, did a summer internship at a startup called Eventbrite and then started working on projects on my own with some friends. By then, I was sure that startups were my passion. I switched my major to Science, Technology & Society so I could take some more computer science and engineering classes. That major also gave me the flexibility to focus on projects outside of school, as well as student organizations.

Did you work on any projects other than BASES?

We started working on building a company my sophomore year. Through BASES and other events I got to know people who might be interested in entrepreneurship. One day we got everybody together—there were about 15 people—and we all just said, "Let's build a company and brainstorm together." There were a bunch of really wild ideas. Eventually, the group was too big and we split up into 3 or 4 separate groups. David Tran was in my group along with 2 other guys and we started working on our first project together, to build the 'YouTube for teachers,' to allow teachers to share their lesson plans with other teachers and get advice and mentorship. We built a prototype but ended up discovering that the problem is a lot bigger.

I think once you start solving a problem, you start realizing there are all these other things that come up. We thought that a lot of the problems that we had to solve were more systemic and not really something technology alone could address. One example is that, teachers don't really know how to use computers, and that's something that as technology people it's hard for us to understand how to really deal with that.

After that, David Tran and I split off and started doing our own things. We applied to the business plan competition at BASES. I was the president of BASES at the time and we didn't even make it past the first round of judging. So that was pretty discouraging.

We had a couple of summer grant programs that didn't work out. Lightspeed Venture Partners has a summer grant program, so does Highland Capital Partners. We just wanted to work on a startup over the summer as well. None of that worked out; this was junior year. David Tran went to work at Mozilla and I went to work at Eventbrite. Every day after work I would go to David Tran's house and we would just hack on different projects. After our summer internships were over I went to stay at David Tran's place and we would just work on different projects during that time too. So there was a lot of searching for ideas, hacking different projects together, and finding time and excuses to do it, because we really wanted to do this thing. After junior year we applied to Y Combinator and got rejected the first time.

I also got rejected as a solo founder.

Our senior year, we applied for the winter cycle and we didn't get in. We didn't even get an interview. Paul Graham sent us a message on Hacker News saying, "Why don't you just finish school, why are you doing this now?" We never heard back from him after that so we were getting very worried because we really wanted to do it. But I think we're both very determined and felt that regardless of what happened after college, we were just going to get a job and moonlight the startup stuff. We would get together like we did during the summer and just work on it at night. We had no doubt we could do it. We sacrificed what was supposed to be our most fun year in college as seniors to work on the startup during crazy hours like midnight to 4:00 AM at random rooms on campus after we had taken care of our other responsibilities. We applied again to a bunch of different programs: TechStars, Launchpad, all these different places and finally, in March, Y Combinator accepted us. Now we have a little more angel money so we can keep going.

You said you had emigrated from Taiwan, did you know anybody going into Stanford?

No, I was the only one from my school.

Did you find other ways to meet people?

I think when you're searching for direction in college you tend to gravitate towards those people who are very clear about what they want to do in their lives. But it wasn't always like that and like I said, I wasn't even interested in business. In fact, my dad lost most of his money in the stock market so I always thought that business was this evil thing that made life miserable.

I never got to do many extracurricular activities in high school because if I wasn't studying, I was working outside of school. In college I was just blown away by the opportunities that I had and the things that I could get involved with; I was basically doing everything. Sophomore year I was in 6 or 7 different organizations whether they dealt with medicine, the stock market, venture capital, or consulting. I was in a fraternity as well. I did all these things and I think that was good. You're supposed to use the opportunity to explore when you can before you enter the real world.

I think the critical moment was realizing, I was involved in some of these groups but wasn't fully committed to a lot of them and I felt really bad. I gravitated towards BASES and as soon as there was a leadership position opened I said, "I'll do it." Same thing happened with my fraternity; I became the president of my fraternity my junior year because I really loved it. So in my junior year I basically said no to the 4 or 5 different organizations that I was in and I made a decision that I really wanted to focus my time and energy on my fraternity and BASES, that's it. I think that was the critical moment, *learning how to say no to all these opportunities and all these responsibilities*, taking a closer look at what I was interested in and just focusing on making sure that I spent my time in a way where I got the most out of it. That's a hard lesson to learn for ambitious people like me.

Do you have any advice on how to find a cofounder in school?

If you join an organization where people are looking to do startups, you go to events where people are doing startups, and you work on your own projects, then you have something to talk about with people and that's really how people come together. David was always there because we work together and shared a passion, and then we found Mark through an event we organized at BASES. We weren't even looking; we just struck a chord with Mark. My best advice is just get out there and start making things happen. Stop saying that you are not getting anywhere because you don't have a cofounder, just move.

Did you work when you were at Stanford?

I didn't work a lot fortunately—I got a lot of financial aid from Stanford. But I did work as a tutor. I didn't want to work for the government financial aid work-study programs at $15 an hour. I wanted to do something where I could get more out of my time. So I tutored kids for $80 an hour. There are a lot of agencies in colleges that match you up with student tutors and they take a huge cut. They'll charge parents $100 bucks and they'll pay the tutor $20 and keep $80. I just basically went to those guys' websites, took their copy, and put it on Craigslist and said, "I can undercut them; I offer the same things, just come work with me."

Did you take some time to relax and party?

I definitely took time to party. Stanford's a pretty fun place and I definitely didn't go out every weekend. A lot of times I just stayed in and tried to take care of the student organizations I was a part of; tried to take care of school. During my junior and senior years, when we were working on projects, whatever free time we had we were coming together to work on them. So parties were out of the question. In fact, freshman year was probably the time when I partied the most, and then sophomore year a little bit.

I think once you find something that you're interested in you really know it and you're just not going to let it go. I really enjoyed the work and I didn't want to miss out if I had the opportunity to work on it. Who knows what's going to happen in the future, right? So, if I had the time in school, there was just no question I was going to go work on a startup.

What were you doing right as you graduated?

We found out we got into Y Combinator in March and we were graduating in June. During that time we were already working on getting the first version out there. We spent all the time we had outside of classes working on our company. The first 2 weeks of Y Combinator we were still graduating and so we were a little bit late in joining. Admittedly, the last week of school was pretty much partying every day, so we lost a week of productivity there. You can't do much when you're graduating—it's a lot of work. The last spring quarter before you graduate, that's probably the craziest 10 weeks ever. We said no to everybody for 9 weeks and then joined everyone else the last week of school.

Any tips for applying to groups like Y Combinator?

We ended up changing what we were working on around week 5 or 6 of Y Combinator. I think it was the fact that PG, Jessica, and Harj, saw the drive that we had, listened to the story about us working together for a long period, and just recognized that we were very persistent people. I was in touch with Jessica before—working in BASES—helping her put together Startup School, which is where we met Mark. She knew that I could do good work because I had helped her out with Startup School stuff, and the fact that we had applied once before, that also helped.

If you know for sure this is what you want to do, do everything you can to show that it's what you want to do. Build a prototype, show that you can actually create something even if it doesn't end up working out; it's what you want to do anyway so who cares. And I think we were pretty determined with YC. Our thought was, if we get it, that's great, we can pay ourselves; if not, we'll still work on it and we'll go find a job somewhere and spend most of our time working on our startup. Nothing was going to stop us, really.

While you were in college, were there any people that really inspired you?

Kimber Lockhart inspired me; she took me on a trip to see all the social enterprises in the Bay Area. She was in BASES, did a startup out of Stanford, and got acquired by Box.net. I really admired her because she was also working on her startup in school. Every Saturday I would go to the Student Union and I'd see her and her 3 teammates just working there all day; they were really intense about it. The door was always closed but you could see through the glass that they were going crazy in there. Like I said earlier, people gravitate towards passionate people and I really gravitated towards her. She told me to join BASES and I did. If I'm going to find other people like her, yeah of course I'm going to join that organization. I hope I did that for other people too, being very passionate about what I'm doing and helping people find their inspirations and their passions.

How did those first ideas get started? What was the thought that came to you, that made you think you should do this?

I think we started—not because we hated anything—because we were just dreaming up possibilities with what could happen if someone figured out something to do with all this Twitter data. We're baseball fans so we wanted a way for us to be notified of critical moments in the baseball game where we could actually turn on the TV and watch if it was tied in the 8th inning, or if it was a rivalry game, or something like that.

So, we created a Twitter account that would just send out status updates of baseball games at the most critical moments. If it was the 9th inning and the closer was coming in with two guys on base, we define that as a *must watch moment* and we have a Twitter account that will send out that information. So if you're following that account and you see that, you will turn on the TV and watch the game. Later on I saw another startup doing this. So I felt pretty happy that someone was working on this problem, maybe we weren't crazy.

So that was original idea, but that one didn't really work out; we didn't think things through well enough. In school, everything is experimental. We were not as committed to overcoming all different challenges. One of the biggest challenges with the sporting application was: how do you pay for all the play-by-play data? There were only two providers and they charged a ton and we didn't have any money to pay for it.

So that was one thing. Another thing that we did with Twitter, had to do with facilitating discussions. So, say you want to have a discussion about The Simpsons episode that you saw today. If you type in The Simpsons, you'll find a thousand forums online, and in each forum you have to read everything, understand the culture, go through the registration process, probably a really nasty looking phpBB board and then you'll read the threads to see if the question is something that you want to ask that has not been posted before and then you post something in one of these forums and cross your fingers that someone will respond and have a discussion with you.

If you just type Simpsons episode in the search on Twitter, you'll see a bunch of people talking about it who are looking to talk more about it just because they really like what they saw. So we thought, okay, there is some way for us to help you find the people who are interested in having a discussion with you about the Simpsons and to provide a way for you to invite them to join you in a spontaneous discussion—a forum thread. We thought that would be super valuable so we built that.

That's what we applied to Y Combinator with, and after the first time we met with Paul Graham we were still working on the idea and he had no idea what we were working on. He literally said, "Why did I fund you guys again?" And I was thinking, "Too late! You already signed the check, I deposited the money." *(Laughs)*

You raised an undisclosed angel round after YC. What was that experience like?

It was super stressful. As first time entrepreneurs, we really had no idea how to go about doing it and Y Combinator had taught us a lot but at the same time you really have to learn by doing it yourself and making mistakes. It was a time-consuming process for us and it definitely felt like we were fighting for our survival. We had money from YC and another angel in the beginning so we had around $45K in the bank and if we don't raise additional money, that's only going to take us so far.

How long did it take to build that first prototype of CrowdBooster? How did you spread the word at first?

The beta took us about a month to build. In week 6 of YC, we decided to pivot. Week 10 was demo day and we were under a lot of pressure to produce the first version of our product so that we could show it to investors and get users on there. We did a lot of the Steve Blank customer development. We spoke to a lot of social media managers at that time and we basically went back to these old contacts.

A lot of it was just saying, "I'm a startup, I'm a student and I'm working on this problem and you guys seem like you're really good at Twitter and I'd love to just learn more about your job and the challenges that you face everyday so that we can create a better experience for you. We're hackers; we can make things and make people's lives easier."

That's the pitch with every single company and, of course, you get rejected or you just don't hear back. You get rejected most of the time, but when you do get in touch with people, they really share everything with you. So, building CrowdBooster came from the pain that we saw when we first spoke to these people a year ago. Our initial users came from that customer development process that we did before.

Were there any moments for you guys when you either thought, "This is going to fail" or you just got really nervous or stressed out?

I think the toughest moment was during the pivot. Mark joined us in early 2010 and, around January or February was when we started working on the idea for Twitter discussion forums. We called it 'On the fly forums for Twitter' and we applied to YC with it. So, beginning of February we were working on that product all the way until mid-July, when we were like, "Okay, we really don't know how to do this, it's not getting very much traction," we iterated on the product a couple of different times and repositioned it. Instead of being a forum, we turned it into a Q&A service on Twitter.

I think the entire process was just really grueling and we were under pressure and other YC companies already had a lot of traction and—for some people—things were coming together and people were taking off. You have this ticking clock and we were just extremely stressed at the time and said, "Let's build something that has more business value that people will actually pay us for."

So those were some of the key criteria we put on this thing we were going to work on. People were going to pay us for it; we started working on a bunch of different marketing campaigns on Twitter. We coded up a system to orchestrate a retweet bomb. So, for the World Cup, we helped one of our peer companies in YC that has to do with sports orchestrate a retweet campaign where they enlisted over 100 of the most passionate users and all of YC, and everyone retweeted the same message on the morning of the final match of the world cup; we wanted to become trending and we thought that was a really clever social network marketing campaign on Twitter. We did stuff like that and it kind of worked, but not really. We then decided to do analytics, because for all the stuff that we were working on, we couldn't really show much for it. So, sure you've got 120 retweets, great. What does that mean?

From our experience it's actually the same problem that every single social manager experiences. We confirmed for ourselves that this was a critical matter and decided to work on Crowdbooster, so that entire time was probably the lowest moment in our company history. If it weren't for David and Mark, I don't know how I would have done it myself. I was basically really depressed every single day and it doesn't help that we had to go to YC every Tuesday and show other people the progress that we had made, or the lack of progress. Luckily, one of the best things about YC is we weren't the only ones in that situation; there were a few other startups that were also struggling and that helped a lot.

I remember one trip from another product we were working on called Conversely. We scheduled four meetings with YC founders who were running bigger companies and we pitched them on how they could use Conversely, from a business standpoint. It was a Tuesday; we spent all day in the city. Everyone had encouraging words, but it didn't really resonate for anyone, even when we showed them the prototype and what was possible. They weren't that enthusiastic, so we drove down and went straight to YC and the entire time, the entire drive down from San Francisco, the three of us didn't speak. We didn't say a word to each other—we were super depressed. The radio doesn't work in Mark's car so there was no music and there was traffic and it was just really depressing until we got to YC, outside the door. We were just hanging out there, just how it usually goes: you hang out a bit before the speaker comes in and the food gets served.

But I was hanging out and another team in our batch walked up to the door and they all had sad faces so I said, "Hey what's up, how was your day?" And they said, "We went up to the city and we presented our idea to all these companies, they all hated it." I was like, "Wow, that's exactly what we just did and it's really great that you guys are here because I was just about to go cry in the corner." So I think that was one of the most memorable moments in YC—surprisingly, the worst and the most miserable time.

We were one of the top teams for office hours. PG has office hours and people can sign up for them. We went to office hours every single week.

Can you talk about the time you most successfully hacked some non-computer system to your advantage?

I wasn't the smartest kid at school. I didn't have a good foundation. English is my second language. There were a lot of challenges at school and so I needed to get tutored for the SAT because that's what you have to do to get into a good college. Usually, I would give money to my dad. Instead I saved up some money and I went to pay for 2 months of SAT tutoring at this expensive tutoring place in my neighborhood and at the end of 2 months I went in and told them, "I have to go, I don't have money to pay for this. The tutoring was great but I don't have money to pay for it." They liked me enough to say, "Hey, we'll tutor you for free" and I was with that tutoring service for the next year and my score significantly improved. I think my first test was on the 1600 scale. Later on they changed it to 2400 during my senior year when I actually had to take it, but it was 1600 and my first score was somewhere around 1000. So I had a significant boost in my SAT score later on.

In college, some finance people get the allure to want to work at VC firms and that kind of stuff, but not too many VC firm hire college students because to be honest we're pretty useless. Instead of submitting resumes, I checked YouNoodle and reached out to Corey Reese at Alsop Louie Partners and he got me a position at ALP. When I started getting more interested in startups, I wanted to work for a growing startup with some senior management that I could learn from, so I contacted the CEO, Kevin Hartz, through the Stanford alumni directory and I said, "Hey Kevin, I would really love to come talk to you about Eventbrite and potentially explore my career options." On the website they weren't posting for jobs and I became the first intern and basically defined my position. He asked me what I wanted to do and I ended up doing everything that I said I wanted to do. I designed a position around it and now they always hire summer interns and called them 'super interns'; I was their first 'super intern'. Now I call my interns 'super interns' and I try to give them the same experience. **CrowdBooster is hiring, why would someone want to work there?**

We're young founders too, so we love to work really closely and learn from each other. We're also really shaping the industry. We're passionate about what it means when businesses get on these social media platforms and have a much more transparent, genuine, relationship-based marketing approach with their consumers. We want to push the world in that direction, so please help us.

James Fong, Listia

Tags: programmer, Y Combinator, coincidental, VC funded, Ivy League, hiring

Overview: Listia is a new kind of marketplace where people trade stuff using virtual currency instead of cash. Essentially, users upload items they want to get rid of to an auction and they get credits that other users bid with. They can then use those credits to bid on other things on Listia. It feels a lot like eBay for free stuff—things found on the site range from handmade jewelry, coins, old baseball cards, and other types of collectible goods. Listia started in 2009, went through Y Combinator, and has since raised over $2 million.

Where did the idea of Listia come from?

For me, it was basically a problem that I had trying to get rid of some of the stuff in my house. I had a pair of old snowboard boots that had only been worn maybe 5 times and I wanted to get rid of them. At first I tried to sell them for money by putting them up for auction, but when nobody bid on them I ended up losing out on listing fees. After that I said, "Ok, I don't want to throw them away since they're perfectly useful, let me try to at least give them away" so I listed them on an online classifieds site in the free section. As soon as I posted them I ended up getting fifty emails that said, "Oh, I'll come get them, I want them." Then, out of all those emails, I had to pick one guy, tell him to come pick them up at my house, and at the end of the day he never showed up. I figured, "There's got to be a better solution to connect people and allow them to reuse the stuff they don't want to just throw away, stuff that somebody else could find useful."

So Listia is a direct solution to a problem I had actually experienced in real life.

Did you do anything that you would consider entrepreneurial while you were in high school?

Not that I can remember. My cofounder Gee and I both graduated college in 2001. We were studying electrical engineering at the time and I had always wanted to start something—create something that everybody used—I just never really had the guts to actually quit and pursue any of my ideas. So I went to graduate school and got a Master's in Electrical Engineering and after that I worked at SUN and Micron for five or six years. Finally, a couple of years ago, I decided to take the plunge on this idea we had.

In college, what classes were you taking?

As an undergrad, everything was all EE; there was some CS and I actually really didn't know what type of job I might get after all those classes. My favorite undergrad classes were web development classes; one taught me about databases, I believe it was a ColdFusion class.

That's back when Macromedia was licensing it? I think it's under the Adobe brand now.

Yes, I learned a lot and that actually peaked my interest in web development. After college I designed my own websites on the side and that got me even more hooked, but I didn't think I should waste my undergraduate education in electrical engineering by going into web development or startups, so to speak. So I decided to go with an EE job doing verification at SUN, instead.

Now when I talk to people my advice is to do what you like. The key is to take risks when you are young and don't have too many other responsibilities.

Did you know many people going into college?

I went to college at Cornell and I actually didn't know anyone going over to New York from California, but I quickly made a few good friends that had the same interests I did, and my cofounder is actually from Cornell as well. We've been friends since freshman year. We didn't live in the same dorm, but cliques form pretty quickly and you end up hanging out with the same people all four years. Classes help; he was also EE, so we stuck together.

Did you do anything outside of class?

Freshman year I experimented with playing water polo but it ended up taking a lot of time, so I didn't do too much outside of classes. I was on the board of Cornell's Chinese Students

Association where I did publicity my junior year, and my senior year I created a Webmaster position for myself. I've always had this desire for people to either see or use something I've created.

So you weren't interested in startups in college, and you weren't looking for cofounders?

Right. Our story is a little bit different; I would say that we are a little bit late to the game. It wasn't really even on my mind to do a startup in college because of the whole bubble. I think I was somewhat interested, but I never really took the option seriously. Dropping EE and trying to do a startup was just out of the question for me. Plus I don't think I had any good ideas at the time.

Was it a grind or did you have time to relax?

I had my fair share of good times in school; had my share of parties, for sure. College is tough though and I wish I could go back and attend every lecture to get the most out of it.

When you were graduating college, what was going through your mind? Were you thinking you wanted to get a job?

Actually, in 2001, the job market got hit pretty hard as I recall. I didn't really have a plan after college, so I decided to continue my education and get my Master's back home at San Jose State. While I was getting my Master's I interned at SUN, which put me into electrical engineering jobs and stuff like that.

You didn't have any interest in startups or entrepreneurship or anything like that at this point?

No. Well, I always had an interest, but I never really had the balls to actually quit and move on any of my ideas. I didn't really know what to do, and then over the course of a few years, post-college, I did more coding, and that actually gave me a little more experience with everything.

Was there a turning point where you got more confident or something happened to make you start thinking you should do a startup?

Yeah. My turning point was probably two years ago when I started reading a lot of Paul Graham essays. We did a lot of research on Y Combinator; we had always known about Y Combinator, actually, but never had a good enough idea to apply with. So once we did come up the idea it was a no-brainer to apply; I think the idea was the thing that was missing in all of this, actually. If we had had a better idea earlier on, I might have made the jump to do a startup earlier, but an idea is something you can't really force, right?

Y Combinator's mantra is 'Build something people want,' and I think it's very important to do exactly that. You can't force a startup to happen; you can't just be looking for the next big thing. It has to come about, naturally.

You and I were in the same Y Combinator class and it may be easy to forget how uncertain times were back then. Sequoia Capital's RIP Good Times presentation was leaked in October of 2008 and I've spoken to founders from the winter class and even I forgot how bad the economic climate was. Today in 2011, it doesn't feel much like 2008 or 2009. I'm curious why you guys chose summer 2009, of all times to apply?

For us it was almost, do or die. When we were applying to Y Combinator we didn't really pay attention to the investing climate or the fundraising climate, we just figured, if we had an idea we should just go with it, try it out. We thought, "It's on our minds right now, fresh in our head, let's just do it."

People were saying that when fundraising is difficult it means the best startups survive, right? So we took that advice and just went with it. You don't want somebody funding you on a crappy idea just because the funding environment is hot. A crappy idea is simply that: a crappy idea. So you want to build something solid and make sure that you know it's the right thing.

How was the interview process at YC?

The application process was pretty straightforward. We had seen the application before and knew what we were going to put down for the answers. When we applied, Listia was just an idea so we really had to sell it on the application. Since we applied pretty late we didn't have any time to make a demo or anything.

It was pretty cool to get an interview, but right away we felt like we had to get started on a prototype so we built something in less than two weeks. For the interview, Gee was actually in Taiwan at the time, but we had planned this whole demo out where he would be on Skype and we'd run through it together. On the day of the interview, Jessica came out to let me know they'd be ready for me in two minutes and suddenly the speakers on my laptop died. I started to panic, but there wasn't really anything I could do. My ThinkPad used to take 10 minutes to restart and by that time the interview would be over, so I had to wing it.

It was definitely one of the more stressful moments in my life, but everyone at Y Combinator was really nice. The interview ended up going really smoothly even with our little demo mishap. We ended up just talking to the team to hash out some ideas; it was more like a brainstorming session than an interview, for us. Paul didn't even take a look at the demo we had worked on for two weeks, night and day.

Any tips for people applying to seed investment programs, like YC?

I think the best thing to do if you are applying to Y Combinator is read all of Paul Graham's essays. Get to know how he thinks, get to know what they are looking for, try and talk to previous Y Combinator alumni. That, I think, is huge. Alumni can give you first-hand insight into their experiences and what to expect from everything.

The selection process is straightforward: you go in for the interview; you'll be sitting on this bench for 10 minutes waiting for your name and then once you go in there will be four people behind a long desk and it could be a deluge of questions, you showing a demo, a brain storming session, you name it. The more prepared you are, the more comfortable you'll be and the better the interview will go.

You went on to raise $400K, what was that experience like?

Overall, the experience was positive because we did walk away with money to keep us up and running. At the time it was pretty stressful because, the fundraising climate wasn't as hot as it is now. We also had a difficult time pitching our idea because we didn't have any traction. We had nothing under our belts; we were very new to the game, so to speak. So, it took a while for an investor to see our vision, believe in us, and give us money.

We both did fundraising together, so the product did come to a halt for three or four weeks, which was pretty scary. Advice you get from most people is to have as few people dedicated to fundraising as possible because it's such a time sink. However, we both wanted to go through the motions together because we were both new to it and wanted to learn the ropes. We took that risk and luckily it turned out to be okay. After we finally got the term sheet, we went right back to work.

How long did it take to build the beta?

The demo beta for the interview was two weeks, but the real one took three or four months. We launched on August 5th, 2009 and we had no code in May, so that's about four months.

TechCrunch wrote about you, did you do anything to grow the company after that?

No special marketing or anything like that. In the beginning we were seeding the marketplace with our own stuff because of the whole chicken and egg problem with marketplaces. If there aren't any items, then nobody is going to get anything, and you have to start somewhere. So we actually ended up seeding it with a lot of the stuff in our homes. We ended up buying a few things from Fry's and listing them ourselves, given our budget—our $15,000 funding—from Y Combinator. From there, it sort of took off. We actually had a TV up as a promotion for our TechCrunch launch. Paul Graham also helped us seed our marketplace with a bunch of old stuff from around his house, including a signed copy of *On Lisp*, which was really nice of him to do.

I noticed you started using game mechanics and badges. When did you start doing that?

After I saw GraffitiGeo. I saw their badges and I was like, "Oh my god, this is the greatest idea ever." I think I added it that week. It's one of the most sought after things on our site. People love their badges.

Badges seem to work really well if they're done right. I think the games like Starcraft, Halo, and Call of Duty are the best examples of using them in a way that seems genuine and fun. Foursquare has obviously nailed this too.

Yeah, we also just added something called *perks* which is modeled after Call of Duty. You pay for a perk and instead of nickel and diming you for listing fees you can subscribe to a perk instead. For that month, you get to use that feature as much as you want for a small amount of credits. For instance, you can set a start time or a longer number of days for your auction.

Did your blood pressure ever go up over stressful matters? Did you ever think Listia would fail?

Your blood pressure always goes up when the site is down. That's probably one of the things that will kill you, especially for an auction site where things are ending all the time. There is no such thing as downtime for us. Another one is Paul Graham's famous 'Trough of Sorrow' when you see user growth flat lining. We had a few moments like that but for the most part we've been pretty lucky over the past year, year and a half. To answer your question though, I think my blood pressure is permanently higher these days.

It seems like launching can make a lot of founders nervous. Were you nervous?

Definitely. We were worried about any and everything that could happen. We were worried that the site would go down, we were worried about the comments, and we were worried about how people would react to the idea. Anything that you can worry about, you name it, we were worried about it.

Have you focused on revenue?

Since we've launched we haven't spent an enormous time focusing on revenue. We are mainly focused on user growth right now and making sure we build the right product. Our revenue actually scales pretty well with our user growth so when we get more users our revenue will increase as well. For a marketplace that's pretty natural.

How do you split up the work?

Gee and I work really well together and have ever since our lab work at Cornell. We always manage to split up the work and make sure we play to each other's strengths.

The schedule was and still is: all day, every day. We wanted to launch before Demo Day, that was our goal, and in hindsight that was pretty fast. It only took us three to four months to build the entire site out from scratch. We actually didn't even know Ruby on Rails before May, so we had to learn Rails and then go from there. It was a lot of work but it was fun at the same time.

Even with all the hardships, stress and constant work, I can say that I've never had a better time in my life, than this. It's highly rewarding to make something that people actually use and see every day.

What's your biggest challenge today?

I think that our biggest goal for the next year is continuing to gain user growth and traction. We want to eventually get to the point where Listia is a common household name.

It's normalized happiness, in a sense. When you reach a new high the next day that new high is old news and it's normal. Every day you should be raising the bar higher and higher. If you ever become satisfied with what you're doing then that should be a big red flag, something is wrong.

How would you describe the Listia culture?

At Listia we have a strong startup culture. People can work on their own time; we have a lot of fun at the office as well. We work long hours but there is always time to kick back and have some fun.

Were there any times where being productive became difficult?

Gee and I know each other really well, so if one person sees the other heading downhill, he picks him up—it's a very delicate balancing act. If I'm worried about one thing, Gee will reassure me that it's not anything to really worry about. So we work really well together and I think it's very important for cofounders to have that kind of relationship.

Together you have to have each other's backs and keep each other motivated, moving forward. Doing a startup alone is not something I would ever recommend or want to do. It's not an easy ride at all, so there always needs to be somebody there to help you along the way, even if you don't think you need it.

What do you look for in people, when hiring?

Sometimes it's hard to tell. You can ask the standard questions for developers, but at the end of the day you have to ask yourself, *"Do I want to be spending ten hours a day with this guy? Can we work together? Can he get the job done right?"* And for people that I'm interviewing I usually say, "Be yourself, because you are going to end up being yourself at the job. If somebody doesn't see that you are a good fit because of who you are, so be it, but just be yourself and see where it goes from there."

You want the people you work with to also be your friends; especially in the early days when the number of employees is in the single digits, right? You are going to be spending a lot of time with these people, so be yourself.

Do you have any general advice for a student interested in doing a startup?

If you know that you want to do a startup, definitely go for it as early as you can because I made the mistake of waiting a bit too long. Yeah, maybe the idea wasn't there, but I do wish that I had done all of this a lot younger, because when you get older you have a lot more responsibility; you are married, you have kids, you have a mortgage. Earlier on when you are in your early 20s, you don't have those things to worry about and you can really grind out great products when you are living very minimally.

If you are non-technical and you want to do a technical startup, you have to have a friend that is technical, or try to learn the ropes yourself. Hiring a contractor to do your programming sounds like a bad idea.

What were the most beneficial parts of Y Combinator for you guys?

For me, one of the most beneficial parts was being around so many other cofounders going through the same things I was; meeting and engaging with those people, being able to talk to them every Tuesday and say, "Oh, I'm going through the same shit you're going through. Oh dude, we have badges, you guys should totally have badges." Networking is important, but when you're in Y Combinator you actually make some good friends too.

Paul Graham's advice resonates and echoes in your brain and the speakers he brings in are awesome. You get a lot of advice, education, and motivation straight from the people that have gone through it and have been successful at it. I think Y Combinator was one of the best experiences I've ever had.

Why would someone want to join Listia as an intern or employee?

We're still in single digits as far as employees, so now is the best time to join. We offer good equity and we're fun to work with. Oh, and we're going to be huge.

Adam Goldstein, Hipmunk

Tags: Y Combinator, programmer, hiring, VC funded, design-focused, profitable

Overview: Hipmunk was recently started in 2010 to find flights online as easy and fast as possible. Hipmunk understands the trade-offs between the myriad of flight options and they use a visual format to display the flight information in a novel way, and they also do the same for hotel searching. Hipmunk went through Y Combinator in 2010 and has since raised $5 million. Alexis Ohanian and Steve Huffman, the cofounders of Reddit, are now both working on Hipmunk.

How did you get involved with startups? Take me back as far as you can remember and let's talk about where all of this began for you.

Though I don't recall what I was doing in kindergarten or preschool, I've been told that I set up a little museum in my room, charged admission, and had little cut-outs of different sea creatures that I found in various books, and I charged $0.25 or something, to enter.

The first thing I *do* remember is, when I was about 13 or 14, I started developing shareware, sort of try-before-you-buy software, and I did really bad programs. I can't believe that anyone actually paid for them, but they did. I was in school so when I started out, it was things like a calculator for fractions.

Later on I developed a little board game and eventually, by the time I was 15 or so, I actually had a pretty cool program that added an auto-save feature to any program on your Mac. That was on the software side. At the same time, I decided I really wanted to be involved in writing about the stuff that I knew, so I picked up AppleScript—a Mac scripting language as the name suggests—from a series of reference books.

Trying to learn AppleScript was a really terrible experience. I started writing out little how-tos for it and, somehow, I got it into in my head that I should just write a whole book about AppleScript or some particular portion of it, so one summer I just sat down and tried to write a book about it—and, I kind of did!

It wasn't very good; I went to a few different publishing companies and none of them actually wanted to publish it. It was really specialized. It covered this facet of AppleScript where you could make full-fledged programs using it, which is what I used to make my shareware stuff. So, it just stayed on the back burner. Coincidentally, though, I went to a book signing where I met a guy named David Pogue who was, and still is, the tech columnist for the New York Times; he had this series that I thought was really cool that was called the *Missing Manuals*—an understandable, funny, well-written series on how to use different programs, operating systems, or devices.

We talked for a while—I was 14 at the time—and I showed him some tips that he didn't even know about in terms of things you could do with a Mac. About a month later he emailed me that he was close to his book deadline, and he wanted some help with technical editing. He wanted someone to look through a few chapters and make sure the information was accurate.

I agreed to do that for him. From there, I ended up writing a chapter, updating a chapter here and there, and eventually got to the point where I gave him this idea I had for a book. He passed it along; I got the deal from there. So, when I was 16, I got it published—I did have to rewrite the entire thing from scratch, but it was a book about AppleScript that got published, and then after that I wrote one with him about switching to the Mac. So that was the start in high school.

What was your motivation when you were 12 or 13 doing shareware and building board games? Was it for money? Intellectual stimulation?

I don't think making money was, in and of itself, the goal. I liked money, yes, but I think it was more that I wanted to see whether I could build something that people would actually be willing to pay for. More importantly, I was interested to see how many would actually try it. I would just follow statistics on the number of downloads, and that was a really cool thing to watch.

In terms of why I wrote it in the first place, I think it started out as curiosity; I would realize that there was a problem with doing something, like calculating or adding and subtracting different fractions. There was no easy program I could find to do it, so I would write something to do it and the next thought would be,

"Well, if I have this problem, other people probably do as well," so I would share my solution.

It was the same with the book. I figured I couldn't possibly be the only person who had a difficult time learning AppleScript. That's a trend throughout all the stuff I've worked on—I write something to help people with a problem, and make sure that solution is well shared.

Did you work on any other projects in high school?

I continued to work with O'Reilly, the tech publisher for this series. I interned there the summer after my junior year, which was significant, because that's where I met Steve Huffman who five years later became my Hipmunk cofounder. The next summer I interned at Apple, working on a replacement for AppleScript. That was basically high school. I stopped writing for the series once I started applying to colleges.

What was college like?

There were a few things that took up my time in college. At MIT there was a department called Electrical Engineering and Computer Science, and I double majored in that joint program and Mechanical Engineering, which was a pretty heavy course load.

I also minored in economics, and, as a side project in college, I worked on a new startup with a guy named Chris Anderson who is the editor of Wired Magazine; not to be confused with the Chris Anderson that runs the TED Conference. But he found me through Paul Graham. I met Paul when I was working at O'Reilly the same summer I met Steve. So yeah, all these connections.

I ended up working with Chris Anderson on a website where authors could find interested audiences, sort of an event-tracking site. It had two components: one was, you could see who else was coming to your area, and the other was: if you were an author, you could see where authors like you had gone. This whole group still exists.

So, I started that with Chris and another guy, my freshman year, working on it full time over the summers and part time during the year for a few years. The final thing I worked on in college, my other big hobby, was the debate team, where I competed for MIT in the U.S. and internationally.

That was great fun. We went to England, Thailand, Turkey, Ireland, a bunch of places, and represented MIT on two-person teams in competitions against other schools; we did pretty well. My senior year, the crowning achievement was my two-person team won the North American Debating Championship.

How did you meet Paul Graham at O'Reilly?

O'Reilly runs this conference every summer, or at least they did, called FOO Camp which stands for Friends of O'Reilly. It's basically Camp O'Reilly but the founder invites two or three hundred people to his headquarters and has them create their own conference.

There's no agenda. Steve was part of Reddit, which was founded that summer, and Paul Graham was there, representing Y Combinator. So this was the first summer of Y Combinator. I'd read a lot of Paul's essays and made a point of introducing myself to him there. I think I'd heard of Reddit before that, or maybe I heard about it there—I was definitely one of their first users.

Did you go into college knowing many people?

There were two other people from my high school class in New Jersey that ended up going to MIT my year. Besides them, I think there was one other person that I knew. My first couple of weeks I was just getting to know people; after that, it was as if I'd been there for years.

I didn't go into college thinking, "I'm going to find a cofounder here", but I definitely did go in, thinking, "When I'm done with college I'm going to do a startup." That was never in question. So it was probably an oversight on my part not to make a bigger attempt, in college, to find people who would be good cofounders.

As a by-product of going to entrepreneurship events and classes, I met people who I definitely would be comfortable bringing on as cofounders in the future, but I wasn't actively trying to find them. I think it was probably an oversight. I definitely should have been doing that.

Did you do anything else outside of class?

No, the debate team was like a sport. Literally, every weekend, I was competing somewhere. It had all the time-consuming elements of a sport, without the exercise.

Did you have a work-life balance? Was school a grind for you?

I wouldn't call it a grind. I enjoyed all of it and that's why I continued to do it. I was never a big partier and I was never actually on campus on the weekends because of debate. There were definitely periods in college where I felt somewhat overwhelmed, but overall, I think I worked pretty efficiently at most of the stuff I was doing. So, it didn't become a big, stressful, time drainer. Also, it has always been important to me to get enough sleep and I was pretty much always able to do that in college, which to me is a sign that I wasn't going too crazy.

So what were you doing right as you graduated college?

During my senior year it occurred to me I wanted to start a company. I didn't really know what I wanted to do. I interviewed at one Y Combinator company and talked to a couple others, but I never really applied for a job like you would normally; I never sent my resume anywhere.

I mostly just wanted to see what the market rates and market norms were for someone right out of college. So, I started thinking early in my freshman year about what I would work on and I realized that I ended up building up this interest in the airline industry in general, just over the course of my time in college. Traveling for the debate team had introduced me to a lot of these interesting intricacies of the industry, like the way fares are calculated, the way routes are scheduled, how different airlines cooperate or compete; all sorts of interesting operational and logistical things that I just thought were cool.

It occurred to me, as I'd started flying more and gotten better at finding flights, that even with all the knowledge and insight most people didn't have, I *still* was not that much better than anyone else at searching for flights online. It would still take me half an hour, an hour, two hours to actually make sure I felt like I'd found the best flight and the best deal.

It was very much a situation where I found myself trying to 'scratch my own itch.' I felt like there was this problem that I recognized and that I knew how to fix, so by my second semester of college, I was thinking about how I was going to fix it, and who I was going to fix it with.

I graduated in June 2010. I went straight from graduating to Y Combinator; even before graduation I had convinced Steve, my cofounder, to join me and we both decided to move out to San Francisco, start it, and be in Y Combinator. We did all these things at once so there was really no transition. The day before I graduated I started getting moved in and the day after I graduated I moved out to San Francisco for good.

Were there any people that really inspired you when you were in college?

Yeah, I read Paul Graham's essays when I was in high school. That was very early inspiration in terms of startups, working in technology, and just generally feeling good about being a computer nerd. Paul Graham is definitely an intellectual inspiration. I had always been a fan of Steve Jobs; I had been an Apple nerd since early on and had seen a bunch of his keynotes at Macworld and other conferences.

Keep in mind, this was back before Steve Jobs was a cool figure; this was before the iPad or the iMac first came out—a long time ago. He was someone I just thought was fun to watch and I thought the products were fantastic and well-designed, so that was definitely an early inspiration as well, and my dad also was someone who was reasonably fluent in HyperCard—one of the precursors to AppleScript as a programming language.

He had written his own little programs and was one of the people who helped me learn the basics of scripting on a computer. So those three things, together put me in the mindset where I not only realized that I could write code but that I could maybe write it in a way that is cool and useful to people, and potentially even turn that into a startup at some point. Those are probably the three biggest factors, early on, that pushed me in this direction.

What was your fundraising process like?

I've been saving up since middle school, literally, so that if I wanted to start a company myself, I'd be able to live off of savings for a while. But I'd also known about Y Combinator a few years before I got started, and Steve did Y Combinator the first summer it existed with Reddit. So there was never really any question in our minds that we were going to apply to Y Combinator because it gives you so many unfair advantages in the startup world, from motivation, to advice, to connection, to press; neither of us needed the money to get started but there was never any question that we were going to apply to Y Combinator.

Do you think the $150K from Yuri Milner is a good or bad thing?

I don't think it's enough to matter, and I don't say that because I don't think $150,000 is a lot of money, but because most Y Combinator companies end up being able to raise that much fairly easily, anyway. I mean, in the last batch, it was something like 80 or 90%. So for that 10 or 20% that wasn't able to previously, it's great, it gives them some extra runway; probably it gives them another six months to a year to hack away at whatever they want until they can get something cool. For the remainder, I don't think it actually makes any real difference.

How long did it take you guys to build out that first beta of Hipmunk?

From the code perspective, I think we were near release-ready in about a month and a half. We had some difficulty acquiring the data supplies we needed in order to actually launch something publicly. So, in practice, it turned out to be about two and a half months until we had something that was truly ready to go public.

How did you spread the word, initially?

We called up TechCrunch; they covered it and it just spread from there. It was amazing, the first day we were covered in TechCrunch, VentureBeat—a bunch of different tech publications. The second day we were covered in CNN and a couple of others. It was completely out of control; way, way more coverage than we were expecting.

There was some point where Ashton Kutcher tweeted about it and, we were doing tons of searches—I don't know how much, but, way more than we have since then. We're not at the point where it's a clear success but I'd say we're out of the trough of sorrow!

We've been almost entirely focused on product development because we didn't, until recently, feel the product was at a point where we wanted to be advertising it to non-technical people. Within Silicon Valley, we had a product that was pretty understandable. People appreciated it; they understood how it worked just by looking at it.

But, it's a pretty radical departure from other travel sites. It doesn't work like anything else most people have ever seen. So we wanted to get to the point where we had the coverage we wanted so that people wouldn't find a better deal elsewhere. We also wanted to polish up the experience to the point where people wouldn't be asking for how-to guides whenever they looked at it.

We're starting to get to the point where we're playing around a bit with display advertisement and stuff, but it's a pretty tiny percentage of our revenues that we're spending on that. So we're really still working on the product and haven't gotten to put an effort into marketing.

Have you guys ever had any pivots with your startup?

I wouldn't say there's been anything that would qualify as a total pivot, but early on we didn't look or feel anything like we do now. We displayed all of the results in a text format. It was similar information, just harder to parse because it was all text and it was ugly as anything; you would not recognize it as Hipmunk at all. The similarities between that and today were very minor, superficial ones. So we did have innovations, but I wouldn't call it pivot.

Is it coincidental that you've focused on design and experience?

Yes and no. I don't think we set out saying, "We're going to build something that looks nice." But anytime there was a feature or a section that didn't look nice, both of us would notice and comment on it. Steve and I are not designers at all. We have no design training; no design knowledge, really. But we are both *critics* of design. We're both people that are irritated by bad design.

So, as we were developing, we went through a long criticism process until we got to a point where we felt like it was usable; so it wasn't some design stuff, it looks a lot nicer just from a pure user-design standpoint than it did before. The fundamental experience hasn't changed much since we launched, and I think all of the changes on the experience side came on our own.

Was there any point for you guys in Hipmunk that you started to feel depressed, or anything that was really difficult to deal with?

Yes. Before we launched we were really, really nervous. Steve, even more so than I was. He had founded this site that had become hugely popular and was worried that this time, the expectations of version 1.0 would be too high for him to meet. I was definitely nervous the day before we launched because I thought the site might break or we might get too much traffic during a spike and not be able to keep up with the demand, or something like that.

As it turned out, it was fine. We were way more worried than was justified, but most of our worrying came about during that first period; after that, things generally were better. There was never a point where the site completely died or we got a super harsh review in a press outlet that we really liked. There was never any point that was really depressing and I think that's pretty unusual. We were pretty fortunate in that respect.

We've been unusually fortunate to have such a positive reception from the day we launched and not to have had any huge disaster, since. I would be shocked if that lasted forever, but so far I've never felt, "Man, we really screwed that up." There were definitely things that we didn't expect, for example, there was an airline—I can't tell you which one—that decided it was going to pull its data from us the day after we launched, so we wouldn't be able to display their flights at all. It was only after several months that we managed to get a deal in place with them.

But, there was no way we could possibly have seen that coming; or I should say, there wasn't any way given our relative inexperience in the industry that we could have seen that coming. So I don't beat myself up too much about that. It was a disappointment, but it wasn't a fiasco.

Was there a point where you guys started to notice revenue picking up?

We launched and on our first week we sold hundreds of thousands of dollars in tickets, so that was a pretty cool milestone—way earlier than we expected. After that, every time there was a positive press piece we certainly noticed the uptake, but there was never a similarly large step function jump that was as easily traceable as the day we launched.

How do you guys split the work up?

When we were writing the site before we launched, Steve and I split it pretty much, both working on code full time, with a few exceptions where I would go out and do business development with airlines or travel agencies. So effectively, we were both working on the same thing.

After we launched, we realized very quickly that there was going to be too much for the two of us to do, period; but also, too much stuff besides code for the two of us to only be working on code. So within a week of launching I switched to doing everything *but* the code, which was primarily business development investor relations, and Steve continued to be the CTO; as we've hired more programmers they've all worked under him. We've currently got four other engineers.

Was it a chaotic schedule when you guys first started out and, is it still, today?

Early on there were definitely crazy periods, primarily just before we launched. But it's actually pretty chill when there's no one using your site and complaining about bugs and stuff. I think we were way more stressed that first week *after* we launched than the three or four weeks before we launched. All in all, we probably work nine or ten hours per day on Hipmunk.

What is your biggest challenge right now?

The biggest challenge overall—and it has gotten easier recently—is just getting deals done with large companies. Enormous, multi-billion dollar companies dominate the travel industry. There are airlines and travel agencies and we need to work out deals with them in order to even be able to provide options for our customers to book tickets. So that has been the biggest ongoing challenge, just getting them to return our phone calls, to negotiate contracts in good faith, those sorts of things. While it has gotten easier, it still from my perspective is our number one challenge and our number one priority.

What's the culture at Hipmunk?

I think our culture is a little more laid back than what you'd find in a lot of startups. We don't, for example, work late nights in general, and there's no expectation that you're going to show up on weekends. I think we pride ourselves on the facts that we're small and everyone's voice can be heard. There is a hierarchy of responsibility, but I think all of our programmers would trust one another to write whatever feature they're writing. There's no possessiveness among the staff.

So it's probably too early to think what this would transcend up through a larger company, but I think we're very fortunate to be able to hire smart people, that we personally respect, and who I think, respect us. Having a community of people who like each other and respect each other's work means there really aren't arguments or much tension in the office; it's a pretty relaxed place.

What single piece of advice would you give to an undergraduate student, thinking about doing a startup, but who has no idea where to begin?

Learn to code.

So, even if they're non-technical, you're saying they should learn to code?

Yeah, if you're going to do a web startup. I don't know if it matters if you're going to do a media startup or something, but if you're going to do a website, absolutely. First, because you might not find a cofounder and you might have to write the site yourself; if you can, you'll be able to and if you can't, you won't. Second, because if you take classes in a technical field you're much more likely to meet technical people and eventually be able potentially to persuade one of them to join you.

I think the biggest complaint, to which I'm unsympathetic, is someone who says, "Oh my god, it's so hard to find a technical cofounder; I don't know the first thing about writing code and I really need someone who can do it." The response I have, which I don't usually tell them, is, "If it's that important that you feel like you need someone to be able to do it, why don't you teach yourself so that you can at least hack it for a while?"

Can you talk about the time you most successfully hacked some non-computer system to your advantage?

In high school I ran for class president against several people who were substantially more popular than me. A bunch of people had always given me a hard time for not wearing a belt (I'm not sure why I opposed the idea for so long). So I promised that, if elected, I'd wear a belt every day. And I hung "Vote Goldstein" posters around the school, from belts.

I won and I kept my promise.

Why would someone want to work with Hipmunk?

There are a bunch of reasons. I think an engineer would join us because our engineering team is top notch; smart people who've got great experience building big, successful websites who also just care a lot about the quality of their code. They're not like,

"Patch it and fix it when it breaks;" they're like, "Let's build this thing right the first time."

I think another reason would be because they find the industry that we're in interesting. I know that was my main motivation. I just think the technical and algorithm challenges surrounding pricing and scheduling plane tickets are really fascinating, and I don't think you need to be interested in that to be interested in working with us, but it helps. The other reason would be because you want to be part of an early-stage startup that has the potential to do well.

It's certainly true that every early-stage startup has the potential to do well, but we've done a Series A round, which takes out a fair amount of the risk, at least for a couple of years. So, I think you can get a lot of the benefits of working on a small team without the huge dilution problems that come out when you're five years into it. That's another attractive feature.

Is there anything that you really look for in applicants, that kind of, X-factor?

Yes. There are two things. To illustrate the first one, we were looking for someone to do user support—respond to emails and chats on the website, stuff like that, and we got a bunch of applications. We were about to decide, when we got an application from this girl who said, "I'm a big nerd for flights. I live near Sacramento and I can hear the planes overhead and I can often tell you which flight number it is, just based on what time of day the plane is leaving because I know the schedules."

So, while that's impressive, Sacramento doesn't have that many flights so, if you put your mind to it, anyone could have done that. But, it's cool that that's something someone thought was worth doing, so it stood out as dedication to this field. We figured somebody who knew a lot about it might bring an interesting perspective.

To illustrate the second, one of the ways that we found our main contract designer, was, he put up a blog post where he talked about what he did and didn't like about Hipmunk's interface and what he would do to improve it; he basically put up a sketch of how he would have made Hipmunk himself if he'd started it from scratch. So, he already knew about us and thought that we were going in the right direction, but recognized that there were things he could contribute and improve upon; that was really appealing to us.

The takeaway shouldn't be that Hipmunk is going to hire people who say that they love Hipmunk, because that's not what I'm saying. Hipmunk really likes it when people say that there are certain things that they like about it but certain things they don't and then offer us constructive suggestions or improvements on how to make it better.

People who do that, and there have been a couple, tend to be great hires. They're self-motivated and have interesting product ideas and we are always happy to have people like that around.

Jessica Mah, Indinero

Tags: designer, Y Combinator, undergrad founder, Ramen profitable, programmer, VC funded, design-focused

Overview: Indinero was started in 2009 as an easy way for businesses to track their expenses. Jessica finished high school at 15 years old and has been covered in publications such as Inc. Magazine, Wall Street Journal, and has been featured on PBS encouraging students to pursue entrepreneurship. Indinero went through Y Combinator in 2010 and shortly after raised $1.2 million.

You're still pretty young, so this might be an easy question for you, but when did you get started with entrepreneurship?

In middle school you had basically two options. You could get a job, a really crappy job raking leaves or helping your parents do chores, or you could start your own business. It's just easier to start a business I think. It's not necessarily for the money or the interest; it's just more convenient. So I thought it would be more fun to do.

I think the first thing I did was build websites for people. I knew how to build websites and I knew that I could make a few hundred dollars for a person who wanted a website built and it was pretty easy money, so I thought it would be the point to start.

I'd say that I did one big project in a few weeks and it was perfectly fine, except that I wanted more business so I started trying to sell website templates on eBay. It's about making a few extra hundred dollars a week for doing pretty much no work at all, and then I started to look for more things like that to do. The market got really bad in 2004: too many people started reselling templates, so the price went from $12 to $2 within a few years.

How did you get interested in computers?

I think I got really interested in 6th grade, since my dad sent me to computer camp. There are computer camps where you learn about programming and all those cool things, so I did that in Massachusetts.

What kinds of classes did you take in college?

My first year was all liberal arts classes. I was trying to figure out what I wanted to do with my life, so I took basic core classes and tried to narrow down from there.

Did you know a lot of people going into college?

No. I didn't know anyone.

How did you meet your cofounders?

I met my current cofounder during the first or second week of class. I transferred into Berkeley as a junior—it was my first year there and I met them in classes we took together. There are four total cofounders who went through YC, but I primarily started Indinero with one other guy. I met two of my cofounders through the computer science club at Berkeley called CSUA, the Computer Science Undergrad Association.

Did you do anything else outside of class?

Not really but my good friend Andy and I had built some side projects before, so Indinero wasn't actually our first project. We were building a site called InternshipIN.com and we wanted to help students find internships and that was our first project together and then after that we thought well, it's a cool idea but it's not going to make money and it's not world-changing so we thought about what to do next and that's when we started thinking about ideas for what led to Indinero. Half our time was spent doing class, and the other half was on these projects we did.

My GPA ended up taking a hit from the projects we worked on. Yeah, I was a terrible student.

Did you take time to relax in school?

I think my first year while doing InternshipIN, I went out a lot more because it was my first year at Berkeley so I had to have that Berkeley experience. I did a lot of that the first few months and then I guess it became boring after a while. Then we moved on to Indinero, and Indinero was such a blast.

We worked actively on InternshipIN through January and February of our junior year and then my idea for Indinero came up in February: we started coding on it in March. I think we were just throwing around some ideas, and we wanted to know what the really big problems we could solve in the world were, and helping people with their money was a hot topic of the night. So we didn't have the idea yet, we just knew it was just money related.

What were you doing right when you were graduating college?

We worked on Indinero through that summer and we tried to raise money in August before our senior year and back then if you remember it was bad for fundraising. I pitched a bunch of angels and not a single one of them wanted to invest so I didn't think very highly of myself back then. No one gave us a penny; it was so depressing.

We couldn't drop out of college, so we went back to college for our senior year reluctantly. Actually I was talking to one of the founders at Rackspace, I was telling him that I was dropping out and I'm trying to raise money and he said, "No, you're going back to college and here's why," and I ended up going back to college. That's a true story.

Would you have dropped out if you had raised the money?

If I had raised the money, yeah.

What were you wanting to do right as you were graduating?

We wanted to be fulltime on Indinero and we wanted to raise money so we could hire people and in January two other classmates told us they wanted to join in. Drew Houston gave a talk at Berkeley about why he did Y Combinator, why YC was so awesome, and the early days of Dropbox. It was packed: so many people showed up, so that day I decided we were going to apply for YC.

Did you have other ideas before Indinero?

Yeah, I think the idea was at first trying to help people manage their investments because people are really bad at planning their money and planning their investments. Another idea was to help people get out of debt and personal finance stuff.

We definitely had a few ideas and I looked up Paul Graham's lists of ideas, which are at ycombinator.com/ideas.html. I went through every single one, thinking, "Let's find an idea," and I knew that one of my criteria was building our own company. One of my other criteria was that it would generate revenue so that it wouldn't be a bullshit photo sharing website. I felt really strongly about that, so I was going through this list and it was a Friday morning. I was doing interviews with someone and idea number 17 I thought was really attractive, which is about doing new payment methods. I guess Square is doing that now and then I saw number 21: "Finance software brings the jewel to small businesses." And so like shit, Paul Graham thinks this is a good idea, it must be a good idea. "Alright, fine, we're going to do that."

We thought of the idea for Indinero beforehand, but looking at this list validated what we were already thinking.

You believe very strongly that the company should have revenue from the beginning. Not everyone takes that approach, so why do you feel it's particularly important?

I think our experience at InternshipIN was such that we were getting users and we were helping them find internships, and that was really cool, but it wasn't making any money. So it wasn't very fulfilling and that's when I personally decided I wanted to focus more on revenue.

You moved to California and covered your living expenses. Any advice you can offer to students on how to live cheaply?

I think the best way is for everyone to live in the same house. We just got a place for $2500, a four bedroom house in Mountain View and we cooked for each other: we had a shopping list and a budget for going out to buy groceries. So we kept to the budget and so out total costs were about $3,000 a month for the house.

How long did it take to build your beta?

It was kind of weird because we spent all of our summer between our junior and senior year trying to build the product, but about halfway through the summer I started trying to raise an angel round and of course we all know that I failed at that. The lesson learned from that was don't waste time on fundraising because then you get nothing done on the product—that was the big take away.

Did you guys build it with the goal of going out to a customer for the first version?

Yeah, we actually wrote our first lines of code at something called Startup Weekend San Francisco which means we show up on Friday night and we start hacking away and then we present it to the audience on Sunday.

Between Friday and Sunday, we might have slept a couple hours.

We got absolutely no publicity from this though. We didn't get publicity until the tech blogs covered us (TechCrunch, VentureBeat, etc).

How did you sustain growth after the blogs?

We knew that press is really good at making us money. After a press spot you make a bunch more money and it's like, "Alright, we've got to get to Ramen profitability before demo day," and the weekend after our launch, we were halfway there already. So we thought, "We just have to do the same thing one more time to be Ramen profitable." We worked our asses off and we got more press, and we were profitable weeks before demo day.

Was there any type of particular press that you noticed worked really well?

Since our audience is just a bunch of business owners, entrepreneur publications really helped. TechCrunch and Mashable have a bunch of entrepreneurs coincidentally. It's tech-focused, but there are a lot of entrepreneurs. Inc magazine, Fast Company, New York Times and CNN all have huge entrepreneur followings.

Were there any stressful moments for you at Indinero?

Not many. I fundraised for the first time and I wasted an entire month. That was so bad. It was really depressing. But during YC things were pretty stable. I slept eight hours every day, and I'm pretty sure everyone else here slept 8 hours. We took Saturdays off sometimes, and sometimes I felt guilty like, "Why aren't we working as hard as the other YC companies?"

When did revenue start to take off?

I think on launch day we saw the most promise of our revenue. Launch day was huge for us because that's the first time we'd find out what our funnel looked like, and we'd know what our conversion numbers looked like, and they were way higher than we expected them to be. Press was the single best thing for us in terms of revenue.

How do you split the work up at Indinero?

Well, it's six people. Four guys are coders and then we have one other girl who was one of my college roommates. She does all of our support, operations, bookkeeping, and legal work. I'm the product designer and the public spokesperson.

I haven't done much coding lately and I do a lot of the design work now. Most of the work on the site is from me, and we have an army of design contractors right now. I have about six designers that I keep on top of every other day to get designs done.

What's the work schedule like?

I think we're in chaos mode in stages. This week we got a lot of press, so this entire week we worked our asses off to get that push done. But next week it'll reset itself. During that week after demo day, you have to take a break.

What is your biggest challenge?

Today the biggest challenge is fixing our funnel. The way I think about product strategy is based on how to get more PR and how to fix the funnel because I'm the official businessperson.

I'll explain what I mean by 'fixing the funnel.' Let's say you're a new user on Facebook. If you join Facebook, Facebook wants you to add as many friends as possible into the service because if you don't add friends you're not going to be active, same thing for us. If you sign up for Indinero but you don't add your bank accounts to the site, you're not going to be active. So our goal is to increase that percentage by as much as possible. If you add your friends on Facebook you probably want to be active. Same thing for us, if you add your bank accounts to Indinero there's over an 80% chance you're going be active.

What's the culture like at Indinero?

I'd say really close knit; a lot of inappropriate jokes. There's a big game culture here—people play video games at night. Every night, the company stops working and they play video games and it's kind of like a college environment.

Do you have any advice for students interested in doing startups?

I say start small. Just find people who are willing to buy the thing you're building and so you don't have to make it a big business overnight: that's what we did. For the first prototype we wanted to find five people who are willing to use it, then gradually increase that number. Every time we get more users, we have a new goal for where we want to be for the next milestone. A lot of people ask for certain features so hopefully by doing that we'll get more users.

I'd say don't be afraid of starting small, and just incrementally build it up to get more happy customers because a lot of entrepreneurs, they think they need to have money and full time employees and a full product build, and you really don't need that much to get started.

If you're not technical, I recommend either figuring out how to be more technical yourself or come up with a different business idea. There are plenty of business ideas out there that make hundreds of millions or billions of dollars that don't require technology and if you want to build a technology business then you really ought to know technology.

Can you talk about the time you most successfully hacked a non-computer system to your advantage?

Back when I was 10, I was the target of teasing and bullying by classmates. Instead of fighting back, I started a 'corporation' to rally together the smartest and strongest people in my grade. The big and strong guys in my grade would join my 'corporation', act as my bodyguards, and it was my dorky way of evading bullies. The company didn't do anything other than make my bodyguards feel important.

Indinero is hiring—why would someone want to work there?

We're a bunch of CS grads out of Berkeley, so you're in a company with other smart people. And we're going to build a billion dollar company. Those are two reasons to join Indinero.

Matt Gornick, OrangeQC

Tags: self-funded, side project, undergrad founder, programmer

Overview: OrangeQC was started in 2009 in Chicago to help manage food and janitorial services used by companies in quality control. I met Matt Gornick as a sophomore after I started a student entrepreneurship group that eventually merged with another group on campus. Matt helped me with the challenging aspects of managing a student organization: recruiting members, spreading the word, working with partners and faculty, and putting together social meetups. As an undergrad, Matt was working on a project that would eventually become OrangeQC.

A big part of what you do involved quality control, which isn't your typical Silicon Valley startup. Can you describe a little bit what you mean by quality control and what value OrangeQC provides?

Quality control is a process for checking that certain processes were followed and the end result meets an expected level of quality. Hospitals are a great example of a quality-sensitive environment where a certain level of cleanliness is necessary. Our first user was a contractor for the University of Chicago Medical Center.

If you were to monitor the quality, manually, you'd have somebody like a janitorial supervisor or a facilities manager walk around and inspect all the janitorial work that was done; this person's report would include their seal of approval to say, "Yes all these things were done according to certain criteria." Maybe the medical facility needs to be cleaned three times a day, or maybe certain steps need to be taken during the cleanings. This person's job is basically to go around and make sure that those steps were followed.

Typically, what happens in these kinds of situations is that there is a huge file on the services, and nobody really knows what's in it. So, say somebody forgot to do something, or they missed an area, it would be documented somewhere and hopefully would get to the right person. What we do is simplify the whole process so you can notify the right people as soon as there's something that was missed or that needs to be documented and signed off on; we ease the hassle of using paper records and make them digital.

How did you first get started in entrepreneurship?

It sounds cheesy but my parents were always of the mindset that, "If you want something, you have to work for it." My parents ran a little accounting firm in the area; in accounting, after seven or so years, you have to purge all your documents, you don't need store them any more. So when they got to that point, they just said, "Well, we have all these boxes of paper that we don't need anymore." They offered to pay me $5 a bag to shred the paper. I would literally work hours and hours just shredding paper. I was young and this idea does not scale. It scales with more bodies shredding paper. I must have been 10 years old when I was doing this and then shortly after, I worked at a pizzeria for a bit.

That summer at the pizzeria was horrible. I was scrubbing pots and pans all day long and this was when minimum wage was really low, maybe, $5.15 an hour. I'd work all night scrubbing pots and pans and make $40. It was bad. So, when some of my parents' clients had computer problems and would get completely aggravated, my parents would say, "Our son is really into computers, maybe he can fix it." At that time I was always taking things apart and building computers, just tinkering.

I knew I could fix some of these computers. It was doing things like: removing spyware, installing antivirus, setting up printers, stuff that I already knew how to do. I quickly realized I could make money by just fixing computers and not scrubbing pots or shredding paper; all I had to do was this computer stuff quickly and I could make a lot more money.

In high school, I developed a little AdSense plugin for Google AdSense, where you can log in and check how much money you made through ads. I wrote something Java back then that would basically log in and get my amounts so I could just run this program instead of logging in, and it would do all that stuff for me; I could look at how much I made, that day, on my Google AdSense ads.

I was also into security, around this time. I think the program was called Snort—it was an intrusion detection system that produces all these log files of when people try to break into your network. I thought it would be really cool to build an analyzer for all these logs that simplified the whole process because all you get is a massive log file which is worthless at that point; it's almost like paper.

So I built a little analyzer. I looked for certain kinds of triggers, like denial of service or if someone was doing some scanning, I would just scan through the logs and try to find those things and then email out an alert. Basically, you just import this massive text file and then it summarizes everything so that it can then identify, for example, an IP address that tried to do conduct various attacks in your network.

What kind of classes did you take in college? Did you do any projects there?

I graduated with a BS in Computer Science, but the classes I really enjoyed were the ones that were similar to my experience in high school. Then, you're working on what you're really passionate about and you ask when you have questions. I feel like I learn better that way, as opposed to sitting in lectures and listening to somebody for hours. I think I took a programming studio and they had projects that you would work on where they would ask you to write a program to do something but they didn't specify languages. It wasn't terribly difficult to build what they asked, but you could use just about any language you wanted so you got to experiment with stuff; that's how I got introduced to Ruby in a setting that was valuable because they liked and encouraged code quality and readability.

I felt like that experience showed me that the quality of your code matters quite a bit, especially if you're working on a team like that. We'd do code reviews and you got graded based on what other people thought of your code. I thought that was really interesting, really different. We had a little bit more freedom—we were graded on how well we could build the system, versus, could we pass certain unit tests?

I took a class that I actually enjoyed for multiple reasons, but it was the database class at UIUC, CS 411.

I took CS 411 and you're mentioned in one of the slides for creating Illini Crime. What does that app do?

A lot of schools have iPhone apps except U of I. So my friend Blaine—who I met through the entrepreneurship group—

decided to build one because he thought we should have one as well. At UIUC, we get all these crime alerts. So if someone gets robbed on campus or something, we get notified in our e-mail. Blaine wanted to put the alerts in the iPhone app. He thought we could have a map of all these crimes that happen. He tried to build it and the data was structured horribly. That was pretty bad in retrospect.

What data format did you guys get back?

I think the public safety has kind of a pseudo blog, if you will. From that, he asked, "Do you have an XML feed?" They sort of had an XML feed, except it was injected with HTML. So it was not really structured in any sense—it's not like the XML had a key for the location or a key for some of these other metrics, like for offenders, it would say who the offender was.

It was just a big blob of text. It would be like, XML incident one, and then a blob of text. Just having him use that XML feed on the iPhone was not practical because he would have to write all this crazy parsing code. So I said, "How about I just write a Rails app and then I just provide it to you like an XML feed, nice and clean; you can format it however you want and we can do all the geolocation work on the server?" He agreed. I started building it and then in CS 411 they were like, "Well you guys could do whatever you want and then you just have to use a few SQL queries, and that's it."

People in my group didn't really know Ruby on Rails so I got to expose them to it a little bit. I feel like UIUC is focused on C, C++ and Java, but outside of that realm, very few people test the waters, so then when you show people Git, and explain to them, "This is how we're doing source control," people are like, "Oh my god, this is crazy," and then pushing code is easy. I showed them Heroku and people were shocked by how easy it was.

Do we even need programmers any more? (sarcasm)

It's unbelievable, so we built this app. I can't remember when we started, but it was sometime within that second semester of 2010. We built this app and then we added a heat map to it; we did some basic analytics.

We are probably the only students that can see where all the crimes happened. Maybe the police know, and maybe a few dedicated people would do it by hand. But at the time, I think we were the only ones to do it, and that could see that data.

I remember reading about it in the newspaper. How did you meet Blaine? Was this before the student group we started?

I met him right around when we started forming Illini Entrepreneurship Network (IEN); Blaine was a part of Collegiate

Entrepreneurs' Organization (CEO). It was an organization and, at that time, I was good friends with you and we were always talking startup stuff. We were always talking about starting an entrepreneurship group at UIUC.

There were two groups: CEO, a student organization on campus that was business focused and part of a national system, and University Business Developers (UBD) through which we were trying to approach startups and do some kind of consulting arrangements, but mostly it was a networking thing. It was a way to meet other students on campus that were involved in startups. I think we actually interviewed members and the people we ended up working with had all pretty much had startups before. So, I met Blaine through the merging of those two student groups.

So that's how you met Blaine and Blaine is a designer.

Yep, and then he picked up iPhone development just because really wanted to build the app; somebody wanted a project built near his hometown, so he was like, "Yeah, I'll just learn iPhone development and build it." So he took it upon himself, which is pretty rare to go out on a limb and just teach yourself this because you think it's going to be awesome.

So he picked up Objective-C on his own, as a designer?

Yeah, he learned it without knowing much about programming, and then I did the Rails stuff.

Did you know a lot of people going into UIUC?

I knew a handful of people from my high school. I think I might have seen the people from my high school five times the entire time I've been at UIUC. So, it's not like I was there hanging out with high school friends, for the most part I came in with a clean slate. I was there to meet new people.

If you sit by the same group of people in CS 125 and you've done that for the whole semester, you're probably pretty likely to be in that same group unless you're really trying to break out of the mold. Your other classes, you default to going out with the people that you always hang out with.

Did you do anything outside of IEN and classes?

I dabbled in a bunch of different clubs and sports. I was in UIUC rock climbing. It was something that I just enjoyed doing. I'd be able to advance or go climb. I did look at a lot of small business or entrepreneur groups on campus and I really didn't see any that made any sense to me. None of them clicked with me, personally, or what I wanted to do; it just seemed like it wasn't for me. I spent quite a bit of time just looking for something. I think that's one of my main motivations when I helped start IEN, nothing really existed for people who just wanted to build startups because it's awesome. It seemed like there wasn't a place to do that.

I sort of dabbled around in ACM a bit and not to diss ACM or anything—it's a great group and I got my first experience in Silicon Valley through ACM—I found that a lot of members seemed interested in going to Microsoft and Google out of college as opposed to taking some risk and doing a startup. So I felt like there was an opportunity to meet students interested in startups through other groups. I don't know if you felt the same.

I know some people in ACM and that's definitely a great group. But, with computer science or engineering in general, I feel like it's very easy to assume that you need to go to Microsoft to be successful. There's definitely a stigma, it's along the lines of, "If you're not getting a job at Microsoft then what are you doing?"

On the other hand, it has changed a lot as well. My freshman year I think a lot of people were interested in full-time jobs. Then, by senior year, I felt like there were still a lot of people interested in full-time jobs out of school, but I knew more people who wanted to do startups. It's becoming increasingly common.

I went to OrdCamp this weekend, it's like a FooCamp in Chicago. There are lots of startup people there; I feel like that kind of energy would have changed the playing field. I live in Chicago now; you can walk down the street, say "Ruby on Rails" and get a job immediately. In Champaign, you would never know that. You would never know the skills you have are in that much demand and maybe that's why you feel like you have to go to Microsoft.

If students could spend a little time in the Valley or even in Chicago, they might realize they could work at *any* company right now, because everybody is doing stuff in technology.

You participated in a new program at UIUC for students called iFoundry, what is that?

They basically want to shake up and modernize engineering education. So the big problem is that you just keep hammering engineering, have them do more calculus problems, have them do the same problem or the same physics problems, over and over again, until you just force-feed engineering into somebody's head. Now, they're magically engineers, and so iFoundry basically says, "That idea is not right." There are better ways of making a great engineer where they're thinking outside the box and not just thinking, "I've got to solve this equation and use the inner growth."

You've got to think outside of that, and so they focused on learning things from the humanities—engineering from the standpoint of, "I want to tinker with stuff, I want to build cool things, what do I need to do to build cool things?" I want to build stuff because I enjoy tinkering and that's what I think it's all about.

So I spoke with Karen Hyman, one of the directors of iFoundry. There was a big focus on entrepreneurship and students that are coming in, it's seems like they're getting younger and younger. There are kids coming in from high school who want to do a startup. I don't know how many people were thinking of doing that when I was in high school, but when I was in iFoundry, it seemed like there were lots of students saying, "I want to build and sell stuff, we've got to figure out how to manufacture it, we've got to figure out how to program it." People were thinking about this their freshman year, so I basically got involved by being a student advisor.

At the end of the day, everything we're building is solving a problem for people, so the whole iFoundry idea was dealing with that aspect of, "We're building products for people, we're not just solving integrals, we're building real things." I feel like bringing in the business aspect of it and bringing the startup aspect is what students are excited about doing.

How did the idea for OrangeQC originate?

I started OrangeQC, May 2009. It basically came about through this consulting work I was doing with Total Chaos Networks, that was my little consultancy that I was running and that was where people were complaining to us about this problem they had with managing their janitorial services. So, I did some research and looked at different products. Every time I set up these third-party apps for them, they just stopped using them after a few months.

It was so aggravating, so much more of a burden. Paper was just simple. None of the existing software was solving the problem, so it was a matter of fixing that.

I asked myself, "Why doesn't the software exist to do this?" If there's a problem and I just have to build a solution and then sell it to the people that want it, that sounded simple. There were all these solutions that had a lot of bloat and were too complex. So we wanted to simplify that.

You have a cofounder at OrangeQC, how did you meet him?

I met him freshman year in the computer science classes.

Did you ever raise any money?

We won the Cozad competition, so we had several thousand dollars in winnings through that. There was a local venture capital firm there that invited us for one of their programs but it just wasn't what we thought of as the best way to grow a business.

How long did it take to build your first beta?

We had a wireframe in May, and we brought the idea up with some of these potential customers. We asked people, if we built it, would they buy it? And so we literally had wireframes put together and they said, "Oh yeah, this is really good. How soon can we use this?" It was a wireframe so there was nothing to be used. It was June, and we're like, "Okay, we've got to build this entire thing in 30 days to get this demo, we better get started." It was an immense undertaking, but it was a lot of fun.

Where do you guys work? Is it out of your apartments?

We've been trying remotely, I'm not a fan of it but I've done coffee shops, I actually have some rolling office space at the Illinois Technology Association in Chicago, which is a pretty cool place. It's more or less like an incubator in the middle of Chicago, so they have a ton of events there and it's just a great place to network.

Did you guys ever have to do any big pivots along the way?

We're doing pivots constantly. We started out in this janitorial area. We still are, but we never really captured the medical industry, it seems to be a really good fit for what we're doing. A lot of what we're doing now is focused on medical— improving the process of making it easy for someone doing hospital or emergency rooms or nursing homes. Basically, the whole gamut of healthcare facilities; we feel there's a lot of value we can provide in that area.

Have you had any points where you've been really stressed about something that happened?

Constantly. After we built this thing in 30 days, demo day was like, "Oh, this is great. Yeah, let's talk about using it, let's talk about price." We quoted them a price and they countered that it was way too expensive, and we had just spent all this time building it. We didn't really anticipate that they weren't going to pay for it; we basically had no real revenue at all. We were just burning cash that whole summer and then around that time I thought I better start looking for a job because we're not making any money. We've spent all summer building something that's not making any money. It's constant ups and downs.

Are you making revenue?

We are bringing in revenue. We're all doing stuff on the side too. We'd like to reach Ramen profitability in 2011. Our challenge is that our revenue is based on building relationships with the contractor, where the sales cycles are months.

For us, it's a matter of getting enough sites, enough contracts to make that work. So, we originally started cold calling. That just did not work; it was just too hard and our conversion rate was basically zero.

We can always be blogging more but when people would call and say, "I saw your article, you guys wrote about how you set up Chicago Public Schools and that's really awesome, we were interested in bidding on something and we might want to use your software," and so something like that I think got us further than picking up the phone and beating our head against the wall. I kept wondering why we couldn't close deals with random people on the phone.

A lot of people just search for us. So they'll search for 'janitorial quality control' or 'janitorial software' and they'll email us from there or from Google. I think we're decently ranked for that category and it's a very small category. If you search "'janitorial quality control" we're probably on the first page.

So you guys have explicitly worked on SEO then?

We have. Abi, our third cofounder, came in several months after we already started. He was pretty pumped about getting started. He was coming in from iFoundry and I just told him about what I was working on. He eventually dropped out as a freshman, so he was in school for a semester.

How do you guys divide the work up?

Ryan does almost all of the mobile development, so iPhone and iPad. I do most the Rails back-end work and Abi does most of the Rails front-end and any sort of SEO marketing stuff. He worked at a web design shop in Chicago, so that's where he picked up a lot of the SEO.

What are the hours like?

We work better when we're all together. We got together at my apartment a few weeks ago and basically had a three-day hack-a-thon; it works out really well.

Abi and Ryan really like doing remote work; I can't get it to work for my personality or work schedule. It's not a particularly huge time commitment, we're at the stage where we want to get more customers before we allocate a ton of time to development, so if we can get one or two more sites using us then we could have four sites telling us what we should build. If we're only dealing with two paying customers, it would be better to have a few more to get more feedback.

We're kind of reluctant to focus on developing new features without getting some necessary feedback from customers on what they actually use.

Sounds like your biggest challenge is getting the customers with a slower sales cycle?

Definitely. It's business-to-business. A typical sale in enterprise software might take much longer, but I can just put together a proposal over e-mail. It means a lot of waiting around for two weeks and getting revisions done on an agreement.

What advice would you give to an undergraduate student who wants to do a startup?

Find a problem that you have or that you think would be interesting, and start immediately. When you're in school you can fail and nothing will happen, so you might as well start and try something that you think is really cool. Just build something that you enjoy using or building.

Starting is half the battle and I think even when I was at UIUC, you get worried when you start hearing in a class on entrepreneurship that you're supposed to write some 50-page business plan and you've got to talk to VC's and you've got to have a five-year growth plan and you're like, "oh god, I don't even want to do this, I'd rather just go party." It scares people because there's a huge level of work and they think they'll mess up a business plan. So just start if you have a gut feeling that something would be awesome to build, or try to hash it out with a potential customer.

What if you're a non-technical person? Should you learn to program?

Blaine is a good example of the "business guy." He thought he could teach himself how to program and be awesome at it, and he did. So it's definitely possible to do and maybe some people just don't have the mind or discipline to do it, but I would say, it's either you can build it or you can sell it. If you're the business guy you need to be able to sell it. If I did a startup with a non-technical founder, the guy would have to have connections and be able to sell.

David King, Camino Real

Tags: programmer, acquired (previous company acquired by Playdom), funded, hiring

Overview: David King is an ex-Googler who recently started Camino Real, but before that he started and sold Little Green Patch to Playdom, which was ranked as one of the top five most popular Facebook applications with over 500,000 active users per day. Little Green Patch raised over $90,000 for the Nature Conservancy and saved over 70 million square feet of Costa Rican rain forest according to Fast Company. David King's current startup, Camino Real, builds mobile communication products and has raised approximately $500,000 from angels.

How did this whole entrepreneurship thing start for you?

Actually, I had about 25 different types of jobs/entrepreneurial ventures growing up, and most of them I didn't keep for very long but I liked to try a lot of things. I used to do telephone surveys; I was a golf caddy; I was a night watchman at a pool; I ran an IT consulting company, writing software for people when I was in elementary school; and I made music remixes for people for money. I was always hustling for new projects. I was always into trying new things out of a combination of boredom, restless energy, and just wanting to make things. I don't even know what you'd call the first thing that I was doing.

I began doing entrepreneurial stuff around age six or seven. I had a paper route, but I basically ran the whole business (customer acquisition, billing and payments, finances, delivery, etc). In college, I think I was looking for interesting economics arbitrage opportunities. I noticed that at the end of the spring semester, every year, everybody wanted to get rid of their bikes. Nobody wanted to deal with shipping them wherever they were going for the summer. And, right before the start of the fall semester everybody wanted new bikes. One summer when I was staying in Champaign, I bought up all the bikes. I just tied them up to the same stands and sold them back, three or four months later, at a profit; it was just something I did for fun. It wasn't like it could scale really well but it was just a way of hacking the system.

I started working on more Internet-related projects in the '90s; my first funded thing was a mobile content transformation platform we built in 2000. I also did an online ecommerce project where we sold recycled traffic lights and turned them into high-end pendant lamp fixtures. I'm not really involved in that any more but I think they still sell them. It's called Greenlight Concepts. In L.A., they have all these traffic lights that the city was just throwing out. They moved from colored glass lenses to LEDs. Some friends and I built pendent lamps out of the colored lenses and started marketing and selling them online.

Did you get the lights for free? Did you have to buy them?

There was some cost. They were sitting at a holding plant. We had to pay rent, effectively, to have them sit in storage and not take delivery of all of them at once. We did that to practice selling things online. Again, it wasn't a super scalable business, but it was a fun project to try things out.

Was this after college?

This was 2004. I was at Google at that point. I was just doing it as a side project. When you're at Google you have 20% time for most Internet related things you're doing, so I also worked on non-software projects for personal enjoyment.

What was your favorite class at UIUC?

My favorite, by far, was a computer architecture course that includes a lot of assembly language programming. We got to write some games, we wrote a Dig Dug clone. The whole class was assembly language. Every few weeks we were doing fun projects. I later went on to be a TA for the class.

Did you go into school knowing a lot of people at U of I?

Yeah. A lot of people from my high school went there. My brother was also in ECE and he was a year or two ahead of me so he knew a lot of people.

Did you do any groups or sports or anything like that?

I didn't do many organized activities. I've played piano since I was a child, so I actually took a bunch of Jazz piano classes and played with some ensembles. I also got into running in college but not in a group setting, it was more solo long-distance running. It was an extracurricular, but not really an organized one.

In college, did you know you wanted to do a startup and were you looking for cofounders?

Yeah, I was always working on some sort of project while I was in college. I don't think I was explicitly looking for cofounders in school. I think it could have been useful to focus on trying to find people that were really excited about startups. College is a great chance to meet people and you can figure out if you work well together and like the same kinds of things. I think that's a really healthy attitude. At the time, I was just doing projects. I think I could have taken a more focused approach to recruiting people.

Did you work any jobs in college?

I had a bunch of jobs. I got paid for TA'ing for ECE 291. I also used to work in the engineering workstation labs; I was the guy who sits in the front of the lab answering questions and changing passwords and doing Unix sys admin stuff.

Did you take time away from class to relax and party?

I had kind of a strange college experience. It wasn't very coherent. When I was at school I was pretty focused on jamming through school, but then I also spent a lot of time off campus. I went there for two semesters, stayed a summer, and then I left and went to California and did an internship at Intel and another internship at Microsoft up in Seattle. I went back to school for another semester, then I went and lived in Spain for six months, came back to school and did another semester and then I think I was done. So, yeah, I was there for five semesters but when I was there I was jamming pretty hard.

Right when you were graduating college, what were you doing? Did you want to do a startup; were you planning to go to work somewhere?

I still wanted to work on startups. I had been working on startup-type things throughout school. So I wanted to keep doing that and this company called Trilogy was supportive and basically said, "Come down to Austin and we'll fund you to do this thing; whatever you want to do." I think what they were they really trying to do is get people to show up and then they were going to be like, "Oh well, your startup didn't work, but here, we've got a consulting job for you", but they ended up supporting what I was doing.

I ended up building that over the course of a year. It was a mobile content transformation platform. It was 2000, so, way too early, but we were trying to build ways to make it easier to use mobile devices given that they have access to the Internet, which is what I'm doing again now.

After about a year, making that successful and selling a bunch of it, making their business better, I threw everything in my car and drove from Austin to San Francisco. In San Francisco, I talked to a bunch of people and got plugged in with this crew of really talented engineers who were working on this web marketplace software. While that was a great learning experience and it evolved into what is now a reasonably successful enterprise business, it wasn't something that I was super excited to continue to work on.

It's a good business, but I came out wanting to work on more consumer-focused things. The dot com stuff had collapsed; everybody was all hyped on the wrong things. I was thinking, "This makes no sense. Let's just find good people to work with, at least that will be fun and useful and interesting." The more I thought about it, the more frustrated I got with the culture of stupid startup stuff. I thought, "Maybe I'd be happier doing something more academic/science-oriented to I began to explore studying bioinformatics."

So, I started taking biology classes at Berkeley, thinking there might be an interesting way to apply computer science to biology. I ended up not being super excited about the courses, the way I had been as an undergrad in computer engineering. So I decided not to do that.

Around the same time, a friend of mine that I had met when I first moved out here and kept in touch with over the course of a couple of years was applying to Google and suggested that I also apply. I thought he was a really smart guy so I was like, "Okay, I'll try this." I did and ended up at Google for about four years, where I worked primarily on AdWords and mobile stuff.

Why did you leave Google?

At that point it was sort of this bigger company. When I went to Google it was this really interesting time; the company was evolving and there was so much changing, it was really exciting. It was still reasonably fun and fast paced when I left, but it felt like it was more of a big company, and I knew I wanted to do startup stuff because I'd been doing that my whole life.

Is this when you started doing Facebook apps?

No. Facebook hadn't launched the platform when I left Google. At the time, I was first working on this mobile social network thing; a WAP-based social network.

Like foursquare?

It wasn't really around the idea of locations and checking-in. It was more around the idea of trying to move SMS over IP channels. So, it was basically a way to do richer messaging—let's say over the web but in a messaging format, which fits well into a mobile device screen; this was pre-iPhone. This was for devices like Motorola RAZR. I tried to make an IP-based messaging system work better (mapping SMS as signaling for richer messaging on mobile web pages).

Did these phones have browsers?

Yeah. Plenty of phones had browsers but they ended up being really hard to use. SMS as a distribution or communication mechanism was difficult. Users just weren't comfortable with it, weren't accustomed to it. You can't build great social software doing carrier deals. I think the stuff that Foursquare did, somewhat proved that hypothesis to be correct, but they did it with the launch of the iPhone, which made a ton of sense—there was a lot of new distribution available around data-connected devices. I was doing it in late 2006, so, it was a little bit too early. I think if I tried some of this right when iPhone was launching, it would have been better timing.

That worked reasonably well and it ended up becoming, sort of, a dating network. People were messaging, in a dating context, because it wasn't attached to a really strong identity or reputation. So, people would just go there and look for pictures of people they like. You could submit pictures via MMS. We could buy traffic, monetize that traffic, and make it into something; it was a business. You could fund it as a business but it was clear to me this wasn't going to be really huge. I messed around with that and a bunch of other ideas around web-based distribution for communications products.

I did about a year's worth of playing around with various projects after I left Google. I was unemployed for a year and didn't really make any progress towards what eventually became the gaming network, until December 2007. Basically, a bunch of my friends had been doing stuff on Facebook and there were reasonable product ideas but nobody was really using them and we couldn't get a lot of distribution for them.

This was around the time when Facebook's platform launched. I thought there would be something there if we could build something that would take advantage of all of the new Facebook's distribution that was made available.

So, we started building stuff on Facebook and social SMS mobile, trying to convert users from Facebook app nonsense into a mobile experience. We realized that wasn't super compelling and then said, "Hey, let's try the kind of viral stuff that we know will work." We started putting up silly pictures of cute things that people could send to each other. We got a bunch of cute pictures together, put them up and designed it effectively, as what is now thought of as a game.

I guess we thought of it as a virtual world, but a very simple one; it's just some graphics and you've got this garden you're managing and you can get points and currency for growing flowers. We put together a pretty reasonable design of what we thought would be more interesting than just sending gifts to each other; sending gifts where gifts have a purpose because they help you accrue a virtual currency which can be used to buy other gifts, or special gifts. I played with a bunch of these virtual world and gaming sites online, not as a player but more as an intellectual exercise.

We launched it and it was obvious to me, from day one that this was going to be a huge hit. We were doubling users everyday despite being a fairly incomplete product.

Did you do anything to grow that way or was it organic?

It was organic, but viral. We designed the game to work better if you distribute it and share it with friends. The only way to get plants in your green patch, for example, was to have people send you plants. The only way to tell people to send you plants was to send them plants.

We were just building a viral hook. But, so many people who were building stupid viral tricks were just like, "Hey, I'm going to send you these cute things", and then you said, "Thanks for the cute thing", and that message is very ephemeral. We thought the message could be a type of transport to help accrue value to the user who received it and make them more engaged and give them more to do with it.

If you play Little Green Patch by yourself, there's nothing to do because you show up and you have a green patch with nothing in it and you're like "Okay, how do I get some plants?" Well, the only way to get plants is to send plants to your friends, so they'll send plants back. If you're the only player, the game makes no sense. If you have 20 friends playing, you're having a lot of fun, and we designed it that way because we knew that would be more viral.

I sort of likened it to—and this is kind of a lofty ambition— but I likened it to Skype. Skype is a terrible user experience if you're the only person on Skype and it can be awesome once you have 20 friends on, right?

So you just kept growing from there?

Yeah, we kept growing and fine-tuning things, and we realized more about how viral distribution works, how different messaging channels get used, how to convert users through the channels, and how to assess user value.

We hired a bunch of people, raised money, and built out more games. We started with something small and it ended up working, so we just compounded and threw more money and people at it; built it up to become one of the biggest networks of games on Facebook.

And then Green Patch got acquired, right?

Yeah. We sold the company to Playdom in late 2009, and Disney later bought Playdom.

What was that process like? Was it a positive or negative experience?

It was generally a positive experience. In many cases with acquisitions, there's some sort of dance that you're doing. We knew of Playdom and they knew of us before we actually did anything; we had been talking on and off, getting to know each other, and figuring out whether or not there was something we could do better together.

It was like a courtship, in a sense. We had talked to them, they had talked to us, we had a bunch of mutual friends, and people were like, "Hey, you guys should do something together".

How big was the team at Little Green Patch?

We were 2 cofounders and a total of 16 employees.

Did you stick around at Playdom for a while?

I stayed around for about five months. I was basically helping to transition the team over and get all the pieces in place. My cofounder at Green Patch was really excited about running, what was previously, the independent company; I was like, "Okay, you do that, and I'll go find other interesting things to do at Playdom."

After Playdom, what did you want to do?

Well, I knew I was going to start another company and I thought it would be reasonably soon after. I had met a friend who was also excited about doing something new; we started a little project and did things like browser sharing and a SMS web marketplace. We built a few different projects, over the course of a year, after leaving Playdom.

Each one we built, we would look at and say, "Well, we have a good reason for wanting to do this, why we think this could be useful, but we just don't feel super excited about this particular product", and so we would abandon it and move on. We weren't both getting excited about anything. We kept deciding, "It's fun to try these things, but we don't feel like they are things we want to build a company around."

So, we kept talking, trying, and hacking on things on the side; playing around with ideas. I had been meeting a lot of people, advising, and investing. I wasn't really excited about any of our ideas so I ended up leaving to travel throughout Europe and Asia for three months. I wanted to unplug from Silicon Valley. I'd been there so long and was so focused on how Silicon Valley does things. Our network of people is really strong, but it was all the same people, same parties, etc. I wanted to try branching out, unplugging my brain and resetting and recharging the batteries.

How did the idea for Camino Real come about?

Before I left to go travel, I had worked on a bunch of projects with my cofounder, Abhay Vardhan who is also an Illinois guy and ex-Google guy. We had worked on these projects and built some things, but hadn't been really excited about anything. When I came back from traveling, we sort of doubled down on our effort to find something interesting enough that we both wanted to commit to. We took a much more focused approach to looking at how these markets were evolving.

There was this theme that I have continually been drawn to and continually failed at around how data availability in mobile can create much richer experiences for users. I did it in 2000, again at Google in 2005, again as I was leaving Google in 2006 and 2007, took a detour to Little Green Patch, and now I'm coming back to that same idea, 11 years later. I feel like I have unfinished business that will play out over the next 18 months; these changes are now hitting the tipping point. Essentially, the things we've been trying to do for 10 years, are finally going to be possible.

What was the process of fundraising like? Was that a positive or negative experience?

We're in a fortunate position that raising money was actually a very pleasant and happy experience. Initially we were only raising from non-institutional sources—so, only from individuals. I made a list of 30 people that I wanted to get involved and I talked to all of them. Within the first hour, every one of them committed. These are all my friends and people I know already; they're super supportive and they're going to be helpful in helping us build this.

So if you got 30 people, each to agree to do $10K, then you could have just raised 300K.

Yep, and we raised more than that, but that's basically what we did. We've been in a fortunate position where institutions are throwing money at us on crazy generous terms. We've had a lot of support, financially, at whatever point we want to take it.

Do you have a beta ready for Camino Real?

No. We're going to launch our first product in April 2011.

How did you meet your cofounder?

He was a UIUC guy and a Google guy. We have a mutual friend who introduced us a while back and we've just been kind of talking and working on projects ever since.

How do you split the work up?

We're both fairly collaborative. We just decide what products we want to build and jump in, wherever possible. He's a strong hacker, so he'll just dig into anything and crank stuff out really quickly. I work a lot on product stuff, design, wire frames, and general wrangling. We sort of split the work and we stay super focused on the product and getting something out.

What's the work schedule like?

We're pretty excited about what we're building so we sort of work most of the time.

What's the biggest challenge today for Camino Real?

The core is we need to get our product launched. So my biggest thing is, "What can we do to accelerate our ability to launch this product quickly?" and also, given that I've done this before, I know that one of the things that we're going to have to be ready for is the ability to recruit really quickly when we get our product growing.

Would you basically take the same approach with Green Patch? Where you want to make it viral by nature, is that how it's working?

Yeah. That's how it works overall, but this is more of a communications product than a game. So, I think Green Patch happened because that was the opportunity available at the time, though it wasn't really my lifelong dream to build it.

Do you struggle with motivation or productivity?

No. At Green Patch we certainly had some super stressful times, but we always made it work. With Camino Real, we're both super committed to making this work; things will get stressful, but we're also both fairly logical and rational people and we're very calm about how we solve problems. But we're extremely motivated to get this launched.

Do you have any advice for undergrads interested in doing startups or finding cofounders?

Meet everybody. Figure out where all the great people are. Be authentic and just meet people that are great. I wouldn't be too focused about being on the hunt to find the one or two guys, but find people that you work well with. Be active about meeting people, not so much for a hunt but just to expand your network of great people and ideas.

Cory Levy, One

Tags: businessperson, undergrad founder, hiring

Overview: One started in 2010 as a mobile application that allows you to meet people nearby that have similar interests. For example, if you indicate you are interested in a certain type of music, and someone nearby also has the application, you might get a recommendation to meet each other at a café nearby.

Can you take me back as far as you can remember about how you got started with entrepreneurship?

Tennis has always been a big passion of mine. I started playing when I was five years old and still play today. There was a professional tennis tournament coming to Houston so I signed up to be a ball boy, ended up getting autographs from the players, and sold doubles on eBay. That is kind of when the whole entrepreneurship bug hit me; it was an eBay business in elementary school and I was making a lot of money. It happened every single year when I was a ball boy. My hero at the time, Andy Roddick, had just won the U.S. Open in 2002 or 2003 and I really wanted to meet him.

So I poked around on the Internet and searched for Andy Roddick's email address. Of course nothing came up but I did find his mother's email address on Andy Roddick's charity; the charity that I started. So I sent her a cold email—I was 11 or 12 years old—and I told her I really wanted to meet her son and that he was my hero; surprisingly, she responded.

From that moment on, I believed that I could do anything and that nothing could really stop me from doing stuff. I ended up meeting Andy Roddick. I moved forward with the eBay business, got more autographs. I arbitraged buying stuff when tennis wasn't popular and then sold it when it was popular during the U.S. Open.

I didn't know what the word entrepreneur meant at the time, but I was finishing my last year of summer camp and thought the best way to actually learn was to start a business. I went onto Facebook because I had a big idea right as LinkedIn was being built, which is what I wanted to create. The first step I took, was market research. I manually cold-messaged over 750 people from all of the startup groups. I asked them if they would use this different idea; I didn't know about LinkedIn at first. When a few people brought it up, I asked them what they were not getting out of LinkedIn. Long story short, it was a failure but the things I learned from that experience paid off.

I realized the people I was contacting were pretty influential. I got them on the phone and picked their brains. These were people at Founder's Fund, Union Square Ventures, TechStars, founders, students, a congressman. A diverse group of people was willing to help, so I asked for and took on internships, learned about venture capital, and learned about startups. I went into specific Facebook groups and just interviewed these people, told them what I was doing, and then asked them a bunch of questions.

I got my Facebook account banned trying to do this when I was a sophomore. Did you get into any trouble?

One of the people I contacted worked at Facebook. I never used my real name and I was honest with people about that, up front. I remember one of the Facebook guys responded in detail, he was like, "I work for Facebook; you're not allowed to do this but I'm not telling anyone." That was the only time I almost got kicked off, but I don't think I ever actually did.

This was pretty early. I was probably one of the first Facebook spammers, because Peter Thiel was one of the people that I reached out to and he responded. So, this was when there was either no spam or very little Facebook spam.

Did you work with any of the people you contacted?

I ended up working with a bunch of them. I thought, "I love startups; I love the early-stage stuff, what's the best way to learn more about it?" Working in a startup is the best way to learn. At the time I thought working in VC was the best way to learn because then you work with a variety of different startups every day. That's what they live and breathe.

So, I reached out to TechStars, Founders Fund and Union Square Ventures, and asked for an internship. They all said, "No, we don't take on high school interns. Finish your resume and we'll see what we can do." I had no work experience, no resume, no idea how to write a resume. But one of the people I reached out to on Facebook was a professor at U.C. Berkeley and he helped me write a resume that outlined my accomplishments and skills up until I was 15 years old; I think that's still on my website.

Eventually, TechStars and Union Square Ventures said, "Yes," but Founders Fund vehemently said, "No." I was bummed about that since those were the guys I really wanted to surround myself with, but I was still happy to be working with Albert Wenger and Fred Wilson at Union Square Ventures.

Here's another funny story. One day, Albert Wenger, the guy who I was with 98% of the time, said, "We are going to lunch and then to a board meeting with a guy from the Founders Fund." When they told me the name of the guy, I realized it was the same one who had turned me down, before.

Sure enough, we sit down at lunch and introduce ourselves. I said, "Do you remember me?" I told him I was that kid who had annoyed him for that internship; he remembered me and was kind of shocked that I was with his colleague at Union Square Ventures and said, "Keep in touch and maybe something will work out next summer." So I did. I kept in touch and reached out to him periodically, and sure enough, that next summer, I was at the Founders Fund.

Was there anything that stood out on the resume that allowed you to work in VC at a young age?

No, I just thought it was creative. I remember the Founders Fund: specifically, they ripped my resume apart. They said it wasn't in the proper format, and offered to show me an example. With TechStars and Union Square Ventures I didn't have to change the format of my resume, but with the Founders Fund, they walked us through how to write a resume and sure enough, in its standard form it looked awful because I had no work experience, no education, nothing, and that's what is usually highlighted in a resume. I had 'middle school degree' down, which didn't look impressive at all.

What kind of work did you do with Union Square and Founders Fund?

I analyzed different companies, met with entrepreneurs; pitched and went to different meetups to interact with new entrepreneurs; wrote reports, went to, and learned how to run, board meetings, stuff like that. Essentially, I was at their side all the time and, at the Founders Fund, people thought I was a partner, not an intern.

Before those, I interned at NutshellMail, as it was getting started, during the winter of my sophomore year of high school. They were recently acquired by Constant Contact. The next summer I was at Union Square Ventures and TechStars, and the following summer, I was at the Founders Fund.

What were you doing after your junior year, then?

I did an event at Stanford that summer, a meetup. While I was at the Founders Fund they inspired me to take the network I had built since then and share it with everyone. So, I started a conference at Stanford called the NextGen Conference that brings young entrepreneurs, the world's greatest entrepreneurs, and venture capitalists together. I planned it remotely while in high school in Houston, Texas and then flew out to Stanford for three or four days.

It was sold out. I pulled it off and just did it again, recently, a couple of weeks ago; it was sold out again, over 250 people. We had the same caliber of speakers, but the big name was Peter Thiel.

How did you promote the conference and sell tickets?

The first year, I didn't really know what to do. I went on EventBrite and that's where people bought tickets, found out about the Startup Digest, which was just starting, and they promoted it. Thirty days prior to the conference, no one was signed up, so I was a bit worried, but after that, it sold out. Stanford helped promote it among student groups; UIUC sent eight people. So there were students from UIUC, Berkeley, mostly people in the area.

This past conference, a lot of people signed up specifically for the speakers. It was on VentureBeat which helped us reach a bunch of people; it ended up selling out. My capacity was 125 people. I oversold it to 150 and then started a waiting list. In two days' time, the waiting list was around 70 people, so I ended up moving the conference to a hotel across the street to accommodate the large demand. Over 250 people showed up.

How did you get involved with One?

While I was at the Founders Fund in Houston they introduced me to three individuals: the first two were, Tim Seagull at ShareThis and Dr. Goldberg at UIUC. I was then asked to come speak to the iFoundry class.

I did that my senior year and I was on a panel and got introduced to Michael Callahan, the third person. So, after the panel we met and talked about what then came to be One, for about two hours. This was October of my senior year of high school—fast forward about six weeks to November—that was the first NextGen conference and Mike flew out for that. So that was our second interaction and we decided to work together from there.

Did you know many people going into college? Did you have plans to find a cofounder or do a startup?

I knew some camp friends and they were my schoolmates and then I had a bunch of friends from my business year at iFoundry. It was weird being away from my normal group of friends; I went to school with the same group of 70 kids from kindergarten to 12th grade. I wasn't looking for cofounders, but obviously I was looking for talent to help grow this company.

At the time of this interview, you're a freshman in college. What types of classes are you taking and how do you manage your time?

Last semester I was taking computer science and physics classes at UIUC. This semester I'm taking a lighter load since I plan to be out in the Valley a lot. Outside of class I play tennis on the club team. It's not a big commitment though.

NextGen took very little time. Did I have trouble with work-life balance? No, again personally, I just make it work. I might require less sleep than the normal college student. If you look at your work as your life, in a way, there is lots of work-life balance.

You've seen lots of founders. Have you noticed any patterns of success? Do they all have something in common?

Startup CEO salary is a good indicator. There is a correlation between that and success. Some people would take CEOs with a venture fund and start out taking six figures or $70,000 to $80,000, usually sending the signal that they're in it for the money and not building the company. But if you see a CEO taking $30,000 to $50,000, a low salary, that's a pattern that I've seen; that metric yields to greater success.

At one company I worked with, the CEO didn't take a salary for two years. At another, the CEO took a $25,000 salary. That's super low to be living in San Francisco, but those companies tend to be a lot more successful than the company where the CEO takes an $80,000 salary.

The Founders Fund created something called series FF stock—it's for entrepreneurs who may need some money—so they buy the Founders stocks to let them pay their mortgage, start a college fund for their kids, and so on. It all depends on the situation. If you don't have a mortgage, that's a good thing. When you have a family, the situation is different.

Fast forward a little bit to the present, are you guys bootstrapping One, or are you guys raising money?

We're bootstrapping for a while. We've signed a term sheet and now we're in the process of closing our series A.

How long did it take to get a beta? How did you spread the word?

The first beta took six weeks or so to make and we had a core group of people at UIUC that we tested it with. So it was a test launch, not a market launch and it was private. To download the app you had to have a password. I think we're the only people at the app store that were allowed to do that, and we worked with Apple to do that. So we haven't done it live yet, we've just been testing it at the university.

How is the work split at One?

Mike is the CEO and the core technical person. I manage fundraising, operations, and hiring, but we both do a little of everything, and we look at what needs to be done, day-by-day.

Right now it's our legal counsel and our investors. We're working out the series A deal, and tomorrow, it's making sure we're going to launch our second version of the iPhone app and then there's the next stage, how we're going to market that. So there's all these different things that we do every single day, I can't really give it a particular title or role but you know how it is in startups, you do everything.

What's the work schedule like?

Michael wakes up and starts working. Then, 17 or 18 hours later, he goes to bed. We work days, nights, holidays, weekends.

You guys are so early in your startup that it's difficult to gain a whole lot of insight and perspective—but what's your biggest challenge today?

Getting our product into people's hands, so, growth and hiring. Eventually, promoting and putting it in the hands of everyone; we're going to focus on one city, San Francisco, and then move from there. So I expect the next version is going to be public to everyone but our team is focused on launching specifically in San Francisco. That's our focus and that could be our challenge at the same time.

Would you offer any advice to students thinking about doing a startup?

Go work for a startup, would be my advice. As Mark Schuster says, "JFDI – just fucking do it." If you're not technical, you should learn how to program. You'll learn it or find someone that complements your lack of ability. But yeah, either find someone that can do it or you learn it yourself; obviously tech people are in very high demand.

You're passively hiring right now, is there something that would make an applicant stand out?

I think we are a small, smart team of people with an awesome group of advisors and mentors. By working with us, a) you get to experience what it's like to be working a startup and b) you're going to meet a lot of people.

I don't want to see a resume. I've already received tons of resumes—I may open one or two to glance at them. But don't send your resume. Send me your LinkedIn profile; send me a blog; send me your web presence. If you don't have one, send me what you've built; send me a link to an app that you've built; send me screenshots of different things you've made; and *then* maybe send me your resume.

www.ingramcontent.com/pod-product-compliance
Lightning Source LLC
Chambersburg PA
CBHW060113200326
41518CB00008B/815